More than Witnesses

How a Small Group of Missionaries Aided Korea's Democratic Revolution

Edited by Jim Stentzel

Editorial Team

Henry Em
Linda Jones
Gene Matthews
Louise Morris
Pat Patterson

©2008
Nightengale Press
A Nightengale Media LLC Company

More than Witnesses
How a Small Group of Missionaries
Aided Korea's Democratic Revolution

For information about Nightengale Press please
visit our website at www.nightengalepress.com.
Email: publisher@nightengalepress.biz
or send a letter to:
Nightengale Press
10936 N. Port Washington Road. Suite 206
Mequon, WI 53092

Library of Congress Cataloging-in-Publication Data

Stentzel, Jim,
MORE THAN WITNESSES/Edited by Jim Stentzel
ISBN:1-933449-62-4
ISBN 13: 978-1933449-62-3
Christianity/Korea/Democratic Revolution

First published in Korea by Korea Democracy Foundation, Seoul, Korea in 2006
Permission granted to publish in the United States.

Copyright Registered: 2008
Published by Nightengale Press in the USA

November 2008

10 9 8 7 6 5 4 3 2 1

Printed in the USA and the UK

Endorsements

"The stories told in More than Witnesses reflect the sacrifices and dedication of a small group of missionaries who aided Korea's democratic revolution, helping the nation put behind the era of dictatorship. It also tells of the courage of Korean people whose lives exemplified the love and teachings of God through their strong religious commitment.

"During the dark days under military dictatorship in Korea, this group of foreign missionaries, often at their peril, reported to the international community on the adversities and serious human rights violations inflicted by the dictatorships. Through these efforts they solicited international support for Korea's democracy. Some of them were deported by the dictators, but eventually they were able to overcome such hardship through their persevering courage and spiritual belief. The efforts and devotion of the missionary community provided democratic activists, including me, a ray of light and a source of hope and courage. The inspiring achievements of these "Foreigners with Hearts of Koreans" have helped lay a firm groundwork in Korea for freedom, peace, and justice to come into full bloom like pretty, tenacious wild flowers."

—Kim Dae Jung, President of The Republic of Korea from 1998 – 2003 and 2000 Nobel Peace Prize Winner. He is mentioned frequently throughout the book.

"During the most brutal period of the South Korean military dictatorship more than three decades ago, a group of Korean Christians and missionaries chose to stand at great personal risk against the flagrant injustices and murderous excesses of the government. This splendid volume is a collection of their stories, a powerful example of contemporary witness to the faith. Knowing many of the authors personally, I was deeply moved by their courage and constancy under such cruel oppression. All who read these accounts cannot but be inspired."

—James T. Laney, President Emeritus of Emory University in Atlanta, Georgia (president from 1977 – 1983). He served as Ambassador to Korea from 1993 – 1996.

≈ ≋≋ ≈

"As an activist for democracy and as a spouse and sister-in-law of political prisoners, I am personally indebted to the authors of this book, who provided safe breathing spaces for us in the grip of suppression and who kept information pipelines open to the outside world. Their deep involvement in our struggle made them truly "more than witnesses" and shortened the number of years it took to birth our democracy.""

—Heisoo Shin, author, scholar, university professor, human rights activist, women's rights activist, and member of the UN Committee on the Elimination of Discrimination Against Women (CEDAW).

≈ ≋≋ ≈

"There are times in history when small groups of Christians take seriously the biblical command to "bring good news to the oppressed, and ... release to the prisoners." That was the case with a group of Western missionaries in South Korea in the mid-1970s during the Park Chung Hee dictatorship. *More than Witnesses* tells the stories, some never before told, of how this courageous group informed the world of what was happening. It is a challenging and humbling account of being faithful in the worst of times, and has important lessons for all of us."
—**Jim Wallis, President of Sojourners and author of many books including his most recent, *The Great Awakening*.**

⁓ ⧼⧽ ⤳

"*More than Witnesses* is a truly living witness of dedicated missionaries who fought with their body and spirit for peace and justice in Korea. It shows what it means to be true mission partners to share the love of Christ. Korean Christians are deeply grateful for these true partners of mission in our struggle for peace and justice."
—Syngman Rhee, former Moderator, Presbyterian **Church USA; former President, National Council of Churches of Christ in the USA. He was Mission Executive of the Presbyterian Church USA at the time of the events described in *More than Witnesses*, and currently teaches at Union Theological Seminary in Richmond, Virginia.**

⁓ ⧼⧽ ⤳

"This book is a rare collection of moving, first-hand accounts by westerners, both men and women, with broad knowledge, love and respect for the Korean people whose struggle for democracy and human rights in the turbulent '70s and '80s they supported and shared. The book should be read in colleges, universities and seminaries or by anyone who wants to know what it is like for ordinary people to confront a repressive regime."

—Peggy Billings, prominent civil rights and women's **rights activist, poet and author. She was Chairperson of the North American Coalition on Human Rights in Korea at the time of the events described in *More than Witnesses*.**

⋙ ⋙⋘ ⋘

"The stories presented by the authors of these pages are about 20th century suffering servants who, as they offered up their lives, were serving an eternal order. I came to know them as I visited South Korea on human rights and church related missions. Many of them were imprisoned, some tortured, some exiled, only because they sought freedom and justice for their people. We will be forever in their debt. This book should be required reading in seminary classes on mission and should be in the hands of all of those who go to distant lands as servant ministers "

—James Armstrong, **former Bishop of the United Methodist Church; former President, National Churches of Christ in the U.S.A. He is a strong voice for peace and human rights and a frequent lecturer on theology and the practice of ministry in today's society.**

⋙ ⋙⋘ ⋘

"*More than Witnesses* tells the story of how ordinary people can become extraordinary when they respond in faith to extraordinary circumstances. It is told by a group of missionaries in Korea from the U.S. and Canada who unexpectedly found themselves enmeshed in the life and death struggle of the Korean people for democracy and freedom from military rule in the 1970s and '80s. At considerable peril they provided shelter to dissidents in hiding, publicly protested the sham trials and executions of political prisoners, and smuggled information out of the country to build international support for the Korean people. The work of these missionaries provides a powerful lesson of what it means to serve a people in the name of Christ. It should be read by all who ponder the value of intercultural Christian mission today."

—Pharis Harvey, former missionary, human rights champion and former Executive Director of the North American Coalition on Human Rights in Korea.

Acknowledgments

In 2004, five remarkable and dedicated individuals volunteered to assist me as members of the Monday Night Group book editorial team. I am deeply indebted to them, individually and collectively, in ways too many to itemize here. You will get to know three members of the editorial team – Linda Jones, Gene Matthews, and Louise Morris – by reading their chapters. Two other team members labored behind the scenes: Henry Em, assistant professor of Korean history at the University of Michigan (now teaching in Seoul); and Pat Patterson, a retired U.S. United Methodist mission board official who directly and indirectly supported Monday Night Group members at critical junctures during the 1970s and '80s. Henry and Pat brought unique and important perspectives to the content and design of this book.

We are deeply thankful to the Korea Democracy Foundation, especially current president Father Ham (pronounced Hahm) Sei Ung and past president Rev. Park Hyung Kyu. When the humility of Monday Night Group members led to a reluctance to tell their stories, KDF insisted the stories were too important *not* to tell. The book process began in earnest during a July 2004 Monday Night Group reunion in Lincoln, Vermont, and KDF soon agreed to fund the project and to publish the book. For all its support and assistance, we are deeply grateful.

I am personally grateful to several persons for special assistance: John Fullerton, for providing his Colorado home as an editing base; Roger and Jacquie Talbott, for desk space and internet access in their Ohio home; Jean Thornton, for her Florida home and high-speed internet connection; and Cathy Stentzel, not only for her eagle proofreader's eye but also for sharing her excitement about the manuscripts – lifting my spirits at times when I felt mired in the minutia of rewriting and editing.

Because I was on the road a lot during the editing process, I am thankful to Louise Morris for serving as the key communication link between chapter writers, editorial team members, KDF staff, and me. I am grateful also to Gene Matthews for "going the extra mile" in terms of editorial feedback and computer assistance.

This paperback edition would not exist without the inspiration and efforts of Gene Matthews. He worked with Nightengale Press on the publication details, and he oversaw all revisions and updates in the text. The editorial team deeply appreciates his labor of love.

Special thanks go to Valerie Connelly of Nightengale Press whose patience and devotion to getting it right made this paperback edition possible. Thanks also to Carolyn W. Kohler, Librarian Emeritus, The University of Iowa, for her help in proofreading the paperback edition.

The Faye Moon's chapter includes sections adapted from texts previously published in Korean. Sections of George Ogle's chapter are adapted from an as yet unpublished autobiography. We are thankful for permission to use their material here.

Jim Stentzel

We dedicate this book to those Koreans who could not tell their own stories because they died in the struggle for democracy and human rights.

Table of Contents

Acknowledgments *Jim Stentzel*

Dedication

Foreword	*Ham Sei Ung*	*15*
Introduction	*Jim Stentzel*	*19*
Glossary	*Gene Matthews*	*41*
Timeline	*Henry Em and Jim Stentzel*	*54*

Chapter 1	Our Hearts Cry with You, *by George E. Ogle*	*67*
Chapter 2	From Isolation to Collaboration, *by Randy Rice*	*100*
Chapter 3	What Korea Taught Me about My Country and My Faith, *by Louise Morris*	*113*
Chapter 4	Heartaches No Longer, and Some that Linger, *by Faye Moon*	*148*
Chapter 5	Things They Never Taught Us Down on the Farm, *by Gene Matthews*	*181*
Chapter 6	One Community Across All Boundaries, *by Marion Kim*	*223*
Chapter 7	It Was Impossible to Be Uninvolved, *by Willa Kernen*	*240*

MNG Photos   269

Chapter 8   Missionaries, Cows and Monday Nights,
                 by Walter "Butch" Durst   279

Chapter 9   Acting on Our Convictions, *by Sue Rice*   308

Chapter 10   Let It Be an Experience, *by Jean Basinger*   326

Chapter 11   We All Know More Bible than We Live By,
                 by Fran Nelson   348

Chapter 12   A New Day Had Dawned, *by Marion Current*   357

Chapter 13   Now You Are Free to Speak Out, *by Fr. Jim Sinnott* 375

Chapter 14   From Service to Solidarity, *by Linda Jones*   411

Chapter 15   1979-1980: When Violence Peaked and Dictatorship
                 Began to Crumble, *by the Editors*   441

Supplements   463

Postscript Where They Are Now   465

Introduction to Fact Sheets   469

          Fact Sheet #1   Repression Brings Response;
                            The Case of Rev. Hyung Kyu Park 471

          Fact Sheet #5   The "Yushin" Constitution of South
                            Korea and Its Consequences   475

          Fact Sheet #12   Letter to President Ford, From Mothers
                            of Korean Political Prisoners   480

          Fact Sheet #18   The Struggle Continues   486

     Emergency Decree Number Nine   495
     A Tract for Our Times   499

 *Foreword*

The Lives of Missionaries: A Mirror for the Heart

The Korea Democracy Foundation seeks to uphold human dignity and community life through commemoration and preservation of our democratic inheritance. On three occasions in the past five years, the Foundation has invited renowned foreign figures and missionaries to return to Korea so we could express our gratitude for their dedication in bringing about democracy and human rights in Korea. I am delighted that our Foundation now has the honor of cherishing their lives and testimonies through the publication of this book.

I am writing this Foreword on the 31st anniversary of a dark day in Korea's history. On April 9, 1975, eight innocent persons, condemned in the case of "People's Revolutionary Party Incident," were executed under the iron-fisted rule of then-president Park Chung-hee. The international community vehemently criticized the execution as "judicial murder."

In a remarkable coincidence, today, April 9, 2006, also marks Passion and Palm Sunday, a day when Christians remember the crucifixion and meditate on the holy sacrifice of Jesus. Today we pray that all injustice in judicial trials, religious or political, be eradicated.

More than Witnesses

A belated retrial for the PRP Incident was held in late March this year. It was profoundly moving to witness a righting of the wrong perpetrated by the general-turned-president. The wives of the victims wept throughout the retrial. They thanked all those who worked hard to uncover the truth, especially missionaries of the Monday Night Group who showed their encompassing love and deep humanitarianism. Members of the group were true Christians who cared about, loved, and embraced Korea. As these missionaries share their stories and give their testimony in this book, it is like a fifth Gospel or sequel to the Acts of the Apostles. The accounts of their experiences demonstrate in detail how God called them and led them to Korea, a land of oppression and poverty at the time. We learn what motivated them to intervene in the socio-political events in Korea, and we are reminded of the calling of prophets.

The missionaries came from the United States, Canada, Australia, and Germany, leaving security and status behind to befriend Koreans living in every kind of poverty. Members of the Monday Night Group were people of *kenosis* who left behind their fertile lands and, like Christ, sought on their own accord a humble place.

The missionaries also were pioneers. They lived the wisdom of "when in Rome, do as the Romans do" and led lives more Korean than even some Koreans. This deepens my respect for them.

Moreover, the Monday Night Group missionaries were Christians of action who embraced the misery and poverty of Korea after the tragic fratricide of the Korean War. They lived lives poor in resources yet rich in spirit. Practicing what they preached, they were the best kind of evangelizers. Giving up many of the privileges of foreign nationals, they voluntarily walked the path of suffering in the darkest days of Korea's political history in the 1970s and '80s. They read the signs of the times and plunged into the fray. They were true icons of faith and calling. They were the first to share the suffering of imprisoned students, workers, and intellectuals under the dictatorship. They gathered together to pray for those who were persecuted and tortured in their fight for human freedom, dignity, and democracy in Korea. They were Good Samaritans who raised money and collected clothes and books to take to those in prison. The missionaries became saviors of the imprisoned by informing the international community of the human rights situation in Korea. Above all, the missionaries saw first-hand the crucifixion of Jesus in the eight lives unjustly lost in the trial of the People's Revolutionary Party Incident; they realized that the essence of Christianity lies in human liberation. They were truly creative Christians who gave witness to God's salvation breaking into history.

The 1970's were a fearful time of darkness and violence when Park's every word was absolute law. All Koreans suffered, and many were silent. But some – youths, students, and freedom fighters – had the courage and integrity to loudly voice their dissent against the dictator. Members of the Monday Night Group were their greatest supporters.

Koreans have an unquestionable duty to call for a democratic Korea. The marks of military dictators like Park Chung Hee and Chun Doo Hwan still remain today in various corners of our society. Many young Koreans are ignorant of what happened only twenty or thirty years ago; they are losing their historical awareness and humanitarianism, blindly following individualism and selfishness. This is extremely shameful. To us at this particular moment, the lives and testimonies of the missionaries are a mirror of the heart upon which we can reflect deeply on our lives.

As a human being and as part of the community that struggles for democracy, I want to convey my heartfelt appreciation to all missionaries and benefactors whose quiet contributions made possible today's democratic Korea. A human life of close solidarity filled with sacrifice, dedication, care and love is an eternal source of deep emotion. Let us all acknowledge that wellspring of inspiration once again, and may our love for humanity draw us into an even closer unity and bond.

April 9, 2006
Father Ham Sei Ung
President, Korea Democracy Foundation

 *Introduction*

They Had to Do Something

Jim Stentzel

We finish our schooling, follow our intentions, chart our courses, begin our vocations.

But life is full of twists and turns.

I had no intention of becoming a foreign correspondent. Then the Columbia University Graduate School of Journalism awarded me a Pulitzer-funded traveling fellowship, allowing me to go to Japan to consider just that.

I had no intention of becoming a missionary-journalist in Japan until that opportunity was presented by the National Christian Council of Japan and the United Methodist Board of Global Ministries in the U.S.

Based in Tokyo, I had no intention of writing primarily about south Korea. Until some interesting twists and dramatic turns.

The first "twist" was an interview I conducted with Kim Dae Jung in his Tokyo hotel room in 1973. Kim had been narrowly defeated by incumbent Park Chung Hee in the 1971 presidential election – an election marred by accusations of vote fraud. When I interviewed Kim he was still recovering from an assassination attempt in Seoul.

The interview was not remarkable. What happened a few weeks later was.

Kim was kidnapped from the same Ginza Dai-ichi hotel room where we had talked. Korean CIA agents hustled him out of Japan, putting him on a boat that headed into the Japan Sea – where Kim later told me he knew he was about to "disappear" – thrown overboard, never heard from again.

Before that could happen, some aircraft buzzed the boat – were they American military, he wondered – and his life was spared.

That day was a "turn" in my life as a journalist. Although still based in Tokyo and a member of the Foreign Correspondents Club of Japan, Korea became the focus of hundreds of articles I would write for publications including the *Nation, Far Eastern Economic Review, Pacific News Service, New Asia News, Sojourners, Christian Century,* various church-related publications in Asia and the U.S., and several Japanese monthly news-magazines including *Sekai.*

Kim Dae Jung was under house arrest most of the time from 1973 to 1976, so I visited him regularly in his home. Being under house arrest, cut off from most Koreans, meant that Kim had lots of time to talk with foreigners like me. He was a patient teacher, and I received a good education about things Korean – political, economic, and spiritual (Kim is Roman Catholic).

After his own lifetime of dramatic twists and turns, Kim Dae Jung would be elected president of south Korea in December 1997.

❧ ❧ ❧ ❧

Kim Dae Jung was one of many Koreans who would help me begin to understand Korea's culture, history, political landscape, and economic situation. But a considerable amount of my education – including introductions to, and translation help with, those Koreans – came from a handful of westerners in Korea who called themselves the Monday Night Group.

Introduction: They Had to Do Something

Members of the Monday Night Group were good Christian folk from towns like Wapello, Iowa; Pitcairn, Pennsylvania; and Saskatoon, Saskatchewan. When they finished their schooling, they followed their intentions by volunteering to serve as missionaries to Korea.

The younger among them were self-admittedly naïve and idealistic. They arrived in Korea lacking many things, including any certainties about what lay ahead of them personally or vocationally in such a totally foreign culture.

What members of the Monday Night Group did not lack was faith – the assurance that God acts in history in bold and unexpected ways. They didn't lack love – a willingness even to have their hearts broken. They didn't lack courage – an ability to leave risk unweighed as they reached out in faith and love.

But their faith, love, and courage were like mustard seeds, untested by life's twists and turns.

Those seeds would grow remarkably in the cauldron of political and economic upheaval that was south Korea in the 1970s.

~ ❧ ❧ ~

The 1970s were the center of three tumultuous decades not only for south Korea but also for its primary ally, the United States. The U.S. was bogged down in a long, brutal war in Vietnam. Insurgency in southeast Asia provided the rationale for extreme security measures in northeast Asia. It was no coincidence in April 1975 that, as helicopters evacuated the last American personnel from the roof of the U.S. Embassy in Saigon, the south Korean government increased its crackdown on all forms of opposition.

The U.S. government did not object. The Korean peninsula, located so close to the Soviet Union, China, and Japan, was central to its Cold War strategy. More than democracy, the U.S. wanted "stability" in south Korea.

South Korean President Park Chung Hee took maximum advantage of this situation. He granted himself dictatorial powers; imprisoned opponents; demolished civil liberties; denied freedoms of press, assembly, and speech; crushed workers' rights; sent Korean Central Intelligence Agency personnel into every corner of society; and fabricated communist plots to justify those actions.

The U.S. government issued statements objecting to some of the more brutal acts of the military dictatorship, but it was mostly political theater. At root, the United States and its primary Asian ally, Japan, saw the benefits of regional security outweighing the costs of Park's oppressive rule.

Knowing he could depend on political, military, and economic support from the United States, President Park moved swiftly and aggressively to mobilize support at home. A well-oiled propaganda machine began churning out not only "news" of imminent north Korean invasions but also "reports" that communists had infiltrated south Korean schools, factories, and churches.

One problem with this tactic was that dozens of foreign missionaries were well-connected in some of those schools, factories, and churches. They knew or heard about Korean coworkers, students, friends, and neighbors who were being harassed, arrested, interrogated, tortured, imprisoned, blacklisted, and/or fired from their jobs.

The majority of missionaries remained silent. Fearful for their jobs, families, and well-being, they also reasoned that, as guests of the south Korean government, they should avoid "meddling in domestic politics."

A small minority of foreign missionaries, however, saw a clearly emerging divide between good and evil. They could not just stand on the sidelines; they understood no biblical or other basis for neutrality. They had to do something. They had to stand with those who were struggling for justice.

But what should they do?

Initially some of those missionaries, Protestant and Catholic, agreed just to get together to share news about what was happening to their Korean colleagues, students, and neighbors. How about Monday nights? Fine. How about meeting in different missionary homes each week? Okay. How about putting on the agenda ways that they might respond to what was happening? Good idea.

So the "Monday Night Group" was born (see Randy Rice chapter). It was modeled after a similar but larger group that had met in the 1960s. The Monday Night Group was small; usually eight to 10 attended, sometimes as many as 20. They were American, Canadian, Australian, and German. They included Presbyterians, Methodists, Roman Catholics, members of the United Church of Canada, and others.

Initially, they felt intensely powerless: Koreans they loved and admired were suffering gross indignities at the hands of the government, and all the missionaries could do was report those indignities in their small living room circles each Monday night and in letters back home.

That sense of powerlessness gave way not so much by design as by accident. First, the Monday Night Group began filling the void of information coming into and going out of Korea. Electronic communications in and out of Korea were unavailable or unaffordable for 99 percent of the people at that time. Domestic and international print communications were heavily censored (even *Time* and *Newsweek* articles on Korea were carefully blacked out by government censors).

If few Koreans knew what was really happening, even fewer people abroad knew the extent of the emerging harsh realities. Most international media reported on Korea from news bureaus in Tokyo.

When those foreign correspondents did come to Korea, they often came only to Seoul, only briefly, and only in crises. When in south Korea, they tended to rely heavily on government and embassy sources.

That is, until those reporters began running into Monday Night Group members – missionaries who shared news that embassy officials either didn't know or wouldn't share. Soon these reporters, and representatives from international church organizations and human rights groups, began drawing from the pool of information shared weekly at Monday Night Group meetings.

By the mid-1970s the Monday Night Group had become a key international conduit. The group received materials from abroad, including banned foreign press reports, to distribute judiciously inside Korea. More importantly, it arranged for letters and documents (such as political prisoner lists, torture reports, and pro-democracy declarations) to be smuggled out of Korea, hand-carried to Tokyo and points beyond.

I was only one of several members of the Foreign Correspondents Club of Japan who made good use of the knowledge and insight of the Monday Night Group. We benefited not only from the information and Korean contacts provided by the group but also from their backgrounding us on Korean cultural sensitivities and political nuances.

Some of the better-known Tokyo-based American reporters who benefited from the Monday Night Group were Don Oberdorfer of the *Washington Post,* Richard Halloran and Fox Butterfield of the *New York Times,* and Elizabeth Pond of the *Christian Science Monitor.*

The Park Chung Hee regime sometimes could not understand how media in Japan and the U.S. could within 24 hours report arrests and beatings that supposedly only the Korean CIA and a handful of other Koreans knew about. The Monday Nighters can now confess: They often had a hand in it.

As the group's international network grew, so did the importance of solidarity groups in Japan and the United States such as the Korea Support Network and the North American Coalition for Human Rights in Korea.

Today, with the internet, the Monday Night Group's methods of global communication seem terribly quaint. It's difficult to comprehend the need for, or the difficulties of, transporting so much paper around the globe.

◈ ◈◈◈ ◈

Koreans bear the scars of their three-decade struggle for democracy and human rights. But their foreign missionary friends did not escape unscathed. Three members of the Monday Night Group were deported, and others were threatened with deportation. Two members of the group suffered as their Korean husbands endured torture and imprisonment; all group members dealt regularly with various forms of government surveillance.

That was the cauldron in which the mustard seeds grew.

Members of the Monday Night Group were mostly missionaries, sent to Korea to transform people's lives. When they eventually returned to their home countries, they were as much transformed as transformers.

The transformations were political, economic, and spiritual.

Members of the Monday Night Group were shocked out of any political naïveté they may have brought into Korea. They could not comprehend the pain that the Park regime inflicted on some of the country's finest Christians and truest patriots. But they were shocked also by U.S. tolerance for and rationalization of those abuses.

Monday Night Group members were also introduced to some

of the dark side of capitalism. International media heralded south Korea's "economic miracle." But these missionaries personally knew too many workers at the bottom of the economic ladder who were paying dearly for that "miracle." Twelve- to 18-hour days, six to seven days a week. Poverty wages. Insufferable working conditions. On-the-job losses of eyesight, limbs, or life itself. Sexual and other exploitation of women workers. Labor "unions" controlled by government and management; labor organizers beaten and arrested.

Of all the transformation and growth experienced by Monday Night Group members, I believe none is more important than their spiritual transformation. For that, they had good role models.

God may be an inscrutable mystery to many of us most of the time, but God's handiwork was clearly evident in the Korean Christians who moved to the forefront of the country's struggle for democracy and human rights. God gave those Koreans wisdom, courage, hope, determination, and endurance that continue to astonish.

As you will see, some of the qualities of those Korean Christians rubbed off on the contributors to this book, deepening their faith, expanding their hearts, and changing them forever.

Just by going abroad, living in a new culture, missionaries anywhere discover that the *world* is larger than they knew or imagined. By working in solidarity with south Koreans in their Spirit-led struggles for democracy and human rights, Monday Night Group members discovered also that *God* was larger than they knew or imagined.

Part of that discovery was that God has a sense of humor. Amid the pain and pathos recorded in these pages, there are also some just plain funny incidents. The humor often involved encounters with, or attempts to avoid, the Korean CIA agents assigned to follow and report on all suspicious persons – including Monday Night Group members.

Introduction: They Had to Do Something

Members of the Monday Night Group were under continual pressure to "stop interfering in Korean domestic affairs." The pressure came from various quarters, beginning with missionary colleagues in Korea and extending as far as members of the U.S. Congress. For example, here are remarks made in the summer of 1975 by U.S. Rep. Otto E. Passman (D-La.):

"Without the form of government you have in South Korea, the great people of South Korea would be under the domination of the policies of North Korea. If you missionaries would teach religion rather than reform and let the South Koreans run their own government, then all people concerned would be better off. If the missionaries cannot attend to their own business and preach religion, they should go home," he said.

The congressman was hardly alone in such criticism. Some American missionaries in south Korea wrote impassioned letters to their U.S. mission board officials protesting the "political involvements" of Monday Night Group types. They detailed how such involvements put all missionaries and their mission work at risk, and they begged the mission boards to rein in the activists.

In every case I know of, including Korea missionary letters to my mission board attacking me as a "communist sympathizer," mission board officials firmly supported the Monday Night Group's witness (and my journalistic work) as compatible with Christian mission and the teachings of Scripture. The importance of this support should not be underestimated. Group members often were surrounded by opponents, hounded by critics, and trailed by government agents, but they never felt abandoned by their friends at home (the Korean Christians) or allies abroad (on the mission boards and in the Korea solidarity groups).

They did feel abandoned by many of their missionary colleagues. Missionary protests against Monday Night Group activism reached their peak in 1975. The group responded in a letter to all missionaries in south Korea. Among other things, the letter attempted to explain why, as Christians, they felt compelled to speak out against evil; it asked why any government should be allowed to determine what is "proper religious activity"; and it expressed regret that some Christians would try to separate what is inseparable in the New Testament: evangelism and social action.

Gene Matthews sent a copy of the letter to mission board officials in New York City. They considered it timely and important, so they turned it into a pamphlet titled "A Tract for Our Times." The full text of the pamphlet appears in the Supplements.

Also in the Supplements are sample "Fact Sheets," one- to three-page reports on a wide variety of topics related to the struggles for democracy and human rights. Monday Night Group members wrote more than 60 of the Fact Sheets, which were then smuggled out of Korea for reproduction and distribution around the world.

Members of the Monday Night Group got involved in the Korean people's struggles for simple, practical reasons:

- They were human. When a bloodied student or prisoner's spouse showed up at their door, he or she was of course invited in.
- They were godly. Their reverence for God and understanding of Scripture allowed them no choice but to welcome the suffering, help the prisoner, and defend the oppressed.
- They had good role models. They could not help but be inspired by the love and sacrifice of Korean Christians at the forefront of the struggle.

Introduction: They Had to Do Something

• And they had several levels of small but powerful support communities -- Korean church relationships such as the National Council of Churches in Korea; worshiping communities such as the Thursday Prayer Meetings and Galilee Church; and international support from mission boards, ecumenical agencies, and solidarity groups.

Members of the Monday Night Group had influence far beyond their numbers. One reason was that they could do things that Koreans could not; and if caught, the missionaries faced much less severe punishments than Koreans would for the same deeds.

The Monday Night Group had several layers of protection. They were foreigners, mostly North Americans. They were Christians. And they were missionaries, which meant they had quick and easy access to world-wide ecclesiastical structures and media networks. The Park Chung Hee government, which otherwise tended to throw caution to the wind, wanted to avoid charges in foreign media that it was persecuting Americans, Christians, and/or missionaries.

For some of the same reasons, the Park regime appeared sensitive to charges of persecution of Korean Christians. If this stopped the government from even more brutal treatment of Christians, it also exasperated some of the government's more hard-line enforcers.

That exasperation was apparent in the government's response to the March 1, 1976, pro-democracy declaration composed by Korean Christians and delivered at Seoul's Myongdong Cathedral. In a statement clearly intended for foreign media – it was released in English in Tokyo – the south Korean government expressed its frustration:

"These people [the declaration signers and their supporters] deliberately took advantage of a religious ritual in an attempt to give the false impression of religious persecution. Thus they betrayed themselves to be devoid of any religious conscience. We deplore that it was an irresponsible and cowardly act."

≈ ≋ ≋ ≈

Koreans are a proud people. Anti-Americanism is part of the flip side of that pride. Maybe it's better described as a love-hate relationship: Koreans love the U.S. for its Korean War sacrifices (more than 50,000 Americans died), but they hate the "ugly American" behavior around the U.S. bases in Korea. They appreciate the security those bases provide, but they dislike the feeling of being an "occupied country." They enjoy American movies and culture, but they wish Americans would show equal respect for Korean culture. They value the political and diplomatic power of the U.S., but reject the myriad ways Americans misuse or abuse that power.

The anti-Americanism that began to take hold on south Korean campuses in the 1960s mushroomed in the 1970s and '80s, spreading beyond students and into the larger population. The primary cause was U.S. support for military dictatorship. Even though President Jimmy Carter was elected on a human rights platform, his State Department reflected the priorities of the Nixon and Ford administrations: geopolitical concerns ultimately outweighed human rights concerns in Korea. The presence of U.S. military bases and more than 40,000 troops in south Korea was of enormous strategic importance for the whole region. Nobody in Washington wanted to disrupt the status quo of American hegemony in northeast Asia.

The result was that many Koreans felt the U.S. was blind and deaf when it came to their struggles for democracy and human rights.

Ironically, the perception that the U.S. did not care about democracy in south Korea might well have helped bring it about. The lack of visible U.S. support meant that the south Korean people had to do more – had to do it all – themselves. They organized, they fought, they leafleted, they petitioned, they went to jail, they got out and spoke out, they died in some cases. They did everything – themselves.

And south Korea became a living, breathing democracy. By struggle, from the grassroots up; not by force from the top down.

I can only imagine the bloodshed if the United States had tried to impose democracy by military force as it attempted later in Iraq.

One recurrent theme of this book is the strength and courage of the Korean women. You will be introduced to ordinary women who did extraordinary things, and some extraordinary women who surpassed even that. Women often stepped to the frontlines of the struggle – and not just when the frontline men were in prison. They took leadership in their own right, speaking out, signing declarations, leading worship, rallying opposition, and giving courage to others to join and do the same.

But women did more than that. I believe that the democracy and human rights struggles of the south Korean people were as much spiritual as they were political – and often it was women who most profoundly made that connection. They helped everyone, male and female, to keep in touch with, and draw strength from, a deep spiritual reservoir.

Women's stories are perhaps the least told, or the most often under-told, in histories of south Korea's democracy and human rights movements.

The Park Chung Hee military dictatorship was efficient and ruthless in conscripting young men, silencing male students, and intimidating male workers. But one of the government's major miscalculations may have been not taking women more seriously, including the wives of political prisoners. The government could not have imagined, for example, that the "People's Revolutionary Party" wives would ever find a public voice. But speak out they did (see Ogle and Sinnott chapters).

Nearly a quarter of a century later, the government finally acknowledged that the "PRP" was a fabrication and that the Park government had murdered eight innocent men. On August 21, 2007 Seoul Central District Court ruled that the government must pay compensation to the surviving family members. The compensation was the largest ever awarded in a political dissent case in Korea. Thus justice was finally achieved, too late to save the eight innocent men but bringing a measure of closure to their long-suffering families.

⁂

One of the interesting things about the democratic revolution that occurred slowly in south Korea over the last three decades of the 20th century is that the Korean Christians who played such central roles in the revolution were a small minority within the Korean Christian community, which at that time comprised a minority of the south Korean people.

Why is this worth noting? Because self-proclaimed "Christian majorities" – in south Korea today as well as in the United States – lay moral claim to levers of conservative state power.

As a small minority within a minority Christian community in the 1970s, the Korean Christian patriots could never have been accused of such arrogance. Any secret ambition to impose a religious or moral agenda would have been laughable. The Korean Christian patriots were more the conscience of the nation than a power base. They sought not power themselves but the empowerment of others, especially the exploited and oppressed.

Perhaps only minorities within minorities can witness with such integrity.

Introduction: They Had to Do Something

The scores of Christian leaders who spoke out in the 1970s were not embedded enough in the system to have a "hidden agenda". Rather, they had a clear vision: of a homeland where the rights of all people were respected and the government reflected the will of the people.

❧ ❧❧ ❧

What led certain missionaries to get involved and take risks while other missionaries did not? The same question could be asked of the millions of Korean Christians: Why did the vast majority support the government, and only a small minority speak out against its abuses?

Some of it was generational. For many older missionaries and older Koreans, the Korean War and anti-communism remained in the foreground of their consciousness. For the contributors to this book – and for younger Koreans and those with personal experience of the wider church and wider world – that consciousness was beginning to recede into the background by the 1970s. With a larger vision, they saw possibilities for a new Korea; they were ready to move beyond fear of communism to hope for a government by and for the people.

But the gap was more than generational. It was also theological. Then and today a majority of Korean Christians, like American Christians, find it easy to associate Christianity with success, wealth, power, the military, and the state or nation. For these believers, obedience to powerful national leaders like Park Chung Hee came easily.

The Korean Christians honored in this book had a different theology, one based on Jesus' ministries among the poor, the suffering, the outcast, the prisoner. Obedience to that ethic outweighed obedience to the state.

How did so few Korean Christians have such a large impact? What they lacked in obedience to the government they made up for in love of country. Their patriotism was rarely doubted, and that patriotism had historical traction: From 1905 to 1945 Koreans lived under Japanese imperial rule, and churches were sometimes the only places where Koreans could gather and quietly give voice to their dream of a nation freed from oppression and domination.

My seminary training prepared me to appreciate the spiritual journeys of the Korean Christians and their supporters in the Monday Night Group. But my journalism school training initially made me skeptical of some of the claims of MNG members. I wanted two or more witnesses of torture before believing that any U.S.-backed government would do such a thing. So the MNG members would hurry me down some of the more remote back alleys of Seoul, duck into coffee shops, and introduce me to some of the victims of torture, scars and all. These credible witnesses told me some incredible stories. Sometimes more than my heart could bear.

What amazed me then, and does to this day, is how much the tortured persons' hearts could bear. I found it incredible that one of the more common results of torture was that, once physical wounds were healed, the tortured rejoined the movement with deepened faith and commitment, with renewed centeredness and resolve.

In my attempts to be an "objective journalist," I confess that I never came up with appropriate words to describe opponents of the Park Chung Hee dictatorship. Secular western media most often referred to them with either the adjective "anti-government" or the noun "dissidents." Both words rankled; they were negative, oppositional words. "Dissidents" seemed to suggest disgruntled, disaffected, disagreeable persons. But the Korean Christians I knew were none of those things; they were always surprisingly positive –

about life, about their faith, about their nation, about prospects for change, about the inevitability of democracy.

To describe them by what they were against missed the point. They deserved to be described for what they were for: justice for all Koreans, economically as well as politically. They were advocates for human rights.

"Patriots" was a more accurate word than "dissidents," for these women and men loved their country.

"Christians" was also more fitting than "dissidents," because the leaders of the opposition understood they were doing simply what Jesus would have them do.

Democracies are fragile. What happened in south Korea under President Park Chung Hee can happen in any democracy anywhere in the world – even again in south Korea. All it takes is a determined president; an acquiescent legislature and cooperative judiciary; controlled media; strong military and police; fear that an enemy "out there" (communism or terrorism) is "in here" (has already infiltrated and can attack any minute); media that play upon such fear; arbitrary "Emergency Decrees" that broaden powers of arrest and detention; appeals to patriotism and "defending our way of life"; unrestricted electronic and other surveillance; suspension or revision of the Constitution; co-optation of civic and religious groups and leaders; suppression of legal, human, and labor rights; and the use of torture.

Democracies may take decades to establish, but they can be torn down in a matter of months.

From 1973 on, Korean CIA agents followed me almost everywhere I went in south Korea. An agent sat in the Seoul YMCA dining room each morning as I ate breakfast. Occasionally I'd enjoy losing my "tail." After being followed to interviews with well-known opponents of the government, I sometimes would briefly stop by the U.S. Embassy in hopes of adding an interesting twist to the agent's logbook.

To this day I don't know if the KCIA ever associated me with any of my writing, because I wrote under a variety of pseudonyms including Frank Lanich, Hasegawa Kazuto, Brian Woodward, Kim Song Jin, and Malcolm Fleming. Many of my articles on Korea were published in some form in the newsletter of the National Christian Council of Japan. None carried my byline. On the front of the newsletter, though, was the name of the NCCJ General Secretary, Rev. John Nakajima.

When the Korean government published a list of "enemies of south Korea," Rev. Nakajima's name was there, and mine wasn't. He was proud; I was amused.

The "enemies" list included various members of the Tokyo foreign correspondent's club, and it ranked them, I recall, from Number One Enemies (incorrigible, unredeemable) to Number Five Enemies (persuadable, invite to Blue House). While working at the press club one night, I heard a correspondent express his embarrassment at being given a "Three," and another his shame over a "Five" rating. "We deserve better," they said.

I remember having dinner with Rev. Pak Hyung Kyu (Pak Hyŏnggyu) before I moved back to the U.S. in 1976. We got to talking about Christianity in south Korea and in the United States. He said, "I believe America today needs missionaries even more than south Korea does."

That's how I understood my calling when I joined Sojourners community and the staff of *Sojourners* magazine in Washington, D.C., in 1977.

I covered President Jimmy Carter's 1979 visit to Seoul, where I distributed lists of south Korea's political prisoners to the unbelieving White House press corps. That seemed to annoy the south Korean government, which first sought to deport me but settled for keeping me under "hotel room arrest" until President Carter's plane departed Seoul.

In the mid-1980s I was a member of another Monday Night Group – one that met in the Washington, D.C., home of Steve Moon (see Glossary) and Faye Moon (see her chapter). That group was comprised of Seoul Monday Night Group "alumni" and other D.C.-area supporters of democracy and human rights in Korea.

In 1988 I was in Seoul as the primary researcher and writer of a 133-page press packet for media covering the Seoul Olympics. It was published by the North American Coalition for Human Rights in Korea. The packet was intended to help foreign reporters look beyond south Korean government press releases and see the harsher political and economic realities.

෴ ෴෴ ෴

The idea of a Monday Night Group book germinated for nearly two decades. "We should write a book" was said at occasional reunions of the group during the 1990s. But it was never acted upon, in part, I think, because these are not persons who like bringing attention to themselves. Their focus was always on their Korean friends and allies, and they felt that *those* persons were more important and *their* stories a higher priority.

Still, the idea lingered.

The Korea Democracy Foundation (KDF) moved the idea along. In October 2003 MNG folk were among those invited to Seoul to be honored and thanked for their involvement in the Korea Democratization Movement. During that week KDF staff conducted a group interview, asking many of the contributors to this book, and others, to share their Korea stories.

More than Witnesses

With KDF's encouragement, the book began to take shape during a July 2004 reunion of the Monday Night Group in Lincoln, Vermont, hosted by Sue and Randy Rice. An editorial team was selected: Henry Em, Linda Jones, Gene Matthews, Louise Morris, Pat Patterson, and myself. Writing assignments were made, and a book proposal was presented to and approved by KDF in 2005.

After many months of writing, editing, rewriting, and restructuring, we were finally able to send KDF the original manuscript and supplemental material. In 2006 they published a beautiful hardbound edition of the book. After more months of revision, correcting and updating, you now hold in your hands the fruits of our collective labor.

Three editorial notes:

1) Korean names in this book begin with the surname or family name (Kim) followed by the individual or given name (Dae Jung). Exceptions are made for commonly understood reversals of that order: so Rhee (surname) Syngman becomes the more popularly accepted Syngman Rhee.

2) The editors have opted to employ two systems for spelling Korean names and places. Initially, they are spelled so that the average reader will be able to approximate the pronunciation as closely as possible. In many cases, for academic purposes the widely accepted McCune/Reischauer system of Romanization is included in parentheses following the first appearance of the name. In addition, commonly recognized names such as Syngman Rhee and Park Chung Hee are left in their most commonly recognized form. Common Korean words are italicized.

3) Until 1945, Korea for centuries had been one nation, one people. Out of respect for that history, and reflecting Koreans' hopes for reunification of their divided nation, our style in this book is to lower-case the "s" and the "n" in south Korea and north Korea.

Introduction: They Had to Do Something

❦ ❧❦ ❦

Readers unfamiliar with south Korea will appreciate the stories in this book more if they first skim the Glossary and the Timeline – and know they can easily refer back to those sources if names or dates get confusing.

❦ ❧❦ ❦

History has many twists and turns. The tortured and imprisoned "criminals" of the 1970s are now recognized heroes of Korea's struggle for democracy and human rights.

But history that swings one way can always swing back. A new generation is rising in south Korea that has no personal experience of the harsh brutalities of Park Chung Hee's rule. And the old saying remains true: those who forget the past risk repeating it.

When I was in Seoul in late 2004, many Koreans told me about the fast rising political career of Park Chung Hee's daughter, Park Geun Hye (Pak Kŭnhye). That in itself would not bother me; I do not believe the sins of fathers are visited on their children. But I heard something more disturbing: that President Park's reputation is being polished. Increasingly he shines as the hero of south Korea's economic miracle; if he trampled on human rights and brutalized his opponents, well, according to the new mindset, that was a necessary sacrifice. It created the political stability that enabled the economic miracle.

Such revisionist history should remind us that struggles for justice and truth never end; they are always ongoing. Military dictatorship, torture, imprisonment, crushing of human rights, denial of civil liberties, outlawing free speech and press, executing innocent persons, harassing opponents, spying on everyone – these must never be thought of simply as "costs of doing business" or, in today's jargon, "collateral damage."

More than Witnesses

Democracy, once achieved, is never locked in place. It must be defended and fought for continuously. One key is never forgetting those who sacrificed their lives and their livelihoods for today's democratic freedoms. They are Korea's true national heroes. They are the Koreans remembered and honored in this book.

❧ ❧❧ ❧

In 1973, a quarter-century before Kim Dae Jung would become president of south Korea, he told me "democracy in south Korea is inevitable."

I reported what he said, but I didn't believe it. As far as I could see – one, three, five years down the road – all I could see was more repression.

I realized much later that Kim Dae Jung was looking 10, 30, even 50 years into the future – whatever it took for vision to become reality.

September 2008

Glossary

Gene Matthews

CBS - *Christian Broadcasting System*: Established in 1954, after the Korean War, CBS is a network of Korean radio stations that broadcasts not only spiritual content and sacred music but also thoughtful news programs and editorials, some of which the Park and Chun regimes found threatening. During much of the '70s and '80s it operated under intense pressure from the government, and at one point was nearly shut down. In spite of these pressures, CBS has broadcast continuously since December 15, 1954, and is now engaged in all forms of mass communications: radio, internet, and television broadcasting.

JOC - *Jeunesse Ouvrière Chrétienne* (Young Christian Workers): A Catholic organization pursuing the rights of laborers. In Korea it has often worked closely with the Urban Industrial Mission (UIM), a Protestant organization modeled along the lines of JOC.

KCIA - *Korean Central Intelligence Agency*: Created in 1961, this agency combined aspects of both the American CIA and FBI but tended to focus much of its effort on controlling government opposition. Following the assassination of President Park Chung Hee in 1979 by the KCIA director, the agency was reorganized and later renamed the Agency for National Security Planning (ANSP). In spite of the new name, it retained its former unlimited power and continued to be used to intimidate and control the populace. With the transition to full democracy in 1999, the agency was again reorganized, its powers were greatly reduced, and it was renamed the National Intelligence Service (NIS).

KCWU - *Korea Church Women United*: An ecumenical organization of Protestant Christian women that served as a persistent thorn in the side of the authoritarian governments with its bold stances on human rights and justice. In addition to its courageous challenge of oppressive government policies, the KCWU became involved, especially in the 1970s, in combating the sex tourism trade in Korea, in working with Korean victims of the atomic bombs dropped on Japan in World War II, and in seeking justice for so-called "comfort women," Korean women who had been forced into providing sexual services for Japanese soldiers during World War II. It remains active in developing women's theology and dealing with issues of injustice.

KSCF – *Korean Student Christian Federation*: An ecumenical organization of Christian Students which was created in the early 1960s from a merger of the former Korea Student Christian Movement (KSCM) and student chapters of the YMCA and YWCA. Decried by some conservative Christians as a radical organization because of its strong emphasis on social justice, it has long served as the Christian conscience of the student resistance in Korea. Beginning in the 1970s and continuing into the 1980s, its activities were closely monitored by the government and much of its adult and student leadership faced arrest and imprisonment. It continues to challenge students to work for justice in society.

NCCK - *National Council of Churches in Korea*: Self-described as an ecumenical council of churches that confesses Jesus Christ as Savior, responds to God's call, and works for God's glory. With its current membership of eight denominations, it seeks peace and unification in Korea, promotes environmental concerns, advocates gender equality in church and society, and works to protect poor and marginalized persons. It also attempts to work in solidarity with other religious bodies in Korea and around the world. Because of its strong emphasis on human rights, the NCCK leadership faced constant surveillance and harassment under the Park and Chun regimes. At various times during the '70s and '80s, much of its leadership was arrested and imprisoned.

PCK - *Presbyterian Church in Korea*: Korea's largest protestant denomination. It tends to be both theologically and politically conservative and generally teaches the inerrancy of Scripture. The PCK seldom opposed the authoritarian governments.

PROK - *Presbyterian Church in the Republic of Korea*: This denomination resulted from a Presbyterian division that occurred in 1953 along liberal/conservative theological grounds. The more liberal PROK has placed strong emphasis on freedom of thought and conscience. The PROK has provided much of the ecumenical leadership in Korea and has often stood in the forefront of Christian struggles for justice. The denomination is historically related to the United Church of Canada.

PRP - *People's Revolutionary Party*: A fictitious political party concocted by the KCIA in 1965 and again in 1973. Under Park

Chung Hee, countless persons in Christian, academic, and labor circles were arrested and accused of supporting this party and its alleged plot to overthrow the government. In April 1975 eight men listed by the KCIA as leaders of the party were executed by hanging. By 2005, the eight men were retried, exonerated and their names cleared. In a later civil case their families received a large financial settlement from the government..

ROK - *Republic of Korea*: The official name, in English, of the southern portion of the Korean peninsula commonly referred to as south Korea.

SMCO - *Seoul Metropolitan Community Organization*: Originally an organizational name, SMCO became shorthand for urban-poor mission work and the urban-poor movement. The movement was formed in 1971, inspired by urban mission work started by Presbyterian missionary Herb White. The SMCO became a major motivating force behind the development of church work among south Korea's urban poor. The work of SMCO is closely identified with Rev. Pak Hyung Kyu (Pak Hyŏnggyu [see below]).

UIM - *Urban Industrial Mission*: A Protestant organization similar in nature to the Catholic JOC. Dr. George Ogle, deported from Korea in 1974 for his efforts on behalf of those accused of membership in the so-called PRP, was instrumental in beginning the work of the UIM in Korea. Because of UIM's stand on behalf of severely exploited workers, its staff and members were under constant pressure from the KCIA.

April 19 - An anniversary that marks the beginning of a 1960 student-led overthrow of the corrupt regime of President Syngman Rhee. Rhee's ouster and subsequent exile to Hawaii seemed to pave the way for democratic reform, but the democratic process was interrupted by a military coup in 1961 led by General Park Chung Hee. An April 19 cemetery and memorial in Seoul recognize the hundreds of students killed in the revolt.

Blue House – *Korean equivalent of the White House in Washington, D.C.*: The structure, named for its beautiful blue-tiled roof, is the official residence of the president of the Republic of Korea and also provides office space for his staff.

Cardinal Kim - *Stephen Cardinal Kim Sou-hwan (Kim Suhwan)*: Long-time leader of the Catholic Church in Korea, appointed archbishop of Seoul April 9, 1968, and elevated to cardinal April 28, 1969. He served in these positions until retirement on April 3, 1998. Cardinal Kim inspired many with his quiet, humble demeanor and keen mind. Under his leadership the Myongdong Cathedral in downtown Seoul became a center of human rights activity.

Christian Building – Located near Seoul's old East Gate, this building housed a number of agencies that played important roles in the human rights struggle. During the 1970s these agencies included the National Council of Churches of Korea and its human rights office, Church Women United, the Korea Student Christian Federation, and the Christian Broadcasting System. The Thursday Morning Prayer Meetings (see below) took place in the Christian Building. The building was regularly surrounded by heavily armed riot police, especially on Thursday mornings, and plainclothesmen were a constant presence inside the building.

Chun Doo Hwan – Korean Army general who staged a mutiny and then a slow-motion coup following the assassination of President Park Chung Hee in 1979. Chun's seizure of power over the military involved armed attacks on the Department of Defense, arrest of the Army chief of staff and 40 other high-ranking officers, elevation to director of the KCIA, and the violent putdown of the 1980 citizen uprising in Kwangju. He was eventually named president in a staged election, and he ruled with an iron hand until his term ended in 1988. After leaving office, investigators found that he had amassed a fortune while serving as president. He and his successor, Roh Tae Woo, were arrested in 1995, convicted of mutiny and treason in 1996, and sentenced to death. Their death sentences were later commuted by President Kim Dae Jung

Chun Tae Il (Chŏn T'aeil) - Young laborer in Seoul's notorious "Peace Market" sweatshops. When his efforts to improve the terrible conditions in the sweatshops were beaten down by the government, he committed self-immolation on November 13, 1970. Since that day his mother and sister have carried on his efforts on behalf of the workers. Today Chun Tae Il is regarded as a hero of the working class in Korea and is the subject of several books and movies.

Emergency Decrees - A series of presidential decrees issued by President Park Chung Hee, ostensibly to prevent overthrow of the government by outside forces but in reality aimed at stifling opposition to the government. Two of the more sweeping decrees were:

Emergency Decree #4 - Issued in 1974, aimed primarily at controlling academia. Among other things, it forbade students from joining certain student organizations, printing materials critical of the government, or leaving class to participate in anti-government demonstrations. It listed punishments ranging from imprisonment for not less than five years up to and including death. In spite of the severe restrictions and harsh punishments, and the arrest of more than 300 students, the decree was only partially successful in curbing anti-government activity by students.

Glossary

Emergency Decree #9 - A catch-all decree issued May 13, 1975, essentially outlawing all anti-government behavior including public criticism. (Text included in the supplements)

Father Ham (pronounced Hahm) Sei Ung - Catholic priest and long-time activist in the Korean people's struggles for human rights and democracy. He was born in Seoul in 1942 and studied theology at the Catholic University of Korea and the Pontificia Universita Urbaniana. He holds a doctoral degree in theology from the Gregorian University of Rome. Ordained a priest in 1968, he became rector of the Eungamdong (Ŭngamdong) Church in 1973. In 1974 he served as a spokesperson for the "Democracy Recovery National Congress" and became a leading member of the Catholic Priests' Association for Justice. Since 2004, Father Ham has served as president of the Korea Democracy Foundation.

Galilee Church - A small gathering of Christians who met each Sunday afternoon to worship, to share their stories of suffering and of joy, to decry oppression, and to declare their freedom in and through Jesus Christ. Those who experienced this worship said it felt like what Jesus Christ must have intended the church to be.

han - The inner anger and angst of the Korean people arising from their history of oppression. Its theological and political expression is the imperative to acknowledge and respond to suffering. Culturally, Han is expressed as the strength to endure, a spiritual strength derived from that very suffering.

Kim Dae Jung – Long-time proponent of democracy, he was inaugurated president of the Republic of Korea on February 25, 1998, and held office until February 25, 2003. Because of his pro-democracy stance and championing of human rights, he was subjected to harsh treatment by the military regimes. He was nearly assassinated on two occasions and was sentenced to death under President Chun Doo

Hwan, a sentence later commuted. Kim Dae Jung in turn pardoned former Presidents Chun Doo Hwan and Roh Tae Woo after both were sentenced to death. Kim was awarded the Nobel Peace Prize in 2000 for his efforts to promote dialogue and reconciliation between south and north Korea.

Kim Kwan Suk (Kim Kwansŏk) – PROK minister who provided much of Korea's ecumenical leadership during the long human rights struggle. He served as NCCK general secretary and then president of CBS when those institutions were under intense scrutiny and pressure from government security agencies. During his term as NCCK general secretary he was arrested on trumped-up charges and served several months in prison. He died February 4, 2002, at age 80.

Kwangju – City in southwestern Korea, a section of the country long discriminated against politically and economically by the authoritarian regimes in Seoul. From May 18 to May 27, 1980, it was the center of an uprising against the military takeover of the Korean government by Chun Doo Whan. The putdown of the revolt by south Korean military forces, which killed hundreds of Kwangju residents, epitomizes for many the ruthlessness of Chun's dictatorship. (See Chapter 15)

Lee Oo Jung (Yi Ujŏng) – Outstanding theologian and justice advocate, former professor of theology at Hanshin University and Seoul Women's University. Included in her many leadership roles were president of the National Church Women's Association of the Presbyterian Church in the Republic of Korea, president of Korea Church Women United, and president of the Korean Association of Women Theologians. She held leadership positions in the National Council of Churches of Korea and the Geneva-based World Council of Churches. She also participated in the creation of the movement of Asian Women Theologians and the Association of Third World Theologians. During the period of dictatorial government in south Korea, her active leadership in the struggle for human rights meant frequent detention, interrogation, and living under constant surveillance. Through Korea Church Women United, she brought attention to the plight of Korea's so called "comfort women" and also ministered to the Korean victims of the atomic bombs dropped on Japan. In spite of ill health, she worked tirelessly on behalf of all victims of injustice until her death on May 31, 2002.

Lee Tai Young (Yi T'aeyǒng) – Born in 1914, she became Korea's first woman lawyer in 1952. She was a courageous Christian woman who pioneered work on behalf of women's rights in Korea. That work led eventually to the establishment of a Legal Aid Center that provided free legal counsel for poor women. She was the 1975 winner of the prestigious Magsaysay Award for her human rights work. She died in 1988 at age 74.

March 1 – A national holiday commemorating the date in 1919 when Korean patriots and students declared independence from Japan. The peaceful uprising caught the Japanese rulers by surprise, and the Japanese gendarmes responded brutally to put down the uprising. Hundreds of Korean citizens, including many students, were killed and thousands of others were arrested, tortured, and executed or otherwise died in prison.

Minjung – A term somewhat difficult to translate into English: the literal translation means simply "the mass of people." Culturally, the meaning is more complex and overtly political, taking on the idea of the people both as victims of oppression and as the subject of struggles for liberation. In Korea the term has given rise to a progressive Christian theology. Although outstanding scholars have written about *Minjung* Theology, its very definition as a dynamic theology and practice arising from the experiences of the common people would almost seem to preclude any systemization. Another important derivative is Minjung art and literature that convey the experience of suffering and struggle of the common people. The term *han* (see above) is often mentioned in the context of Minjung.

Moon Ik Whan (Mun Ikhwan) – Timothy Moon, PROK minister: Many have described Timothy as the conscience of the Korean church during this era. He inspired thousands with his teaching, preaching, writing, and willingness to go to prison for his beliefs. A constant thorn in the side of the dictatorial regimes, he spent many months in prison on various occasions. At the time of his death on January 18, 1994, the road leading up to Han Kuk Seminary where he taught for many years was lined with thousands of bouquets of flowers from those who came to honor his life.

Moon Tong Whan (Mun Tonghwan) – Stephen Moon – one of a remarkable family of Christian leaders who provided leadership, inspiration, and theological insight in Korea's struggle for democracy. He was a PROK minister like his older brother Timothy, and their lives paralleled each other in many remarkable ways. Minister, teacher, prisoner of conscience, preacher, and prophet, Steve is married to Faye Moon, one of the contributors to this book.

Nam San (Namsan) – A mountain that once marked the southern area of the old walled city of Seoul but now stands more or less in the center of the enormous metropolitan area that has engulfed it. Nam San (literally "south mountain") became infamous and assumed a separate identity when the KCIA established its headquarters on the side of the mountain. Located in the sub-basements of the headquarters were the notorious KCIA torture chambers. When students, professors, journalists, and Christian ministers were taken by the KCIA for interrogation, they were commonly said to have been "taken to Nam San." In a later example of a somewhat macabre sense of humor, the torture chambers were referred to as the "dry cleaner."

Pak Hyung Kyu (Pak Hyŏnggyu) – PROK minister who, early in his career, served as general secretary of the Korea Student Christian Federation and later was closely identified with the work of Seoul Metropolitan Community Organization (SMCO). Because of his continuing efforts to minister to the poor and oppressed in Korea, Pak was despised by dictatorial governments, intent on bolstering Korea's economy through exploitation of poor workers. Rev. Pak was frequently arrested and imprisoned. When he refused to bow under to these pressures, the government resorted to different tactics. Government-sponsored thugs invaded his church and drove him from the building. Undaunted, he began conducting worship services on the street. Following the democratization of Korea, Pak became the first president of the Korea Democracy Foundation.

Park Chung Hee – Dictator who ruled south Korea with an iron hand from 1961 – 1979. He first seized power in a military coup in 1961 and ruled the country militarily until 1963 when he was elected president. He was re-elected in 1967, then amended the constitution so he could run again in 1971. He defeated long-time proponent of democracy, Kim Dae Jung, in that election, which many assumed was rigged. In 1972 President Park imposed martial law and began ruling by a series of increasingly harsh emergency decrees. Finally, he imposed his Yushin Constitution, which essentially established him as president for life and forbade any criticism of his regime. Park survived an assassination attempt in 1974 which took the life of his wife. He himself was assassinated in 1979 by the head of the KCIA. Under Park's harsh rule countless opponents were arrested, tortured, imprisoned and, in some cases, executed.

More than Witnesses

Peace Market –Notorious sweatshop market area near Seoul's historic East Gate. The large multi-story buildings comprising the market consisted of hundreds of small shops on the lower floors where an imposing array of merchandise could be purchased at very cheap prices. The upper floors were divided horizontally into lofts with such low ceilings that the young children workers could not stand upright; they had to work bent over sewing machines. The combination of long hours, bad ventilation, dust, low wages, inadequate diet, and sleep deprivation took an enormous toll on those who worked there. On November 13, 1970, a young worker named Chun Tai Il immolated himself on the street in front of the market to call attention to the plight of the workers.

Sarang-bang (Sarangbang) Church – This remarkable "church without walls" grew out of an effort by Christian leaders from the Thursday Morning Prayer Meeting to be in ministry to slum dwellers in the capital city. The slum dwellers were constantly being uprooted from their meager tents and cardboard shacks as the city expanded and "developed." They usually settled on a vacant piece of property where they pitched crude tents and built shacks that were soon torn down by government-hired thugs. When the slum dwellers then settled temporarily in a vacant section of southeastern Seoul, Timothy Moon and others began holding worship services in the open space between the tents. For a brief time, the Sarang-bang Church brought hope and joy to the slum dwellers. But the government soon bulldozed the entire community – including the Cross under which it worshipped.

Seoul – The capital city of the Republic of Korea: Interestingly, the word means simply "capital."

Thursday Morning Prayer Meetings – When many Protestant and Catholic clergy and lay persons were included in the various sweeping arrests that took place under the regime of Park Chung Hee, their family members and friends began to gather for prayer each Thursday morning in the second-floor chapel of the Christian Building. They were soon joined by others including some who initially had no religious affiliation. The plight of those accused in the fabricated PRP plot first came to light during one of these prayer meetings. Wives of the alleged PRP plotters joined the gatherings and reported on the dire straits of their husbands. Fiery sermons and prayers criticizing the Park regime became routine at these prayer meetings, and participants found great strength in sharing this time of worship. Also attending, stoically taking notes and recording the services, were numerous KCIA agents. The government both despised and feared this powerful gathering.

West Gate Prison – A prison located on what was once the western edge of Seoul's walled city, it was notorious during Japan's annexation and rule of Korea from 1910 to 1945. Japan used it as a center for detention and torture of Korean opponents of Japanese rule. Presidents Park Chung Hee and Chun Doo Hwan also used it to detain and torture their opponents. The 1975 executions of the eight alleged PRP men took place in West Gate Prison. Following democratization, the prison was converted to a memorial park and is now somewhat of a tourist attraction.

Yushin – Title given to a revised constitution in 1972. The word has been translated into English as "revitalizing reforms." In October 1972 the government of Park Chung Hee declared martial law, dissolved the legislature, and suspended the 1962 constitution. The following month, the government introduced the new constitution. It essentially established Park Chung Hee as president for life and gave him unlimited power to stamp out opposition.

 *Timeline*

Henry Em and Jim Stentzel

South Korean
Historical Highlights
Emphasizing 1969-1980

Before 1945

670 - 936 CE: Unified Silla Period

918 – 1392: Koryo (Koryŏ) dynasty

1392 – 1910: Choson (Chosŏn) dynasty

1905: Korea becomes a Japanese protectorate. United States and Great Britain support Japan's takeover of Korea.

August 29, 1910: Korean monarch abdicates, and Korea is annexed by Japan.

March 1, 1919: Nation-wide demonstrations for Korea's independence. Nationalists in exile create a Korean Provisional Government in Shanghai.

Timeline

1930s: Korean communists wage armed struggle in Manchuria against Japanese imperial forces.

☙ ⌘⌘ ☙

1945-1968

August 8, 1945: Soviet Union enters war against Japan.

August 11, 1945: United States drafts General Order Number One, which proposes that U.S. forces will occupy Korea south of the 38th parallel; Soviet forces will occupy Korea north of the 38th parallel.

August 15, 1945: After the atomic bombing of Hiroshima and Nagasaki, Japan surrenders to the United States. Soviet Union agrees to U.S. proposal for a divided occupation of Korea.

1947: Soviet Union proposes simultaneous withdrawal of troops from Korea; United States takes the Korea issue to the United Nations.

May 10, 1948: U.N. oversees separate elections in southern Korea.

August 15, 1948: Republic of Korea (south Korea) inaugurated, with Syngman Rhee as president.

September 9, 1948: Democratic People's Republic of Korea (north Korea) inaugurated, with Kim Il Sung as premier.

November 1948: President Rhee passes the National Security Law through the National Assembly. The law prohibits any seditious organizations; 188,621 people are arrested in the first full year after its enactment.

December 25, 1948: Soviet Army leaves north Korea.

More than Witnesses

June 30, 1949: United States Army leaves south Korea.

1950-1953: The Korean War. More than two million north Korean civilians die, along with 500,000 north Korean soldiers. Some one million Chinese soldiers die. Approximately one million south Korean civilians die, along with about 50,000 south Korean soldiers. U.S. deaths are put at 54,246, along with 3,194 dead among other U.N. forces.

July 27, 1953: An armistice is signed, but the Korean War ends without a peace treaty.

1958: United States deploys nuclear weapons in south Korea. (They are withdrawn in 1991 by President George H.W. Bush.)

Winter, 1958-59: President Rhee amends the National Security Law, mandating up to five years in prison for "knowingly distorting facts...to benefit the enemy."

February 15, 1960: The opposition candidate, Cho Pyong-Ok (Cho Pyŏng-Ok), dies of cancer. Rhee government sets mid-March date for presidential election.

March 15, 1960: Presidential election held; ballot boxes disappear from opposition strongholds; other fraud and abuse committed by the Rhee government.

April 19, 1960: More than 100,000 students and young people converge on the presidential palace in "the April 19 Revolution." Palace guards fire into the crowd.

April 26, 1960: U.S. Ambassador Walter McConaughy and General Carter Magruder urge Rhee to resign. Several days later President Rhee resigns and goes into exile in Hawaii.

Timeline

June-July, 1960: Second Republic begins. Democratic Party wins majority in both houses of Korea's first bicameral legislative body. The National Assembly elects Yun Po-Son (Yun Po-Sun) as figurehead president and Chang Myong (Chang Myŏng) is selected to head the government as Prime Minister.

May 15, 1961: Major General Park Chung Hee and Brigadier General Kim Jong Pil overthrow the Chang Myung (Chang Myŏng) government in a bloodless military coup d'état. Park presides over a military junta. That summer, Kim creates the Korean Central Intelligence Agency (KCIA), with help from the American CIA. A committee within the KCIA, with the help of Harvard political scientist Rupert Emerson, prepares a new constitution.

October 1963: Park Chung Hee is elected president, narrowly defeating Yun Po-son. (Yun Po Sun) Beginning of the Third Republic.

Spring 1964: Student anti-government demonstrations.

August 1964: Government arrests persons it alleges are connected to a "People's Revolutionary Party." Meanwhile, the KCIA grows from a staff of 3,000 (1961) to a network of 370,000 agents and informers.

April 3, 1965: South Korea and Japan restore diplomatic relations under the Korea-Japan Treaty. Japan gives south Korea $300 million in grants and $200 million in loans; the $500 million is called "aid", but is understood as reparations for Japan's colonial rule of Korea.

March 4, 1966: Under the Brown Memorandum, the U.S. agrees to provide $1 billion to south Korea over five years.

1966: South Korea agrees to send 50,000 troops to aid U.S. war effort in Vietnam. By 1973, more than 300,000 south Korean soldiers will have fought in Vietnam.

1968: North Korea seizes U.S. spy ship *Pueblo.* KCIA kidnaps several Koreans living in West Germany and tries them in Seoul for being "pro-North Korea."

~ ～ ～ ~

1969-1980

October 1969: President Park Chung Hee gets a constitutional amendment allowing him to run for a third term.

November 13, 1970: Chun Tae Il (Chŏn T'aeil), a young garment worker, burns himself to death to protest working conditions in Seoul's sweatshops.

April 1971: Park Chung Hee is re-elected to a third term as president, narrowly defeating Kim Dae Jung amidst charges of vote fraud.

May 1971: Kim Dae Jung is run over by a truck and permanently injured in a KCIA-inspired assassination attempt.

July 1971: U.S. Secretary of State Henry Kissinger secretly visits Beijing. North Korean Premier Kim Il Sung is also in Beijing secretly. Seven months later (February 1972) President Nixon visits China.

December 1971: President Park declares a state of emergency because of "rapidly changing international and domestic situations."

July 4, 1972: In a press conference at KCIA headquarters, south Korea announces that it has been engaged in secret talks with north Korea regarding a "broad national unity" – peaceful reunification independent of influence by "outside forces."

October 1972: Park imposes martial law, suspends the constitution, dissolves the National Assembly, closes universities, prohibits all political activities, and begins strict censorship of the press.

Timeline

November 21, 1972: President Park's Yushin ("revitalizing reforms") Constitution is ratified in a national referendum, inaugurating the Fourth Republic. Among other things Yushin allows the president to serve unlimited terms and to appoint one-third of the members of the National Assembly.

April 1973: Tens of thousands of Christians attend an Easter sunrise service where leaflets entitled "Christian Manifesto" are distributed quoting Old Testament prophets and protesting government oppression and corruption. Rev. Pak Hyung Kyu (Pak Hyŏnggyu) and others are later arrested and charged with "insurrection."

August 1973: Opposition leader Kim Dae Jung is abducted from a Tokyo hotel room by KCIA agents and placed under house arrest in Seoul.

January 1974: President Park issues first three of what would become nine Emergency Decrees that enhance his powers to silence, arrest, and imprison those who object to his rule.

April 1974: Government fabricates a new "People's Revolutionary Party" (PRP) plot (see August 1964) and arrests 20 alleged conspirators. Student demonstrations grow in size and frequency. Student groups calling themselves the National Federation of Democratic Youth and Students (NFDYS) issue "Declaration on the People, Nation, and Democracy." In response to the declaration, the government issues Emergency Decree #4 authorizing arrests without warrants. Hundreds of students, clergy, and prominent citizens are arrested in the following weeks, including Catholic Bishop Chi Hak Soon, former President Yun Po Sun (Yun Posŏn), and the staff of the Korean Student Christian Federation (KSCF).

June 1974: The National Council of Churches of Korea (NCCK) denounces the government for using anti-communist ideology to justify repression and to disrupt the ministries of the Urban Industrial Mission (UIM) and the KSCF.

July 1974: Prosecutor asks death sentences for seven persons, including poet Kim Chi Ha, for alleged involvement in the NFDYS case.

August 1974: Military Court sentences Bishop Chi, Rev. Pak, and others to 15 years in prison in NFDYS case.

August 1974: President Park's wife is assassinated in what appears to be an attempt on the president's life.

September 1974: Joint Catholic-Protestant prayer meeting calls for abolition of Emergency Decrees and immediate release of all political prisoners.

November 22, 1974: U.S. President Gerald Ford visits south Korea.

December 1974: U.S. United Methodist missionary George Ogle is deported. *Dong-A Ilbo* newspaper protests government threats against advertisers; launches campaign for public to buy ad space.

January 1975: Christian churches announce campaign to collect 1,000,000 signatures in support of constitutional revision. Police confiscate the signature lists.

February 1975: Two days after declaring a national emergency and putting the military on full alert, the government holds a national referendum on the Yushin system and announces 73 percent approval.

March 1975: *Chosun Ilbo* and *Dong-A Ilbo* reporters demand freedom of press; many are fired.

Timeline

April 1975: Eight defendants in the alleged PRP case are executed by hanging. Five of the bodies are forcibly cremated. A U.S. Maryknoll priest, Fr. Jim Sinnott, is deported for protesting the executions.

May 1975: President Park issues Emergency Decree #9 authorizing sentences up to death for "denying, opposing, distorting, or defaming" the Yushin Constitution (i.e., Park's rule).

May 1975: Gulf Oil admits to U.S. Congress that it contributed $4 million toward President Park's 1966 and 1971 elections.

January 1976: Seven hundred Protestants and Catholics issue pro-democracy appeal at prayer service in Wonju.

March 1976: Eighteen prominent religious, political, and intellectual leaders issue a "Declaration of Conscience" at Myongdong (Myŏngdong) Cathedral (Roman Catholic) in Seoul. Ms. Lee Oo Jung (Yi Ujŏng), head of Korean Church Women United, reads the statement and is the first of 27 who will be arrested in connection with the declaration. The government labels Kim Dae Jung, Fr. Ham Sei Ung, and Rev. Moon Ik Hwan (Mun Ikhwan) "leaders of the conspiracy."

March 1977: "A Declaration of Workers' Human Rights" is issued at Myongdong Cathedral, demanding removal of Emergency Decree #9 and calling for a minimum wage of $63 per month, the right to bargain collectively, and the right to strike.

August 1977: Government forcibly removes urban poor by demolishing some 2,000 riverside and 5,000 hillside shacks in Seoul.

February 1978: Hired gangsters invade the union office at the Dong-Il Textile Company in Inchon, destroying equipment and hurling excrement on women union officers and members.

June 1978: Estimated 10,000 persons demonstrate near government buildings in Seoul. Police brutally disperse the crowd and make 67 arrests.

September 1978: Rev. Cho Hwa Soon, Methodist pastor and Urban Industrial Mission (UIM) leader, is among 27 arrested following a prayer meeting in support of fired workers at the Dong-Il Textile Co.

October 1978: Fired *Dong-A Ilbo* reporters are arrested for publishing a special edition of their newsletter covering human rights abuses in the past year.

November 1978: Rev. Pak Hyung Kyu (Pak Hyŏnggyu) is sentenced to five years in prison on charges of "mismanaging church funds."

January 1979: Some 130 political prisoners in prisons across south Korea conduct a coordinated two-week hunger strike to protest prison brutality.

March 1979: Staff of the Korean Christian Academy are arrested and tortured for their efforts to help farmers and laborers. Rev. Cho Hwa Soon is sentenced to five years in prison for her work with laborers.

April 1979: Nearly 200 workers are injured as riot police disrupt a meeting of 500 women workers at the YH Trading Company. The workers were protesting a decision to close the company rather than allow workers to organize. In a separate incident, 38 students in Seoul's Sodaemun (Sŏdaemun) Prison are brutally beaten by guards.

June 1979: Government puts hundreds of persons under house arrest in anticipation of U.S. President Jimmy Carter's meeting with President Park. Church leaders express regret over Carter's embrace of Park. Missionaries oppose the visit.

Timeline

July 1979: Government releases 86 political prisoners, including Rev. Pak Hyung Kyu (Pak Hyŏnggyu), in response to a request from President Carter.

August 1979: Nearly 1,000 women workers of the YH Company flee a riot police attack on their company dorm and seek safety in the opposition New Democratic Party headquarters. One woman dies as police violently remove the women and their supporters from the headquarters. Nine days later, more than 10,000 persons protest the incident at a Mass for Peace and Justice at Myongdong (Myŏngdong) Cathedral.

October 26, 1979: President Park is shot to death by KCIA Director Kim Jae Kyu during an argument over how to put down growing anti-government protests. Martial law declared. Investigation into the assassination is headed by Major General Chun Doo Hwan. Prime Minister Choi Kyu Ha (Ch'oe Kyuha) named acting president.

November 1979: Under the guise of attending a "wedding," opponents of extended martial law gather at the Myongdong (Myŏngdong) YWCA in Seoul. Army troops and riot police break up the meeting, arresting 96 persons and severely torturing some of them, including revered 75-year-old Quaker elder Hahm Sok Hon and teacher Kim Yong Bok (husband of Marion Kim whose chapter appears in this book).

December 12, 1979: In the first stage of a military coup d'état, Generals Chun Doo Hwan and Roh Tae Woo lead a blitz attack on the Korean Army headquarters, killing an undisclosed number of soldiers and arresting the Army chief of staff and some 40 other top military officers. Separately, the government announces that 25,957 persons had been detained since martial law was declared in late October.

March 11, 1980: General John Wickham, commander of ROK/U.S. Combined Forces Command, tells *Asian Wall Street Journal* that south Korea's military plays a positive political role as "watchdogs on political activity that could be destabilizing."

May 1980: Chun Doo Hwan exercises his military and KCIA powers to extend martial law to the entire country and to dissolve the National Assembly. Protest demonstrations grow in number and size across the country. Protesting students in Kwangju are brutally beaten by south Korean Army Special Forces (paratroopers). More than 200,000 citizens of Kwangju take to the streets to express their outrage; they succeed in driving the Special Forces from the city by May 23. The Army retakes the city on May 27 in a nine-hour assault. Casualties for the 10-day siege are startling, with hundreds of citizens killed and thousands injured.

August 1980: Acting President Choi Kyu Ha (Ch'oe Kyuha) resigns and General Chun Doo Hwan is named president by the National Council for Unification.

September 1980: Opposition leader Kim Dae Jung is sentenced to death by a military tribunal on charges of sedition for allegedly instigating the protests in Kwangju.

October 22, 1980: A new constitution is passed, inaugurating south Korea's Fifth Republic. *See February 1981.*

⤝ ⧫⧫ ⤞

1981-2000

January 1981: Kim Dae Jung's death sentence is upheld by the Supreme Court, but within hours is commuted to life imprisonment as an act of "clemency" by President Chun. Chun dissolves Chonggye (Ch'ŏnggye) Garment Workers' Union.

Timeline

February 1981: Chun Doo Hwan is elected president under the revised constitution.

March 1982: Kim Dae Jung's life sentence is commuted to 20 years in prison.

December 1982: Kim Dae Jung's 20-year sentence is suspended, and he goes into exile in the U.S. through February 1985.

October 9, 1983: A bomb kills six high-ranking south Korean government officials in Rangoon, Burma. President Chun Doo Hwan, the intended victim, is not harmed. North Korean agents are believed responsible for the bombing.

June 1987: Mass movement marks a major turning point in Korea's struggle for democracy; middle-class people join students in continuous street demonstrations in urban areas across south Korea. This is generally recognized as the genesis of genuine democracy.

June 29, 1987: President Roh Tae Woo capitulates to demands for democracy in the face of nationwide, student-led protests. Promises direct presidential elections, an open campaign without repression, amnesties for political prisoners, and easing of press controls. *See December 16, 1987.*

July 1987: Kim Dae Jung is cleared of all outstanding charges and his political rights are restored.

December 16, 1987: Factional strife in opposition party between followers of Kim Young Sam and followers of Kim Dae Jung allows Roh Tae Woo (co-conspirator with Chun Doo Hwan in the 1979 military coup) to win presidential election with less than 36 percent of the vote.

More than Witnesses

1990: Kim Young Sam merges his splinter party with Roh Tae Woo's ruling party and with Kim Jong Pil's party; the three-party merger creates the Democratic Liberal Party.

1992: Kim Young Sam is elected president with slightly more than 40 percent of the vote.

June 1994: Former U.S. President Jimmy Carter visits north Korea.

October 21, 1994: North Korea agrees to freeze and eventually dismantle its nuclear reactors. U.S. agrees to provide North with light-water reactors, to lift economic embargo, and to adopt policy of nuclear non-aggression.

March - August 1996: Chun Doo Hwan and Roh Tae Woo are put on trial for their military coup in 1979 and for the May 1980 massacre of citizens in Kwangju. The two former presidents are jailed, then pardoned and released on December 22, 1997.

December 1997: Financial and economic crisis sweeps Asia. On December 3 the International Monetary Fund agrees to a $57 billion loan to south Korea. On December 18 Kim Dae Jung is elected to a five-year term as president of south Korea.

March 1998: President Kim sends large amounts of food aid to north Korea.

June 13-15, 2000: President Kim makes historic visit to Pyongyang, north Korea, for the first-ever inter-Korea summit meeting.

November 2000: Kim Dae Jung is awarded the Nobel Peace Prize for his efforts to promote dialogue and reconciliation between south and north Korea.

Chapter 1

Our Hearts Cry with You*

George E. Ogle

It was December 1974 – more than 20 years after I arrived in Korea as a Methodist missionary – when things came to a head.

For years the Park Chung Hee government had harassed our Urban Industrial Mission, accusing us of being "communists" or "communist dupes" because of our ministry to laborers. Now the government's anger was focused on me because of my public defense of eight innocent men – men the government was preparing to execute for "plotting communist revolution."

The U.S. Embassy in Seoul passed on to me a message from the foreign minister of south Korea: apologize for the "errors" of my way, and state my intention regarding future work in Korea.

I could not apologize and betray the trust placed in me by so many people. I could not apologize and betray the foundations of my faith and belief. But I could tell the government my future intention as a Christian minister living in Korea. So I wrote and signed a letter that concluded:

Jesus was a poor man. He lived and died for the salvation of man's soul and society. I have intended that my acts as a missionary in Korea should follow that path. I have no political or social ambitions and support no political party. I do, however, intend to practice Christ's message of salvation, freedom and justice and to serve those who are suffering.

The foreign minister found my statement inadequate. Two days later at seven in the morning a black jeep pulled up in front of our home. The process of my deportation had begun.

I was born in Pitcairn, a small railroad town in the mining district of Western Pennsylvania, in 1929, the year of the stock market crash. My father was fortunate to keep his job in the post office. My ears and heart tuned in to the struggles of family and neighbors to survive during the years of economic hardship. The churches in our community had strong influence on our values. Two of my brothers served in the military during World War II. My mother went to work at the Westinghouse Airbrake plant. When I graduated from high school the probabilities were that, like many of my classmates, I would join the ranks of local factory workers, and, like my brother Stuart, eventually go to Korea as a soldier.

The principal of my high school changed the course of my life. He encouraged me to go to college and arranged for special scholarships so I could attend Maryville College in Tennessee. In college I had the good fortune to study under Dr. Verton Queener, who had worked in Washington, D.C. during the days of President Franklin D, Roosevelt. I learned from him how economics policies affect justice or injustice for workers. This helped me to understand the situations I had observed in my youth and gave me some insight into how we might affect a more positive future.

From Maryville I went on to Duke Divinity School. One professor made sure we students became acquainted with the labor movement in North Carolina. Also, I was exposed to the Catholic Worker-priest Movement. Catholic priests exchanged clergy garb for workers' coveralls. They believed that their lives as laborers helped complete the incarnation of Christ into the world of the poor.

During my college and seminary years, the Korean War dominated the news. Because my brother Stuart was serving there, I was especially interested. In my third year of seminary Rev. Mah Kyung Il (Ma Kyŏngil), a new classmate from Korea, taught me much about his country. When the Board of Missions of the Methodist Church came to Duke Divinity School to recruit missionaries, no one was surprised that I agreed to join their three-year mission program in Korea.

I began my journey with the Korean people in September 1954 – just one year after the truce was signed between north and south Korea.

As a single missionary I had the flexibility to move into a Korean house with my language teacher. I immersed myself in the Korean language and took every opportunity to participate in Korean life. My assignment was to teach English at the Methodist Seminary in Taejon (Taejŏn) and the Young Myong (Yŏngmyŏng) Boy's High School in Kong Ju (Kongju), and to work with the youth of the church. I wasn't a very good English teacher, but my experiences during this time helped create a vision for possible future ministry.

More than Witnesses

In post-war Korea people were focused on survival and rebuilding. Anti-communism and fear of war dominated everything. Millions of people were adjusting to the reality of not knowing what happened to family members remaining in north Korea. At the same time one could see the beginning of an industrial revolution that would rapidly transform south Korea from a rural to an industrial nation.

Watching the reconstruction of factories and the development of small manufacturing businesses, I knew that a ministry to labor would be needed.

When I completed my three-year term in Korea, I moved to Chicago where I served as pastor of a small church in the West Side Christian Parish – an interdenominational inner-city ministry. During that time I attended three universities, taking courses that I felt would help me to develop a ministry to labor in Korea. I also met Dorothy, who knew I was headed back to Korea and agreed to marry me.

When I returned to south Korea with Dorothy in February 1960, we lived in a second-story missionary apartment nestled between Paejae Boys' High School and Ewha Girls' High School in the center of Seoul. As we began our full-time Korean language study at Yonsei University, part of our mind was trying to concentrate on learning Korean, and the other part was trying to understand the ongoing political chaos in Korean society.

The week we arrived, students in the southern city of Taegu were demonstrating against government corruption and economic chaos. In March Syngman Rhee, south Korea's President since 1948, was re-elected in rigged elections. Students around the country demonstrated in protest. In early April the body of Kim Ju-yol (Kim

Chu-Yŏl) ,was found in the ocean near Masan. The student had been killed by teargas and his body thrown into the sea by police.

A nonviolent protest at Korea University in Seoul was met by government troops who killed 186 students and injured more than 6,000. Within a few days the conflict escalated throughout the country, resulting in a full-scale revolution that continued until President Syngman Rhee resigned. The students also demanded the resignation of the National Assembly and the removal of former government supporters from the staffs of universities and colleges. The students were regarded as national heroes.

"The spirit of freedom has triumphed over tyranny.... The despotism of twelve years has finally fallen before the wrath of the people," the *Voice of Korea* said in its May 1960 issue. The nineteenth of April (4/19) was declared a national holiday, celebrated to this day.

A parliamentary form of government was established under Prime Minister Chang Myun (Chang Myŏn) and President Yun Po Sun (Yun Po-Sŏn) , whose powers had been considerably weakened under a revised constitution. This new government was faced with the aftermath of years of political oppression and a struggling economy. Splits in Chang Myun's party made it impossible to command a stable majority. In addition, his government adopted a series of measures that were very unpopular. The police force had been so discredited that it could not maintain order. In this atmosphere the students went out of control. They had no plan to govern, but they were frequently out on the streets protesting. While they had no guns or weapons, their actions became increasingly militant.

We read about some of this in the newspaper, but I witnessed first-hand the destruction of the home of my next-door neighbor, long-time missionary Dr. Charles Sauer. He had volunteered temporarily to chair the board of Yonsei University when no Korean would agree to do it. The students were opposed to a foreigner being in that position. Giving just enough warning for Dr. and Mrs. Sauer to leave the house, the students stormed the missionary compound, knocked open the door to the Sauer house and spent an hour or so breaking up all the furniture, cutting the upholstery, and even pulling out the bathtub from the wall, allowing the water to pour out of the pipes. The only thing left standing was a beautiful chrysanthemum that flowed gloriously down to the floor.

By early 1961 there was a campaign to collect signatures in favor of reunification, and in April students were demanding postal, economic, and cultural exchanges with north Korea.

*　＊＊＊　*

About six in the morning on May 16, 1961, the sound of gunfire startled us out of our sleep. It sounded like it was coming from the playground of Paejae High School right below our porch windows. I got out of bed and crawled to the window and peered out over the windowsill. The shooting continued but there was nothing to see.

The first thing that came to mind was that the communists had come. Had the Korean War flared up again?

It could not have been students. They had no guns.

*　＊＊＊　*

Dorothy and I tried to act calm for the sake of our ten-month-old son, who had started to cry. We turned on the radio, but the U.S. Army radio station did not mention what was taking place. The doorbell rang. Was this someone coming to tell us to evacuate? No, it was a beggar who had also been aroused from his sleep and decided to get an early start on his rounds. We asked him what was going on. He said that "the reds had come," but it was clear that he knew no more than we did.

Like many, we breathed a sigh of relief when we learned that a bloodless coup had taken place. But we had no idea how the next 26 years of military rule would cause so much suffering for the laborers we would come to know in the mission work we were about to start.

The United States was slow to comment on the coup. The commanding general of the joint military forces was an American, but this coup was carried out without his knowledge. The Americans liked the coup's front man, General Chang Do Yung (Chang Toyong), but they became apprehensive when they found out that behind him stood the real strong man, General Park Chung Hee. Park and his military junta ruled the nation for two years. By the summer following the coup they had founded the Korean Central Intelligence Agency. The United States reluctantly recognized the coup and pushed for civilian elections to be held in 1963.

Park resigned from the army so that as a civilian he could run for president. He won by a small margin. On the surface there was an acceptable degree of political freedom and democracy, but the Korean CIA grew from a staff of 3,000 in 1961 to a nationwide network of more than 370,000 agents and informers in 1964. Eventually the KCIA would penetrate every aspect of society.

Hunger for power can be satisfied only if there are supporting allies. The Korean army was, of course, Park's most immediate source of support. It numbered about 600,000 men, well supplied with American military equipment. The military also controlled the national police, the riot police, the KCIA, and other secret intelligence agencies. Without all of these control agents, Park Chung Hee would have had no power. The military men pledged that they would crush any internal or external opposition to President Park.

A second source of strength for the Park regime came from political and economic ties with Japan. Relations between the two countries were normalized in 1965. Japan became the dominant economic influence in south Korea as Japanese capital flowed into the peninsula.

The third support for the Park government came from the United States of America. The U.S. government fully supported the Park regime, reasoning that security took precedence over human rights. American corporations, which benefited from the Korean government's suppression of labor, found no contradiction between their registration in a democratic country (the U.S.) and the practice of contributing to a dictatorial, military regime (south Korea).

⤳ ⬤⬤ ⤳

When I finished language school in Seoul, the bishop of the Korean Methodist Church assigned Dorothy and me to begin new work among laborers in the industrial city of Inchun (Inch'ŏn), near Seoul. We found a Korean-style house in the center of Inchun where Dorothy, son Martin, and I moved in September 1961. I invited several of the local pastors to our house to plan the labor ministry. In the post-war period, Korean pastors were accustomed to foreign missionaries offering money to rebuild their churches. They were somewhat surprised when I proposed that this ministry should be the work of the Korean churches. They agreed to help raise local money to support the work. We operated on a shoestring budget. For several years our small house was the only office.

My first day visiting the factory in Inchun was instructive. Imagine a large, freezing warehouse heated by a lone stove cut from a 50-gallon drum. The fire, fed constantly by a sliver of sawdust, burned red-hot. The metal of the drum was at a meltdown pink.

Those of us gathered around the stove were hot in front, but the cold wind that swept through the run-down factory kept our backsides shivering. The roof and part of the walls had been blown away by the war. All that was left was a shell of a building constructed during the Japanese occupation of Korea. The men who worked inside this shell of a building were constantly exposed to the outside elements. The machines were old, often held together only by the welding ingenuity of the Korean workers. Signs of injury and accidents were everywhere. Of the 20 or so men gathered around the fire, seven of them were missing thumbs. The furnaces had exploded on a couple occasions because hand grenades had accidentally been shoveled in along with the scrap metal.

We sat around the stove as the workers began to eat their lunches. Pak Yong Hi (Pak Yonghǔi), a foreman in the shop, and a member of the Naeri Methodist Church, opened the discussion. "We have a foreign guest with us. He's a missionary from America. He wants to talk with us about the Christian faith. I invited him to come and sit with us. He has a Korean name, Oh Myung Gul (O Myǒnggǒl)."

With that, Pak turned the meeting over to me. "I am honored to be allowed to visit you today," I started. "I hope that you will be able to understand my Korean. I am still studying. As Mr. Pak said, I would like to talk with you about faith and its relation to our every day lives, but I do not want to preach. I want to hear about your faith as well as share my own. If you are interested, I will come each Wednesday at lunch time. We can meet right here around the stove and stay warm. Talk it over and if you want, we will begin next Wednesday."

Questions came fast. "Who are you? Why do you want to talk with us? Are you going to preach and try to convert us? Do American workers live well? Are they organized? Are you part of the [American] CIA?

I laughed at the last question and assured them that I had nothing to do with the CIA. My only connection with any American organization was the church. "We don't have time to talk very long today, but I would like to come back next week and talk more."

There seemed to be general agreement, so each Wednesday for the next two months I ate lunch with 20 or so workers around that old sawdust stove. We discussed Christian faith and practices, Buddhism, Shamanism, the Korean War, labor practices in America and Korea, and race problems in the United States.

One Wednesday as I was getting ready to go to the factory, a phone call came. It was Mr. Pak. "Reverend Oh, there's been another accident at the shop. Nine men were injured, two of them badly. They are at the Inchun Christian Hospital. Will you go with me to visit the men?"

"Of course I will. See you in front of the hospital in thirty minutes."

One of the men was unconscious and in critical condition. The other one was conscious, but most of his face was swathed in bandages. Family members stood around, some crying, others quietly waiting. Mr. Pak and I greeted each one of them. I asked the wives if it would be all right for me to pray. Neither was Christian, but both said yes.

I offered a short prayer. "Lord of heaven and earth, look upon these thy servants with mercy. They have labored hard so that their families can live. They have labored so that their nation might grow. Touch them now with thy healing power. Give strength and comfort to their wives, their families and fellow workers. In Christ's name. Amen."

The next Wednesday when I entered the factory, the manager introduced himself and thanked me for visiting the injured men. After that, I became rather widely known in the entire plant. Requests for pastoral visits were brought to me, and after we had completed our two months of discussions in one section of the factory, opportunities came to repeat them in other sections.

Our Hearts Cry with You

The Urban Industrial Mission (UIM) in Inchun was born.

⁓ ⧓⧓ ⁓

Cho Seung Hyuk (Cho Sŏnghyŏk) had been a south Korean Marine chaplain before he volunteered to work with us in Inchun. He resigned from the Marines one week, and the next week he was a day-laborer in the Daesong (Taesŏng) Lumber Mill Company carrying heavy logs and loading freight on to trucks and box cars. Rev. Cho shared the theology that located Jesus among the poor of society. He went to the factory to test out that belief. He found the work grueling and the shop dirty and poorly managed. Workers were in constant conflict with each other. A union, manipulated by the company manager, contributed to the tensions. The first few days and few months were so fatiguing that Rev. Cho thought he could not endure. Neither his body nor his mind was prepared for what he was experiencing. He held on by prayer and determination. Gradually, as he overcame the shock of his new existence, he began to ponder what could be done to improve the situation.

His first experiment was predictable for a preacher. He started Bible study among the Christian workers, sometimes in the factory and sometimes in their homes. He soon discovered, however, that most of the Christians were next-world oriented. This world was to be escaped. Oppressions at the work place were to be endured, not opposed.

In the midst of his frustration over what his witness was to be, a very mundane thing happened to him. He was helping unload a truckload of plywood. The truck man stood on top of the load handing down the wood. Rev. Cho and several others were at the bottom catching it as it came down. An argument arose between one of the men and the guy on top. The truck man began to throw the wood down as fast as he could, endangering the men below. Rev. Cho got hit on the head and knocked down.

Enraged, Rev. Cho yelled up to him, "If you throw one more piece like that, I'm going to come up there and beat the hell out of you." Something in Cho's tone of voice must have been persuasive. The truck man calmed down.

The incident was like a revelation to Rev. Cho. Day in and day out his comrades were being walked over by guys like the truck man. Religion and salvation had to be understood in terms of freedom from such oppressions. The web of rules that governed the work place, the attitude of management and even the labor union were all used as ways to keep laborers under control. Religion, if it wasn't just other-worldly, had to be a religion of liberation. The incarnation of Christ into such a world meant justice and freedom for the oppressed such as the comrades among whom Rev. Cho now lived.

Reverend Cho Wha Soon's (Cho Hwasun's) experience at the Tong-Il Textiles was similar to that of Rev. Cho Seung Hyuk , except her fellow workers were young women from the countryside. About a third of Korean industrial workers were women ages 16 to 25. Rev. Cho Wha Soon described her first day on the job:

"I was told to report to the employment office at 8:00 AM. I told the receptionist who I was. She disappeared for a brief time, came back and said that the supervisor said he would be with me in a few minutes. For two hours I sat there getting madder by the minute. When the guy finally did make an appearance, he looked at me in great disdain and spoke to me in insulting language suitable for a bar maid. 'You help in the kitchen today. Next week you go on the floor.' He left. He didn't even show me where the kitchen was. Finally I found it. As I went in, a girl much younger than I began giving orders in nasty, low talk. I am not sure how I kept my mouth shut. I had always been talked to in honorific high talk. To have this kid talk to be in low talk ignited a fire of anger in my belly. But I did keep quiet and followed her commands. As my indignation churned inside me, I came to realize that this young woman lived most, if not all her life, in a work place and society that showed her only disrespect. She was projecting on to me the anger she lived under every day. It made her feel better to make me subservient. After that, my anger subsided and I went about doing the kitchen work as she ordered."

～ ≈≫≪ ～

The next week Rev. Cho Wha Soon started work on the plant floor. It was agony. In the winding room 90 girls, working three shifts, produced threads used in weaving and making undershirts. The noise was deafening. Lint and dust turned the girls into walking snowmen in a matter of a few hours. There was no rest. The machines demanded unremitting attention. No words were passed. The speed and noise of the machines made it impossible to talk to one another. Fatigue was a constant condition.

When Rev. Cho was first rotated into the winding room, her whole body ached. Her legs swelled so that at quitting time she could hardly make it back to her room. Her colleagues, likewise, dragged themselves back to their one little dingy room, often used on an alternating shift basis by other girls.

Like Rev. Cho Seung Hyuk, it took Rev. Cho Wha Soon a couple of months to get over the shock of her new existence. The question "Is Christ here among these young women?" haunted her. "Am I here to make a witness to his salvation?" she wondered.

Her coworkers began to help her find the answer. The workers had one day off each month. On that day off, Rev. Cho gathered some of them to play, sing, and discuss their common problems. Christians and non-Christians alike agreed that they were being treated unjustly, oppressed by forces they could not understand or control. Their youth was being consumed. They had to do something – but what?

At the time they didn't realize that by meeting and talking things over with each other they were already in the process of overcoming their frustration.

~ ~~~ ~

Both the worker-priest experience and the factory chaplaincy program revealed the need for pastoral concern and mutual care within the factories. To meet that need we recruited some local pastors to visit the shops with us. More strategically we developed a series of training programs for Christian workers. Ten men from steel mills, machine shops, electrical equipment manufacturers, a glass factory, railroad yards, and communication and transportation systems were chosen to take the course. Two women from textile mills also took part. For three months these "12 apostles" gathered after work each Saturday to study, talk, eat, and sleep in the UIM office until time for the 11 a.m. Sunday church service. First we studied Scripture. Then we focused our discussion around four guides: (1) keep eyes open to the needs of fellow workers; (2) discern the causes of each problem; (3) decide what action the apostle could take to help relieve the problem; and (4) take action to help the brother or sister in need.

Each person would share his/her case study involving the first three guidelines. The following week they would share what action they took and what resulted from that action.

The process turned out to be a means of grace. It took only a couple weeks of this in-depth sharing to develop a strong comradeship among us. Problems faced by one were the problems faced by everyone. They were of two kinds. The first kind related to family and fellow workers. Everyone worked six bruising days a week, yet everyone lived near poverty. The country had not recovered from the war, and everyone, except for a few, still carried its burdens. Men often seduced young women textile workers who had just come from the countryside; men would often get into fights over the best ways to share the work; and families became deep in debt to money lenders. In such situations the apostle found he/she could at times do little more than offer a kind word.

The second kind of difficulty was more organizational or institutional. Supervisors would play favorites; wages were not rightly calculated; safety procedures were ignored; and men were laid off or penalized without cause.

As these institutional problems were brought in for discussion, the question was frequently asked, "Where are the unions? Aren't they supposed to help the workers in cases like this?"

This opened a new dimension to the UIM ministry. Unions have a long history in Korea, dating back to 1919. Unfortunately much of the time they have been under the control of employers. In Inchun during the 1960's, most workplaces had union organizations, but they did little to help the worker. When the apostles began to realize that the unions should be strategic partners in mitigating some the workers' suffering, several of them began to take part in union activity.

In the last half of the 1960's, the UIM regularly conducted labor education programs with unions representing metal workers, textiles, foreign employees (those working for the U. S. Army), railroads and transportation, electrical workers, dockworkers and automobile workers.

The government actually encouraged development of collective bargaining in the late 1960's. As our Inchun labor education programs became more widely known, we received invitations to cooperate with national and county departments of labor. Schools such as Sogang University and Korea University established centers for labor studies, and Rev. Cho Seung Hyuk, Rev. Cho Wha Soon, and I became regular participants. But the government would begin curtailing the right of collective bargaining in the 1970's.

❦ ❦❦ ❦

We who worked in Urban Industrial Mission (UIM) believed the Korean labor movement of the 1960's could have led the nation on a path where democracy and economic development progressed together. We carried on a ministry among Inchun's industrial workers for almost a decade before the KCIA moved to shut us down. Unfortunately the military believed that workers' rights and economic progress could not coexist. The military mind could understand our ministries only in terms of communism. Even before the Yushin constitution was proclaimed in 1972 (see Glossary), the Inchun UIM staff was suffering under police and KCIA surveillance, threats, and arrests.

Hurling accusations of "communist," they arrested my Korean colleagues and circulated warnings to the workers in the city that anyone associated with UIM might be suspected of communist leanings. The KCIA didn't like certain facts about our ministry: our missioners labored in the factories; we visited workers' families in their homes; we prayed in the hospital for those who were injured at the plant; and we cooperated with labor unions.

In spite of government harassment, the UIM continued to grow in the early 1970's. UIM staff was working with thousands of laborers and hundreds of labor union leaders. The Inchun staff expanded to include five staff people in addition to dozens of lay volunteers. In addition, UIM work began in several other cities.

During the years of Yushin (1972-1989), however, the military government made it almost impossible for UIM to carry out its ministry. There were longer imprisonments and even torture. The military dictatorship subverted most of the progress that unions and management had made during the 1960's. But as the persecution increased, the resolve of the workers was strengthened. Labor was a big part of the broad coalition of citizens including students, professors, clergy, civic leaders, and ordinary citizens who would struggle against the military dictatorship for nearly two decades.

～ ❦ ～

We worked in Inchun for more than 10 years, becoming deeply involved in the lives of the industrial workers. When I left Inchun on furlough in 1971 it was time to turn that ministry completely over to my colleagues, Rev. Cho Seung Hyuk and Rev. Cho Wha Soon.

After completing my Ph.D. in Industrial Relations at the University of Wisconsin, I was invited in 1973 to be a visiting professor teaching labor relations at Seoul National University's School of Commerce. The bishop of the Korean Methodist Church approved that assignment. This was a time, however, when a significant number of students were more committed to working for democracy than studying. The universities were frequently closed because of student demonstrations against the military dictatorship. So I had few classes to teach. Instead, my ministry changed to supporting Korean colleagues who were suffering at the hands of the military dictatorship.

Among other things, I participated in the Monday Night Group and the Thursday morning prayer meetings for Christian prisoners. That led to my involvement with the families of eight men who were falsely charged by the government of being part of the so-called "Peoples' Revolutionary Party."

～ ❦ ～

The Yushin decrees of January 1972 failed to bring an end to opposition and protests. The regime promulgated a fourth decree which made it a crime punishable by death to criticize the government.

More than Witnesses

In April 1974 the government announced it had uncovered a large communist conspiracy to overthrow the government. A thousand or more democratic dissidents, many of them leaders in the Christian community, were rounded up and thrown into prison. Eight men were charged with being the ringleaders of a People's Revolutionary Party (PRP), an alleged conspiracy dedicated to overthrowing the south Korean government and establishing a communist regime.

The KCIA plucked the name People's Revolutionary Party out of the history book as a useful tool for settling scores with some activist students who had been exonerated by the courts in the previous decade. The communist-sounding name was just what the KCIA needed to fabricate its case – to make it look like the critics of the government were controlled by communist north Korea. It was a ruse to frighten citizens and make them more submissive to the Park regime.

With no evidence against them, the military tortured the eight alleged PRP men, forcing them to confess to being spies from the north. Then all eight were given the death sentence.

Quite unexpectedly my wife, Dorothy, and I became involved in the tragic drama of these eight men. In the fall of 1974 we lived on the campus of Yonsei University in Seoul. One night late the phone rang. A woman's voice said in Korean, "Reverend Ogle, you don't know me. I heard about you from some of your friends. I must see you at once. May I come to your house?"

"Who are you? What do you want?" I asked.

"I can not talk over the phone," she said. "It isn't safe."

Given the political situation in south Korea at the time, I knew she was right. Many phones, including our own, were probably bugged by the Korean CIA.

"It's already late," I said. "Could you come tomorrow morning?"

"That will do. I'll be at your place by 9:00 o'clock," she answered and hung up.

The next morning at the stroke of nine the doorbell rang. Instead of one woman, however, there were eight. I asked them in. After we got all seated, the women began to introduce themselves. As they spoke their names, I had glimmers of recall. I had heard their names before. Then it came to me. These women were the wives of the eight men accused by the Korean CIA as being leaders of the communist conspiracy to overthrow the government.

After the introductions, Mrs. Woo, who had phoned the night before, explained that each week they had to take food and other supplies to their husbands at West Gate prison. While they waited to get in, they had met relatives of some of the Christian prisoners; the relatives suggested that the women come and talk with me.

Several women began to talk at once. "Reverend Ogle, we need your help. We are desperate. Please help us! Our husbands are in prison. They have been tortured and forced to confess to something they know nothing about."

I interrupted. "For me to understand, we will need to talk slowly. I have heard of the alleged conspiracy, but I know only what I've read in the newspapers. Will you each take turns and tell me your personal stories. That way I think I will understand better."

Mrs. Woo began. "I was only eighteen when I first met Woo Hong Sun (U Hongsŏn). I worked as a clerk in a bank where he did business. Love seemed to come at first sight. We married young and quickly had four children. My husband worked as a bookkeeper with a small construction company here in Seoul. Life has always been hard for us, but we always made ends meet, and our love seemed to get stronger. Even after 10 years of marriage, we would walk up

South Mountain holding hands like young lovers.

"It happened on April 16 this year. Without warning, police broke into our house and turned our house upside down searching for what they called 'evidence.' They terrorized me and the children. My husband was dragged out of the house and charged with taking part in an anti-government conspiracy about which he knew nothing. He was tortured and forced to confess. A military court has sentenced him to die. He was given no chance to defend himself. Lawyers were not permitted to talk to him. All appeals were rejected."

After Mrs. Woo, the other seven women each told similar stories. It was afternoon before we finished.

I believed what these humble ladies told me, but I had no idea what I could do for them or for their husbands. As a foreigner, I was not permitted to interfere in Korean politics. I had no influence with people of power.

But the women would not be put off with such excuses.

"You've got to help us," they insisted. "We have no one to turn to. You as a Christian missionary can call for a retrial by a civilian court. That's all we want."

Finally, just to get them to leave and to give me time to think, I said, "I can promise nothing since I have no influence in political affairs, but I will look into the matter." Those last six hesitant words changed my life forever.

After the women left, I went to see two Korean friends who were knowledgeable about political affairs. Both of them told me the same thing. The charges against these eight men were fabrications. The military government of Park Chung Hee wanted to inject a new wave of anti-communist fear into the people of south Korea so that it could tighten its control over the nation. There was no evidence to sustain any of the government's charges. The eight men were innocent lambs going to the slaughter.

Our Hearts Cry with You

⁘

I decided on a plan of action. It wasn't much, but it was all I could think of. The government had arrested nearly 1,000 persons for their pro-democracy, human rights, and labor rights positions. Many if not most of those arrested were Christians. Each week families and friends of imprisoned Christians gathered for a Thursday prayer meeting, held in the Christian Building in Seoul. There they pleaded with God to protect their loved ones and release them from prison.

On Thursday, October 9, 1974, it was my turn to give the meditation and lead the prayers. I decided I would speak about and pray for not only the Christian prisoners but also for the eight condemned men, none of whom was Christian.

Police agents were everywhere. I counted a half dozen black-jacketed police from where I stood. Sitting in front of me were about 100 persons, most of whom had a loved one in prison.

I looked out at the congregation, including the black-jacketed policemen, and I began to speak.

"Christ is often mediated to us through the most humble and weakest of our brothers and sisters. Among those now in prison are eight men who have received the harshest of punishments. They have been sentenced to die, even though there is little evidence against them. They are not Christians, but as the poorest among us they become the brothers of Christ. Therefore let us pray for their lives and souls. Probably they have committed no crime worthy of death."

As I spoke, the "black jackets" assiduously wrote down every word. I found out later that their notes were quite accurate.

⁘

At 5:00 p.m. on Friday, October 10, two agents of the Korean Central Intelligence Agency came to my home to arrest me. I would be gone for only a couple hours they said. My wife, Dorothy, wasn't home at the time, so I left word that I had gone to "Namsan" (euphemism for KCIA) and would be gone for "a couple of hours" (euphemism for indefinitely).

The ride to Namsan was an experience in itself. The driver darted in and out of Seoul's rush-hour traffic like he was on a mission of death. When we arrived at the KCIA headquarters, I was taken to a small room with nothing but three chairs. Two interrogators were waiting for me. They dispensed with normal Korean manners of introducing themselves and saying something nice. Interrogation began immediately. I was told that I would have to write down every question and answer in Korean. So for the next seventeen hours I practiced my Korean handwriting as I never had before.

"Why do you have prayer meetings on Thursday mornings?

Of course they already knew the answer, but I explained how we met to pray for the health and safety of our friends and family members who were imprisoned unjustly.

"What right do you have to pray for the release of criminals? The government has judged them guilty of breaking the law. What right do you have to try and get them out of prison through prayer or any other means?"

Mr. Huh (Hŏ), the chief interrogator, was indignant, even hostile. Mr. Yun, the other interrogator, played the role of my friend. I would answer each question, then Mr. Huh would harangue me for being insincere. I would give a second version. Mr. Huh wouldn't like it, so he would alter the question slightly. I would respond again. At certain points, Mr. Yun would intervene as mediator, trying to find some acceptable answer that could be recorded. I was told that my written answer should be of my own free will, but that seemed impossible given Mr. Huh's attack mode and miserable disposition.

"You gave a sermon at the prayer meeting yesterday," Mr. Huh said "What did you say?"

"I spoke from the Bible where it urges Christians to serve those who are the poorest and weakest in society, and I said we should pray for eight men who have been sentenced to death."

"You said the men of Peoples' Revolutionary Party were innocent. You spoke on behalf of communists, didn't you?"

"I believe I said that the KCIA had presented very little evidence against the eight men, and that they probably had committed no crime worthy of death."

Mr. Huh was outraged. "Such talk is in violation of the anti-communist law. Did you know these men were communists before you gave your sermon?"

I said I knew that the KCIA had declared that these men were communists, but I didn't know whether they were or not. This reply infuriated Mr. Huh even more.

"How do you dare question the judgment of the government? The government decides these things, not you. You, a foreigner, come into our country and insult our people and culture!"

"I insult no one," I said. "I have nothing but respect for Korea, its people and culture. There are a thousand of your countrymen in prison now because they think there should be democracy in the land."

Over and over again Mr. Huh and I repeated our opinions about the right of people to have opinions different from the government. After about 40 minutes he changed the subject. "Yesterday, after you spoke, someone prayed. Who was he and what did he say?"

"I'm sure you know; he was Rev. Pak," I said. "I don't know his first name. His prayers are his responsibility, not mine. Ask him. Anything I say could be used against him."

Mr. Yun assured me that the KCIA did not do things that way. Everything I said to him or Mr. Huh would be kept in strictest confidence, he said. When I stubbornly refused to answer, Mr.

Huh proceeded to read from his notes the exact words of Rev. Pak's prayer.

"That's what he said, isn't it?" asked Mr. Huh.

"You will have to ask him," I replied.

I didn't know it then, but that was exactly what other KCIA agents were doing at that moment somewhere else in the building. Rev. Pak had been arrested a couple hours after I had been. When we compared notes later, we found that similar tactics had been used on each of us: They questioned him closely about what I had said, assuring him that everything he said about me would remain strictly confidential.

Back in my interrogation room, the subject was changed. This time the two agents demanded that I write down the names and addresses of all the people I knew in Korea and the nature of those relationships. From hearing the stories of friends who had been through KCIA interrogations, I expected this question. If I were to give a name, the KCIA would then visit that friend and claim that I had accused him or her of some anti-government action. The friend would then be blackmailed into providing names of more people, and, of course, the trust between all of us would break down.

I wrote down the names of churches and institutions where I had worked in south Korea, but I refused to give personal names.

Mr. Huh's harangue was loud and ferocious. Mr. Yun calmed him down. We were about to return to the topic of communism when a messenger entered the room and said something to Mr. Huh. Our session was discontinued, and I was taken to another room. It was the main office, I believe, of the KCIA's 6th section. One man was sitting behind a large desk. He wore a dark blue suit. I was ordered to sit down.

"Mr. Ogle, I am Mr. Lee. You have been in Korea a long time, but obviously you do not know much about Korea, and you know nothing about communism. You have violated our anti-communist law, but because you are a foreigner, we are going to be generous. I am going to prove to you that these eight men you pray for are indeed communists."

Lee then repeated to me the exact same thing that had come out in the newspapers. His only piece of evidence was a copy of a speech by Kim Il Seung, premier of north Korea. Ha Chae Won (Ha Chaewǒn), one of the eight, allegedly listened to the speech, copied it down, and showed it to a few other people.

Then, suddenly and amazingly, Mr. Lee stopped showing me "evidence" and launched into a tirade. "These men," he shouted, "are our enemies. We have got to kill them. This is war. In war even a Christian will pull the trigger to kill an enemy. If we do not kill these men, they will kill us. We will kill them. If we do not kill them, I will visit the national cemetery and confess before all those buried there that we have sold out our country to the communists. I will go to the United States and tell the brave men who died in the Korean War that they have died in vain. They (the eight men) must die!"

What was going on? Mr. Lee's emotional soliloquy certainly could not have sprung from the "evidence" that he showed me. His eyes were lit up like a warrior about to go to battle. He was on an emotional jag that I found incomprehensible. Later on, a friend told me that Mr. Lee had carried on a personal vendetta against some of the condemned men for more than a decade. Now he was in a position to secure revenge. That may have accounted for his weird actions.

The interview with Mr. Lee lasted for about an hour. I was then returned to the cubicle with Huh and Yun. The interrogation began again. This time they wanted details about Urban Industrial Mission, the mission work I had been involved in since 1960. When did it start? Who was part of it? What were its goals? Why did we have clergy working in factories? Why were we cooperating with labor unions?

I wrote down answers to these and other questions, but each was a struggle. Mr. Huh refused to accept my first answers. We went back and forth until finally we arrived at a response acceptable to both of us.

It was about 1:30 in the morning. Mr. Huh was getting tired. He instructed Mr. Yun to make me write down the names of the wives of the eight men for whom I had prayed. Then he wanted to know how often had we met, and what we talked about. Mr. Huh then stretched out on an army cot and went to sleep. Mr. Yun and I continued for a couple more hours.

Finally, sleep began to overtake us. Mr. Yun said we would rest for a few hours and then finish the interrogation. "In the morning," he said, "you will need to write an apology, confessing your wrongdoings and promising not to repeat them."

The two agents had already prepared an apology for me to sign. First, I was to say that I did not know the eight men were communists when I prayed for them. Second, I had to promise that in the future I would obey all government policies. Third, I was to promise that I would never again pray or speak on behalf of the eight condemned men.

It was 3:30 am when I was given this ultimatum. Mr. Yun said I could sleep on it for a couple hours, then we would discuss it. I crawled into a cot next to the snoring Mr. Huh, covered myself with a khaki blanket, but did not sleep.

We were up and into the interrogation again by 7:00 am. I told Mr. Huh that there was no way that I would agree to the first item in the apology. "The way you have worded it implies that I now know them to be communists. I do not know any such a thing." Much to my surprise, neither interrogator forced the issue. We went to the next point – obeying government policies.

"You want me to say I will obey all policies of the government or all laws?" I asked.

"Policies! You are a foreigner here. You must be obedient to all the policies of the government."

"But there are too many policies, and some I do not agree with. How can you ask me to obey all policies? Not even you do that."

Mr. Huh again jumped on his high horse. "Who do you think you are coming into our country and insulting our ways of doing things? You are a foreigner! Don't think that the American Embassy can help you. You can't break our laws and get away with it."

"I have lived in Korea for more than fifteen years and have never been arrested or charged with breaking any laws," I said. "I respect your people and willingly live under the laws of your land."

About that time a little man in an army uniform came in and ordered Mr. Huh to hurry things up.

The interruption helped me avoid signing the second part of the apology. Only the third item was left – declaring that I would not preach or pray for any of the eight men. Mr. Huh said he would take out the prohibition against prayer, but I must promise not to speak on their behalf. After much debate as to what "speak on their behalf" meant, I finally signed a statement saying I would not speak about them in my sermons – leaving open other forms of "speaking".

At approximately 11:00 am the little army man returned and ordered me to go with him. He took me to the office of the KCIA deputy chief of security. The deputy chief was introduced to me as Mr. Lee. He told me he had lived in the United States for eight years and that he knew Americans very well. He was sorry to see me in this situation, but my offense, he said, was very serious.

"If you ever help the communists again, I will either put you in prison or deport you," he said.

Then he ordered a big black car to take me home.

⌒ ⊱⊰ ⌒

One week later, as I headed toward the dean's office at Seoul National University, a man stepped in front of me. His very bearing told me he was a KCIA agent. In polite Korean he said, "You are Dr. George Ogle?"

"I am."

"Could we have a talk?" He didn't bother to introduce himself.

"If you wish," I said. "We can go to my office. It's cold there, but it will be quiet."

As soon as we were seated, he began, "You are the person who was detained last week for speaking in support of eight communists?"

"I was arrested and interrogated for twenty hours at the KCIA headquarters for praying for eight men who were tortured into making false confessions."

"Did you not understand that you were breaking the law and giving comfort to our enemy, the communists?"

"I have lived in Korea for nearly twenty years and have never been accused of breaking a law. I hold Korea and its traditions in highest respect, but as a Christian minister I always have the freedom to pray for people who are in prison."

He obviously didn't want to pursue that matter. Abruptly, he changed the subject. "Dr. Ogle, we are well aware of your background with the subversive organization called "Urban Industrial Mission." We are not insisting right now that you be removed from the university, but we do need more information about what goes on in UIM."

He had suggested a trade-off: my job security in exchange for inside information about UIM. "I am sure your agency must already know all there is to know about UIM," I said. "There are many agents in Inchun and Yongdongpo (Yŏngdŏngp'o) who keep track of it. As to how I got appointed to the university, I sent my resume to the faculty search committee, and they hired me. Nothing secret about that."

"Will you answer questions about UIM?"

"Certainly," I said. "There's nothing to hide, and it definitely is not subversive. It's a ministry of the church to industrial workers. We carry on a variety of education and pastoral programs and support the right of workers to organize and bargain collectively with the employer. What more would you like to know?"

"Is it true that you have clergymen and students working in disguise in the shops of Inchun?"

"They are not exactly in disguise," I said. "They just don't reveal the fact that they are clergy. But, yes, we do have clergy men and women working in factories."

"Why? That is very suspicious. Who are you trying to deceive? It sounds like something communists would do. Why not just set up regular churches for the workers?"

"The church has many different ways of serving the poor," I explained. "About fifteen years ago the bishop of our Methodist church appointed me and some others to begin a unique type of mission. Clergy who work in UIM take on a special discipline. For at least one year they must be employed at hard labor. In this way they can better understand the circumstances of the workers. Jesus himself was a carpenter. UIM has nothing to do with communism."

"That is what you think," he countered. "We know that the communists are trying to use the church as a front in order to cause trouble here in the south. Why don't you leave the labor unions alone? Unions have always been centers of communist infiltration."

That evening I had supper with Rev. Cho Seung Hyuk and

Rev. Cho Hwa Soon. I told them about the morning visitor and his interest in UIM.

Seung Hyuk gave a smile of understanding.

"It's the military mind," Seung Hyuk said. "You were arrested because you prayed publicly for men the military has declared to be communist. That violates their mind-set. Either you are for them or you are against them.

"And as regards UIM," Seung Hyuk continued, "it's the same thing, partly because of what we have done in UIM over the last decade: workers have become active, and more unions have been organized. The military, and the employers, don't want that. They want an obedient workforce. 'Justice for the poor' makes no sense to them. Communists, they think, have to be behind such talk."

As the three of us parted that night, I had a premonition that we wouldn't be meeting for supper many more times. Events related to UIM, the university, and the eight condemned men were moving too fast.

I felt a shiver of fear as I walked home.

⁂

Things came to a head quicker than I expected. About a week after my interrogation, I received a surprise invitation to lunch from a Mr. Erickson at the American Embassy. He informed me that he had been asked by the foreign minister of south Korea to pass on to me a brief message. I must apologize to the government or be thrown out of Korea. Praying and speaking for men whom the government declared to be communist was in violation of Korean law, said the foreign minister. The foreign minister demanded two things from me in writing within 24 hours: my apology, and my statement of intention regarding future work in Korea.

I didn't want to be thrown out of Korea. It was home for me

and my family. But to apologize would betray the trust I had not only with the eight men and their families, but also with the hundreds of other innocent people in prison.

I finally decided to write a letter stating that, since the day I arrived in Korea in 1954, I had only the highest respect for Korea's laws, traditions, and people. I said I had broken no law. Then I described my intentions for future ministry in Korea, quoted in the beginning of this chapter.

The foreign minister was not impressed with my letter. Less than 48 hours later I was escorted from my home, put in a jeep, and taken to the Office of Immigration.

"Mr. Ogle, there has been an error in regard to your visa and residence permit," the immigration officer said. "You were given a visa as a missionary. That does not qualify you as a university professor. (I had taught labor-management relations at Seoul National University the previous semester.) You have violated our law. Therefore we must ask you to leave Korea."

"How can that be?" I said. "I was hired by the Department of Commerce of Seoul National University. They knew all about me before I came. Besides, there are hundreds of missionaries teaching in Korean schools all the way from kindergartens to graduate schools in your best universities. Why do you select me for this punishment?"

"We are not talking about other people, only about you," the officer said. "You are in violation."

So it came about that on December 14, 1974, I was deported from Korea. The government picked up the cost of the one-way ticket to the U.S.

The government never officially charged me with any wrongdoing. Instead they resorted to chicanery, alleging that my visa had been secured falsely.

Behind the chicanery was a military mind-set that could not tolerate prayers for innocent people or justice for industrial workers.

~ ~ ~

The deportation itself was filled with grief and tears. But there were also moments of grace and hope. Here are two of those stories: The Ring, and The Postcard.

The Ring: As the police were leading me out of my home towards the jeep that would take me to Kimpo Airport, someone reached out and placed in my hand a small, gold ring. As I slipped it onto my little finger, tears filled my eyes. I knew instinctively that the ring was from Mrs. Woo, the PRP wife who had called me that night and then brought all the PRP wives to our home the next morning. On the day of the deportation, Mrs. Woo had been standing outside our house all afternoon. When she saw that I was to be deported, she was afraid that I would end up in Japan or the United States without money or anywhere to go. She quickly went home to get a gold ring. A friend took the ring and threw it to another friend who was inside the line of riot police that blocked access to our yard. As police took me from the house, that friend pressed the ring into my hand.

The Postcard: When Korean Airlines flight 002 was out over the Pacific Ocean, a snack was served. As the young hostess placed the tray before me, she dropped a postcard on my lap and hurried off without saying a word. I glanced at it, but waited awhile before turning it over to read.

"Rev. Ogle, Please go in peace. I am a young man. (I will not use my name.) Many of us know that you work for true freedom and democracy in our country. Our hearts cry with you. Your name will be inscribed in history. I believe that things will change and before too long you will be invited to return to Korea to continue your work.

"Please stay in good health."

I began to cry. It was the last of many tear-filled moments that very long day. As the 747 continued towards the U.S., I gradually fell into a deep sleep, the postcard on my lap.

On April 9, 1975, four months after my deportation, suddenly, without giving the right of final appeal, the government hanged the eight alleged PRP men. Because foreign reporters had left Korea to cover the end of the war in Vietnam, the eight deaths received little international coverage. Human rights activists helped families arrange funerals for some of the men. Bodies of some of the PRP men were not released by the government, presumably to cover up signs of torture.

For 28 years the families of these men suffered public censure and disgrace for being related to "convicted communists." Finally, in 2002, south Korea's Presidential Truth Commission announced officially that the PRP case had been a complete fabrication of the Park Chung Hee government. In December 2005 a "truth-finding committee" of the National Intelligence Service confirmed the fabrication, saying the PRP men were tortured into confessing and that "the charges that they were revolutionary communists flowed from an orchestrated effort of the KCIA, prosecution, police, and the Defense Ministry acting together for the purpose of intimidating other activists." A member of the NIS panel said there was "no smoking gun" proving direct involvement by President Park Chung Hee in the PRP case, but that there was "no proof of Hitler's direct involvement in Jewish genocide either."

🕸 *Chapter 2*
🕸 🕸

From Isolation to Collaboration

Randy Rice

When I departed the U.S. in August 1966, I was an energetic, idealistic, social-action-oriented, thirty-four-year-old Presbyterian minister, father of four small children, sound in mind and body, and still very much inspired by a dramatic spiritual experience which had happened in October 1965: While attending a charismatic praise and prayer gathering at a sister Presbyterian church in Bridgeport, Connecticut, I experienced laying on of hands and prayers by a worship team that lifted me out of a prolonged period of spiritual dryness and depression.

From 1960 to 1965 I had served as an ordained minister of the United Presbyterian Church, USA, first in a rural parish in Ohio (1960-62), then as assistant pastor of an inner-city congregation in Bridgeport (1962-65). My upbringing in the First Presbyterian Church of Lewiston, N.Y. provided me with a biblically grounded faith, with a strong emphasis on Christian ethics, both social and personal. I was also deeply impressed by Sunday School stories about missionaries, and from early on felt a strong sense of call to that vocation. My studies at Pittsburgh Theological Seminary and Yale Divinity School (1956-1962) reinforced and enriched these two themes. In 1965, while I was serving the church in Bridgeport, my wife, Sue, and I were presented with the opportunity to go to south Korea as missionaries. We said "yes."

We first touched Korean soil on September 6, 1966, and we served in Korea until February 1982. Our first two years were devoted to language study. When we graduated from the Korean Language Institute of Yonsei University in June 1968, I was appointed by the Presbyterian Church of Korea to work with the Korean Student Christian Federation (KSCF) as a campus minister and to teach English at Kyunghee University, a large and rapidly growing secular institution in Seoul.

Returning to Korea from furlough in 1971, I was appointed to work at the Christian Literature Society (CLS) of Korea. I also served in the campus evangelism department of the Youngnak (Yŏngnak) Presbyterian Church in Seoul. My involvement with these young people over the following 10 years was the crucible in which I not only became fluent in the Korean language and learned the ways of the Korean people, but also was drawn into an active role in the struggles of the Korean people for social justice and human rights. Through my relationships with Korean college students and the time I spent on various campuses, my "career" took two tracks: (1) my "official duties," noted above; and (2) my unofficial duties related to issues of justice and human rights. The Monday Night Group became a source of both ideas and inspiration for my unofficial duties.

More than Witnesses

"The books are here," I whispered in a conspiratorial voice. There was a slight pause at the other end of the phone line, followed by the puzzled response, "Books? What books?"

"You know, the books we talked about last week."

Another pause. "I don't know what you are talking about. I don't remember anything about books."

These were the opening sentences of a late evening conversation between myself and Walter Beecham, a United Church of Canada missionary who lived just up the road from us behind Seoul Foreign School. It was a time in the mid-1970s when several Koreans being pursued by the KCIA found refuge in the homes of Monday Night Group members. Walter and his wife, Lenore, had opened their residence to a minister of the Presbyterian Church in the Republic of Korea who had come up from the countryside to avoid arrest by the authorities.

During the weeks the pastor had been with them, there had been no contact with his family. The Beechams had arranged a meeting between him and his daughter, whom I recall was soon to be married, and our house was designated as the rendezvous point. Prior to her arrival, Walter and I, suspecting that our phones were tapped, had agreed upon a simple code message. When the young lady had arrived, I was to ring him up and tell him (I thought), "The books are here." Unfortunately, one or the other or both of us had forgotten the code. After a few more fruitless attempts at sustaining the subterfuge, I gave it up and said, "She's here. Send him down," at which point the light bulb came on and we were in business. Within a few minutes the pastor knocked at our door, and father and daughter came together in an emotional embrace, while Sue and I retired to another room.

I tell this story not only for its humor and joy (two things abundantly present during those heady days), but also because it illustrates a characteristic of the Monday Night Group. Considering the magnitude of the powers with which we in our small ways were doing battle, we were not the world's most skilled tacticians when it came to political action. We were a rather unsophisticated bunch. We had zero experience dealing with government surveillance and harassment, or with riot police and arrests, or with KCIA threats and interrogations. The "who's on first?" conversation between Walter and me is a case in point.

Think, however, about the proverbial bumblebee that continues to buzz from blossom to blossom, peacefully oblivious to the fact that science has concluded there is no way she should be able to fly. Similarly, we Monday Night Group members, in our clumsy ways, somehow managed to surprise not only government authorities with our occasional effectiveness; we surprised even ourselves with all that we were able to accomplish in support of Koreans struggling mightily for democracy and human rights. Our final surprise would come nearly 30 years later when we found ourselves numbered among an august company honored by the Korea Democracy Foundation for supporting the democratization movement.

When did the Monday Night Group begin? None of us can pinpoint a date with any degree of certainty. There is, however, consensus about two things. First, the MNG began in the early 1970's; and second, its forerunner was another home-based gathering that I remember as the "Group of Fifty" but others in this book recall as the "Committee of Fifty" (see Faye Moon chapter). Most of its 50 members were citizens of the United States. The group formed in 1968-69 in response to President Park Chung Hee's ramming through a constitutional amendment permitting him to run for a third term. When college students protested this blatant power grab, they were tear-gassed by riot police ferried to the scene in trucks whose doors were emblazoned with the handshake logo of the United States Agency for International Development. The Group of Fifty was formed to object to this public association of the U.S. government with such repression. Among those who gathered to discuss which measures might be undertaken were Ed Baker, a Peace Corps volunteer teaching English at Seoul National University; Dave and Ellen Ross, Southern Presbyterian missionaries; Methodist missionary George Ogle; Presbyterian missionaries Herb and Marge White and Sue and Randy Rice; Faye Moon, and Gregory Pai. I recall that Gerhard Breidenstein, a professor of social ethics teaching at Yonsei University, also was active in the group, and that a Korea-specific study manual he wrote, "Christians and Social Justice," was one of the formative documents first for the Group of Fifty and later for the Monday Night Group.

The group received political and historical backgrounding and guidance from the Rev. Moon Tong Hwan (Steve Moon), Faye Moon's husband. Herb White, one of the group founders, brought experience and expertise as an organizer trained by community organization guru Saul Alinsky. One of the actions taken by the group was to draw up a petition calling upon the U.S. government to withdraw support for President Park's power grab – beginning with stopping those trucks with the highly visible USAID logo. A petition to this effect was hand-delivered to the U.S. embassy by Ed Baker. Shortly after this several members of the group were invited to meet with Ambassador William Porter at the embassy, which they did twice (see account in Marion Kim's chapter).

Apparently the action had some effect: the logo on all the vehicles was painted over. Another action of the group was to meet U.S. Vice President Hubert Humphrey at Seoul's Kimpo Airport when he arrived on a state visit. With an ease that no one can even imagine in these post 9/11 days of ironclad security, some group members walked out onto the tarmac and greeted Mr. Humphrey as he got off the plane. Ellen Ross, a Southern Presbyterian missionary, and Faye Moon were among those who met with Humphrey in his suite at the Bando Hotel.

Within a few years the Group of Fifty quietly "morphed" into the Monday Night Group. The MNG retained several essential characteristics of the group. First was the practice of meeting in one another's homes on a rotating schedule. The rotation, we surmised, would at a minimum provide a weekly challenge for the government agents assigned to surveillance of MNG members. Second, Monday Night Group meetings and membership were open – any foreigner could attend. Koreans were excluded for one very practical reason: any Korean citizen intimately involved with MNG planning and strategy could have faced consequences much more extreme than those reserved for us foreigners. Third, the MNG, like the Group of Fifty, was committed to accurate information and careful reflection leading to concrete action.

※ ※※ ※

Open membership in the Monday Night Group meant that people just showed up. Some may have been invited; others heard of the group by word of mouth. There was no written roster of names and no "attendance" was taken. The fluidity of MNG membership was related also to the fact that new missionaries were arriving and others were departing as they completed their terms or departed on furlough.

By 1972 the Monday Night Group's core membership was comprised almost entirely of missionaries (Protestant) and missioners (Roman Catholic). Some had been in south Korea for decades (e.g., Willa Kernen since 1954, Gene Matthews since 1956); others were newly arrived (Dave and Linda Jones and Butch and Louise Durst in 1972). A variety of nationalities was represented: the United States, Canada, France, Belgium, Germany, Australia, Ireland, Italy, and perhaps others I have forgotten.

Here is my recollection of persons who regularly participated in Monday Night Group meetings during the 1970's: Bill and Jean Basinger, Walter and Lenore Beecham, Dolores Congdon, Marion Current, John Daly, Fran Dunn, Sean Dwan, Butch and Louise (Morris) Durst, Jo-Anne Fisher, Dolores Geier, Madeline Giusto, Robert Jezegou, Linda and David Jones, Robert Kelly, Willa Kernen, Marion Kim, Charlie and Fran (Nelson) Krauth, Steve Lavender, Marty Lowery, Gene Matthews, Angela Mistura, Faye Moon, Dirk Nelson, George and Dorothy Ogle, Christine Ortis, Richard Peterson, Marion Pope, Basil Price, Sue and Randy Rice, Ian Robb, Dorothea Schweizer, Delores Smiskol, Jim Sinnott, Dieder Terstevens, Benny Zweber, and others whose faces I remember but whose names escape me now, nearly three decades later.

These persons brought to the group a variety of theological, political, economic, historical, and cultural perspectives. We could have devoted time to debating our many differences. But we didn't. We remained united and focused, a result of our orientation to practical action combined with the urgency of the times. We were further united and focused due to a common understanding of faith – a non-verbalized conviction that the gospel of Jesus Christ has a social/political dimension. We believed that our mission as Christ's disciples extended beyond the salvation of souls to engagement in people's struggles for justice and liberation.

❧ ❧❧ ❧

Why did people come to the Monday Night Group? There were probably as many answers to that as there were members of the group. But we did have one thing in common. All of us were extremely concerned about the increasingly authoritarian policies of the Korean government. We were deeply disturbed about the Park regime's harsh treatment of academics, students, laborers, journalists, poor people, and clergy who worked among the poor. Quite a few of us were in regular contact with Korean friends, neighbors, and colleagues who were bearing the brunt of this repression. But we were frustrated by our powerlessness. We had no idea how to translate concern into action. The Monday Night Group provided a way for us isolated individuals to move from being solitary to being in solidarity.

At the very least, the Monday Night Group provided an opportunity to share our feelings of isolation and impotence. I think about a person who comes to an Alcoholics Anonymous meeting and hears the first of the Twelve Steps: "We admitted that we were powerless over alcohol...." Instead of "alcohol," substitute "the political situation" or "the Korean government" or "the Yushin Constitution" and you have one of the rationales for the Monday Night Group. We came together because we were powerless. We gathered because we were starved for information. We met because we needed a time and place to tell personal stories of what was happening to our Korean friends and their families. We came together because we wanted and needed to take action; every meeting concluded with consensus on a course or courses of action that we would take together or individually in the week ahead.

We kept coming to the Monday Night Group also because we sensed something was happening that was larger than our individual or collective selves. Perhaps it was the work of the Holy Spirit, stirring up the wisdom in the group consciousness and calling us to witness in faith.

More than Witnesses

The Monday Night Group functioned in two ways: as the group gathered, and as the group scattered.

To help you appreciate the group gathered, I will try to describe a "typical" Monday Night Group meeting: It's 7:00 pm and you have arrived at the front door of our Seoul residence – the home of Randy and Sue Rice. On other occasions you might have gone to the home of Butch and Louise Durst, or Dave and Linda Jones, or perhaps the community residence of the Maryknoll sisters in the western part of Seoul. A glance at the jumble of shoes removed near the door tells you that others have already arrived. The living room is crowded. Most folks are sitting Korean style on the floor; a few others are in chairs. Books and papers are strewn about; a large stack of thick manila envelopes occupies the center of the floor. The atmosphere is casual and lively. People are at ease with one another.

Facilitator Linda Jones calls us to order. This particular evening someone reads a page from the *Radical Bible* to open the meeting. Linda, organized and focused as always, lays out a proposed agenda. It's a full menu. First she draws our attention to the manila envelopes and hands them around. These are the Information Packets, enough for every person in the group and some left over. They contain a variety of "hot stuff": materials in Korean and English including copies of magazine and newspaper articles, MNG Fact Sheets, prayers, letters – many of them resources not available anywhere else in south Korea. Distribution of the Information Packets is a staple at every meeting.

The agenda includes verbal reports from those who attended the Thursday Morning Prayer Meeting at the Christian Building and the Sunday afternoon worship service at Galilee Church. Others give updates on the status of political prisoners and their families. There is a letter to be drafted to send to President Ford in anticipation of his visit to Korea. The meeting progresses as outlined, with some departures from the agenda. Two decisions need to be made: who will write, type, sign, and send the letter to President Ford; and who will take primary responsibility for getting warm clothing (for example, long underwear) to prisoners as winter approaches.

The meeting flows. People feel free to laugh, to be serious, to weep. No one dominates. Everyone has an opportunity to speak. Consensus is reached on the wording of the letter. Someone takes responsibility for getting the clothing for prisoners; we hear that money is available. Another person will see that the clothing gets to the prisons.

The meeting closes with a reminder of where we will meet next week. A few people linger to converse and make plans for the week. Back at the front door, you find your shoes – and you notice it's 10:30 pm. You have just 90 minutes to get home before the midnight curfew sirens sound.

～ ～ ～ ～

To help readers understand the group scattered, I will describe the large number of activities that took place each week between Monday night meetings. I should mention first that it was good that the MNG met weekly. First, it allowed sufficient time to carry out decisions, make contacts, collect and duplicate materials, attend prayer services, and more. Second, the awareness that we would gather again in just one week kept us focused on getting things done – and "getting MNG things done" meant finding time within our regular, full-time missionary assignments.

What follows is my attempt to categorize 13 areas of work involving the "scattered" Monday Night Group.

1. Political prisoners: Attending trials of prisoners, meeting with and supporting their families, accompanying family members on prison visitations, collecting and passing along funds to help prisoners' families with school fees and with food, medicine, and

clothing purchases for those in prison, and documenting stories of treatment of prisoners – particularly if there were rumors of torture.

2. Prayer meetings and worship services: Attending Thursday Morning Prayer Meetings at the Christian Building in downtown Seoul and worship services at the Galilee Church. (More Monday Night Group members gathered at the Thursday Morning Prayer Meeting than at any other occasion during the week.)

3. Meeting with college students and with staff members of the National Council of Churches in Korea, Korean Student Christian Federation, and Urban Industrial Mission.

4. Arranging meetings between Koreans and persons visiting from overseas (reporters, church officials, congressional representatives, State Department personnel, etc.).

5. Writing letters to people in government (ambassadors, senators, presidents, State Department officials). Although the majority of group members were citizens of the United States, those of other nationalities also corresponded with their governments.

6. Gathering, duplicating, translating, preparing materials for the Information Packets.

7. Researching, writing and duplicating the Fact Sheets.

8. Arranging to get materials out of the country by hand. This was not always easy – as readers will discover in the following chapters of this book.

9. Maintaining the Monday Night Group "files." We gathered a wealth of material over the years related to the struggle for democracy, human rights, and social justice in south Korea, particularly during the 1970's. These records, which filled several large boxes, were added to and updated periodically. Periodically the files were moved from one location to another.

10. Relationships with fellow missionaries: There were many more western missionaries in south Korea in the 1970's than there

are today, and a segment of that missionary community was highly critical of MNG activities. This opposition had both theological and practical dimensions, and MNG members responded on both levels.

11. Hiding fugitives: A number of MNG members opened their homes to Korean students, pastors, and other activists being sought by the KCIA. Among those who opened their homes as places of refuge were Dave and Linda Jones, Bill and Jean Basinger, Walter and Lenore Beecham, Willa Kernen, Butch and Louise Durst, and Sue and Randy Rice. Other missionaries who did not attend MNG meetings were also helpful in this regard.

12. Participating in demonstrations and other forms of public protest. And when members of the MNG were arrested and detained, other members went to their aid and gave emotional support to their spouses and family members.

13. Miscellaneous activities: The Monday Night Group had a small lending library, and books were brought to each meeting. Included were works of Martin Luther King Jr., Gandhi, Saul Alinsky, and others. We also occasionally sought the instruction and guidance of visitors to south Korea. They would either come to a regular Monday night meeting or, like Richard Deats, director of the Fellowship of Reconciliation in Nyack, New York, guide us in a weekend retreat. Deats taught us about nonviolence, including methods of nonviolent resistance.

❧ ❧❧ ❧

Why did the Monday Night Group appear to have an impact far beyond our numbers or our actions? I can only speculate, but I believe the size of the "stage" had something to do with that. South Korea is a relatively small and compact nation. If the MNG had been operating in as large an arena as China or the Soviet Union, our impact would necessarily have been much smaller. We also benefited from the fact that Seoul was the absolute center of everything political, ecclesiastical, economic, military, diplomatic, and journalistic in south Korea. The excellent transportation system of trains, busses, and taxis made it easy to travel around the capital city and also put the rest of south Korea within easy reach. Thirty percent of the nation's people resided in Seoul, and that's where the major universities and the church and mission headquarters were located. Whatever went on in one part of the metropolis reverberated throughout the nation – and sometimes around the world.

Every MNG alumnus would respond with a hearty "Amen!" when I say that we received much, much more than we gave. This book is a group production, but each one of us could write another volume speaking about the kindness, the generosity, the courage, and the remarkable faith of the Korean Christians whom we were blessed to know personally. When Sue and I returned to Seoul in the autumn of 2003 to be honored with forty-plus others by the Korean Democracy Foundation for our small part in Korea's great struggle, my mind was constantly occupied with the thought, "We shouldn't be here... The real heroes should be here – the wives, the children, the students, the UIM pastors, the professors, the widows."

Chapter 3

What Korea Taught Me
about My Country and My Faith

Louise Morris

When my husband, Walter (Butch) Durst, and I arrived in Seoul in September 1972, it didn't take me long to realize that learning the Korean language would be more difficult than learning Japanese. I had learned Japanese while serving as a short-term missionary in Japan in the late 1960's. At that time, Butch had been a "short-termer" in Korea, and we met after returning to the U.S. from our respective three-year mission assignments. After a year and a half of long-distance courtship (he in Colorado, I in Tennessee), we married and began preparing to return to the mission field. We decided to go to Korea. I had no idea how that decision would change my life.

As we began our two years of language study, we were given the second floor of a two-story Western-style stone house in one of the missionary compounds in Seoul. The house on the missionary compound came with a housekeeper – a middle-aged Korean woman we called "*adjumoni (ajumŏni)*," which literally means "aunt," but is also used to refer to any middle-aged woman. *Adjumoni* came two or three times a week to clean and cook. I didn't know enough Korean to communicate with her, so I thought I'd try Japanese, since I knew that many Koreans learned it during the Japanese occupation that ended in 1945. When I asked the *adjumoni* if she spoke Japanese, she responded curtly, "Why?!" I was taken aback by her abruptness and mumbled something about not knowing Korean yet, and hoping we could communicate in Japanese until I learned more Korean. She softened a little, but it was obvious that she was not interested in speaking Japanese. Then a light bulb went on. Of course! During the Japanese occupation (1905-1945), Koreans had been forced to take Japanese names, were forbidden to study Korean history or learn the Korean alphabet, and were not allowed even to speak their own language. She simply didn't want to speak the language of her former oppressors. It was a good lesson, and I never again tried to speak to Koreans using Japanese. It motivated me to try even harder to master Korean as quickly as possible.

Living in the missionary compound, Butch and I felt somewhat isolated from "real" Korean life, so within a few weeks we moved in with a Korean family who rented us their upstairs. One October 1972 morning we awoke as usual and got ready for another day at language school at Seoul's Yonsei University. The night before, I had been studying my flash cards, trying to memorize *Hangul*, the Korean alphabet. Butch had the radio on. He was practicing Korean by listening to the news, but he wasn't understanding much of what was being broadcast. After breakfast, Butch and I walked the 15 minutes to the bus-stop and caught the city bus to Yonsei University for language school. We got off the bus and started toward the front gate, as usual, but to our great surprise, there were tanks and armed soldiers blocking the gate.

We had no idea what was going on. What did this mean? Why were the gates blocked? Had a coup taken place in the night? Was Korea being invaded by the North? A million questions swirled through our minds. We hesitantly approached one of the soldiers and asked if we could go through the gate to the language school, just up the hill on the campus. After consulting among themselves, they allowed us to pass through the gate. The campus was eerily quiet – no students anywhere, none of the buzz and activity of a normal day on campus. Where was everyone? We learned later that only because we were foreigners were we allowed on campus, and that no Korean students would be allowed back for weeks.

When we got to our class there was a buzz of conversation. We quickly learned that the previous night, President Park Chung Hee had declared martial law. All banks, government offices, and universities were closed to the public and placed under guard by armed soldiers with tanks. Butch then realized what he had been hearing on the radio the night before – President Park's announcement of martial law. With a master's degree and an additional year of graduate work, I was fairly well-educated, but I had no idea what martial law was or what it would entail. Looking back today, I realize that was when my *real* education began.

꿈 ꤯ ꤰ ꤍ

At language school we learned about a group of Americans and Canadians who were working in Korea and wanted to get together to try and sort out what was happening around them. We had noticed that the tanks in front of the public buildings had "USA" marked on them, and we wondered what connection the U.S. had to Korea's martial law. We were eager to find out what others might know. There were about fifteen of us at that first meeting – missionaries mostly, but also Fulbright Scholars, Peace Corps volunteers, and others. This was our introduction to the regular weekly meetings of what became known as the "Monday Night Group."

In subsequent weeks we learned more about martial law and why it had been declared. According to the media, ostensibly there was a threat from communist north Korea. What we found to be the real reason, however, was that President Park Chung Hee was using this communist scare as an excuse to promulgate "National Security Laws" and "Emergency Decrees" that gave him nearly unlimited powers to control the populace and quell dissent. Perhaps President Park was also making a preemptive move, because soon he would also change the Constitution to allow him to remain in office indefinitely.

≈ ≈≈ ≈

When I went to Korea I thought I was fairly well-informed about the world, or at least about that part of the world. I had lived in Japan for four years, had completed a graduate degree, had been through two summers of mission orientation, and had undertaken an additional year of graduate school focused entirely on Korea – the country, the culture, the church, the political and economic history, and the people. The U.S. churches – at least most mainline denominations – had gradually become more broad-minded about mission work and no longer believed that Western Christianity was the form that had to be adopted by everyone. We'd made at least some progress in that direction, in contrast to earlier days when most Western missionaries assumed that anything Western was more advanced, more developed, even more "civilized." In fact, the Korean Methodist Church, the denomination with which I was affiliated, had become autonomous from the U.S. church years before, had developed its own theology, written its own hymns, and trained its own clergy in its own seminaries. Even though I was part of this more "enlightened" era of missions, I still carried with me an underlying, perhaps subconscious, belief in the superiority of Western institutions, systems, and structures – certainly in matters of democracy and economic development.

I would soon learn the extent of my ignorance and arrogance. In spite of my wonderful education and supposed open-mindedness, Korea immediately expanded my view of geopolitical realities; it impressed upon me the nobility of the human spirit; and it exposed seeming contradictions in my understanding of Christianity.

※ ※※ ※

After a few weeks of martial law, students were allowed back on campuses, and widespread demonstrations started. It was not unusual to see riot police in full battle gear at the front gates of Yonsei University, hurling tear-gas canisters into the crowd, roughing up the students and arresting them. When we noticed that the tear-gas canisters were imprinted with "Made in USA," we were puzzled. The tanks that enforced martial law also had the raised letters "USA" on them, even though the letters had been painted over. What did all this mean? Was the U.S. government supplying the Korean government with the means to oppress its own people? At the Monday Night Group meetings we discussed these issues and what we should do, if anything. Finally, those of us from the U.S. decided to meet with the U.S. ambassador and get some answers.

During those first few months in Korea, I had been reading more in depth about U.S. history, its relations with other countries, about multinational corporations, the World Bank, the International Monetary Fund, etc. The more I read, the more astounded I was. Unlike the history I had learned in school, I was learning about things left out of or glossed over in textbooks. The U.S., perhaps the number one superpower in the world, was spreading its form of capitalism around the world, and in the process, wielding enormous power over other countries' political leaders and economies, forcing its rules on others, taking control of others' resources through trade agreements, and supporting less than democratic leaders in many countries. The list of such behaviors seemed to go on and on. It seemed that if other countries didn't conform to U.S. efforts to advance U.S. interests, it would go to great lengths, sometimes resorting even to violence to achieve its goals. Was this the way an advanced, "enlightened," Christian nation was supposed to act in the world? Was this the way U.S. capitalism worked – controlling weaker nations, tipping the trade balances in our favor, always going for the almighty dollar, often at others' expense? Was this how the U.S. had become such a superpower – not because of our way of life, or our desire to promote democracy and freedom? Were we simply following the example of Britain in its era of colonization of Africa, India, and other countries? How could this be true of my beloved country? My naïveté was becoming more and more apparent.

With these thoughts swirling through my head, I went with others from the Monday Night Group to meet with the U.S. ambassador. We entered the massive gates of the embassy, were escorted into a large "parlor" and were seated around a big fireplace. Ambassador Philip Habib served us tea and made small talk for a few minutes as though this were a social occasion, but soon we launched into our questions. What was the U.S. government's involvement in Korea's martial law? Why were the tanks in front of the campuses from the U.S.? Why are the riot police using tear-gas canisters *Made in USA*? What is the U.S. relationship with the Park regime? What is going on?

The ambassador made excuses, pleaded ignorance, and essentially trivialized our concerns: "Of course we are concerned, but our hands are tied. Korea is a sovereign nation, and we cannot interfere in the domestic affairs of a sovereign nation," he told us.

Never mind that the U.S. had tried to assassinate Cuba's Fidel Castro. Never mind that the U.S. was in full support of Ferdinand Marcos, the dictatorial president of the Philippines, giving him aid and remaining silent about human rights abuses there. Never mind the release of the Pentagon Papers and revelations about what we were doing in Vietnam. Never mind that the U.S. would soon be directly involved in the overthrow and assassination of democratically-elected President Allende of Chile. In the face of all these realities, Ambassador Habib had the nerve to tell us that the U.S. never interfered in the affairs of another nation, that its hands were tied.

We in the Monday Night Group were not buying it. Especially when we later learned that not only does the U.S. have a "say" in how our aid is used, but that Congress has to approve any sale by a U.S. company of "instruments of torture." Does that mean that there *are* occasions when we willingly sell instruments of torture to other countries? Needless to say, we left the ambassador's office disgusted and angry. We had been lied to by a high official in our own government, a government supposedly based on the ideals of truth, democracy, freedom, and good will toward others.

I wondered how our country had come to this sorry state.

While trying to make sense of all that I was experiencing, I came across the book *Bury My Heart at Wounded Knee,* which documents the U.S. treatment of American Indians. Again I was shocked, but I was beginning to see a pattern, borne out in our treatment of the Indians. We took advantage of their trustfulness, tricked them into "selling" us land or, if that didn't work, then stealing it from them outright and running them off the land. So many "treaties" were forced on them, which were then violated when these "contracts" got in our way of further expansion south and west. We would oust the Indians from their traditional territories, send them on long marches to some unfamiliar part of the country, and even kill them if they tried to defend their territory – almost the complete opposite of the stereotypes promoted by the cowboy and Indian movies I saw as a youngster. As I read about the atrocities committed against the Indians, I felt the wind knocked out of me. "Oh, my God," I thought, "we in the U.S. have been treating people like this for centuries! It's not like we started out with pure intentions and somehow became corrupted along the way. We've been running over people who get in our way since the very beginning of our history."

One Saturday afternoon, not long after finishing *Bury My Heart*, Butch and I decided to go to a movie. There were usually a few "foreign" films (English movies with Korean subtitles) showing, and that day we went to see one called "Soldier Blue," which seemed innocuous enough. It turned out to be about the Sand Creek Massacre in Colorado. The U.S. Cavalry went into a peaceful camp of Indians and literally massacred them, carrying out all kinds of atrocities in the process. In spite of the fact that one of the soldiers tried to protect some of the Indian women and children, the overall picture was one of cruelty and violence by the whites toward the helpless Indians – all in the name of what? As the movie ended and the lights came on in the theater, I wanted to hide my American face. Walking out of the theater – two white faces in a sea of Koreans – I realized that, for the first time in my life, I was ashamed to be an American.

From that time, I began to view politics and economics with skepticism, especially U.S. policies. I began to grasp the depth of the suffering we had inflicted in the past and continue to inflict today. The more I witnessed in Korea, the more the picture began to fit together; I began to see history in a new light. It was more than rich nations taking advantage of poor countries. It seemed to be a whole system – a way of treating other people – based on exploitation and violence, starting with the treatment of the Indians, then slavery and continuing racial injustices, gender inequality, economic disparities between the "haves" and the "have-nots," and ultimately, war itself.

I found evidence of this system – of getting what we want at whatever cost – in other obvious (though faraway) places: control of Guatemala by the United Fruit Company and U.S. support of apartheid in South Africa; U.S. support for the Shah in Iran, Somoza in Nicaragua, Noriega in Panama, and Saddam Hussein in Iraq – all rulers the U.S. supported until they no longer served our purposes.

I began to look behind the public messages and PR statements given by our U.S. leaders, our politicians, our ambassador to Korea, and the U.S. corporations doing business in Korea and other third world countries. What I discovered was that there were two different stories – the one fed to the public about "liberty," "democracy," and "free trade;" and the other story, about what was really going on: unfair trade, propping up dictatorships, supporting runaway companies that leave the U.S. and go elsewhere for cheaper labor where unions are not tolerated and where we can get advantageous tax arrangements like the "free trade zones" in south Korea.

There was also U. S. Public Law 480 – Food Aid, sometimes referred to as "Food for Peace." It was purportedly to be used for countries experiencing food shortages, but if that were true, why then was this "aid" going mostly to countries in which we had a political interest? In fact, the way it was being used in Korea produced quite the opposite of aid. (I later read the prize-winning series by Don Bartlett and David Steele of the *Philadelphia Inquirer*, called "Food Aid: The Flawed Dream." Researching several recipient nations, they concluded that very little U.S. food aid reached hungry bellies. Instead, this program was used as a political weapon.)

More than Witnesses

In the case of Korea, first of all, there was no food shortage. Korean farmers were very productive. In spite of that, Korea was receiving tons and tons of rice through P. L. 480, for urban markets, causing the price of Korean rice to drop. It created a chain reaction: Korean farmers were no longer able to get a fair price for the rice they produced; they could no longer provide a sufficient livelihood for their families; they would have to send their children to the cities for work. Especially when these children were young girls, they were easily exploited in the cities. Completely ignorant of city life, many of them were pulled into prostitution, a shameful existence that they could neither reveal to their parents nor could they escape from. Many of the children ended up in factories working for a few dollars a day. This chain of events (food aid leads to low rice prices leads to cheap urban labor) provided the basis for much of President Park's "economic miracle" – but the cost to both the rural farmers and the urban workers was enormous. Of course, the pressures on farmers and exploitation of workers were never part of the government's public message. What I was seeing in Korea did not jibe with what the public was being told. A huge gulf existed between propaganda and reality.

❧ ❧❧ ❧

At the Monday Night Group we shared what we were learning from our Korean colleagues and what we were hearing from outside international sources. But when we attended our respective denominational missionary meetings, there was no mention of these things. Surely, we thought, it was just a matter of oversight on the part of the other missionaries. When we'd bring up these issues, however, we'd get blank looks, or comments about how we hadn't been in Korea long enough to understand the culture, implying that we were misinterpreting things or at least exaggerating; that at any rate, we shouldn't be "getting involved" in political things, that such activity was not "appropriate" for a missionary. This was not the attitude of *all* the other missionaries, but it seemed to us that some of them, at least, were simply ignorant of what was going on around them. Surely, we thought, they would understand if they just had the facts.

Jim Stentzel, a Methodist missionary-journalist in Japan who reported also on Korea, suggested that we write Fact Sheets as a way to get the word around. "Yes," we thought, "this would be a way to inform some of our fellow missionaries as well as the outside world about what we are seeing and hearing directly from the Koreans in the movement, especially from the Korean Christians."

Our first Fact Sheet was about the arrest of Rev. Pak Hyung Kyu (Pak Hyŏnggyu), one of the most revered Presbyterian ministers in Seoul. We wrote furiously – wanting to get the word out as quickly as possible.

At our Monday Night meetings we would discuss what issues to cover and assign someone to write the Fact Sheet. I tried to help keep the effort somewhat organized, editing and typing the papers and preparing them for distribution. With limited copying facilities in those days, I had to type some of them several times over with as many layers of carbon paper beneath the original as possible. Sometimes, if I had access to a mimeograph machine, I would cut a stencil and run off the number of copies needed. It certainly was a much more laborious process than it would be today with copy machines on every corner, or with personal computers and printers.

The Fact Sheet titles showed our broad range of topics – Urban Industrial Mission, Changes to the Constitution, Arrested Dissidents, Student Demonstrations, Korea-Japan Relations, the "People's Revolutionary Party," the Death Penalty for Korean Youth, the Emergency Decrees, Imprisoned Poet Kim Chi Ha, Galilee Church, U.S.-Korea Relations, the Plight of the Korean Factory

Workers, the Detention of Christian Young People, and on and on. The topics were endless. (With so many contributors, so many differing experiences and writing abilities, it reminds me somewhat of our combined efforts to write this book!) Throughout the mid 1970's to the early eighties we wrote and distributed more than 60 Fact Sheets (see Appendix for samples).

To get information out, we put together and distributed monthly information packets. In addition to the Fact Sheets, the packets included statements written by Koreans, international articles from sources such as the *Washington Post*, the *Christian Science Monitor*, the *New York Times*, and the *Guardian*, as well as Japanese sources. Packaging them up as innocuously as possible in plain brown envelopes, we would then distribute a set of packets among the various missionary groups in Korea – the United Methodists, the Presbyterians, the Canadians, and others. We also made sure that the Fact Sheets were distributed outside of Korea, in Japan, Canada, the U.S., and Europe. In the end, the MNG mailing list included several hundred individuals and organizations around the world.

Whether the information packets resulted in a better informed missionary community inside Korea was hard to gauge. Did the packets help explain things more fully? Were they even read? We didn't know. Very few people commented on them one way or the other. Some, of course, were already sympathetic, others seemed opposed, but perhaps most were somewhere in the middle – not wanting to rock the boat, maybe fearful of what might happen to them, or maybe just not seeing our activism as part of their calling. However, there were a few who did object to what we were doing, which resulted, sadly, in our theology being challenged. The implication was that the missionary role was to preach, teach, provide social services, medical care, etc.; in other words, direct services; but we were not to go beyond that to oppose certain policies, even if they caused harm to those very same people we were serving. Church and state should be separate, we were told, meaning that we should stay out of politics. After all, we were allowed to be in the country and to carry out our mission work at the behest of the Korean government, so we should not be challenging its policies or be involved with those who were.

We were surprised and yes, even hurt, that our understanding of the Gospel would be questioned – not by strangers, but by some of our own fellow missionaries. But even in this challenge, God was acting. In order to clarify our beliefs, we took it upon ourselves to write our "theology of mission" (see "A Tract for Our Times" in the Appendix). The exercise helped us clarify for ourselves (and hopefully to others) the faith that undergirded our actions. We tried to articulate how our understanding of the Gospel included not just giving direct help to those in need, but also standing up for justice, fairness, and proper treatment of others, even if it meant opposing the actions of those in power. The fact was, we were following the example of our Korean Christian colleagues, some of the key leaders in the Korean church. It was a strange juxtaposition being admonished by one group of Christians while being encouraged by another – two different views of Christianity by two groups of equally devout Christians.

In the early 1970's, some of the more progressive Korean religious leaders began holding Thursday Morning Prayer Meetings at the Christian Building, a building of about seven stories on the east side of town that housed the offices of the National Council of Churches of Korea (KNCC), the Korean Christian Student Federation (KSCF), Church Women United, The Christian Broadcasting System, and others. In January 1974 a handful of ministers working in the Urban Industrial Mission (UIM), a ministry to poor factory laborers, decided to hold a demonstration at the KNCC office in the Christian Building, to protest the government's Emergency Decrees and admonish the churches to get more involved in opposing the Park regime's crackdown on the country.

Butch had been working closely with some of the UIM ministers and decided to join them in solidarity and support. Back home after the event, he told me about what had taken place, about the statement the ministers had read and the big banner they had unfurled. He had half expected the gathering to be broken up by the plainclothesmen, but nothing like that happened. Butch said he took some pictures of the whole thing and hoped they would turn out okay. And that was the end of the incident – or so we thought.

Early that afternoon, two men from the KCIA appeared at the house, insisting that Butch go with them to be investigated about the demonstration. They wouldn't tell me where they were taking him, but they assured me that he wouldn't be gone long and would return home shortly. Being the naïve person I was, I initially took them at their word, but soon I began to have doubts. I knew the kinds of tactics the KCIA used to get information out of people, so I realized they would have no compunction about lying to me, and I worried about what they might do to Butch to pry out information. I decided to call Monday Night Group member and our nearest neighbor, George Ogle. He had been in Korea for most of the past 20 years, so maybe he would know what to do.

It was January 17, 1974, which happened to be George's birthday. He was in the middle of his birthday dinner with the family, but without hesitation he apologized to his family and left to try to find Butch. George contacted Gene Matthews and they discussed what they should do. Finally, they bravely decided that they would go together to Nam San (South Mountain) where the dreaded KCIA headquarters were – the place dissidents were taken for questioning (and torture). George and Gene thought that, at the very least, the authorities needed to know that others were aware that Butch had been picked up.

According to George, "It was a dumb thing to do, we knew, but we didn't have any other ideas. Making an inquiry at the KCIA could quite possibly get us both locked up. We finally located the main gate to the KCIA compound and banged on the gate. The armed guard was a bit flabbergasted. 'What do you want?' he barked. 'We came to see about a foreign missionary who was arrested this afternoon,' we replied. In a few minutes, a man in civilian dress came out and invited us into his office. He was very cordial, remarked on the fact that both of us spoke good Korean, and served us tea. He listened closely to what we had to say, but assured us that such problems were not under the jurisdiction of the KCIA, and that we should go instead to the Seoul Police Headquarters. He wrote down the address on a piece of paper and gave us directions. As we left, he bowed and gave the usual Korean farewell greeting, '*annyonghikaseyo (annyŏnghi kaseyo)*' (go in peace)."

The trip to the police station, however, yielded no results either. Some time later that evening, George called me: "We haven't found him yet. We've gone to Nam San and the police station but they said they don't know anything about it. But don't worry. We'll keep looking."

I wasn't sure what to do. I was at home alone pacing up and down with worry. Where was Butch? What are they doing to him? Will they release him tonight? What if they don't? The KCIA were infamous for using various torture methods to get whatever "confession" they wanted from people. They had never gone that far with an American, so I was pretty sure they wouldn't do anything to harm him physically, but there were other things they could do – threaten him, deprive him of sleep, hold him incommunicado for days on end. But I had faith that George and Gene would be able to help, so I tried to put my worries aside.

In the end, George and Gene were not able to locate Butch, but later that night, much to my relief, he was released and made his way back home. Imagine my surprise when he told me that he had been held at the Nam San KCIA headquarters! It turned out that while George and Gene were drinking tea with the KCIA man – the man who had denied any knowledge of Butch's whereabouts – Butch was in the very next room being interrogated!

After that, our phone was tapped, and for weeks there was a special plainclothes KCIA agent stationed in the street outside our house, watching every move we made, every place we went. Butch was obviously very shaken. He was almost like a prisoner, staying mostly at home and going out only when necessary. He worried about the other people who had been picked up. He worried about getting picked up again, or possibly being deported to the U.S. I'm sure it was only his faith and the support of others that helped him through that time. Eventually he ventured out and resumed his participation in prayer meetings, demonstrations, and other ways to support the movement, but that experience left its mark on him.

This was the first time we had personally experienced any direct harassment. Although it was frightening not knowing exactly what the authorities might do, the consequences of Butch's actions turned out to be minimal. Such light treatment of Westerners was certainly in contrast to the way Koreans were treated. The "norm" for students who were picked up was two solid weeks (sometimes longer) of "interrogation" in the bowels of the KCIA headquarters at Nam San. During that time, they would be beaten, starved, shocked with electric cattle prods, given the "water treatment" (held suspended upside down, with water continuously dripping into their noses hour after hour), and be forced to listen to friends in the next room screaming from the torture being inflicted on them. The list could go on and on. There were even incidents of so-called suicides or fatal "accidents." The Koreans were certainly not treated as leniently as Westerners were.

Who knows why the Korean authorities shied away from more brutal treatment of people like us. Without a doubt, Korea was very much dependent on the U.S. – militarily and economically, and therefore politically. The U.S. had fought in the Korean War on the side of the south Koreans. (The U.S. was one of the parties, along with Russia, that made the decision at the end of World War II to divide Korea into two countries at the 38th parallel.) Many Korean intellectuals have been educated in the U.S. The Korean people, in general, seemed to have very positive feelings toward Americans, even if some might disagree with U.S. policies. Perhaps roughing up Americans was just not something the Korean authorities considered a good idea. Such treatment, especially if it got widespread media coverage outside Korea, could have unintended negative repercussions. Whatever the reasons, there was certainly a double standard. Westerners were treated with kid gloves compared to the Koreans. We did not have to fear physical mistreatment, other than perhaps long hours of questioning without food or rest. The worst might be expulsion from the country, which eventually did happen to at least three missionaries in the next couple of years – two from the U.S. and one from Australia.

In the spring of 1974, we read in the newspaper about a new case of communist infiltration. The Korean government had apprehended eight men who apparently had ties with north Korea and had formed an organization called the People's Revolutionary Party (PRP). The PRP, the newspaper said, was plotting to overthrow the government.

More than Witnesses

By that time I was suspicious of anything the government announced; because warnings about the threat of communism, especially from north Korea, were commonplace, I didn't think much about it. However, at the Monday Night Group meeting, I learned that it was definitely something to pay attention to – but not in the way the Park regime wanted people to pay attention. We were suspicious of the PRP arrests; perhaps, we thought, these men had been unjustly accused. Apprehending a dangerous group like the PRP was a way to instill even more fear among the Koreans, and to divert people's attention away from the increasingly serious crackdowns the government was perpetrating against anyone who opposed its policies. If the government didn't have a real case of communist infiltration, it could simply fabricate one. Very easily. Too easily.

George Ogle had been approached by the wives of some of the accused men, asking for his help. George learned from them that their husbands – ordinary people, really just political "nobodies" – had been picked up on their way home from work one day and had not been heard from since. The only news about them was what was being reported in the newspapers. George remembered a similar case years earlier of another group with the same name, charged with the same crime. The earlier case, however, had been dismissed for lack of evidence. It seemed clear that the Park regime was trying the same tactic as before, and with more control over the courts and the media, this time they could make it stick. In retrospect it revealed a government desperate to maintain power and control over the populace – even accusing innocent men of the most serious crimes against the state.

☙ ❧❧ ❧

Shortly after George Ogle was deported in December 1974, Butch and I prepared for a short trip back to the U.S. to spend

Christmas with our families and to speak at some of our supporting churches. We arrived at Seoul's Kimpo Airport, checked our bags, and were going through the check-in line as usual. We were always nervous at the airport, because we often smuggled articles or statements out, or brought in books and other materials that the Korean government wanted to keep out.

This time, as we got to the head of the line to have our travel documents checked, the agent looked at Butch's passport for what seemed like a very long time. Then he excused himself and told us to wait. When he came back a few minutes later there was another man with him. The man told Butch to follow him into another room. This man was from the Immigration Office; our names were obviously on some kind of a blacklist. The agent told us that, if we left the country, he could not guarantee that our visa (which unfortunately was due to expire while we were in the U.S.) would be approved for re-entry into Korea. When we asked why, all he would say was, "You are a threat to the national security of Korea." We protested, but the agent shrugged it off, saying we would have to straighten it out at the Immigration Office downtown. We knew this meant they could, and very well might, decide to keep us out of the country for good.

We made our way back to our house and called Gene Matthews who had been in Korea since the mid 1950's and had much more experience dealing with the Korean authorities. Gene dropped what he was doing and accompanied us to the Immigration Office. As we went in, Gene explained to the clerk that we needed a return visa. The clerk, who had no idea who we were, very confidently said, "Oh sure, I can take care of that. I will just call our staff upstairs to approve it." He picked up the phone, dialed a number, and in a relatively loud and confident tone said, "We have two missionaries here who need return visas. Can you okay their visas for them? Their names are Walter and Louise Durst." Then he hung up and waited for the "okay".

More than Witnesses

When the reply phone call came, his voice dropped several decibels, "Oh, really?" As he listened further, his mouth dropped open. Then he hung up the phone and walked over to us, much less confident than when he had started. "There seems to be some kind of problem. You'll have to talk to my supervisor."

We went in to his supervisor's office. "You are suspected of anti-government activities. I will have to check into this matter." Gene jumped in, "It will not look good for Korea if missionaries are not allowed to return." But the supervisor repeated that he would have to check with his superiors. "Come back tomorrow," he said, dismissing us.

Over the past months, Gene had gotten acquainted with a couple of Korean CIA agents, and sometimes he could get information from them "on the side." As we left the Immigration Office, Gene said he would see what he could find out. He contacted the agents and told them what was going on. He stressed that if we were not allowed to leave and go speak to the U.S. churches as we were scheduled to do, that it would look really bad for Korea. Gene no doubt had to do some serious pleading; after all, we did have a "police record." Butch had been picked up by the KCIA for taking photos of the UIM ministers' protest, and we both had been seen regularly at the Thursday Morning Prayer Meetings. There were plenty of reasons why we had come to the attention of the authorities.

We waited to hear back from Gene, but no word came that day. The next morning Gene heard from his KCIA contacts: "They think your re-entry visas will be approved." We headed back downtown to the Immigration Office. This time the visas had been approved. As they were handed to us, we were warned to stay out of trouble and to obey Korean laws. We left on a plane that afternoon, hoping we'd eventually meet up with our luggage that had left Seoul the day before. We knew that this was just another effort to intimidate us, to keep us quiet.

Back in the U.S., when we told church audiences about the incident and about the other things going on in Korea, they were amazed. In previous visits to the U.S. churches, they had been reluctant to believe that the U.S. government was in support of the Korean dictatorship. Finally, after several years of hearing stories from us, and reading about things like the "Koreagate" scandal in Washington, church-goers became more receptive to our message. Of course, what happened to us at the airport was nothing compared to what Koreans were enduring day after day. It was just a way to harass us and keep us from making waves. Meanwhile, the Koreans were literally putting their futures and their very lives on the line.

❧ ❧❧ ❧

The arrests of the alleged PRP leaders devastated the men's families. The wives were completely dependent on their husbands' wages for their family livelihood. The children were ridiculed at school as children of dirty communists. They were all treated as outcasts.

George knew that someone had to expose this charade. He researched the identities and histories of the men, wrote an account of what he found, and distributed his findings as widely as possible. It was *not* something that endeared him to the Korean government. Because he risked speaking out and even publicly praying for these families, he was taken in for questioning by the KCIA on more than one occasion. Finally, to silence this trouble-making truth-teller, the government decided to deport him. So, in mid-December 1974, he was ousted from the land and people he had loved and served faithfully for nearly two decades, changing the course of his life and that of his whole family. However, it was a much smaller price than the one the "PRP" men and their families would be forced to pay.

More than Witnesses

In April 1975, a year after the men were arrested, it was announced that there would be a final Supreme Court hearing of the "PRP" case. This massive old-style courthouse was difficult to get to, down narrow old roads in a neighborhood of old establishments. A driveway led to the front entrance of the imposing building surrounded by a high wall and with a spiked iron fence blocking the driveway. The day was overcast – raining off and on all day. Hundreds of supporters gathered outside the courthouse. As we milled about outside, plainclothesmen were everywhere. It seemed likely that they might try to disperse the crowd by hauling folks off in paddy wagons, as they often did at demonstrations or other large public gatherings like this.

Some of us expatriates decided to go inside and up to the courtroom to support the wives, and to witness the hearing. Butch, Father Jim Sinnott, and I went into the courtroom and sat behind the wives. The judges walked in. We waited for the prisoners to be brought in, but they never appeared. Then, without testimony from defense lawyers, the prosecution, or statements from any of the accused, the judges pronounced that there was no need for testimony because the men were guilty. Their death sentences would be upheld. Then the judges turned and walked out of the courtroom. It happened so quickly, we stood there stunned and silent. When it finally began to sink in, the wives began screaming and beating the seats with their umbrellas. Such an outrage! The Supreme Court "hearing" was exposed as a complete sham. Soon leather-jacketed men entered the courtroom and began firmly escorting the protesting women out of the building.

Finally, everyone was ousted from the courtroom, except us three foreigners. I felt so strongly that we had to do something to protest this unbelievable travesty of justice. For some reason, feeling more anger than fear, I decided I would just refuse to leave the room.

It was a completely irrational and unproductive action, but I had to do something to defy them, to *not* go along with the program. One of the court bailiffs came over to us and said, "You need to go now. It's lunch time."

None of us moved. The bailiffs were at a loss as to what to do with us. They murmured among themselves. Then one of them approached and said loudly in English with a slight mispronunciation of the letter "s:" "You must leave. Remember, this is, this is ... Supreme Court."

Jim yelled back, "Supreme Court? Supreme Court?! This is not Supreme Court! This is Supreme Sh*t!" Jim continued shouting at them, and when they saw we had no intention of leaving, they began to physically push us toward the back stairway. At that point I lay down on the floor. Butch and Jim followed suit. This surprised the men; once again they huddled to consult with one other.

Deciding there was nothing to be done but to bodily carry us out, four men grabbed Butch and took him down the back stairs. Next was Jim. Finally, three men came over to me. This was a little more "touchy," because it is not proper for a Korean man to physically handle a woman, and I was an *American* woman, to boot. But I wasn't budging and there was no other way to get me out of the building, so the three finally picked me up and started carrying me somewhat gingerly toward the back stairway, obviously uncomfortable with this task. I was determined not to make it easy for them, and decided to resist in any way I could. As they were carrying me down the stairs, I grabbed hold of the banisters and held as tightly as I could. As they tried to pry my hands loose, I overheard one of them say under his breath, "Man, she is really strong." That just gave me more courage, and I continued to struggle against them. As they grabbed at my raincoat sleeves, trying to pull me off the banister without actually touching me, I let my arms slip out of the sleeves, and they were left holding an empty coat. They were momentarily baffled: "What in the ...?" Of course, eventually they did get my hands loose from the banister, carried me down the stairs, and deposited me on the concrete plaza outside the back door.

There were Jim and Butch, sitting on the pavement, not quite knowing what to do next. What a motley threesome we were. There was not another soul around. Suddenly, realizing that we must look like the Three Stooges, we all burst out laughing, relieving a bit of our tension and frustration.

We made our way back to the front of the courthouse and joined some of the other Monday Night Group members who were still there. It was a horrible day – such an outrageous sentence handed down on these eight innocent men. Little did we know that the following day would be even more horrendous – in the early morning before dawn, all eight of the men would be hanged. Their wives and children had no chance to see them or talk to them since they had been snatched off the streets and taken into custody almost a year earlier.

At the Monday Night Group meeting that week, we knew we had to do something to protest these deaths. Because we felt the U.S. had stood by and done nothing, we decided to hold a demonstration in front of the U.S. Embassy. It is not illegal for Americans to demonstrate on the embassy grounds, as this is considered U.S. soil, so we wouldn't be breaking any laws. And, as U.S. citizens, we felt it more appropriate to focus our displeasure toward our own government and its complicity. In previous months we had tried to urge the U.S. Embassy to protest the PRP case, and had always been assured that they were "working behind the scenes," using "quiet diplomacy." We were never quite sure what they meant by that, or how it was supposed to work, but we knew that the U.S. would only have had to say the word and these men's lives could have been spared.

We designated eight of the Monday Night Group men to be in the demonstration. It would be a silent protest, with the eight wearing black hoods and nooses around their necks, symbolizing the eight men who had been hanged. The day of the demonstration, they stood in front of the embassy in silence holding signs that read, "Is this your silent diplomacy?" A photo of the demonstration made the front cover of that week's Asia Edition of *Time Magazine*. (See Walter Durst's chapter for more about the embassy demo.)

In the summer of 1975, my parents came to visit us. I flew to Tokyo to meet them. While in Tokyo I met with Oh Jae Shik (O Chaesik), a graduate of Yale Divinity School who was living in Japan and serving very important roles in support of south Korea's human rights movement. He had prepared some materials for me to take back to the church leaders in Korea, as well as medicines for opposition politician Kim Dae Jung, who was imprisoned at the time.

The night before my parents and I were to leave for Korea, I was trying to pack the medicines in my suitcase in a way that wouldn't be noticed by the Customs officials. If the medicines or materials were found, it could mean trouble for everyone involved. Unexpectedly, my father questioned me: "Aren't you just helping the communists by smuggling these things in?" I was so surprised I didn't know how to respond. What did my taking medicines and other information to the brave Korean defenders of human rights have to do with "the communists?" Did my father think that we were involved in some kind of underground communist movement?

At the very least I realized that he had no real understanding about the situation in Korea. Maybe he was just reverting back to the only clandestine, sinister thing he was familiar with – the McCarthy-era communist scare. Of course, communist north Korea was just a few dozen miles north of Seoul, a fact of which he was well aware. But Butch and I had been writing home about the chain of events taking place in south Korea since our arrival there – and my father obviously had not "gotten" it. I tried to explain to him who Kim Dae Jung was, why he was in prison, that he was in poor health without access to medicines, and that this was the right thing to do – the Christian thing to do. I wasn't sure how much I was able to convince him, but I'm sure it didn't alleviate his fears about the danger.

Once in Korea, my parents got a first-hand picture of what we had been trying to tell them in our letters. They came to the Monday Night Group and saw that the people involved were all church people – Protestant missionaries, Catholic priests and nuns, mission interns, and others from all over the world. They listened to the stories of Korean Christians, students, journalists, laborers, farmers – people from all walks of life – being picked up, arrested, tortured, imprisoned (and sometimes worse) for their courageous stands against oppression and for the restoration of democracy.

Of course, we showed my parents the beautiful Korean countryside and the temples and cultural sights. But we also took them to see the teenage workers in the "Peace Market" garment sweatshops and to meet some of the ministers of the Urban Industrial Mission. They accompanied us to Galilee Church and to the Thursday Morning Prayer Meetings, and they met the wives of imprisoned ministers and the mothers of imprisoned students. They went to the gates of the military prison where poet Kim Chi Ha was held, and they saw the plainclothesmen that followed us everywhere we went.

And they got it: What a beautiful country – its mountains, temples, rich history, villages, lush rice fields, lively markets, bustling cities, and magnificent people. And what a tragedy – widespread fear of the government and its KCIA, police, military; brutal oppression of those trying to defend freedom and restore democracy; constant fanning of the fears of the communist North (a tactic to make people swallow restrictive government policies); and the people's fear of questioning what was happening, so much so that they would even refrain from whispering to a friend in a coffee shop, for fear that the person in the next booth might be an informant listening for something that could be reported to the authorities.

When my parents returned to the U.S. they helped us get the word out as best they could. They wrote letters to Congress and the White House, and they told the story as they had witnessed it. From then on, their letters to us included concern for those they had met or learned about. How was poet Kim Chi Ha (Kim Chiha)? Was he out of prison yet? What had happened to the outspoken Christian leader, Rev. Timothy Moon?

As I watched the transformation of my parents, I relived my own. Like me, they received quite an education. They saw beneath the surface of the U.S. connection to Korea and now understood the world in ways they had not imagined before. They also saw that Korea was not an isolated case. When they heard news of other countries where dictators ruled and people were oppressed, where economies were hand-in-hand with U.S. business, where the U.S. supported the ruling class that kept getting richer while the majority of the population got poorer, where Christians and others who took a stand would disappear or be assassinated, like Archbishop Romero in El Salvador – now they understood. Now they saw world events through different lenses.

❧ ❦❦ ☙

When Jimmy Carter was elected president in 1976, for the first time in U.S. history, an Office of Human Rights was set up. This gave us hope. Perhaps now U.S. policy would have a positive effect on human rights in Korea. Three years later, in the spring of 1979, when we heard that Carter was planning a visit to Korea, we wrote a letter to him, asking him not to come unless President Park agreed to stop the abuses. By now there were hundreds of political prisoners in jails and prisons, surveillance by plainclothesmen was rampant, and hundreds of students were in hiding. The Korean government was clearing the shacks off the Seoul mountaintops, along the route where Carter would be taken. These were the homes of Seoul's poorest citizens who had to eke out a living as day laborers and factory workers.

We knew that our letter would never make it through the Korean mail system without being apprehended, so we asked Pat Patterson, a United Methodist mission board staff person, to hand-carry the letter out of Korea and to mail it to President Carter once she got back to the U.S. Unfortunately, the letter was confiscated at the airport. The next thing we knew, all who had signed the letter were called to the Immigration Office. They handed us a note with a statement written in English; we were told to write the statement in our own handwriting and sign it. The statement went something like this: "I promise never again to write letters to the U.S. government concerning the affairs of Korea." This was outrageous! American citizens were being asked to promise that we would not exercise our democratic rights to communicate to our own president. The immigration officers must be crazy, I thought.

In fact, they were very insistent. If we didn't sign, they said, there would be consequences. Again, illogic and naïveté took over, and we refused to acquiesce. Instead of the statement they had prepared for us, we wrote "As American citizens we acknowledge our democratic right to communicate our opinions to our government." The officers took it into another room to get it translated. In a few minutes they came back, obviously displeased, and said it was unsatisfactory. In fact, nothing we came up with satisfied them. It was getting late, so they told us to go home, think it over carefully, and to come back the next day.

The next day we still were not willing to sign their statement. After much discussion back and forth – maybe they were getting worn down – they finally accepted this statement from us: "We recognize the Korean government's right to implement its laws, and we will accept the consequences of those laws."

After that incident, each of us who signed the letter to Carter had our residence permits shortened. Now we had to renew them every three months rather than once a year.

≈ ✍≈ ≈

What had happened at the airport was that, after the letter to Carter was confiscated, Pat Patterson's flight was delayed while officials dealt with it. Eventually she got the letter back, and her plane was permitted to depart from Seoul. The letter and signatures were delivered to the White House. And the resulting publicity was good for the Korean human rights cause. *Washington Star* columnist Mary McGrory defended us in our claim that U.S. citizens have the right and responsibility to communicate with our government. Her April 29, 1979, syndicated column was entitled, "Carter's Trip to Korea One More Blow Against Human Rights." However inconvenient it had been for us who signed the letter, the publicity was valuable to Koreans in their struggle.

≈ ✍≈ ≈

Back in 1972, when we first arrived in Korea, we began attending a Korean Methodist church not far from where we lived. It was a typical church with typical sermons – mostly focused on one's personal relationship with God, living a sin-free life, and spreading Christianity. Not much was said about issues related to justice – hunger, poverty, homelessness, unfair treatment of others, and certainly nothing related to the abuses being perpetrated by the Park regime. When we would bring up the subject to the minister or some of the parishioners, they would say, "Christians can't get involved in politics. It's not our place. Anyway, it's too dangerous!"

Months later, some Korean church leaders active in the human rights movement decided to start a new kind of church where the truth could be spoken freely. So Galilee Church was started, and we began attending regularly. The weekly Thursday Morning Prayer Meetings and the Galilee Church services were so meaningful and so different from anything we had experienced before. Here were places where the scriptures were searched for guidance about how to live faithfully in challenging circumstances, about what Jesus said regarding "principalities and powers," about the risks he took defying the authorities of his day, about how he stood up for the poor and oppressed.

Galilee Church was a place where truth was spoken to power, where the Korean government's anti-democratic policies and repressive treatment of the people were directly challenged. It was based on the belief that we are called to act on behalf of those suffering, and that if we don't, "the very rocks will cry out." These worship services always included lots of singing, praying, and sharing news of those who had run into trouble with the authorities or been arrested or imprisoned. Much energy went to providing Bibles, books, supplemental food, and warm clothes for those in the unheated prison cells.

The Galilee sermons were powerful. No platitudes or clichés spoken here. These people were calling on the depths of their faith daily, to get through the trials (figuratively and literally) they faced, and to live out the Jesus story. There was no mincing of words about the actions of the government against innocent people, about its efforts to catch any whiff of opposition, or about its ruthless treatment of the students, who traditionally have been Korea's lightning rod in protesting injustice.

Each Sunday afternoon we would take the hour-and-a-half bus ride to the church where the Galilee congregation gathered after that church's regular morning service. We would trudge up the hill, walking past the plainclothesmen watching us from adjacent buildings. Government agents even came to the services, sitting in the back pews to listen and observe, though few if any of them were Christian. I often wondered what the plainclothesmen thought about what they were hearing at those services – the scriptures they heard read and interpreted, the application of them to the situation in Korea. Did they ever doubt the government? Did they ever wonder what their role was – whether they were doing the right thing or not? When visitors were welcomed and introduced at the services, the plainclothesmen would also be asked to introduce themselves. One Sunday an agent said, "I probably attend more regularly than any of you," bringing good-natured laughter from the group.

Watching the Koreans take great risks, even by worshipping in such an open way without watering down the message, challenging us all to be faithful servants even if it meant experiencing some type of persecution, caused me to really look at my faith in a much deeper way. I was amazed at how courageous the Koreans were – speaking out not for themselves personally, but for those with less standing in the community, for the most vulnerable, those without a voice – from the slum-dwellers who eked out a subsistence living with sporadic day labor jobs, to young women working in sweatshops trying to help subsidize their families' shrinking farm income, to journalists being persecuted for reporting what was really going on instead of giving the government party line, to newspaper publishers having all their advertising yanked because they were not willing to turn a blind eye to what was really happening. And of course the students (with support from some courageous professors), who were out in the streets week after week, issuing statements about this travesty of "democracy," being pelted with tear gas, being arrested, or if they were lucky, escaping into hiding to avoid arrest.

I remember the day a young Methodist minister came to our house and asked if we were ready to pack our bags (implying that if we agreed to what he was about to request, we could end up getting kicked out of Korea). He had come to tell us about a student who needed a place to stay, because the authorities were looking for him. We knew what that meant. If he were caught, it would mean torture, forced "confession," implication of others, arrest, and imprisonment. We were not at all as courageous as the Koreans; but how could we say no?

On two occasions we kept students in our home for several months, until things were safe enough for them to be out in the open again. They had to be literally inside the house – if they went outside even briefly for a breath of fresh air, they knew they were taking a chance on being seen by someone who might report them.

As always seems to be the case, we benefited at least as much from these arrangements as did the students we were trying to help. During the weeks and months that students lived with us, we spent many hours engaged in conversation about liberation movements. Though in our missionary work lives, *we* were supposedly the seminary and university "professors," we were almost completely ignorant of some of the things we were learning from these youth – about peoples' revolutions in other parts of the world, past and present; about upheavals and changes in Korea's long history, brought about by the *minjung* (see Glossary); even about struggles in the U.S. such as the labor movement and the civil rights movement, which they knew in much greater detail than even we did. They were diligent in analyzing how these movements occurred, which strategies were successful, which were not and why.

Of course, in addition to the serious discussions, there was always plenty of good-natured teasing and laughter; such as the night at the dinner table when we were told that our *kim-chi (kimch'i)* (fermented Chinese cabbage laden with cayenne pepper, served with every Korean meal) was "wimpy" and just not hot enough. Not hot enough?! It had taken us months to get used to this spicy hot staple! "No, no," we were told, "if you aren't sweating by the end of a Korean meal, you haven't really eaten."

These young people were not just passively sitting at home during their "confinements." They were reading and writing, thinking and planning. They were so committed – willing to risk getting expelled from their universities, to spend years in prison if necessary, to literally put their lives on the line for what they believed in: democracy, human rights, freedom of speech, freedom of assembly. In other words, they wanted a brighter future for their country and were willing to sacrifice for it.

I was so impressed by these young students. Some of them were Christian, some were not. Some were even atheists, though it seemed to me, they were living in a more Christian way than some who professed to be Christian (perhaps, including myself). As I pondered more deeply, I realized that just *calling* oneself Christian means nothing if we're not willing to act on our faith. I began to wonder about what seemingly had always been the church's dominant focus, its highest priority: to convert others so that eventually everyone would profess Christianity, would accept Jesus as Savior, or at least would believe in God. I had studied world religions in college, and at the time had wondered whether God really required that we all become Christians. So many common themes ran through all the major religions – compassion, kindness, sacrifice, service, obedience to a higher calling, faith in God. It seemed to me that there were many paths to God, and that Christianity was only one of them.

I began to think that maybe God doesn't care so much about the things many Christians care so much about. I began to believe that God doesn't discriminate among his/her children – whether they be Christian, Jew, Buddhist, Hindu, Muslim, or even atheist. I became more and more convinced that the most important thing was to *live* compassionately. As Christians we had a pretty good guide: Jesus' life, teachings, and example – all of which might, at times, call us to go against the status quo.

From that time on, I felt that the purpose of faith was neither about getting a ticket to heaven nor about becoming Christian; it wasn't about being "saved" in order to be loved and accepted by God. It seemed to me that faith was a gift to the person who had it, not necessarily a gift to God. It was something that would hold you in good times and give you strength during bad times, something that called out the best in you, especially when times were hard and sacrifice became necessary. Jesus was certainly a model for us in defying authority and sacrificing himself. This was also what the Korean opposition leaders – a significant number of whom were Christians – were doing, and I came to see that this is what Christians are sometimes called to do.

I began to see faith as a personal experience, not something you push onto someone else. Who was I to insist that others believe as I do? Not that I was reluctant to share my faith with others, but I just didn't see the wisdom in trying to pressure or persuade others to believe what I believed. Faith is something that must come from their own hearts, belief from their own conviction, from their own experience of God's grace. Furthermore, if I *lived* according to my beliefs, hopefully that would be the strongest personal witness I could make to others. The Koreans were certainly such witnesses to me. In fact, I was seeing "God in action" on a daily basis, as I observed the way the Korean Christians were living their lives, anchored in their faith. Furthermore, I was also witnessing God in the actions of the *non*-believers as well. It was an awesome eye-opening.

How humbling and joyful to be accepted – even welcomed – as a part of the Galilee Church family, this brave community of faith. How wonderful to have our infant son baptized there by Rev. Stephen Moon, one of the founders of the church; to dance and sing as our friends passed him from person to person, rejoicing with us. Even today whenever I hear or have occasion to sing "Oh Freedom" or "We Shall Overcome," I am transported back to Galilee Church, where we were moved to tears as we held hands in a circle at the end of each weekly service, singing those "benedictions" and gathering the strength to go out and meet whatever faced us in the coming week.

～～～

For me today, true faith and authentic worship has to include the social justice gospel. It has to go further than a personal relationship with God; it has to speak to the principalities and powers, to acknowledge wrongs being perpetrated by civil authorities, to acknowledge our responsibility as Christians, not only to *support* others who are resisting evil, but to be willing to take those risks *ourselves* as well. I now feel compelled to speak up against injustice and oppression, against falsehoods and manipulation, against exploitation and violence, wherever it occurs. And it seems especially important for me, as a United States citizen, to do so when these things are being supported, and even perpetrated, by my own country. It is this conviction that followed me back to the U. S. and that motivates my actions to this day.

⁂ *Chapter 4*
⁂ ⁂

Heartaches No Longer…
and Some that Linger

Faye Moon

As a middle-class, white girl, growing up in Guilford, Connecticut in the 1940s and '50s, I didn't know how much I didn't know.

I didn't know about Koreans or Korea until I married one and went there. I didn't know about dictatorship or repression until my family and friends went to jail for fighting against them. I didn't know about U.S. foreign or military policies until I saw their impact abroad. I didn't know about poverty, drugs, or prostitution until I began helping vulnerable persons caught in those snares. I didn't know about culture gaps and identity crises, or loneliness and depression, until I experienced them. I didn't know how much I needed others' friendship and understanding, until I became a member of the Monday Night Group in Seoul. And I didn't really know about theology or democracy until I saw them both rise from the Korean grassroots – and saw my husband become not only a well-known theologian but also a member of south Korea's National Assembly.

⁂

I had two reasons for going to graduate school: one was to get a Masters in social work, the other was to meet a good, mature man. Both missions were accomplished at Hartford Seminary where I got my Masters and I met Stephen Moon who was from Korea. He was working on his doctoral thesis in Christian education. I found out much later that he was fifteen years older than me. He was definitely mature! When I learned his age, I thought, "Oh, my God! He's almost old enough to be my father!" When I was born in 1936, he was already in high school. I was stunned by the realization, but by that time it was too late – I was already in love.

The only thing I knew about Korea then was that it was somewhere in Asia and that there had been a war there. What I knew came from movie newsreels depicting bombed-out buildings and wandering orphans searching for food. Stephen had wooed me with stories of the refugee days and by singing Korean folk songs to me, but I knew nothing of the political and economic realities of Korea. He was born in Manchuria, bordering north Korea, during the Japanese occupation of Korea (1905-1945). He spent his childhood there until his family escaped to the south during the Korean War. Compared to his life, mine – growing up comfortably in Guilford – seemed more like the life of a greenhouse flower. I was impressed by his depth; I admired his tenacity to overcome adversity; and I could sense his love for his country.

After finishing his thesis, Stephen returned to Korea, but it was two more years before I finally made the decision to marry him.

More than Witnesses

I arrived in Korea on December 10, 1961. Six days later we were married. None of my family was at the wedding, but I was so happy to be marrying the man I loved, I never gave that a second thought. My vows were all in Korean – and I didn't understand a word that was said. One might conclude that I was never really married, but whether I understood the words or not, my heart had definitely made that commitment. In fact, that was my one and only reason for going to Korea – to become Stephen's wife and to have a family.

Three of our four children were born within the first five years. We were creating one child after another so that Steve, then in his mid-forties, would not be too old when we had grandchildren. In the meantime, I was busy trying to become Korean as fast as I could. I wore only the Korean-style dress, ate a totally Korean diet, breast-fed my babies in public like Korean women, and stayed away from Westerners. We lived on the campus of Hankuk Presbyterian Seminary in northern Seoul where Steve was a professor. We lived in a completely Korean environment. Our three-room house had no insulation, no central heating, no refrigerator, no modern stove, and no washing machine. It felt like being on an extended camping trip.

I spent most of my time at home with the children, and studying Korean. Learning new languages was not one of my strong suits, but being immersed in the Korean culture made a big difference. My mother-in-law, the only person in Stephen's family who didn't speak English, would come to our home and talk to me even though I couldn't understand what she was saying. She, more than anyone else, helped me learn Korean. At times, when I went to the market, people would stop me and say, "Hey lady, how is that you speak with a Hamkyung (Hamgyŏng) Province (north Korean) accent?" "I learned it from my mother-in-law," I would answer.

By the second year, I was beginning to feel very lonely. Aside from Stephen I didn't have any friends. I wanted to have a relationship with people in the neighborhood, but that was limited because my Korean still wasn't very good. I began to feel very isolated, so we agreed that maybe I should try to meet some westerners. I decided to visit a missionary prayer group that had been recommended, but these missionaries seemed to have just picked up U.S. culture, brought it to Korea, and planted it there. Their houses, furniture, and food were no different from what they had in the U.S., and I felt very strange being with them. My life and theirs seemed as different as heaven and earth. I later learned that not all missionaries lived that way, but at that time I had the impression that they all did. I even felt some anger toward them, because my life was much harder than theirs. But I have to admit, I also felt a bit of envy. I too wanted the things they got at the U.S. Army PX – butter, cheese, orange juice, ham. It was hard to become friends with people whose lives were so different from mine. I was struggling with questions they couldn't understand – where do I belong? Am I Korean or am I American?

When Stephen became pastor of a church in downtown Seoul, I took on a new role as the "pastor's wife." Surprisingly, this role seemed to suit my character very well. I enjoyed interacting with other people and creating an atmosphere for lively conversation. When Stephen made his pastoral visits, I would go with him. While he was more serious, I tended to joke around in a friendly way. We made a good team.

One day, riding the bus downtown, we passed in front of Korea University, and I noticed a commotion going on. The students were demonstrating. It turned out that they were protesting against the normalization of relations with Japan (1965). Japan's occupation of Korea had ended with World War II, but the Japanese had never apologized for their brutal treatment of the Korean people. The students refused to accept normalization of relations with Japan without an official apology. Soon demonstrations were being held on all campuses, and the Park Chung Hee government quickly dispatched soldiers to break them up. The trucks used by the Korean troops displayed a picture of an American and a Korean shaking hands. It was a symbol of the relationship between the U.S. and Korea, but in this case it seemed to show U.S. support of the repressive Park regime. It was hard for me to believe that the U.S. would support someone like Park who, as a soldier, had seized power in a coup d'état and was very oppressive. It showed how completely naïve I was about politics at that time.

In response to this, Herb White, a Presbyterian missionary working in the area of urban development, discussed the situation with some other Americans who were also concerned about U.S.–Korea relations. They decided to organize themselves and thought they could recruit at least fifty people, so they called themselves the "Committee of 50." This group met regularly to share what was happening across Korea's changing political landscape. I found these missionaries to be very different from the ones I had met in the prayer group. They didn't limit their concerns to service; they wanted to support Korean efforts toward democracy. I fit into this group of progressive missionaries much more naturally, and for the first time since coming to Korea, I felt I could open up and express myself with other Americans living in Korea. It was still a struggle for me to talk to anyone other than Stephen about deep or intimate matters, but at these meetings my heart felt refreshed; I could talk to these new friends about common concerns and even personal feelings. It was then that I began to think again about who I really was. I had come to realize that, no matter how hard I tried, I could not become Korean. Finally I gave up that idealistic idea, and began seeing myself as American again.

One thing the "Committee of 50" did was to meet with the U.S. ambassador to Korea to discuss our concern that the U.S. was increasingly supporting the oppressive Park regime. The ambassador tried to skirt the issue by bringing our attention to Korea's rapid economic development and telling us what a fine job the Korean government was doing creating many new jobs, even for women. Yes, it was true that economic development was taking place, but the working conditions that accompanied those new jobs – especially for the women workers – were extremely harsh. It seemed to us that the ambassador wanted to look only at the surface of things, not the underbelly of the politics being used to create the look of success. After that unsuccessful meeting, whenever anyone from the U.S. government came to Korea, we would try to meet with them, to give them a fuller picture of what was going on in the country.

When we heard that Vice President Hubert Humphrey was coming in February, 1968 to attend the inauguration of Park Chung Hee, we made plans to meet with him. We were so eager that we had to draw straws to see who would get to go. I drew one of the straws, along with Barbara Ross, a conservative southern Presbyterian with a heavy southern accent. We hoped her presence would keep us from appearing to be a bunch of radicals. We felt nervous to be meeting with the vice president of the United States, but Herb White coached us, saying, "Remember, Vice President Humphrey puts his pants on in the morning just like every other man." The meeting went well; we were impressed with Humphrey's willingness to hear our concerns. It may not have had much effect on U.S. policy, but at least he didn't treat us like the ambassador had.

As opportunities came up, the group met with other U.S. officials, church leaders from around the world, and representatives from international human rights organizations. We would always describe to them what was happening in Korea and ask them to support Korea's movement for democracy and human rights.

When Herb White left Korea in the late 1960's, meetings of the

"Committee of 50" became more sporadic. Then in the early 1970's, when newly arrived missionaries expressed interest, the meetings were revived and the new group became known as the "Monday Night Group." It met in a different home each week, moving from house to house. I felt completely at home in this group and made close friends with many of its members.

Back on the home front, Steve and I started an experiment of living in "Christian community." It grew out of discussions at Steve's church about the early Christian practice of sharing all things in common. Several young people from the church were very interested in this concept. After a year of study and discussion, 13 of us made a commitment to live together communally, sharing what we had in common with each other. We called the community the "House of Daybreak."

About that same time, Steve and I became aware of the large number of orphans, resulting from the rapid industrialization of Korea. Young women from the rural areas would come to Seoul to work in the factories. They were poor, uneducated, and very naïve. It wasn't unusual for a girl to get pregnant, but there was no way to raise a baby while living in those squalid conditions and working such long hours. The Bible instructed Christians to care for widows and orphans, and Steve and I felt that if every family would adopt one child, the orphan problem could be alleviated. We decided we should start with ourselves, so we adopted Younghae, a little girl who had been abandoned at a police station. She became our fourth child.

Living in the House of Daybreak community was like heaven to the children. They thrived in that setting, living in a household with others who filled the roles of sister, brother, grandmother, grandfather, aunt, uncle. It was a bold experiment which inevitably had its ups and downs, but it lasted for almost a decade. It probably would have lasted longer were it not for the political situation, which affected us very personally, coupled with the unexpected early death of one of our key members.

Having spent most of the first decade of our marriage raising the children, I began to feel frustrated with the role of stay-at-home mom and wanted to put my degree in social work to good use. Unfortunately, it was not easy for an American woman to find a social work job in Korea. One of my new Monday Night Group friends, Linda Jones, told me about a social worker position available at a U.S. Army base. My reaction was immediate: "Are you crazy? Me work at a U.S. Army base?!" Although I understood why the U.S. had entered the Korean War and continued to remain in Korea, I had strong feelings of repugnance when I heard the words "army base." I was aware that the U.S. was supporting Korea's military dictatorship, and I viewed the U.S. Army as a big part of that support. There were 40,000 U.S. troops in Korea then (nearly that many even today), stationed all the way from the demilitarized zone (DMZ) to the southern tip of Korea.

I wasn't having any luck finding a job otherwise, so I decided to at least check out the position, which was at Camp Casey, north of Seoul near the "front line." When I first stepped on to the base, I was overcome with anxiety, seeing hundreds of Americans living on a compound which looked just like a typical American town. The men were tall and wore flashy clothes, but many also were minorities or poor white farm boys, and this was their first time abroad. I wondered, "How can I relate to these men?" I had been living in a Korean environment for twelve years; this was definitely culture shock for me.

More than Witnesses

At the office, they told me they were looking for someone to work at one of their drug and alcohol rehabilitation centers. If I took the job I would be paid in U.S. dollars at an American standard of living. I realized the salary would be quite good, and there would be many other benefits such as health insurance. However, I knew nothing about drugs or drug rehab. I couldn't tell the difference between marijuana and hashish. But I was so anxious to finally work in my field of study, I decided to take the job. I was the only professional social worker at the center, but I was as green as grass. Knowing nothing about how to relate to these young addicted men, I had to rely on the younger staff who knew a lot about the drug culture even though they did not have much formal education. It was definitely on-the-job-training for me, and it took a while to learn enough to be of any help to the soldiers. My learning gradually increased and, for the next eight years, I was supervisor of social work and clinical director at the Yongsan U.S. Army Headquarters.

❧ ❧❧ ❧

Other problems came to my attention on the base. I became appalled at the treatment of the Korean men who worked there, cleaning and doing laundry for the U.S. military personnel. They were called "house boys" and they acted as meek as mice. I had never come across meek Koreans before, but these men had worked on the base since the beginning of the Korean War in the early 1950s and seemed to have learned their "proper role." It was very much like the way Blacks were treated in the U.S. before desegregation and the civil rights movement.

One thing I did was establish an "Alternative Day," to try to introduce the U.S. soldiers to Korean culture. I would take them to see downtown Seoul, visit a Buddhist temple, taste good Korean food, and generally experience "real" Korean life. Even just walking down the street without pimps directing them to brothels (a common occurrence in the town next to the base) was a new experience for the soldiers.

The base towns were full of Korean women who became prostitutes in order to survive financially. They suffered much psychological abuse from the soldiers. One of the highest-ranking chaplains once told me, "The soldiers receive rigorous training in killing people week after week. On the weekends they must get off the base and relieve their stress." I soon discovered that prostitution was being promoted behind the scenes for the effective operation of U.S. military life. This was a huge problem in my eyes.

~ ≈≈ ~

While I was working diligently for the United States military and enjoying my job as a social worker, the political situation in Korea was heating up even more. The Yushin Constitution, issued in 1972, gave Park Chung Hee unlimited powers; and a series of "Emergency Decrees" began to be declared in 1974, to control any criticism of the government. Stephen and his colleagues began participating in anti-government activities and making speeches calling for the restoration of democracy. The government threatened to close down the seminary if the professors weren't fired. The seminary acquiesced, and Stephen was one of those fired.

Of course, without jobs, the professors now had even more time and energy to give to the pro-democracy movement. Steve and some of the other professors, as well as his older brother Timothy, decided to start a church where they could openly speak their minds. They called it Galilee Church. They also developed a new liberation theology that was unique to Korea. It was called "Minjung Theology," meaning theology of the common people. It focuses on the struggle for survival of the ordinary people and says that God is to be found primarily through them, rather than in schools of theology.

More than Witnesses

One of the things that Stephen, Timothy, and several other well-known Koreans did in 1976 was draft a statement titled, "The March First Statement for Democracy to Save the Nation." March 1st is a very important date to Koreans. On March 1, 1919, Koreans rose up in a nonviolent demonstration against the occupying Japanese and declared Korean independence. Even though they were unable to accomplish independence at that time, March 1st has ever since been recognized as Korea's Independence Day. The "March First" statement of 1976 was an attempt to declare independence from dictatorial rule and to establish a true democracy for the people of the nation. The signers fervently believed that if democracy could not be achieved, the nation was doomed. The statement was made public at a worship service in the Catholic Cathedral in Seoul, where it was boldly read by Ms. Lee Oo Jung, president of Church Women United. Not surprisingly, all the signers were arrested and some, including Stephen, were put in solitary confinement while they awaited trial. The Park regime considered this March First statement an attempt to overthrow the government. In reality it was a declaration of conscience and a statement of faith.

Our House of Daybreak community fully supported Stephen's participation in the movement for democracy. Our house became a meeting place for planning and carrying out actions. Just before Stephen's arrest, however, our community had moved to a rural area three hours north of Seoul where we farmed and tried to become even more self-sufficient. Of course, the community continued to support Steve, and I certainly was not opposed to his participation, but I never dreamed that he would go to prison for his actions, and that I would become a prisoner's wife. He was in solitary confinement, so I now had the sole responsibility for our family; furthermore, I was the only member of the Daybreak community earning a salary. All working members contributed to the community pot, but when we moved to the country they had to leave paying jobs in Seoul to concentrate on raising crops and growing our food. In our new rural setting, I was actually closer to my job at Camp Casey, near the town of Uijongbu (Uijŏngbu). Luckily, my income was enough to support all of us. The rest of the members were, in turn, supporting me psychologically as well as taking care of my children, even filling the substitute father role for them. Our diet was very simple, the cost of living was much lower, and I was happy to be able to provide the funds needed. I even had money left for savings.

Even though I wanted to visit Stephen in prison, it was a three-hour trip to the prison, and I could only go on the weekends because of my work schedule. I could not take off during the week and even had to miss the first visitation, which was on a weekday. For that visitation, I decided to send our oldest son, Changkun. The other prisoners' wives wouldn't let their children miss school to go visit, because they thought it would be too much of a shock to see their fathers in prison. On the contrary, I thought it would be good for the children to see Stephen as often as possible. I also wanted to teach them to be proud of their father for taking such a risk for their country.

Changkun was a young junior high school student at the time, and one of the House of Daybreak members took him to the prison to see Steve. At first, he was overwhelmed by the prison environment – how stark and cruel it was – but he also felt really proud of his father. He took some thick socks and clothing to give his father and hoped it would keep him warm in the unheated prison cell. When Changkun left the prison, he did not have any of the usual feelings of shame a person would have if a family member were in prison. He believed that what his father was doing was the right thing and it felt good to be his son.

More than Witnesses

At this point, the Monday Night Group became even more important to me. Although I often arrived late after work, I did not want to miss one of those meetings. They warmly accepted and cared for me, giving me positive support. After talking with them and telling them how things were affecting me, I would feel completely unburdened. My kids would often complain, though. "Mom, are you going to that Monday Night meeting again?!" It meant I would be coming home very late, which was already frequently the case when I had to work late. They missed having their father around, so they wanted me there are much as possible. Fortunately, because we lived in community, there were other people who could be with them. One of the community members, Mr. Choi, was a wonderful father substitute for the children in Stephen's absence. They loved being with him and followed him around everywhere.

When the "March First" group's trial began, fortunately the sessions were held on Saturday, which meant I could attend. However, when we wives arrived at the courthouse, we learned that the trial was not to be open to the public, a "first" in Korea. Passes were issued only to family members to attend the trial sessions. As a group, we decided to refuse the passes and instead chose to demonstrate in the streets where the press and other citizens would learn what was going on. As we carried out our silent demonstrations, we drew a crowd of onlookers and became a hot news item for the foreign press. During the next few weeks of the trial, we continued to protest in the streets. We refused to enter the courtroom and boycotted all 14 of the trial sessions.

We were very creative about the visual effect of our demonstrations, so every week we would come up with new ideas. First we put black tape across our mouths to show that the trials were being held in secret and that there was no freedom of speech.

Heartaches No Longer … and Some that Linger

One week we took folding fans on which we had written "Free the prisoners for democracy." We took to the streets and at the appointed time we unfolded the fans for everyone to see. At first the police were hesitant to break up our demonstrations. It was not proper to physically touch a woman, so they couldn't easily rough us up as they were used to doing to break up such actions by men. But they had to do something to get us under control, so they took away our fans. The next week we would do something different to keep the police off guard. One week we held purple umbrellas with our message about restoring democracy written on them. Again, as soon as the police saw what was written on the umbrellas, they snatched our props away, but not before we had walked down the busy street near City Hall to let people see our demands.

Next, we made purple dresses to wear, purple being the color of suffering and victory in Korea. We embroidered our husband's prison numbers on the upper pockets of the dresses. I put Stephen's number "6907" on mine – a number I will never forget. Since the police kept taking away our props, we decided to sew big crosses on the front of our dresses. We put on light trench coats and began our demonstration with our trench coats on. At first the police didn't notice anything, but their mouths fell open when we took off the coats and they saw the crosses tightly sewn on our dresses. For once they were stymied! What could they do? Tear them off with their bare hands?! All that summer on the streets near City Hall, we fearlessly demonstrated and protested the trials. The authorities must have known that if they had arrested us, we would have created even more sensational news.

Then the group had another idea: they began crocheting shawls. Though crocheting is not one of my skills, of course I supported the project. Again we used the color purple, because of its Korean meaning, but also because it is the color of the Christian season of passion. Coincidentally, it is also the color of Korea's national flower, the Rose of Sharon. The shawls were made in three shades: purple, lilac, and indigo. Because they were V-shaped, we called them Victory Shawls. Each small unit of the shawl was made of four stitches, and as the wives stitched each unit, they would say the four syllables, "*min-ju hoe-bok*," meaning "restore democracy." This phrase became their chant and their prayer. It takes exactly 10,000 stitches to complete one shawl. Rather than crying as they thought of their husbands' plights, they became determined in their desire for democracy as they chanted and stitched.

At first we gave the shawls to friends and asked for their prayers and help. Later some missionary friends suggested that we sell the shawls both in Korea and outside the country, to raise funds to support the movement.

The project grew and the wives made more and more shawls. They would carry yarn and needles in their handbags wherever they went, and whenever they had a spare moment, they would pull out their needles and crochet. Of course they needed lots of yarn, so they made frequent trips to the big market near East Gate, getting enough yarn for several shawls and making sure it was the same dye lot. They made so many shawls that it finally came to the attention of the authorities; they were not at all happy about it, especially since these shawls (and the stories of their husbands) were also making their way overseas. Government "inspectors" were sent to the market to stop the shopkeepers from selling us any more purple yarn, but the saleswomen just hid the yarn when the inspectors came by. Then, when the wives came to stock up on more, the saleswomen would pull the yarn out from the hiding places and gladly sell it to them. Even friends from overseas began to send us purple yarn.

The money raised from the sale of the shawls was used to support the movement and sometimes to buy long underwear for prisoners who didn't have anyone to visit them or help take care of them.

I may not know how to crochet, but I do know how to pack boxes. I packed box after box of shawls and, using my access to the U.S. APO mail, was able to send them overseas. I also wrote the story of the Victory Shawl to accompany each shawl, so that it could be shared far and wide. We wives of the "March First" prisoners were definitely a thorn in the government's side.

I was invited to the U.S. to speak at the July 1976 gathering of the Women's National Assembly of the Presbyterian Church USA at Purdue University in Indiana. I stood nervously in front of thousands of women and told them about the Korean struggle for democracy. I wore my purple dress and the Victory Shawl and told them the story of the shawl. When I finished, the auditorium became silent. I thought, "Maybe to these women, Korea is just a faraway country, and perhaps the subject of human rights and fighting for democracy is too abstract for them." But I was mistaken. They were silent because they were so emotionally moved. They were able to identify with me, an ordinary American woman telling her story. They were shocked to hear that the United States government was supporting a dictatorship in Korea, so they bought Victory Shawls and started a letter-writing campaign to their members of Congress and to the presidents of both the U.S. and Korea. They also wrote to me, and we were so encouraged as their letters began piling up. Their prayers and letters were a huge comfort to me and to others in the movement.

Life was hard for me when Stephen was in prison. Of course this was a noble cause, and I was proud of his courageous action, but in a corner of my heart I also felt a sense of betrayal. I spent many sleepless, lonely nights, angry that he had abandoned me, our four children, and our House of Daybreak community. However, being with the other prisoners' wives was a big comfort, and taking part in actions with them was a constructive way to defuse my anger and sadness.

Even though I was an American, I did not feel any different from the other wives; we were all facing the same difficult situation. Not knowing when our husbands would be returning home was depressing. Our homes were scattered throughout the Seoul area, so we would often go to the Christian Building in downtown Seoul, to the National Council of Churches of Korea's Human Rights Office, just to be together. I would go after work and meet them there. We prayed together, supported each other, and came up with ideas for our peaceful protests. Even though our husbands were in jail, the atmosphere was full of joking and laughter. Just like the saying "only a widow can understand the feelings of a widow," we understood each other and gathered strength and encouragement from being together.

Sometimes we would be laughing loudly about something when we would learn that a foreign reporter was outside the door waiting to interview us. Immediately, we would change our expressions and try to look more serious. Through these women and the situation we shared, I came to appreciate the value of humor and learned how it can make one's difficulties more bearable.

Needless to say, the international press was amazed by our demonstrations, which provided them with wonderful photographs. Reporters came from all over the world to cover the trials. On one occasion – Easter morning at sunrise – we gathered outside the prison to sing hymns to our husbands. The men could hear the singing, but at first they didn't know who it was. Then they recognized the hymns as ones we often sang at Galilee Church, and finally they realized who was singing to them.

Heartaches No Longer ... and Some that Linger

The next day when I arrived for work at the Army post, the staff showed me that day's edition of the Army newspaper, *Stars and Stripes*. There on the front page was a big photo of us singing in front of the prison with the headline, "Enemies of Chunghee Park." My face could clearly be seen in the picture, and my name was printed just below it. Soon I received a telephone call from Colonel Zane Finklestein, a judge advocate at Yongsan Base, the main army headquarters in Seoul. He said very gruffly, "I'm flying up to your base in a helicopter. Do not leave the area!" That was all he said.

I had never been in any kind of trouble, and I was filled with fear. Instead of a helicopter, the colonel pulled up in a jeep, jumped out, and confronted me. "It is illegal for a citizen of the United States who works on a U.S. Army base to blaspheme as "enemy" the country where he or she resides. You have three options: (1) leave the Republic of Korea, (2) quit your job on the base, or (3) be quiet," he said coldly. Then he walked through the mud back to his jeep and left.

What a dilemma. Thoughts whirled through my head: I may get deported if I keep demonstrating. On the other hand, then I could tell the rest of the world about the stand my husband has taken. I could raise the human rights issue with churches abroad. It might be hard on my family, but the "March First" incident could become more well-known outside Korea.

Then I would think of the other consequences: what would happen to my family? I need to think of the children. The House of Daybreak community is depending on my salary. What would they do if I lost my job?

Then my thoughts raced off in another direction: if I stay and stop demonstrating with the other wives, I will have to apologize to them. They may think I'm a coward or that I'm selling out. What should I do? I felt that if I didn't demonstrate with the Korean women, I could no longer identify with them and, I reminded myself, I'm not really a part of their Korean history. At the same time, I didn't feel that I could identify with Americans either, because they were not going through the same intense struggle that I was. I was reminded of the feelings I'd had in my early years living in Korea: feelings of frustration and the loneliness of living between two cultures. One part of me identified with the American expatriate culture made up of human rights activists; another part of me identified with Korean human rights activists like my husband and his brother. It was impossible for me to totally identify with either.

I vented my anger at the Monday Night Group. When they would sometimes ask me what the Korean human rights activists thought or felt, I would be angry. This was not a fair question – how could I speak for the Koreans? Once though, I did not hesitate to speak out, loud and clear. It was just after the group had sent a letter to President Carter, asking him not to come to Korea because of the human rights abuses. The letter had been discovered at the airport as Pat Patterson, from the United Methodist Mission Board, was trying to smuggle it out of the country on her way back to the U.S.

At this particular Monday meeting, the night seemed to be especially dark and stormy, but perhaps it was only because of the stormy feelings being expressed by the group. The group members had not anticipated that the letter would be intercepted, and they were visibly upset. They talked about the possibility that their Korean visas would be cancelled, or they might be deported – and what would that mean for their individual lives, their work, their families? The discussion seemed to go on and on and the tone grew angrier and angrier. Suddenly, I couldn't contain myself any longer. "You people and your GOD-DAMN VISAS!" I shouted at them. "People like my husband are in prison, people are being tortured and are dying, and all you can think about is your god-damn visas!" You could have heard a pin drop. No one said a word. Then, gradually, the ice began to thaw and the group thanked me for bringing them back to reality.

～ ☙☙ ～

As I agonized over Colonel Finklestein's warning, John Saar from the *Washington Post* contacted me for an interview. His article (*Washington Post*, August 6, 1976) was titled, "The Unequal Battle of Faye Moon; U.S. Army Curbs American Wife of Jailed South Korean Christian." Saar wrote, "Did the crisis of Connecticut-born Faye Moon's life begin fifteen years ago with her marriage to a brilliant South Korean theologian? Or just a few months back when he told her, 'I think it is my turn to go to prison'? Mrs. Moon ... recently has dropped out of the spirited demonstrations that the wives of the other prisoners stage outside the Saturday courtroom sessions. . . . She stopped because of pressure from her employer, the U.S. Army in Korea. . . . Mrs. Moon lost sleep and weight and worried herself to exhaustion before concluding she had no choice but to comply. . . . 'I decided being in Korea was the most important thing for me. I wondered what would happen to my husband in prison if I was forced to leave. . . . We agreed I should cool it.' She is still torn by the identity crisis it brought on – bewilderingly somewhere between being Korean and American. As she explained, 'Americans here are outsiders. Yet I'm involved. I can't leave here with my husband in prison, so my situation is not like other Americans,' she said."

The other wives understood my predicament and comforted me by telling me how sorry they felt. When I was with them, when we cried and struggled together, I gained new strength. But when the trials ended, the men were sent to different prisons all over the country, and opportunities to meet the other wives began to diminish. Stephen was sent to a prison in Mokpo, a port city on the southernmost tip of the Korean peninsula. We were allowed only one visit a month, and it was a seven-hour trip to Mokpo. I was like a widow who felt empty inside after the bustling funeral has ended. I couldn't go home to my parents for comfort; and when I went home to my children, they were waiting for my love like hungry baby swallows.

I think Stephen and I were an unusually close couple, and it is quite possible that I relied on him excessively. Now I had to handle all the responsibilities alone. I wanted to escape, but there was no place to go. I had to miss many of the Monday Night Group meetings because of the distance, but the group remained a vital support group for me and I met often with individual members. Louise Morris and Butch Durst would come up from Seoul to visit; I would sit for hours talking to them, airing my frustrations and trying to make decisions about major issues in my life. Linda Jones became another top advisor, and Sue Rice was a dear friend I could always count on. She went with me the first time to see Steve at the Mokpo prison after the trial was over. I was nervous about taking the long train ride alone, then trying to find my way to the prison, so I will never forget Sue's kindness and support.

I hated the Park regime that had put my husband in prison, and the plainclothes policemen who tenaciously followed me everywhere I went. When I went to work in the mornings, there was a checkpoint on the bus route. A Korean military policeman would board the bus and yell in a loud voice, "Is there an American woman riding this bus?" The eyes of the other passengers would turn to me. As soon as it was confirmed that I was on the bus, the policeman would get off, having fulfilled his duty. When I took a taxi from the bus stop home at night, the taxi would be stopped so the military police could shine his light in my face to confirm that it was me. Inside the dark taxi my frowning white face would appear in the light. To this day I cannot forget the contempt I felt. Although it occurred every day, I never got used to it, and would often feel afraid when I went home at night. I wanted to escape from all this surveillance and tailing that never seemed to let up. There seemed nothing left in life to enjoy; all I could do was endure the situation.

Then I discovered another big benefit to my job. I could no longer demonstrate with the other wives, but there was another role I could play. Articles from the foreign media were not allowed into Korea if they were critical of the Park regime. However, I could easily and safely send and receive mail through the army APO mail system. I was able to use this communications channel to send information to the outside world about what was happening in Korea. Equally important, I could get articles from foreign news sources that could be shared with Koreans in the human rights movement. Some of the information I received were newspaper articles that criticized U.S. support for the Korean dictator, criticized President Park for putting religious leaders in prison, or revealed other oppressive measures of the Korean government. Sometimes I received transcripts from congressional hearings, such as the hearings led by Rep. Donald Fraser (D-Minnesota.) on human rights abuses in Korea. It was also a way to find out what the U.S. government's stance was toward Korea, especially how it was propping up the Park Chung-Hee regime. This kind of information was vital to the movement leaders in Korea and to the student leaders. They could learn the direction the U.S. government was taking in relation to Korea.

I would also send information about the movement to friends, churches, and human rights organizations in the U.S. and other countries. For example, I often sent Fact Sheets written by Monday Night Group members (see Appendix), or reports of harassment of the Urban Industrial Mission leaders' because of their work with laborers, or lists of political prisoners that included why they were arrested, the length of their sentences, etc. Of course, I also sent box after box of Victory Shawls to the U.S. through this channel as well. This means of communication turned out to be very useful for the movement inside and outside Korea, and I was happy to do it.

One day, however, the Army base postal inspector came to see me. Some mail that had come in had gotten rained on and had come unsealed. He took me to the post office and there my mail was, spread out all over the floor like laundry. It contained material critical of the Korean government. He asked me, "Are you aware that sending and receiving this kind of material is illegal?" I stood there nervously, not knowing what to say. Then the inspector, who had no idea what I had been doing, asked me, "Are you a teacher?" Without blinking an eye, I lied, "Yes, I am." "Well, since you're a teacher I can understand why you are getting these news articles, but in the future please be careful."

After this incident, I thought to myself, "So, you will lie when it's convenient, eh?" I was now doing things that were secretive and illegal – but for a good cause. From that time I tried to be careful and not be misleading any more than was absolutely necessary.

❧ ❧❧ ❧

In December 1977, after the first snow fell, the children were, as usual, clamoring to celebrate Christmas and to get ready for the gift exchange. I wondered inwardly, "Could I possibly have the gift of my husband this Christmas?" But it was a guarded hope. I had hoped before only to be met with disappointment. Yet as long as it arose again, I hung on to that glimmer of hope. Christmas came and went without a sign of Steve. Then, after twenty-two months in prison, eighteen of those months in solitary confinement, he was released on December 31, 1977. He arrived by taxi with his bundle of belongings and his hair cropped short. He was very thin and his face was cracked and dry. He looked very old. But we were ecstatic. We embraced tightly, then the children came running, along with the other community members, all laughing and hugging him.

Finally, the person I loved, whose life had been suspended, had returned to my side. I was overjoyed and filled with gratitude. Even though it would take a while to adjust to each other and to living together again, I felt that life could now return to normal. I don't know exactly what "normal" would have been in the midst of such a political situation, but suddenly and unexpectedly a certain tension began to surface between us. I guess the anger I felt during Steve's imprisonment did not easily subside. I was still upset at having been left alone and at having to be responsible for everything at home.

In prison Steve had been formulating a new kind of theology that he called "Joy on the Way" (published in the *Christian Century*, 1978). The more he talked about this "joy" the angrier I felt. I certainly had not experienced any joy while he was gone! The experiences he had had in prison were completely unfamiliar to me. Likewise, he did not understand what I had been through, and we fought often.

As we lay in bed at night talking, inevitably our voices would rise. Then the children would shout in annoyance, "Mom! Dad! Are you fighting again? It's noisy, we can't sleep!" We continued over a period of time arguing and talking and trying to work out our feelings and differences. As time went by, with constant dialogue and a commitment to work things through, even going to counseling for a while, we were able to gain more understanding of each other's experiences and to appreciate what each had been through.

⁂

"Oh, my gosh, we're under house arrest again today," I said, noticing several plainclothes policemen stationed in front of our house. Invariably we found ourselves under house arrest when some important event or demonstration was imminent, or even when a rumor of such circulated. It was like being in a prison without bars. One Saturday, just a few days after Steve's release, we had planned to go to the hospital to see the doctor and to get Steve's blood pressure medicine. We asked the policemen for permission to go, promising to come straight back. It was no use, they would not hear of it. Steve had already spent three days confined to the house.

Just then a rascally little scheme began to form in my mind. "Honey," I said to Steve, "since they're watching just the front of the house, let's slip out the back." There was a barbed-wire fence around our backyard, instead of a stone wall like most Korean homes had. There was one spot in the fence where the children had made a hole, so they could go in and out. Stealthily, Stephen and I slipped out through this hole and sprinted for the woods. Our hearts were pounding. We huffed and puffed to get over the big hill behind our house, but finally got to the other side and hailed a taxi.

We made it to the hospital without incident, and after getting the medicine, Stephen began to worry about whether the policemen would get in trouble with their superiors, if they discovered that we had gotten away. He wanted us to hurry back home. But I was not ready to go back; I wanted to thoroughly enjoy this new-found freedom. I was not as sympathetic with the police as he was, and to be honest, I really wanted to give them some trouble. I suggested that we go to his brother Timothy's house; he was also under house arrest. "We could see your mother there, too," I said, persuasively. Off we went again. In order to evade the police who were also guarding the front of Timothy's house, we again had to climb a hill and try to enter the house from the back. Unfortunately, there was a stone wall around the back of Timothy's house, but we finally managed to scale it and eventually made our way up to the house. When Timothy, his wife Young-gil, and his mother saw us, their eyes got as round as saucers. They hurried us inside, and we all hugged each other, laughing and talking.

We shared some food together, and when we had stayed and talked as long as we wanted, Stephen and I leisurely walked out the front door. The ten or so tough-looking, plainclothesmen immediately grabbed us and stuck us in a car to take us home.

The next morning when we looked out our back window, we noticed that a sturdy fence had been erected around our backyard, like an iron curtain. And as one might guess, there were now five more plainclothesmen guarding the back of our house as well as the front. We chuckled, thinking of the saying about "fixing the gate after the cow got out." Later, whenever things got difficult, we would laughingly recall our day of adventure and how we had escaped by wiggling through the hole in the fence. We still enjoy talking about that.

It was 1979. Two years had passed since Stephen had gone to prison. He had more enthusiasm than ever about the human rights movement and he became even more involved. That summer, he tried to help the women workers at the YH factory who were protesting their working conditions and low pay (see Sue Rice chapter). The incident snowballed and in the midst of the chaos, Stephen was again arrested. Unlike the March First event, this time the arrest was totally unexpected. No one had suspected that people would be arrested for helping workers with a sit-in demonstration. I was worried about Steve's high blood pressure because the prison authorities would not give him the medicine I brought for him. Finally, I had to protest to the U. S. ambassador before the prison guards would give Stephen his medicine.

More than Witnesses

Unlike Steve's earlier imprisonment, this time there seemed to be no one I could reach out to. There were no other wives or family members to meet with and consult with, as there had been with the March First incident. This time I was even more depressed. Again, the feeling of being unable to endure returned. Having gone through the tunnel of depression once, this time it was even more frightening. Each day it felt like I was walking on thin ice.

Then, on October 26, 1979, President Park Chung-Hee was assassinated. Somehow I had to let Stephen know. Our visits at prison were closely monitored and we were absolutely forbidden to talk about politics. We were also not allowed to use English because the guards couldn't understand it well enough to take good notes of our conversation. The children and I came up with the idea of taking a copy of the newspaper article and somehow showing it to him. When I was in the visitation area, I reached into my handbag and flashed the article headlines, "President Chunghee Park Assassinated," and put a finger to my head like a gun. Stephen quickly got the message. Secretly, we hoped that after the assassination, there might be an amnesty and Steve might be released, but it would be almost two more months before that happened.

In the spring of 1980 Stephen went to Europe to attend the World Council of Churches board meeting for education and church renewal. By then, with Park Chung Hee gone and a new moderate interim president in place, many Koreans had a swelling expectation that democracy would soon return. Little did we know what was soon to occur in the southern city of Kwangju.

In Seoul, Stephen's brother Timothy and many other pro-democracy professors and students were arrested, but none of them had any idea what was really going on during those dazzling green days of May. Then one day, Stephen's mother called and told me to contact him quickly and tell him not to return to Korea. If he did he would surely be arrested again. We began to hear rumors of something happening in Kwangju. I knew that if Korean troops were involved in putting down any unrest among the people, they would have to be given permission by the U.S. Army Command. That was the only way Korean troops could be pulled off the front lines. I asked some friends at the Yongsan U. S. Army Base, thinking they might know what was going on in Kwangju. Their only response was, "It would be better if you left Korea right now and don't plan to come back any time soon. It'll be fifty years before there's any return to democracy here!" From that I guessed that they did know what was going on and that things were really bad in Kwangju (we found out later that the Korean military had massacred hundreds of anti-government protesters; see Chapter 15). I had the ominous feeling that something worse than the Park regime might be coming.

I got plane tickets as quickly as possible and arrived at the airport with my four children, full of anxiety but struggling not to show it. We made it safely through customs and got on the plane. I sank down in my seat sighing with relief, thinking, "We are safe now." Just then, an announcement came over the intercom system, "Please do not leave your seats. Remain where you are. Our departure has been delayed. We ask for your understanding." Our plane sat there for a seemingly interminable period, while my heart pounded heavily. I suspected that the authorities were holding up the flight and going through my checked baggage, or contacting their superiors to see whether they should let me leave the country. It seemed clear to me that I was the cause for the delay. My children were squirming in their seats and fussing, "Why aren't we taking off?" Finally, after about an hour, the plane slowly started to roll down the runway. It must have only been a mechanical problem. Gradually my fears subsided and I gave another deep sigh of relief.

I never imagined that I would leave Korea that way – like

a fugitive escaping. As I looked out the window, I saw the neatly arranged rice paddies. Images from when I first arrived in Korea some twenty years earlier came flooding over me, one after another. The rounded thatched roofs were now covered with colorful slabs of tile, and the meandering rice fields now were so straight they appeared to have been marked off with a ruler. Cars were speeding up and down the highways. Just as the scene outside had changed over two decades, I too had changed a great deal from when I first flew into this country. Many tangled emotions were tumbling over me as I looked out the plane window – emotions about leaving my "second hometown," words my Korean friends used to acknowledge my love for their country.

Finally, after many hours on the plane, we arrived at my mother's house in Guilford, Connecticut. That's when we heard news reports about the massacre that had taken place in Kwangju. The children and I cried when we heard what had happened. So many innocent people slaughtered by their own soldiers. So many brave people mowed down in the streets. And I knew that the U.S. military had looked the other way, if not given outright support. Our dreams for the restoration of democracy were dashed.

❧ ❦❧ ❧

About a month later I received a very strange letter from a Colonel James A. Mundt, a judge advocate with the U.S. Army. He said he was writing me at the suggestion of the U.S. Embassy. I was shocked when I read: "It appears that the ROK authorities believe you imported through the APO certain seditious material written by a prominent north Korean official and that you delivered it to a member of the Korean opposition. These same authorities have emphasized that the ROK Government reserves the right to prosecute you under appropriate Korean laws if and when you return to Korea."

Heartaches No Longer ... and Some that Linger

I had no idea where they had come up with this preposterous notion. I had certainly never, to my knowledge, received anything written by a north Korean, but I imagined that the authorities weren't necessarily interested in what I had to say about it. It was one more dark cloud hanging over my head.

~ ❧ ~

It would be five years before our family returned to Korea. A military coup took place shortly after the Kwangju massacre, followed by more years of dictatorship under military-general-turned-President Chun Doo Hwan, and more harsh oppression of the people. Finally, when things seemed to have calmed down somewhat politically, we began to think about returning. By now Chun Doo Hwan was no longer president, and things seemed to be loosening up a bit. Hankuk Seminary was open and the administration felt that, for now, its faculty wouldn't be under as much threat of losing their jobs or of being hassled by the authorities. They invited Steve to resume his professorship.

For me, however, there was still the problem of the threatening letter from Colonel Mundt. In addition to that, I had other concerns about going back. The children were older now, and most were out of school. What would my role in Korea be now? Would I just take a back seat? I certainly wouldn't be able to resume my old position at the Army base. Would there be something for me to do? I decided not to return unless I had some meaningful work to do. I applied to the Mission Board of the Presbyterian Church U.S.A. for support in fulfilling a long-time dream of mine: to open a counseling and education center for Korean prostitutes living around the U.S. army bases. The U.S. soldiers had all the resources – recreation centers, medical clinics, chaplains, snack bars, movies, whatever they needed. Korean women were also readily available to them. But the women had nothing – in fact, the only thing provided for them was a clinic to periodically test them for venereal disease.

This dream felt like a calling from God. I knew I was the perfect person for this work. The Presbyterian Mission Board accepted my proposal and I became a missionary to the women in Korea. Partnering with the Presbyterian Church in Korea, we were able to establish a center we called "My Sister's Place." The center's purpose was to provide a spiritual home for women who had been rejected by their families and by society at large because of their means of making a living. It would also offer them some practical skills.

It took a while to gain the trust of the women. When we opened the center, only three women were willing to come. But gradually trust grew, the staff became strong advocates for the women, and the group became a loving community. We held counseling sessions, awareness education, health classes, English classes, cooking classes – whatever was needed. We hosted special Korean dinners and invited the soldiers, to help them learn more about Korean food and culture. We even started a small bakery for women who wanted to seek other employment.

Of course, I learned more from these oppressed Korean sisters than I was ever able to give them. One day we were at the home of a woman who had married an American soldier. They had a small baby, and as we were studying English together, I noticed that she had just purchased a small quilt to carry her baby on her back. "How much did you pay for that quilt?" I asked. She answered, "8000 *won* ($16.00)." "You paid too much!" I said. "You should have bargained." She responded, "Think of how difficult it is to do all that quilting on the sewing machine. You have to consider the women who work in the factories." I was speechless. This woman lived in one room with only a bed, a potbelly stove, and a radio, yet she was willing to help those less fortunate. I thought I knew how to live a Christian life, but I was being taught by a prostitute how to truly live as a Christian. She became a modern-day Christ for me.

This is just one example of the many ways these women – the most down-and-out, the most despised and rejected by society – ministered to me and taught me compassion, generosity, and love. The years I spent at "My Sister's Place" were wonderful in so many ways and I am proud that its work continues to thrive today, twenty years later.

Though I am now retired and living in the U.S. again, I sometimes find myself contemplating the role of the U.S. in the world and the effect it has on other countries. Having learned first-hand about the plight of Korean women in their relationships with American soldiers, I realized that these relationships are taking place all over the world, wherever American troops are stationed. Women are always available to the soldiers, especially in countries where there is much poverty. The women may be hoping for a better life – to marry an American man and go to live in that rich, bountiful country called the United States. Sometimes these relationships result in the soldiers divorcing their wives who are waiting back home in America. More often, they result in devastation for the local woman who had hoped to find love and security in her relationship with the American, only to find that he was just satisfying his sexual needs.

I remember advising a young American soldier in Korea to stop dating the Korean woman he had met in a bar unless he planned on marrying her. He told me he had made it clear to her that he had no intention of marriage. I warned him that she would likely continue to hold out hope and that his actions would count more than his words. The day before he was to leave for America, his girlfriend committed suicide.

American soldiers are not given proper orientation to other cultures and peoples; they do not understand other nations. Aside from the horrors of war and killing, we in America often do not realize the damage we cause to other countries. Thankfully, My Sister's Place provides a ray of hope for some women in Korea, but when I think of the women all around the world hurting from broken relationships, estranged from their own families, returning to the bars, suffering from mental illness or worse, it still makes my heart ache.

My heart no longer aches, however, for democracy in south Korea. Free and open elections began to happen in the 1990's, as first Kim Young Sam and then Kim Dae Jung were elected president. Stephen took a seat in the National Assembly (south Korea's congress), serving one term as an at-large assemblyman appointed by the Party of Peace and Democracy. A new day had dawned. The long, dark nights of struggle were finally over.

Chapter 5

Things They Never Taught Us
Down on the Farm

Gene Matthews

"No, there is...no...not any torture in Korea."
—Former South Korean Foreign Minister Lho Shin Yong (No Sinyŏng) while being interviewed by BBC television crew in 1975. There is a possibility he believed what he was saying.

"Koreans are remarkably resilient. You can take them to prison and beat them with a baseball bat. They will recover and seek opportunities to do the same thing."
—Former U.S. Ambassador to Korea William F. Gleysteen to a foreign guest escorted by the author.

More than Witnesses

I really can't remember just when it was that Chung Jai Ryong (Chŏng Chaeyong) appeared in my office. I remember being struck by the appearance of this tall, slender and ruggedly handsome man of indeterminate age. In his hand he carried a cloth bundle, the ubiquitous *pojagi* which the Korean people find so useful for carrying just about anything.

He explained that he had been sent by my friend, Dr. Lee, Oojung (Yi Ujŏng) (now deceased), college professor and, at that time, Executive Secretary of Church Women United. He opened the bundle to reveal a thick, hand-written manuscript which he said described his years of torture by the Korean Central Intelligence Agency (KCIA). Because it was impossible to publish such a manuscript in Korea, he explained, Dr. Lee had suggested that I might be able to smuggle it to America for translation and publication there. Mr. Chung then proceeded to tell me his story — revealing to me forms of human behavior for which my upbringing in rural Iowa had done little to prepare me.

꽃 ✿✿ 꽃

Growing up in rural Iowa, I learned early in life how to milk cows, drive various kinds of tractors, bale hay, pitch manure and all the other delights of farm life. One of my childhood chores was caring for the chickens and cleaning out the chicken house every Saturday, a chore which provided a serious challenge to the olfactory nerves. Though it was during the great depression, it was a treasured time for me.

My father was lucky to find work as a school teacher and his meager pay check, paid out only nine months of the year, was supplemented by various odd jobs during the summer. His salary plus an enormous garden, a flock of chickens and a couple of pet hogs kept food on our table. My mother was one of those remarkable mid-west women who seemed to thrive on work. She was also a school teacher but dropped out of her profession while my three brothers and I were growing up. She was constantly cooking, sewing, washing, ironing, canning, baking, churning, cleaning. Her good efforts stretched the meager income and assured that we never went hungry.

Every Sunday we were driven into town for Sunday School and church. It was not a democratic process. We were simply bundled into our 1937 Ford and off we went. In Sunday School we memorized the 23rd Psalm and the Ten Commandments, sang "Trust And Obey" in the Junior Choir and learned that we should always "be ye kind, one to another," which is still pretty good advice. We learned many other things as well, but we never learned about torture.

Mr. Chung had been imprisoned for twelve years, during which time the authorities tried to force from him a confession that he was a communist spy. At the end of that time they gave up, in effect telling him that if he refused to confess after all they had done to him, he must, indeed, be innocent of the charges.

All that they had done to him, however, left Mr. Chung in bad shape. At one point he peeled back his shirt and showed me where a severe beating with a club (the ambassador's baseball bat?) had caved in a couple of ribs. He described years of agony from the resulting lung problems and chronic pleurisy. A very visible scar and indentation on one side of his face testified to another beating. He seemed to have difficulty breathing and would occasionally stop talking, squint, and roll his eyes back up into his head.

When I pressed him, he said that among the many tortures he endured, several had damaged his sinuses and he had a chronic infection which was slowly eating back up into his brain rendering him constantly dizzy and short of breath. His tormentors took delight, he explained, in stripping him naked, standing him outside in sub-zero temperatures and pouring ice water on him. They also subjected him to what may be a uniquely Korean form of torture which consisted of strapping him on his back and forcing water laced with red pepper down his nose. On other occasions they would force water down his throat with a hose then jump on his distended belly. At one point he opened his mouth and peeled back his lips, showing me where a number of molars were missing. The KCIA brethren, he said, had pulled these out one by one with a pair of rusty pliers, very slowly and, of course, without anesthesia. Some of the ordeals he described left me physically ill.

When I asked him to describe the worst thing they had done to him, he surprised me by describing the use of food and drink as the most devious of all instruments of torture. At one point he was kept locked up without food for several days. He explained that after a period of time without food, one ceases thinking about it but until that time comes, thoughts of food occupy every waking moment. They somehow knew when his hunger pangs would be their sharpest, and when he reached this peak, they brought him into a room and tied him to a chair. Then tables laden with food were brought before him and he was forced to look at them. Suddenly, the doors opened and several people entered the room, sat down at the tables and began to devour the food. He nearly fainted from hunger. When they finished and left the room, the tables were cleaned up and more food was brought in. Abruptly, Mr. Chung was released and invited to eat. He rushed to the table and began to eat greedily. He was well into the meal until he realized that the food was salty and there was nothing on the table to drink.

He was then tied back into his chair and a man appeared bearing a large tray weighed down with various kinds of cool drinks. Mr. Chung was forced to watch for several hours. He became so thirsty he tried to bite his tongue and drink the blood. His guards bound his tongue in an old rag so he was unable to bite it. This, explains Mr. Chung, was the nearest he came to breaking during the entire twelve years.

Things They Never Taught Us Down on the Farm

On several occasions I invited Mr. Chung to have lunch with me but gave up when I discovered that he merely nibbled at the food set before him. I've often wondered if his ordeal somehow caused him to feel that food was his enemy.

❦ ❧ ❧

It was during my senior year in high school that a young pastor was assigned to our little home town Methodist Church to replace the (to me) ancient gentleman who had led the flock for far too long. Young Rev. Leonard Tinker began to suggest that central to the Christian faith was the notion of justice. "What does God require of you," he asked in the words of Micah, "but to do justice, and to love kindness, and to walk humbly with your God?" The idea that there was far more to the Christian faith than a lot of things I was supposed to avoid (so I could go to heaven) — working on Sunday, drinking and smoking, swearing, etc. — was a most refreshing concept which I eagerly embraced. And although nothing was said by my exciting young pastor about the kinds of injustices Mr. Chung would experience, the seeds of a concern for justice were firmly planted

❦ ❧ ❧

John Somerville, a Presbyterian missionary friend, was able to arrange medical care for Mr. Chung which quite likely saved his life. Eventually, his body more or less healed. But his mind and his soul were forever tormented. Although I had successfully smuggled his manuscript out of the country and turned it over to friends in the Korean American community, they deemed it too disorganized and confused for publication. They said it appeared to be the work of a mentally disturbed person. Indeed! Undeterred, Mr. Chung became obsessed with torture and embarked on intensive research into torture both historically and as it is utilized around the world today. On his own he published a thick book on the subject. He dedicated the book to Dr. Somerville and me. The book contains many pictures of various forms of torture including those inflicted on him. He and members of his family posed for the pictures. In one of the pictures, Mr. Chung is bound and laying on his back while a man appears to be striking him in the face with a hammer. The hammer is shown landing precisely where the scarred indentation still resides on his face.

My four years at Iowa State College (now university) in Ames, Iowa, beginning in 1952, was a profound experience. Exposure to excellent professors who became lifelong friends and a grasp of new knowledge produced an experience that was really like stepping into a much wider world than I knew existed before. Collegiate Methodist Church and Wesley Foundation in Ames expanded my spiritual life as well. Sunday after Sunday I gathered inspiration from the sermons of Rev. Samuel Nichols, named by Christian Century *as one of the outstanding preachers in America. As I look back his sermons were profoundly prophetic in a society still torn by racial segregation and the gloom of the cold war. Associate Minister Dean Walters and Wesley Foundation Director Mae Gautier were superb spiritual guides who further watered and fertilized the seeds of justice planted by my home town pastor. It was through this combined experience that I felt called to devote my life to missionary service. To qualify for such service it was necessary to subject myself to intensive prodding of my body, mind and spirit by a team of doctors, psychologists, and church leaders. Lengthy training sessions were devoted to helping me better understand the Bible, assess my linguistic abilities, and render me sensitive to cultures different from my own. The training was excellent, but not once during that time of preparation did anybody mention torture.*

Obviously, torture is not unique to Korea. But Korea is where we gained first hand knowledge of it and witnessed its effects on so many of our close friends and colleagues. Eventually, I found myself wondering about the ones doing the torturing. At what point in one's career does one choose to become a torturer? Are there aptitude tests to determine one's suitability for such a career? How does the torturer unwind at the end of the day? One can only imagine how valuable those willing to inflict torture must be to a dictatorship determined to stay in power at all costs. It can be used to extract false confessions from innocent persons. It can be used to concoct fabricated plots to overthrow the government as Park Chung Hee's KCIA did with the "Peoples' Revolutionary Party" case. But perhaps the most devastating use of torture in Korea was as a means of intimidation. People who had done nothing were rounded up, tortured, and released. The government's expectation was that this would cause anyone who might be thinking of opposing the government to have second thoughts.

Those of us who participated in the Monday Night Group were almost overwhelmed with the ubiquitous nature of torture and the almost nonchalance with which the government seemed willing to employ it. Our feelings of shock, anger, sadness and despair were at times almost unbearable. They were, however, strong motivation for our own meager involvement in Korea's struggle for freedom and democracy. We tried to get the word out, to arouse a sense of moral indignation in the world and to persuade our government leaders to intervene. In this we were only moderately successful. They seemed aware of it and upset by it but to our frustration were not sufficiently concerned to try to take steps to stop it. We were only slightly better at trying to pick up the pieces, to arrange medical care and provide comfort to the victims and their families. In spite of their experience, however, many of our friends who endured torture emerged from the situation with their faith intact, their courage strengthened and their resolve firmer than ever.

More than Witnesses

In October of 1999, Lee Kun-an (Yi Kunan), a former police captain accused of torturing hundreds of political prisoners (dubbed "Torture Artist" by former victims), emerged from twelve years in hiding and turned himself into a regional prosecutor's office. One of his countless victims was a young man named Kim Kun-tae (Kim Kunt'ae), a champion for labor and for pro-democracy activities, who in 1987 was named winner of the prestigious Robert F. Kennedy Human Rights award.

On February 7, 2005, Kim Kun-tae, then a three term member of the National Assembly, later Minister of Health and Welfare, and often spoken of as a future presidential candidate, traveled to the prison cell where his torturer Lee Kun-an is living out his seven-year prison term. In the course of the thirty minute meeting, Lee bowed deeply to Kim and apologized saying "I bitterly repent my crimes against you. I'll seek your forgiveness until I die. Please forgive me."

Kim replied, "I forgave you long ago!"

Be ye kind, one to another.

❧ ❧❧ ❧

I honestly can't remember if I sought out and found the Monday Night Group or if they found me. I only know that participation in that remarkable little band of faithful Catholic and Protestant missionaries, most of us woefully unprepared for the directions toward which God led us, resulted in some of the richest and most disturbing involvements of my life. In my childhood and youth, Monday was the day we resumed work in the fields following the carefully observed day of worship and rest. Nothing in my own past prepared me to battle the riot police in Seoul, attempt to aid victims of torture, or comfort the widows of innocent men executed by a militant government. We were drawn together almost inevitably, I suppose, through our mutual concerns over the injustices imposed on the Korean people in the name of progress.

Things They Never Taught Us Down on the Farm

When I applied and was accepted for service as a missionary, I was assigned to Korea, a country I had not known existed until the outbreak of the Korean War just six years earlier. My initial assignment there left little time or opportunity for political thought. I lived in rural Korea where I worked with farmers, carried out relief work and taught English. Korea was desperately poor and, technically, still in a state of war. Syngman Rhee was president at the time and, because he was "Christian," I just assumed the country was in good hands. I tended to discount stories of police brutality and oppression of laborers as minority complaints, irrelevant to a nation with one of the lowest per capita incomes in the world trying desperately to rebuild itself following the devastation of the war.

By the time I completed my term of service and left Korea in 1959 with my lovely new wife Insook, however, the stories of brutality and oppression had built to a crescendo. While attending Garrett Seminary in Evanston, Illinois, I wasn't surprised to hear that President Rhee had been overthrown in 1960 by a student-led revolt against the corrupt policies of his administration. When we returned to Korea two years later, the faltering, fledgling democracy that followed Rhee's overthrow had been shattered by a military coup. Martial law was in effect when we arrived.

On May 16, 1961, Park Chung Hee suddenly and dramatically burst onto the Korean political scene, staging a military coup that overthrew the moderate government of Premier Chang Myon (Chang Myŏn). Park had immediately disbanded South Korea's National Assembly (parliament) and ruled by decree until he resigned from the military and narrowly won election as president in 1963. Four years later, he was re-elected by a wider margin to a second term as permitted by the Constitution.

Thus we returned to a Korea whose meager aspirations for democratic freedoms had been ground under the heels of martial law. At the same time, we saw surprising evidence of economic and political progress. Because I was busy with language study from 1962-64, then an assignment to youth work and rural church development in Pusan, I more or less watched from the sidelines. Park alarmed me as a person because of his arrogance and sternness, but these seemed to be qualities much admired by the Korean people. And he produced some pretty remarkable economic results. In a move not without controversy, relations with Japan were normalized. The country began to pull itself out of the desperate poverty that had characterized it since the Korean War. Under Park, roads were built, factories sprang up, and almost overnight this poor, centuries-old agrarian society was on its way to becoming a booming industrial giant. His economic policies opened the country to foreign trade and created the beginnings of the great industrial revolution which ultimately brought Korea to its present state of prosperity.

It was really not until leaving Pusan and moving back to Seoul in 1969 for a new assignment, however, that I began to be aware of the enormous cost of the economic progress. Exploitation of workers was rampant and, although Park had long since resigned from the military, the country was still being run as a dictatorship. Some of my close Korean friends were arrested for no apparent reason and many of them were cruelly tortured. Stories of immense profits reaped by entrepreneurs through blatant exploitation of young factory workers became commonplace. Learning that many of the entrepreneurs were prominent Christians initially led to feelings of disappointment but later to anger.

In spite of the severity and brutality of Park's regime, the genuine economic progress brought about through his policies would likely have brought him honor had he simply quit at the end of his constitutionally-permitted second elected term. Megalomania reared its ugly head, however, and in 1971 he rammed through a constitutional amendment which allowed him to run for a third term. In the ensuing election he narrowly defeated his democratically inclined opponent Kim Dae Jung. Kim, who years later finally won election to Korea's highest position of leadership, had been seriously injured in a mysterious traffic accident during the election campaign. Many assumed that this was a clumsy attempt on his life. Park's victory in the election was generally considered to be based on fraud.

In 1972, while riding to the Monday Night Group meeting one October evening, we were alarmed to see armored vehicles, tanks and troops rumbling through the city and pouring onto the campuses of major universities. We spent much of the session that evening trying to determine just what had happened. It would be several days before we could fully grasp the situation. What had happened was that Park had suddenly imposed martial law on a nation that was growing increasingly restless under his harsh rule. It was almost as if he had staged a coup against his own government.

With the nation firmly in his control, Park again shut down the National Assembly and introduced his Yushin Constitution (referred to as "Revitalizing Reforms" in the English press at the time). The Constitution named him president for life, authorized him to issue emergency decrees, and imposed harsh penalties on any who dared to criticize him. With the new Constitution in force and the powerful KCIA to implement it, Park was able to retain power until his assassination in October, 1979, seven years later. His regime will ultimately be remembered for its cruel exploitation of labor, ruthless clamp down on all opposition, rigid control of the media, and the inevitable paranoia which besets all dictators.

A major tool of the Park regime was the National Security Law. First enacted on December 1, 1948, ostensibly to protect south Korea against infiltration by the communist north, the law was repeatedly revised and amended over the years to enhance the power of the military dictators who successively ruled the country. Park used its vaguely written Article Seven, which, for example, provided punishment for membership in organizations deemed to "benefit the enemy," plus a series of harsh emergency decrees to harass, intimidate, arrest, torture, and imprison thousands of real and imagined opponents.

Those of us who joined in the activities of the Monday Night Group should probably not flatter ourselves into inflating our importance in the overall scheme of things. The fact that we collectively and individually experienced intense scrutiny and some degree of harassment does not in itself indicate that we occupied a special place of interest for the various agencies of the Korean governments. The ruthless dictators who ruled the nation during that time were characterized, as are all dictators, by an abundant supply of paranoia. They felt threatened by anyone who stood in opposition to them, and they had a vast array of agencies and bureaucracies in place to enforce their paranoia.

≈ ◔◔ ≈

I personally experienced pressure from at least five government agencies. First and foremost was the Korean Central Intelligence Agency (KCIA). This all-powerful organization was modeled after and received training from its U.S. counterpart, but it was used almost exclusively to control and intimidate any real or imagined opposition to the whims of the dictators. Ultimately, an agent of the KCIA was assigned to me. He moved into a building near where I worked and visited me at least once every day, usually inviting me out for a cup of *sangwha tang (ssanghwat'ang)*, a bittersweet herbal drink. His approach seemed to be to cultivate friendship, in part by "warning" me of threats from others in his own organization as well as other government agencies.

Things They Never Taught Us Down on the Farm

Surprisingly, ours became a relationship of genuine friendship that lasted for many years. He called me on the phone several times a day to check up on me, and whereas the phone calls were a nuisance in the beginning, I eventually found myself looking forward to them and to our morning bowl of *sangwha tang*. Eventually, he affirmed my long held suspicion that my phone was tapped and on various occasions quietly suggested that some things I had discussed on the phone with friends might better be discussed in person.

～) ～～ (～

Following the assassination of President Park in 1979, my KCIA friend disappeared for several months. He reappeared quite suddenly one morning by calling and inviting me out for a bowl of *sangwha tang* as if nothing had happened. We greeted each other warmly but he was very vague about where he had been during his long absence. Almost by accident, I noticed that he seemed to be hiding his hands. Without warning, I reached across the table, grabbed one of his arms and pulled his hand toward me across the table. On the back of each finger nail was an indented, discolored scar. I finally pressed him into revealing that because Park Chung Hee had been assassinated by the director of the KCIA, the martial law authorities investigating the case had rounded up all KCIA employees, one level at a time, and tortured them to determine whether or not they had been involved in a plot to assassinate the president. My friend had been cleared of suspicion only after surviving torture which included attachment of electrodes to each of his fingers through which enough electric current was discharged to discolor and scar each of his fingernails.

Since my retirement from Korea in 1997 I have lost track of this agent. Make no mistake. He was trained in brutality and was a willing agent of a ruthless government. But somehow, almost mysteriously, we became friends. Because I wish him no harm, I shall not reveal his name.

The KCIA also assigned agents to the post offices to inspect mail from abroad. Even though technology is available to do this unobtrusively, in my case they obviously wanted me to know my mail was being opened and read before being delivered to me. The envelopes were opened and resealed with thick gobs of glue which stuck not only to the envelope flap but usually matted the envelope to the letter inside making it impossible to open without tearing the letter itself. Beginning in college and continuing until my retirement, my father and I had developed a habit of exchanging letters every week. I wrote to my father and mentioned that his letters were being opened and read by the KCIA. The next letter from my father had a note on the outside of the envelope in his nearly impossible to read handwriting. It said:

Dear KCIA guy. I'm sorry my handwriting is so bad. I know it makes your job more difficult. Please accept my apology. You have a very difficult job. Have a nice day.

Dad's notes to the KCIA continued from that day until I was finally able to inform him after many months that the mail inspection had stopped. He was always polite, asked the inspectors about the weather in Korea and their families, commiserated with them on their fate at having to read his handwriting, and continued to encourage them to have a nice day. At length, my KCIA agent informed me on one of his daily visits that he and his friends were really enjoying the notes from my father.

Phone tapping was so commonplace as to boggle the mind at the enormous resources that must have been invested in keeping a whole phalanx of agents occupied monitoring boring phone conversations. On numerous occasions evidence of the wire tapping was revealed in humorous ways. While speaking on the phone with a City Ward officer about an issue related to a missionary colleague's residency, I mentioned that I had discussed the matter with the KCIA and they were in favor of resolving the issue. Immediately after I hung up, "my" KCIA agent called me and scolded me for mentioning the KCIA's role in the matter.

The KCIA's tentacles were far-reaching. A very close friend in the Korean Methodist Church who was planning a trip to the United States asked if I could arrange a speaking tour of churches in America. I contacted several churches in my home state of Iowa and worked out a visitation schedule for him. While he was still in the United States, the KCIA visited me to inquire why Dr. Kim was visiting churches in Dunkerton, Humbolt and several other towns in Iowa. They even knew the content of his talks.

An agent from the National Police was also assigned to check up on me from time to time. He did not seem to take his assignment as seriously as my KCIA friend. He was quite personable but limited his contacts to occasional phone calls and even less occasional visits, ostensibly to check up on my well-being. He spoke English well and generally preferred to use it. On one occasion he told me he was not happy with his current assignment. When asked the nature of his assignment he described it as "milling-around." He let me know that "milling-around" was not a suitable assignment for a man of his caliber. I tended to agree. Keeping track of me was also a waste of his talents. My assumption is that many employees of the government found themselves wasting their talents merely milling around.

In addition to the KCIA and National Police, various elements of the local police also kept tabs on our comings and goings. I discovered almost by chance that shops I had visited to make minor purchases were subsequently visited by police who wished to know what I had purchased and what I had discussed during my visit.

More than Witnesses

For a period of time, a rather nondescript car was parked in a city construction office across the street from my home. When I traveled in my car, this nondescript car carrying a nondescript driver and equally nondescript passenger would follow. This thrilled my children who took delight in making faces out the rear window and imagining us involved in some kind of James Bond fantasy.

I found myself wondering how much money it was costing the government to keep track of me. I even became a little paranoid and found myself wondering if they would need to fabricate something about me in order to justify the expense.

The agency most responsible for keeping the pesky foreigners in check was the Office of Immigration. We remained in the country at their mercy. The means they used to control us ranged from outright deportation, as in the case of George Ogle, to simply refusing to renew Alien Residence Permits when they came due, as in the case of Father Jim Sinnott. The forced departure of missionaries from Korea appeared to be aimed at least in part at warning the rest of us to behave.

Following the executions in 1975 of the eight innocent men accused of being the ringleaders of the KCIA-fabricated "People's Revolutionary Party" (PRP), a group of us staged a demonstration in front of the U. S. Embassy to protest America's apparent unwillingness to intervene on behalf of the men. The Office of Immigration was given the task of rounding us up later that day and subjecting us to several hours of interrogation.

Following this incident — and related perhaps to other involvements on our part — several of us in the Monday Night Group were placed on very short tether by the immigration officials. For example, some of us were issued Residence Permits good for only three months rather than the normal one year. Persons seeking extensions of their residency were required to fill out copious forms and submit them to the Office of Immigration, along with pictures and revenue stamps, well in advance of the expiration date. Failure to meet the deadline resulted in a substantial fine.

This meant that every three months I would gather my forms, fill them out, and trek to the Immigration Office carrying my pictures and revenue stamp. I would then be told that because of unusual circumstances there would be a delay while my application was being investigated. A month or two would pass before I was called into the Immigration Office to pick up my Residence Permit good for another three months. By that time, however, much of the three months had already passed and I would be reminded that in a week or so I would need to apply for a new extension. During the three-year period that this reality prevailed, I became well acquainted with the clerks at the Immigration Office. They began to joke with me about being their *tan gol sonnim* (tan'gol sonnim) (regular guest).

A final bureaucracy with which we had frequent contact was the multi-faceted Ministry of Culture and Information. This bloated establishment has since been divided into two organizations, but at that time was one and it wielded power far beyond that implied by its innocuous name. The ministry was responsible not only for putting a positive face on the government, a task it pursued aggressively and zealously through rigid control of the media, but also of holding in check all religious organizations in the nation. It achieved the latter responsibility with incredible success through control of property. Korean law required that all property owned by religious bodies be registered by the Ministry of Culture and Information. No sale, donation, or transfer of property or construction of buildings such as churches or temples could take place without approval by this ministry.

More than Witnesses

The churches of Korea were emerging from a long period of destitution mirroring that of the nation itself. As they grew and prospered they were eager to build bigger and grander church buildings, offices, and institutions. They quickly learned that approval for such property-related development was not only enabled by not criticizing the government but was often remarkably enhanced if the church made some outward, dramatic display of support. Some church leaders believed quite firmly that the business of the church was the salvation of souls and considered any effort at combating injustice to be outside the church's realm. But others were genuine apologists for the dictatorial form of government, apparently believing that an authoritarian government protected them from such anti-Christian evils as communism.

One notable example was Campus Crusade for Christ. Following the Korean War, when much of the country was overrun by refugees, indigent squatters occupied practically any available space. Many set up house along the downtown streets in crude little shacks made of cardboard, plywood, and tin. Many more had moved into the area surrounding the remnants of the old Russian Embassy in Chung Dong near the center of Seoul. One fateful day in 1967, squads of police descended on the area without warning, herded the dwellers into trucks and hauled them out into the country. They were dumped on a barren piece of land where they were expected to survive with no resources, no materials for housing, and no transportation to their meager places of work. A friend who lived in the neighborhood at the time, in what was probably an embellishment, described billows of tear gas and "rivers of blood" flowing down the hill.

A short time after this forced evacuation, Campus Crusade for Christ became the registered owner of this extremely valuable piece of land. On it they constructed a training center and a large office building which generated income from businesses that rented office space. Rumors abounded that not only was the land donated to Campus Crusade for Christ but that government funds were also provided for construction of the building. Whether these rumors were true or not, the indisputable fact was that from that time on Campus Crusade for Christ provided the eager spearhead for the frequent pro-government "Christian" demonstrations and rallies.

Many church leaders, though lacking any genuine commitment to the dictatorship and even abhorring the brutal oppression and torture inflicted on the people by the regime, nevertheless went along with it. They gave every appearance of being supportive because of the threat that their property growth would otherwise be curtailed. In fact, they participated in pro-government rallies and prayer meetings and tried to rein in the missionaries related to them. Because critics of the abuses by the government, both at home and abroad, tended to view the Christian church as a proper judge of such violations, the government felt it needed support by at least a segment of the Christian community for some semblance of credibility.

Many potential critics responded simplistically to the situation by saying in effect, if the church supports the government, the government must be good. This resulted in an appalling system of mutual back-scratching. Certain Christian groups were supported financially by the government and the government, in return, was able to call on these groups for public displays of support whenever such a need arose.

Most of us in the Monday Night Group were missionaries and as such were assigned to work with Korean churches and denominations. Our assignments to Korea were endorsed by our related Korean denominations, but they were obviously instructed to keep us out of trouble. On numerous occasions we were called before our denominational leaders and alternately scolded, threatened, labeled communist sympathizers, pled with, or ordered to "just do your jobs and forget politics."

We all became more or less skilled at appearing to comply, but it was a strain, because many of the denominational leaders were our friends and respected colleagues. We had to tread a fine line between helping those who were being victimized by the government and, on the other hand, risking the well-being of our friends in church leadership positions.

Some of our missionary colleagues were also critical of us. They reminded us that we were guests in the country and ought, therefore, to behave properly. We tried to counter by saying that we were, indeed, guests but that our hosts were the ones being oppressed by the government.

There were happy exceptions to this pragmatic tendency of church leaders to turn a blind eye to government abuse. In addition to numerous brave leaders within the various mainline denominations, the progressive Presbyterian Church in the Republic of Korea (PROK) provided courageous leadership in the struggles for human rights (unlike the more conservative Presbyterian denomination which was far more likely to be supportive of government policy). The pastors and leaders of the PROK paid a heavy price in terms of arrest, torture, and imprisonment. In addition, the leadership of the Korean National Council of Churches, the Korean Student Christian Federation, and the leaders in Urban Industrial Mission also spoke and acted courageously and suffered similar consequences.

Throughout this period it was quite evident to most of us that the United States Government had allied itself closely with the governments of Park Chung Hee and his successors. North Korea was depicted as the nastiest of the various Cold War nations, and every effort was made to justify the continued presence of a large U.S. military force in south Korea. In the struggle against the various regimes of south Korea, we in the Monday Night Group tended to hope for more support from the U.S. Embassy than they were willing to give. Furthermore, our own positions called for caution in how we approached the embassy. For example, many U.S. missionary sending agencies had policies in place forbidding their missionaries from working in any capacity with the American CIA. We agreed with those policies, and were aware that many agents of the CIA served in key U.S. Embassy positions.

Our Korean friends in the struggle for justice, however, encouraged us to enlist embassy officials to bring pressure on the oppressive regimes. In this we were only moderately successful. Most of our contacts were with staff of the Political Section of the embassy. For the most part we found them receptive to our reports of human rights violations, and we were assured on many occasions that information we reported to them was being relayed to Washington. Many of them expressed personal frustration and dissatisfaction with the dictatorial regimes, but they also gave the clear impression that political reality required cooperation with them.

Attitudes of the embassy staff quite logically shifted to mirror the feelings of whoever was the U.S. President. During the administration of Jimmy Carter, a great deal more attention was devoted to ferreting out and reporting on human rights violations committed by the south Korean Government. During that time we were often sought out and encouraged to report our knowledge of such violations. Although in reality the U.S. administration accomplished very little in terms of actually assisting the victims during that time, President Carter's frequent and sincere rhetoric about human rights lent great encouragement to the struggle.

More than Witnesses

The replacement of Carter by Ronald Reagan brought an abrupt end to this encouragement as Reagan began to speak openly of quiet diplomacy. From our perspective quiet diplomacy seemed to be a euphemism for aggressive support of the status quo. It also set the stage for the late Ambassador Dixie Walker's very unfortunate "spoiled brats" incident.

Richard (Dixie) Walker (now deceased) was a specialist in Asian Studies who was connected with the Institute of International Studies at the University of South Carolina when President Reagan appointed him ambassador to south Korea in 1981. He served with honor in that post for five years and was generally well liked by the Korean people. He was personable and, as a former college professor rather than a career diplomat, was not overly concerned with diplomatic niceties. Many of us who knew him found this to be refreshing.

He made one serious mistake during his term, however. During a home visit in the U.S., he was interviewed by a small-town newspaper reporter who asked him a question about the dissidents in Korea who were opposing the Korean government. Dixie, probably taken off guard, replied that some people in Korea felt the dissidents were nothing more than spoiled brats.

Within a day or two government-controlled Korean newspapers carried bold headlines stating "Ambassador Calls Dissidents Spoiled Brats." The incident served the dual purpose of infuriating opponents of the government and enabling the government to gloat over this apparent putdown of their opponents by the U.S. Government.

I received a call from a friend on the staff of the embassy asking how I thought Walker might extricate himself from a situation that was becoming increasingly awkward by the moment. I told him I felt that nothing less than a very sincere explanation and apology would suffice.

Things They Never Taught Us Down on the Farm

The opportunity for the apology occurred a short time later when then Vice President George H. W. Bush paid an official visit to Korea. Ambassador Walker used the occasion of the visit to invite a large group of Korean dissidents and some of their American supporters to his home for breakfast with the vice president. This was an extremely bold and generous move on Walker's part, because the group included many professors who had been imprisoned, tortured, and ousted from their jobs; and it included a number of prominent clergy and other leaders who had been at the forefront of the struggle for democracy. I found myself sitting beside Bush, who immediately launched into terribly superficial conversation about how much the Korean people must love Americans, referring to the streets lined with school children smiling and waving American flags when he rode in from the airport in his limousine. I remarked sarcastically that I was sure he realized they were all ordered to be there and that the reception might not have been as genuine as it seemed. He appeared taken aback by my comment.

Following breakfast, Ambassador Walker delivered a heartfelt speech in which he quite genuinely apologized for his remarks. Though his words had been uttered when he was off guard, then were taken out of context, he said he never should have spoken them. He begged the forgiveness of all present. Walker then introduced Vice President Bush who made a few forgettable remarks about "our great nations" standing united against the evils of communism or something along that line. Those present were then allowed to raise questions or make comments.

The Rev. Pak, Hyung Kyu (Pak Hyŏnggyu), a Presbyterian minister who had been imprisoned on several occasions, rose to his feet and expressed appreciation for Ambassador Walker's apology. He accepted it on behalf of the group and suggested that it had completely settled any resentment the "spoiled brats" comment had originally created. When he sat down, another man rose and directed his remarks to Bush. "Mr. Vice President," he began, "when Jimmy Carter was president he spoke often of the human rights violations in Korea. Although he was unable to make much progress in persuading the Korean government to discontinue such violations, we were, nevertheless, encouraged by his rhetoric. Since Ronald Reagan has become president, the rhetoric criticizing human rights violations has ceased. We now feel that we are worse off than we were when Carter was president. Can you persuade President Reagan to resume the criticism?"

Bush leapt to his feet, eyes flashing and chin quivering. He thrust his finger at the questioner and cried out in his metallic twang, "we spoke about human rights in Vietnaaam and now there is no Vietnaaam. We spoke out about human rights in Eye Raan (Iran) and now there is no Eye Raan. We are now carrying out 'quiet diplomacy,' and I'm going to call on Donald Gregg from the National Security Office to explain to you why you're better off now than you were while Carter was president!"

The inanity, the arrogance, the condescension embodied in this statement seems to have completely escaped the vice president. He was addressing a roomful of people who had paid dearly for their pro-democratic stands. Most had been imprisoned. Many had been tortured. Many more had been ousted from their jobs. Common sense would suggest that they were in a better position to judge their situations than this future president of the United States who so obviously had no comprehension of their struggle.

Donald Gregg slowly rose to his feet and mumbled a few words about progress then sat down and the meeting broke up. The mood of apology and forgiveness was effectively destroyed. As we left the Ambassador's residence, Dr. Kim Chan-kook (Kim Ch'an'guk), former dean of the School of Theology at Yonsei University, who would later become president of that high ranking university, sidled up to Bush and said "Mr. Vice President. When Jimmy Carter was president I had a job. Now that Reagan is president I do not have a job."

A few years later when Gregg himself was appointed ambassador to Korea, he told me that the vice president's visit was not one of the finest moments of his life. Gregg went on to become an eloquent spokesperson for justice and democracy on the Korean peninsula.

If there is a focal point to the Monday Night Group's small contribution to Korea's struggle for democracy, it is the terrible week in April of 1975 when the Korean government blatantly executed eight men. The men were innocent of all charges, as determined by independent investigation at that time and later borne out by history. As part of his ploy to name himself president for life, Park Chung Hee had arranged for his notorious Korean Central Intelligence Agency, modeled after and trained by its American counterpart, to fabricate a supposed plot by communist sympathizers to overthrow the government. Hundreds, including many of our friends, were arrested, tortured and sentenced to various terms in prison on trumped up charges, all to persuade the Korean citizens and the world that Park's dictatorship was necessary to protect them from the evil communists. At the top of the fabricated plot were eight men accused of being the ring leaders of a secretive "People's Revolutionary Party (PRP)."

At the request of the wives of these eight men, Dr. George Ogle, a United Methodist missionary, conducted an investigation and wrote a paper in which he announced that the men had been chosen more for their obscurity than their genuine involvement in a plot. In fact they did not even know each other. However, through torture, threats, and pressure on them, their wives, and their children, the KCIA extracted confessions. This "evidence" was used to bring them to trial in kangaroo courts where they were found guilty of treason and sentenced to death.

Following the sentencing, the Monday Night Group inevitably became involved in the events that rapidly occurred that week. For many of us, it became the worst week of our lives. No one really thought the government would be so brazen as to actually execute the men.

The week began quietly enough with church on Sunday morning, followed by lunch with Vanya Kewley, a British producer-director-commentator from BBC television. Vanya was in Korea doing a documentary on the Korean situation. After lunch I accompanied her to a home where we met the Methodist pastors involved in Urban Industrial Missions. The rest of the day was uneventful.

Monday afternoon marked a futile attempt to arrange a meeting at my home between a visiting Amnesty International lawyer and one of the recently released prisoners. A combination of visitors from abroad was making the government nervous. In addition to the BBC crew and two Amnesty International lawyers, U.S. Congressman Donald Fraser (D-Minnesota.), a fervent champion of human rights in Korea who later became mayor of Minneapolis, was visiting Korea. The government responded by giving all recently released political prisoners the choice of either leaving Seoul and taking a guided tour of the outlying provinces (where they were allegedly provided with call girls by the government) or remaining in Seoul under house arrest. My friend — the recent prisoner whom I wanted to introduce to the AI lawyer — had chosen to remain in Seoul under house arrest, believing he could elude his house guard. But he was unable to do so.

That night was the Monday Night Group meeting. Much of the evening was spent being interviewed on camera by the BBC crew.

Things They Never Taught Us Down on the Farm

We expressed ourselves frankly to them and when the crew finally left, we devoted the remaining time to discussing the recent arrests of church leaders including Rev. Kim Kwan-suk (Kim Kwansŏk), Rev. Cho Seung-hyuk (Cho Seunghyŏk), and Rev. Pak Hyung-Kyu. They were charged with misappropriating/embezzling funds from the German church. A German-based organization, Bread for the World, had a made a grant to the Korean National Council of Churches. Bread for the World told the Korean court in writing and through a representative sent to monitor the trial that its grant had been used as intended by the KNCC. Nevertheless, the church leaders were found guilty and sentenced to prison.

At that same Monday Night Group meeting, we also reminded each other that the Supreme Court's decisions on the "PRP" and other cases were due the next day. We decided that as many of us as possible should try to show up at the courthouse. It seemed unlikely that the court would uphold the PRP death sentences, but on the off-chance that it did, we signed a special letter we had written to President Park pleading for clemency for the eight men. At that point, however, none of us really believed the government would dare go that far.

Tuesday morning, quite a few of us gathered at the courthouse. At the beginning of the trial I was busy outside, helping the BBC crew, when word came out that all sentences except those of two Yonsei University students had been upheld. I grabbed the arm of Vanya Kewley, the BBC producer, and together we managed to talk our way past the guards and into the building. We reached the courtroom on the third floor where we were momentarily stopped by a plainclothesmen. We could hear agonizing sounds of woe and misery emerging from the courtroom. We made our way in and were confronted by a scene that Dante might have conceived. The PRP wives and other women were sprawled across the benches of the courtroom in various stages of shock and hysteria -- screaming, moaning, and wailing. A couple appeared to be in shock. Several missionaries and reporters explained to us that the austere judges took a grand total of five minutes to uphold the death sentences of eight men and lengthy prison terms for thirty others. At one point several of those in attendance had jumped to their feet screaming "fabrication, injustice," but the judges, ignoring them, stiffly left the room. Neither the defendants nor their lawyers had been in the room during the proceedings.

The women spontaneously staged a sit-down demonstration in the courtroom. At Vanya's urging, I left to fetch the BBC camera crew. But by the time I had rounded them up, the doors were barricaded, and we were not allowed back in. We remained outside the courthouse glaring at the police until around 1:00 pm when we got word that everybody inside was being forcibly evicted through a side door. We dashed around to the side of the courthouse but were stopped at the top of a little hill by a contingency of riot police. Down at the bottom of the hill we could see the wives being loaded into a bus. They were not going peacefully. Bus windows were broken and bitter cries of despair and condemnation filled the air. We responded with cries of our own, but could not get close enough to comfort them. The bus finally left, taking the women to some unknown destination. We learned later that they were taken some distance from the courthouse and released. The Monday Night Group members who had managed to be present in the courtroom were carried bodily from the building, dumped outside the back gate, and locked out.

Wednesday morning, I was in my office, trying to dig into an impossible backlog of work when the phone rang. Woo Hung Sun's (U Hungsŏn's) twelve-year-old daughter was on the phone asking hysterically if it was true that her father had been executed. I nearly passed out from the shock but gathered my wits enough to explain that it was probably just a rumor because Korean law did not allow death sentences to be carried out in less than twenty-four hours after final sentencing. I told her I would check and call her back. I dashed over to the Christian Building where I learned that all eight PRP men had indeed been hung early that morning. I found out later that their wives had all been told to come to the prison early that morning to "visit their husbands." They were kept outside the prison gate until they heard by radio that their husbands were all dead.

We called Woo's daughter back from Lee Oo-jung's office and confirmed the report. Nothing in my lifetime had prepared me for making a phone call to a little girl confirming that her innocent father had been killed and she would never be able to see him again. She and I both disintegrated over the telephone.

Around 2:00 that afternoon we got word that the wives were still all at the prison and were being invited inside to identify the bodies of their husbands. A bunch of us jumped into a taxi and hurried to the prison. We found a major contingency of riot police surrounding the front gate, keeping everybody clear across the street, away from the prison entrance. Maryknoll Father Jim Sinnott and I were able to make our way through the contingency of riot police and up to the gate of the prison. Suddenly, I spotted Mrs. Chun, the spunky woman, known to us fondly as "the hat lady" because of her fondness for wearing hats. She was standing across the street hanging onto a light pole and crying hysterically. Her husband was not one of those who received a death sentence; but she had become totally involved in the emotional lives of those who had. I dashed back across the street and we embraced and cried together. She then led me to a second-floor tea room directly across from the prison. Many of the other family members were there, including Lee Soo-byung's (Yi Subyŏng's) wife. After we embraced, she told me that although the other PRP wives had been admitted into the prison, the prison guards had not let her in. I half led, half carried her down the stairs, across the street, through the riot police, and up to the gate guard, where I demanded that she be let in. After lots of words, gestures, and raised voices, she was finally admitted.

Father Sinnott and I, along with Willa Kernen and a couple of missionaries from the Maryknoll Sisters, set up shop in front of the gate. We had become very close to these women during the past year as we joined in their struggle to proclaim the innocence of their husbands. We had cried with them numerous times and even laughed with them during unexpected moments of amusement. During that time we never ceased to hope that the end of their story would be a joyful one. Now they had been brought to a state of ultimate hopelessness and despair.

Eventually the wives began coming out of the prison yard one by one, most of them in near-total states of shock. As they came through the gate, they collapsed into our arms. We comforted them; we cried with them; we propped them up as they vented their anger at the world. We embraced them as they cursed the president, the riot police who sat in their bus taunting them, and in one case cursed even God. We felt totally helpless.

At one point, Father Sinnott forced his way through the gate and stood inside "preaching" to the guards. A plainclothesman arrived and pled with me to talk him into leaving. I refused and they finally carried him out bodily.

~ ❦ ~

The events of that day seem almost frozen in time. As I reflect on them, I often think of them in the context of all the words produced by the established church. I have nothing against such words, and I have produced a substantial quantity of them myself. But suddenly I was in the middle of a situation where the church which I represented had no words. There was nothing we could possibly have said to those women at that time that would have made any sense to them. So we took them in our arms and cried with them. It occurs to me that the church would do well to find itself from time to time in situations like that — when all it can do in the name of Jesus Christ is cry, because injustice has burned a hole in its heart.

As the afternoon wore on, the wives became weaker and weaker. Two of them passed out completely and we had to put them in taxis to be taken to hospitals. One dashed into the street and threw herself in front of oncoming traffic. Under police escort, she was carried by relatives to a nearby inn. At one point we got word that the bodies of Woo Hong-sun (U Hongsŏn) , Lee Soo-byung, and Kim Yong-won (Kim Yongwŏn) had been released but that the others would not be released until 9:00 the next morning

Around 6:30 that evening — after all the women had been accounted for and we had gotten them off to their homes — a group of us (several Korean priests, several women whose husbands had lesser sentences, and I) went off to Woo Hong-sun's house to pray with her and console her. When we arrived we were blocked by several plainclothes police who told us that only family members were allowed in. More yelling, more cursing, more pleading and gestures finally put the police in embarrassed retreat and we entered the house. That's when I finally went to pieces. I had cried a great deal that week, but I just began sobbing uncontrollably. Mrs. Woo and her daughters, along with many relatives and friends, were in the room with the body. She was, of course, almost totally incoherent, but as she went on and on, I was able to pick up the following.

In addition to her overwhelming grief, she felt terribly guilty because she believed that the "confessions" extracted from her by the KCIA several months earlier had contributed to her husband's death. In addition, her husband had been a very handsome man. She was secretly very proud of him and had looked forward to the day when she could show him off to her many newfound friends. She had opened the crude coffin to let her daughters look at him one last time and discovered him gruesomely mutilated from the tortures and the hanging. Again I was in a situation where I could offer only my tears. I did not sleep that night.

For any family needing it, Cardinal Kim had arranged for bodies to be stored in the morgue at St. Mary's Cathedral. He had also offered the use of the Cathedral and the Myong Dong cemetery if needed or desired by any of the families. Apparently, plans were made to bury Woo, Kim, and Lee in family plots. It was then discovered that the St. Mary's morgue was already full of bodies, so plans were set up to take the remaining five bodies to a Catholic church in the northwestern part of Seoul where Father Ham Sei Ung, long active in the human rights struggle, served as priest. A memorial service was to be held there at 3:00 pm Thursday. Plans were also made to examine the bodies at the church for evidence of torture and to photograph them. (The bodies of Woo and Kim were examined early Thursday and photographed.)

That week an enormous crowd assembled for the Thursday Morning Prayer meeting at the Christian Building. BBC filmed the whole thing. Cho Hwa-soon, courageous Methodist Urban Industrial Mission minister, prayed one of her very remarkable prayers. Steve Moon, who along with his older brother Timothy had long been at the forefront of the struggle, preached an unbelievably courageous sermon on the Christian's responsibility in the face of innocent suffering. He said that Christ, who also died innocently, urged us to do three things in the face of innocent suffering: pray, demonstrate, and die. Reporting it that way sounds strange, but he presented the whole thing with brilliant logic combined with enormous charisma. The blood of these eight innocent men, he said, would ultimately bring new life and hope to all Koreans as evil was overcome in their names. Many were weeping as he spoke, and my own eyes were far from dry. The front of the hall was covered with special banners; my favorite was "Away with the Murderous Dictator."

During the prayer meeting, we got word that the five remaining bodies had not yet been released, so many of us agreed to go to the prison. I escorted the BBC film crew to the British Embassy for safekeeping, then I went to join the others at the prison. Rumors were flying thick and fast: some bodies had been released, but one had been lost; no, all bodies were released, but were sent to individuals' homes and the homes were barricaded so that no outsiders could enter. Finally, word was handed down that all of the bodies were being released and sent to Father Ham's church. We all piled in taxis and took off. Five of us were stuffed into my taxi and when we got to the church we were told that none of the bodies had arrived, but that one had been stopped by the police back up the road. The five of us hailed another taxi for a dash back in the direction we had come.

Some two miles back from the church we found the prison hearse was turned around and pointed back toward town. In it were the body of Song Sang-jin (Song Sangjin), his wife, and several family members. Some motorcycle police were parked a little way up the road, and a small group of people were gathered around. We learned later that the motorcycle police had been escorting the body to the church when they got orders to turn around and take it to the crematorium to be burned instead. The family had refused to let it go to the crematorium; a struggle was starting just as we arrived,

Gradually, more persons from the Thursday Morning Prayer group as well as Monday Night Group friends arrived. At the same time more police arrived. We argued, we cajoled, we threatened, but the police would not let us take the body to the church. Neither would we let them take it to the crematorium.

More than Witnesses

Finally, two busloads of riot police arrived — big, ugly guys for the most part — with their padded clothing, masks, helmets, and made-in-USA tear gas grenades (Father Sinnott referred to them as the "Darth Vaders"). More arguing, more pleading, more crying – then the order was given for the riot police to advance.

Several priests and missionaries locked elbows and surrounded a cluster of women in front of the hearse. A similar group was behind it. I watched in horror as the door of the hearse was jerked open and Song Sang-jin's wife was dragged kicking and screaming out onto the pavement. She threw herself on the ground in front of the hearse where she was joined by her teenage daughter. Our cluster of people was finally broken up (pushed, shoved, wrestled, prodded with clubs). I was bodily thrown back some distance but got back through the riot police to try to protect the mother and daughter. The mother held onto the hearse bumper with her hand while a burly policeman kicked her arm with his combat boots. I foolishly grabbed his foot and up-ended him before being driven back again. As I was being tossed back, I saw a policeman pick up a woman missionary and fling her so hard she crashed into another woman and both tumbled into the gutter. A bit more adrenalin flowed, so I grabbed the policeman from behind, gave an enormous swing and very nearly succeeded in tumbling him. He jumped at me with his club but backed off when I folded my arms and stared him down.

I must pause here and make two points. One is obvious. I was not being brave. Had I thought about it, I would have been terrified. But I was angry and anger, though sometimes unavoidable, is never characterized by wisdom. The riot police could have beaten or even killed me had they desired. Their lives and their training were all focused on beating up people on the street. It was likely that only their bemusement at confronting so many foreigners kept them from inflicting serious damage on us.

Things They Never Taught Us Down on the Farm

The second is that by nature and principle, I am a pacifist. That day, however, I learned that I am not a very good one. As any good pacifist would point out, our violence that day accomplished nothing. I am still, by nature and principle, a pacifist. But should I be thrust into that kind of situation again, I assume I would behave just as foolishly as I did that day.

These are all just fleeting glimpses of an incredible scene which, by that time, was swirling around the whole, wide intersection while a growing crowd of onlookers cheered us on. At length we were pried away from the hearse. An enterprising priest had managed to snatch the keys and stuff chewing gum in the keyhole. A wrecker had been called, however, and it quickly hooked onto the hearse and pulled it away from the scene and back to the prison where the body was cremated.

After the hearse left, the battle gradually died down. An Irish priest was kicked quite intentionally in the stomach, but there seemed to be no other deliberate attempts to injure anyone. With their mission accomplished, the riot police retreated across the street, climbed aboard their buses and prepared to leave. Most of us were bleeding from superficial wounds. Three of my fingers had been ground into the pavement while trying to protect the women. Our clothing was torn and we were all dazed, embittered, angry, and sad.

Much needed comic relief was provided when a woman emerged from the large crowd of onlookers just as the first bus load of riot police was departing. She carried an enormous hunk of concrete and, with some difficulty, lugged it up to the side of the bus where she let fly with all her might. There was a great crash, creating a marvelous dent in the side of the bus. The driver slammed on the brakes, throwing many of the riot police to the floor of the bus.

Three or four riot police standing outside the bus grabbed the lady's arms and waved the bus on. She spoke very quietly to the men holding her. I don't know what she said to them, but they released her. She calmly walked over, picked up the concrete again and let fly, once more producing another enormous dent. This time the police did nothing to stop her. I found out later that the brave woman was the mother of Chun Tae-Il (Chŏn T'aeil) who in 1970 died by self-immolation in front of the Peace Market in downtown Seoul to protest the terrible working conditions in that sweatshop textile market district.

Following the fray, we gathered ourselves up, marched back to the church for a memorial service minus the bodies, then slowly made our ways home. Friday night I learned that Steve Moon and Father Ham had been arrested. Saturday morning I learned that Kim Sang-keun (Kim Sang Gŭn) and Lee Hai-dong (Yi Haedong), the two pastors who had led Thursday Morning Prayer Meetings, had been arrested; both of them would spend time in prison.

Some questions still haunt us. Why were the bodies not released? The enforced cremations did not make much sense. We have since heard and/or speculated that the bodies could not be released because to do so would reveal to the public that they had been hideously mutilated by torture. We may never know if this is true, but there seems to be no other sane reason why three out of eight were released but the other five were forcibly cremated.

These many years later, it's important to know that the eight men have been exonerated. They were retried in 2005 by the then democratic government and found to be innocent of all charges. Their families have been awarded a large financial compensation. This action goes a long way toward righting a major injustice of the past. It may even bring a certain comfort to the wives and family members of the men. It will not, however, bring them back to life. Their executions on false charge will continue to haunt their families and friends. The eight hangings stand as a stark symbol of Korea's long struggle for democracy.

Things They Never Taught Us Down on the Farm

⥈ ⥈⥈ ⥆

The Korean men who suffered arrest, torture, rigged trials, and harsh imprisonment under the Park Chung Hee and Chun Doo Hwan regimes inspired us all by their courage and faithfulness. We marveled at the calm dignity that seemed to sustain them through indescribable hardship and suffering. Time and again they emerged from their prison experiences with stories so inspiring they moved us to tears.

But at least equally inspiring were the incredible women who confronted the government on behalf of the imprisoned men. This remarkable collection of wives, mothers, sisters, and friends organized prayer vigils, marched in the streets, attended trials, and issued statements of protest. With little more than their wits and their resolute courage, they not only confronted the unjust government but also played a major part in helping the outside world understand what was happening. Their creativity knew no bounds. I played a minor role in one such latter undertaking which seems far more humorous now than it did at the time.

On March 1, 1976, the anniversary of Korea's Declaration of Independence from Japan in 1919, eighteen prominent Christian leaders signed a statement calling for the restoration of democracy. The statement was read aloud during a special Mass at the Myong Dong Cathedral in central Seoul. The 18 were promptly arrested and sentenced to varying prison terms in an obviously pre-determined "trial." The wives of some of the 18, upset by the fact that the trial was not open to the public, boycotted the trial. One of the things they did, in addition to demonstrating each week during the trial sessions, was to crochet purple "victory shawls." (See Faye Moon's Chapter).

The shawls were rich in symbolism: purple, the color of Korea's national flower and the Christian color of suffering and victory; the V-shape of the shawls for victory; the 10,000 top stitches in each shawl calling for ten thousand voices of support. As production of the handmade shawls grew, some were sent to friends as gifts to thank them for their support, while some were sold to raise funds to support the movement for democracy.

When I mentioned that I would be traveling to New York to attend some consultations, they asked if I would mind carrying "a few" of the shawls and deliver them for sale to friends in New York. Mindful of all the surveillance focused on my activity, I was hesitant, but the women were hard to turn down. As I reflected on all they had been through, I decided that any minimal risk to me was unimportant. I would just scatter them among the clothing in my suitcase and hope they would be overlooked.

On the day of my departure, I had not yet received the shawls. I assumed the women had forgotten. But shortly before leaving my house I received a phone call informing me that the shawls would be delivered to me at the airport. There went the idea of discretely hiding them in my suitcase! I still wasn't alarmed, however – until I arrived at the airport and was met by a young lady struggling with two enormous bundles that she was pushing across the floor of the airport. She turned them over to me and, with a gracious bow and words of thank, she departed. Each bundle was wrapped in brown paper and firmly tied with heavy twine. And each bundle reached from the floor to my chest. Each weighed between 40 and 50 pounds. The only way they could be carried was to hold them out at shoulder length. Discretion, thy name is folly!

I struggled through the lengthy line to the check-in counter. When I was asked if I had any baggage to check, I gestured vaguely at the two bundles sitting beside my battered little suitcase. The cheerful checker of baggage patiently weighed the whole lot and informed me that although I was really only allowed to check in two pieces, she would make a special concession and allow me to check in all three. However, I would have to take them all to a special customs agent for inspection. I was impressed by my own calm demeanor as I carried/pushed/pulled the bundles and suitcase to the customs agent's counter.

The agent and I chatted as he opened my suitcase and rummaged through, finding nothing of interest. He then asked what was in the bundles. "TEXTILES!" I almost shouted. The agent then asked if they were samples I was taking for potential sale in America. "YES" I barked. "SAMPLES." He then asked if he could see them. With trembling hands I finally managed to undo one of the knots in the twine and peel back a corner of the paper wrapping. The brilliant purple of the shawls seemed to fill the whole airport and I was certain I could hear the words "*Min-ju hoe-bok*" being shouted out loud. Mr. Customs Agent came around from behind his counter and reached down to feel the topmost shawl. "Those are beautiful," he said. "They should sell well in America."

The rest of the trip is pretty much a blur. The 18-hour flight from Seoul to New York (with a six hour stopover in Anchorage) seemed interminable. In Anchorage, I dragged the bundles through U.S. Customs. Fortunately, that part was not too bad. But when I arrived in New York at LaGuardia Airport, I was faced with an impossibly long line of people waiting for taxi rides into Manhattan. Finally I opted for loading everything into a bus that took me within a couple of miles of my hotel.

Where I got off the bus, people there too were clamoring for taxis – but this time they were not standing patiently in line. Standing at that curbside, I quickly learned that New Yorkers are neither very patient nor very considerate. Surely if they had only known that I bore Korea's democratic future in my two bulky bundles they would have stood aside. I was at a great handicap because each time a taxi pulled up to disgorge passengers, I had to carry/push/pull my bundles and battered suitcase to that vacated spot — and long before I had made it there, somebody not nearly so encumbered had jumped in the taxi and sped away. Finally, discarding all patience and any semblance of good manners, I caught a taxi by using the bundles as a battering ram.

When I finally tumbled into bed that night after over-tipping the bellhop for getting the two bundles and suitcase up to my room, it was well past midnight. I had been awake for nearly thirty hours, my arms and shoulders ached from trying to carry the bundles in my outstretched arms, and I was totally exhausted.

Jet lag brought me wide awake at 2:00 am. I tossed and turned for an hour, then gave up and read a book until our mission board offices opened at 8:00 am. I then realized my journey was not over. The trip from the hotel next to Lincoln Center to the mission offices in upper Manhattan was best accomplished by subway. However, this required a short hike on the front end and a hike of several blocks on the other end, plus all the travel through the turnstiles and up and down the dirty subway stairs. Buses were another possibility, but they were packed at rush hour. I finally settled on a taxi that stopped willingly but seemed on the verge of taking off when he saw my two bundles. Reluctantly he watched as I carried/pushed/pulled the bundles into the trunk of his car.

We chatted on the drive to the Upper West Side of Manhattan, and by the time he let me out we were more or less friends. I carried/pushed/pulled the two bundles into the portals of the nineteen-story building at 475 Riverside Drive, past the receptionist, onto the crowded elevator and up to the 15th floor mission offices. There, excited staff took them off my hands. We were all overjoyed – they, to get such a bountiful supply of the treasured shawls; I to have completed my task successfully, and to finally be shed of the heavy bundles.

Things They Never Taught Us Down on the Farm

From there the beautiful shawls were distributed for sale in Christian communities throughout North America. They generated income for the movement but, more importantly, they helped to enlighten many people about Korea's struggles and the brave, creative women to whom the shawls represented still another method of outwitting the government and all of its forces. One New York mission board staff member who was busily unwrapping and stacking up the shawls paused, turned to me, and said, "It must be really rewarding to take part in such a significant project." I thought a moment, remembering the terror of being discovered at Kimpo Airport, the nearly impossible task of herding the bundles through various forms of transportation, and now the heavy ache that seemed to have taken up permanent residence in my arms and shoulders, and found myself saying, somewhat to my surprise, "Yes. It really is."

Time has an interesting way of resolving things. Over the years, both the KCIA agent and the national policeman assigned to me became my friends. About a year before I retired from mission work in Korea in 1997, I bumped into a man on a Seoul street. We both recognized each other, but weren't sure where we had met. As we talked I learned that he was the immigration official who had interrogated me after the demonstration in front of the U.S. Embassy. He said he always appreciated how I had enlivened the interrogation with humor and had not used the occasion to attack him personally. He was now head of security for the Immigration Office and suggested that I contact him if I needed help with anything. Later when I needed help to obtain a visa and residence status for one of our missionaries, he helped expedite the process.

We occasionally met for lunch and one such time he informed me that he had destroyed the large file which the Immigration Office had compiled on me over the years. He held his hands apart to show how thick the file had become. Although he never said so directly, I gained the clear impression that he was somehow grateful for the little band of foreigners who stood up to the dictatorial governments of the past. Shortly before I left Korea he informed me that he had arranged permanent residency for me in Korea. No longer would I have to trek to the Immigration Office regularly to renew my Residence Permit. Regrettably, I was scheduled to leave Korea in a week and was unable to take advantage of this generous offer.

These experiences have shaped my life. When I retired from missionary service in 1997, I had been related to Korea's challenges, struggles, and trials for forty-one years. During that time, I had laughed joyfully because my Korean friends found unflagging humor even in dark times. And I had wept bitter tears because the Koreans had also shared with me their deep sorrows. I still cry at times when sudden memories of their courage and sacrifice overcome me.

Praise be to God.

Chapter 6

One Community Across All Boundaries

Marion Kim

I had never set foot in south Korea before leaving my American home to move there in 1969. My Korean husband, Kim Yong-Bock, had told me moving stories about Korean Christians' involvement in the March 1, 1919, Independence Movement against Japan. He had also told me about Christian students' major role in the overthrow of the corrupt government of President Syngman Rhee in 1960, and the role of Christian ecumenical leaders and churches in the Korean democratization movement.

When I arrived in Seoul, my introduction to things Korean became much more practical. I got to know my mother-in-law and the rest of Yong-Bock's extended family – and I learned all over again how to shop, cook, and eat. I occasionally took the wrong bus and got lost. While I enjoyed the many surprises of life in a new and unfamiliar culture, I diligently studied the Korean language in hopes of repairing my self-image, which had been severely eroded by my sudden inability to communicate with the people around me. And I began attending meetings of the "Committee of Fifty," the predecessor to the Monday Night Group.

The committee's name referred to the impressive number of missionaries and other overseas residents of Korea who paid a group visit one day to Ambassador William Porter at the U.S. Embassy in Seoul. Through a barrage of polite but critical questions, we asked him to convey our strong request that the U.S. government stop assisting the Park Chung Hee dictatorship in its suppression of Korean citizens. For example, we asked that the U.S. stop supplying armored trucks and other crowd-control equipment to the Korean government. Ambassador Porter responded, "Korea is a cup of pink tea compared to a lot of places." Margaret White, an American professor at a Korean university, challenged the ambassador: "My students are being denied their fundamental right of free speech. Are you saying I should go back and tell them, 'Just relax, this country is a cup of pink tea'?"

The embassy meeting – though lacking in positive results – was an inspiring demonstration to us of the group's potential to organize and mobilize foreigners living and working in Korea. The group continued to meet regularly to discuss U.S. foreign policy, especially ways in which the U.S. might actually support the Korean people.

I joined some of the Committee of Fifty members a few months later on the occasion of a visit to Seoul by a U.S. congressional delegation. Some of the American members of the group went to Walker Hill Hotel to try to meet the congressmen. After a considerable wait, we finally saw them and their wives arriving back from dinner. We set about trying to engage them in dialogue about U.S. foreign policy, with poor results. My Ohio representative, slightly drunk, cursed at me and slammed the door of his hotel room in my face. We were fortunate to meet the wives of Birch Bayh and Walter Mondale. Both women looked very pretty with their hair newly done (Korean hairdressers were world-famous even in those days). The wives were friendly and kind, and they invited us to sit with them. They listened to our comments on the Korean situation and our calls for a U.S. foreign policy that would promote respect for human rights and democratic development. When Senators Bayh and Mondale arrived on the scene, the wives had them sit down and talk with us for a while. Both senators listened attentively and promised to follow up on the issues we'd raised. But we never heard whether they kept their promise.

꿈 ❦❦ 꿈

Yong-Bock and I returned to the U.S. in 1970, then went to Japan where we lived for four years (1973-76). In Tokyo we served as part of the international communications and support network for the Korean democratic movement, led by the Christian ecumenical network in Korea. We had a small but dynamic Korean community in Tokyo that included the families of Oh Jae-Shik (O Chaesik), Kang Moon-Kyu (Kang Mun'gyu), and Chi Myung-Kwan (Chi Myŏnggwan), recently revealed as the author of the famous, serialized *Letters from T.K.*.

While in Tokyo we enjoyed a visit by Linda Jones, who also dropped by Yong-Bock's office, Documentation for Action Groups in Asia. DAGA was sending and receiving materials to and from Korea. It was one of several key contact points in Japan for getting and distributing information about south Korea. My main work in Japan was teaching English to middle school, high school, and college students, but I also edited many materials for Yong-Bock, including the 1973 "Theological Declaration of Korean Christians."

More than Witnesses

By the time our family – now numbering four – moved back to Korea, it was January 1978. Thanks to the kindness of my mother-in-law, I was able to take a job with the Korean Christian democratic movement, entrusting our two small sons – and the bulk of the housework – to her care. To this day I am grateful to her, beyond my capacity to repay. It was hard being away from our children when they were so small, but I made the most of our time together in the evenings and on weekends.

I started work that year with the National Council of Churches in Korea. I had met the general secretary of the NCCK, Rev. Kim Kwan-Suk (Kim Kwansŏk), in Japan once and was invited then to help him with English-language documentation. I still consider it one of the greatest privileges of my life to have worked with this tall, gentle man who, despite his calm and kind countenance, was forthright in speech and firm in his convictions. When he said something, you knew it was from his heart, and you knew you could put your full trust in him. I will say more later about Rev. Kim and the crucial role he played in organizing and energizing a broad base of Christians to advance the causes of democracy and human rights.

My work was to help NCCK translate the many statements and declarations coming out of the movement for democracy and human rights, preparing them to be sent to a growing network of concerned individuals and church and other groups abroad. I also translated reports of multifarious human rights violations, documenting in English not only the detentions, torture, and house arrests, but also the prosecution and imprisonment of students, laborers, clergy and others who dared to speak, write, organize, or demonstrate against the Park dictatorship.

At NCCK I met a lot of brave fighters for democracy including

Kim Hallim, mother of student activist Kim Yun and Lee So-Sun (Yi Sosŏn), mother of Chun Tae-Il, who committed self-immolation in protest of inhuman labor conditions. They and others would stop by our office, often bringing statements or information about important incidents. We translated these and other materials from the movement – especially from the NCCK Human Rights Commission – for delivery internationally.

⁌ ⁙ ⁌

I had heard many reports about the work of the missionaries in the Monday Night Group, and I had met Louise (Morris) and Butch Durst on earlier trips to Seoul from Tokyo. When I started coming to the MNG meetings in 1978 I found a warm, friendly group of Christian missionaries who cared deeply for the Korean people and church. They cared enough to risk their own status and safety to help Koreans who were suffering under the oppressive political situation. These missionaries didn't live like typical foreigners – or even typical missionaries – in Korea; that is, they did not reside in separate compounds isolated from Koreans, and they enjoyed no special privileges. They shared their time, resources, and love with their Korean neighbors.

Jean and Bill Basinger, Sue and Randy Rice, Willa Kernen, Faye Moon, Marion Pope, Marion Current, Gene Matthews, and Ian Robb were the MNG members I remember meeting with most often. John Somerville sometimes came from Taejon, and there were frequent visitors, including large church groups needing basic orientation on the Korean situation, something which the MNG supplied generously. In those days, the group met in the missionaries' homes. Typically, we opened with a brief reading or reflection and prayer, then shared personal stories and information we'd collected on the disturbing or promising events of the past week. Sometimes there were tasty home-baked cookies. Always there was an abundance of jokes and stories lampooning the main actors in the theater-of-the-absurd that Korea had become under the military dictatorship.

Then, and even now in retrospect, the Monday Night Group meetings were very important for me. First of all, we depended on each other for accurate information about the political and social reality in which we lived and worked. The heavy censorship and prohibitions on freedom of speech, press, and assembly blocked the regular news function and rendered it untrustworthy. So every tidbit of news at the MNG meetings was precious, and I diligently took notes to be included in my "Chronology of Events in the Korean Democratic Movement," an ongoing production of mine at NCCK. The chronology was photographed and sent to Japan and Germany to be used by overseas supporters of the Korean democratic movement. I continued producing the chronology even after Rev. Kim Kwan-Suk began work at the Christian Broadcasting System-Korea in early 1980; I accompanied him in that move.

The Monday Night Group was precious for another reason. Because I lived and worked in a Korean-language setting, and felt deaf and mute so much of the time, the MNG meetings were an opportunity to re-open my English ears and verbalize my accumulated thoughts. The MNG was my only non-Korean community in Korea, due to my choice of a "Koreans-only" lifestyle – adopted in the vain hope of assimilating myself into Korea as quickly as possible. The language of the MNG was extraordinary English: inspiring words and stories of suffering and courage made me look forward to the meetings all the more. I would leave the meetings refreshed by this opportunity to become my real self again, having communicated in my own language.

The Monday Night Group also functioned as a warm community of mutual encouragement and support for all its members. This solidarity extended through our individual lives and into our work in support of Korean Christians, students, workers, and others involved in the risky endeavor of democratization. This support was a major source of strength for all of us.

One key MNG partner was the National Council of Churches in Korea, and I served as a link between the two. The NCCK collected and prepared many materials to inform the overseas churches about what was happening in Korea. The MNG members were trusted links in the process, risking their status in Korea to arrange for materials to be distributed world-wide – materials deemed "illegal" under harsh Emergency Decrees that banned all expression of the realities of struggle in south Korea.

One of the most important contributions to the struggle – kept secret until recently – was made by Monday Night Group member Marion Pope. Just after Yong-Bock and I returned from Japan in February 1978, Rev. Kim Kwan-Suk asked my husband to write a secret report on the human rights situation in Korea. Yong-Bock had just set up the Christian Institute for Study, and Rev. Kim Kwan-Suk was the chair of its board. Yong-Bock asked Marion Pope for help, and she went to the NCCK Human Rights Commission and gathered many materials. Meanwhile, Yong-Bock collected more materials from other sources, and the two of them collaborated in the production. Marion edited the final report. It was photographed, and the film was taken out of Korea by Victor Hsu of the World Council of Churches (WCC). The investigator at the airport glanced at the rolls of film but did not inspect them.

The WCC published the report, as did others including the National Council of Churches of Christ in the U.S.A. More importantly, it was published in the U.S. Congressional Record as part of the official report of the Hearing on Human Rights in Korea held by Rep. Donald Fraser's Committee on Asia-Pacific Affairs.

And most important, U.S. Secretary of State Cyrus Vance brought a copy of this same "Report on Human Rights in Korea" to present to President Park Chung Hee during President Jimmy Carter's visit to Korea in late June 1979. President Carter referred to it in his public speech at a state dinner in the Blue House, criticizing Park Chung Hee on human rights issues. Government agents interrogated Rev. Kim Kwan-Suk regarding the origin of that report, but of course he didn't give them a clue.

❧ ❧❧ ❧

Members of the Monday Night Group helped my husband greatly during the two-month period beginning May 19, 1980, when he was in hiding from the new military group led by Chun Doo Hwan. Yong-Bock had already been beaten nearly to death by Chun's Counter-Intelligence Command, and interrogated by the Special Investigation Unit of the National Police, for allegedly being a major organizer of the "fake wedding" incident. The incident took place November 26, 1979, under martial law following the assassination of Park Chung Hee. (The "fake wedding" is described in more detail later in this chapter).

Yong-Bock had been cleared of the original charge by summary trial, after spending 25 days in prison, but news of the Kwangju massacre in May 1980 meant that democracy movement leaders were in renewed danger of arrest or worse – so he made himself scarce for a while. He stayed with a relative, then with a friend, and then – because he had to keep moving around to avoid detection – we asked Monday Nighters Randy and Sue Rice for help, and they kindly offered him a room in their home.

Yong-Bock stayed there until we got word that the police had been listening in on our phone conversations and likely knew where he was; Randy helped him leave quickly to avoid capture. Yong-Bock stayed next with a Korean friend before being invited for an extended stay by a German diplomat. Our German missionary friend, Dorothea Schweizer, had introduced us to the diplomat, who was working as a labor trainer for the Korean government. I visited Yong-Bock at the diplomat's home on weekends, taking a bag of clean clothes and bringing his laundry home to wash.

The MNG members supported each other's activities, cooperated in raising emergency funds for families of prisoners, and provided refuge for many persons wanted by the police or Korean CIA. Their "Fact Sheets," reporting and analyzing the Korean situation, kept people overseas informed. Personally, I was blessed in having Willa Kernen as a kind "elder sister" and spiritual supporter during the years we both worked in the Christian Building. Willa was always helping someone – usually several persons at a time – through communications, translating, editing, and providing shelter or financial support. I was not in Korea in the mid-1970s, but I was told that Willa was a great help to Rev. Kim Kwan-Suk at that time, preparing and transporting documents.

My closest MNG mate in terms of shared culture was Faye Moon, like me a U.S. citizen married to a Korean pastor and raising bi-cultural children with an emphasis on Korean identity. Faye used her APO access to help the NCCK mail out sensitive materials; this was a particularly valuable contribution to the work of the Korean Christian ecumenical movement.

꿍 꿍 꿍 꿍

Life in the closing days of the Park regime and the early days following the Chun Doo Hwan military takeover was constrained by the need to be on constant alert against surveillance. Plainclothes agents tailed people, eavesdropping on their conversations, and visiting their offices to ask questions. We whispered any critical

231

comments we might want to share as we walked along the street, and when inside, we turned on the radio to confuse whatever hidden "bugs" might be present to catch our comments.

The heavy "national security" atmosphere made me nervous, especially whenever I was carrying critical documents in my bag. I feared being stopped and having my bag checked – a common occurrence for young Koreans. The Christian Building, where I worked, was often surrounded by rows of riot police, blocking entrance and exit to anyone they suspected might be trying to contact "impure elements" or conduct "impure activities." During the transition period between the military regimes of Park and Chun, and for a long time after the Kwangju massacre, huge tanks were positioned directly in front of the Christian Building, and armed soldiers stood at the top of the stairs at the entrance to the Christian Broadcasting System.

The "fake wedding" incident at the Seoul YWCA on November 26, 1979, will always remain a stark memory. It took place one month after the assassination of President Park Chung Hee. Under the repressive martial law, all gatherings had been banned except for religious services, weddings, and funerals. So the Democratic Youth Council decided to hold a "wedding" to get people together and to publicize its message. Only a handful of people knew it wasn't a real wedding. Many democratic figures attended, as the bridegroom was Hong Song-Yop (Hong Songyŏb), a well-known youth leader.

Among the "unaware" participants was my husband. At the time, I had no idea that Yong-Bock had gone to the event; I simply worried because he didn't come home on the night of November 26. The next day my office colleagues informed me there had been many arrests, but said there was "no need to worry, because Dr. Kim doesn't usually take part in such public protests." But as several more nights went by and still there was no word from him, the children and I, and Yong-Bock's mother, grew increasingly uneasy and afraid.

I heard later that the "wedding" had started out typically, with the groom taking his place in front of the gathering. Then the bride's entrance was announced. But no young lady in wedding attire appeared. Instead, respected Quaker leader Hahm Sok-Hon, presiding over the ceremony, read a strong statement demanding an end to martial law. The plan had been carried out so carefully and quietly that even the police had had no inkling of it. When they realized what was happening, they rushed to arrest the participants, and there was a mad scramble. Yong-Bock and others began walking out, not imagining they'd be arrested, since they'd had nothing to do with the plan. But they were grabbed and taken away.

A few days later, writer-activist Lee Chol-Yong (Yi Chŏlyŏng) visited my office with a terrible story: He had been arrested and taken away with others at the "fake wedding," and subjected to unspeakably brutal treatment by the military troops of Gen. Chun Doo Hwan, then head of the south Korean Army's Counter Intelligence Corps (CIC). "They set upon us with 'specialist' teams," Chol-Young said. "First was the karate team, who hacked at us with karate chops. When they finished, a second team came and beat us with wooden clubs. A third team kicked us with their military boots," he said. Chol-Young described people passing out under the torture. They would be left alone until they regained consciousness, then beaten and kicked again. He himself was beaten senseless, and when he opened his eyes he saw a man laying beside him whose face was "swollen to twice its normal size." Chol-Yong paused then said, "I wondered who it was ... and finally it dawned on me... it was Dr. Kim Yong-Bock."

I was shocked into action. First I had to find out where my husband was. His mother and I went to the notorious CIC center at

More than Witnesses

Sobingo-dong (Sŏbinggo-dong) to ask about Yong-Bock and appeal for his release. The guards checked with their superiors and told us no one there had ever heard of him. I wracked my brain for ways to get him freed. I remembered Yong-Bock's comment that the regime was quite sensitive to pressure from abroad. For the sake of safety, with intelligence agents everywhere, I went to a hotel and faxed several friends in international organizations that I thought might be able to help us. At night, his mother and I held each other's hands and cried, but in front of our young children – then ages seven and three – I put on a strong front and said, "Daddy was arrested by the bad guys, but he has many friends all around the world, and they will help him." Aside from my imaginings about the pain Yong-Bock had already suffered, and my fear for his life, my strongest emotion was outrage. Though it was un-Christian of me, I wished I could put General Chun Doo Hwan and his gang through the same suffering they had inflicted on my good, brave husband.

About ten days later, after inquiries here and there, our ecumenical movement friends found that Yong-Bock had been transferred to Mapo Police Station, and that his mother and I were now permitted to visit him. We went out before daybreak the next day, taking a taxi to the police station. Yong-Bock looked awful: unshaven, wearing the same clothes he'd had on since the time of his arrest, and his face mottled in black and blue. We had to talk through a metal grate. He said his whole body was bruised but recovering, though he had some worrisome pains in his chest. He also had an infected foot, another result of the beating-torture.

Following that first brief encounter, his mother and I had two more meetings with him, face to face with no intervening screen. Both times, a police agent sat beside us, took notes on our conversation, and warned in menacing tones of punishment that would befall us if we mentioned the visits to anyone else.

One Community Across All Boundaries

Upon the advice of the NCCK, we requested a summary trial; if approved, it meant Yong-Bock could be released from jail earlier. So about twenty-five days after his arrest, he came home, pending the trial. He didn't want to talk about his ordeal, but he said he had been classified as a member of the "A" group – "ringleaders" of the incident – and had been beaten and tortured at the CIC, then kept in solitary for days in a brightly lighted, all-white cell at the National Police Headquarters (NPH), then interrogated by the Special Investigative Unit of the NPH, before finally being moved to Mapo Police Station.

The summary trial was a farce. The judge, after listening to brief statements from the prosecution and defense, flipped back and forth through a six-inch-thick book of records on Yong-Bock and his activities. The judge appeared to have a dilemma over how to rule in an obvious case of wrongful arrest. At last he declared Yong-Bock guilty of minor wrongdoing in relation to the "fake wedding" incident. Yong-Bock was sentenced to twenty-five days – the length of time he'd already been in prison – thereby letting the government off the hook regarding any compensation for wrongful arrest. Several weeks later, an officer from Mapo Police Station visited our home. He bowed to Yong-Bock again and again, apologizing to him and to our whole family for the authorities' mistake. Fortunately, Yong-Bock suffered no permanent physical damage except for a big scar on his foot.

❧ ❧❧ ❧

The Rev. Kim Kwan-Suk, first as general secretary of the NCCK and then as president of Christian Broadcasting System, played a crucial role in putting the Christian ecumenical movement at the center of south Korea's resistance to the unjust, violent dictatorship.

Rev. Kim was a quiet person, a deep thinker, and a committed Christian. He and others recognized that the NCCK, as a Christian network linked with the world churches, had more leeway to act for democratic reforms than did other organizations in south Korea. The NCCK could not be accused of being "communist" – the regime's usual tactic to silence its critics. During the years of harsh military rule, south Korea's denominational leaders did not always agree on how to respond. NCCK Executive Committee meetings often were difficult, with many different opinions expressed. Rev. Kim always ensured full discussion and hearing of all opinions, and he patiently persuaded the members to work together until they reached consensus.

Rev. Kim's strong consciousness of the rights of the *minjung* (grassroots people – workers, farmers, urban poor) made him their consistent advocate. He introduced social justice issues to the Korean churches, got them concerned about laborers' problems, and obtained their support for the urban poor, particularly through the Seoul Metropolitan Community Organization. Rev. Kim's SMCO connection led to his arrest and imprisonment. Along with Revs. Pak Hyung-Kyu, Kwon Ho-Kyung (Kwŏn Ho'gyŏng), and Cho Seung-Hyuk (Cho Sŭnghyŏk), he was tried on charges of misusing funds granted by Bread for the World. The charges were eventually dropped.

Rev. Kim's concern extended to students who were arrested as a result of their work for social justice, including those who had organized night schools for laborers. Their friends and family members came to NCCK for legal assistance and other help.

With Rev. Kim Kwan-Suk as its leader, NCCK accomplished many things. One of these was the establishment of the NCCK Human Rights Commission (HRC). Rev. Kim drafted the proposal for its creation and, together with Rhee Kyung-Bae (Yi Kyŏngbae), the HRC's first director, got it approved by the NCCK Executive Committee. Rev. Kim got the HRC established as a legally separate entity from NCCK, in order for it to operate independently. His strong leadership was what made NCCK's human rights work possible.

Rev. Kim Kwan-Suk became president of the Christian Broadcasting System-Korea in early 1980, just a few months before the Kwangju people's uprising (see Chapter 15). Piece by piece, as eyewitnesses came to Seoul in late May 1980, we got news about the Korean military's massacre of hundreds of citizens. The more we learned, the deeper our shock became. Under the government's oppressive rule, it was impossible to speak openly about it; the mass media offered not a shred of the truth; and a blanket of fear covered everything.

When I visited my family in Ohio that summer, my tongue was freed and I recall talking about nothing but Kwangju.

Years would pass before the full story of the Kwangju Massacre became known to the general Korean public.

The Christian Broadcasting System was targeted for destruction by the new Chun Doo Hwan military regime. The Chun group closed down the National Assembly, mangled the Constitution, dragged thousands of persons off to "purification camps" from which some never returned, and threw up various other roadblocks to democratic progress. One of the Chun regime's key programs was the merger of mass media. The government closed several television stations and combined others, shut down various print media, and imposed new rules to prevent "wayward journalism." CBS, as a nationwide Christian radio network strongly supported by the churches, could not easily be closed or merged by the government. So CBS was ordered to stop all news broadcasting and advertising. Rev. Kim fought back by organizing a nationwide CBS Supporters Organization. With the assistance of Cho Sung-Ho (Cho Sŏngho) and other key CBS staff, new kinds of cultural programs were created and aired – programs with content that challenged the anti-democratic regime. Eventually CBS's news and advertising functions were restored. CBS's campaign was supported not only by the Korean churches but by many civil society action groups who recognized defense of CBS as an important step toward the recovery of a free speech and press in Korea.

During the 1980's, Rev. Kim Kwan-Suk and the other leaders and members of the Christian ecumenical movement continued to make significant advances in the movement for peace and reunification of the divided Korean peninsula. They also helped pave the way for Korean churches to participate more fully in the process of political development that would, finally, lead to a democratic south Korea in the 1990's.

The Monday Night Group continued to meet throughout the scary, difficult period of Chun Doo Hwan's rule. Then, as the political situation gradually improved through the election of increasingly more democratic presidents, MNG meetings were reduced to one per month. The group's discussions became less intense and more relaxed. Our focus remained on issues of justice and peace.

In recent years, Monday Night Group topics of concern have included environmental issues and the difficulties faced by foreign migrant workers in Korea.

The Monday Night Group has been a home for me in Korea. It has helped me keep my faith in the goodness and power of the human spirit. It has helped me to realize we are one community across all kinds of boundaries. Together we have shared the experience of solidarity with the Korean people, learning from their courageous actions to transform their society. We have also learned from each other's compassionate acts as we tried to practice the two greatest commandments: "Love God and love your neighbor." Those words were the fundamental theological principle of the Korean Christian ecumenical movement. Those commandments also guided us well in the Monday Night Group.

Chapter 7

It Was Impossible to be Uninvolved

Willa Kernen

The church has been central in my life as far back as I can remember. It started with Sunday School in a little village church in Canada. By age ten I was involved in many activities in a large congregation in the city of Saskatoon, Saskatchewan. After high school I worked in business offices and took special commercial courses. Then, believing I should be working where my heart was, I went to Toronto and enrolled in a two-year in-residence course that trained women church workers for unordained ministry.

It was 1951-53 and the Korean War was in full swing. Two of my classmates were Korean. My missions class was taught by Dr. Katharine Hockin, who had been forced out of China. She opened church and world up to us. "The church is one and it is worldwide," she said. "Where you serve the church depends on where you are called and where you are needed." I applied for mission appointment to war-torn Korea. After language study at Yale, I arrived in Korea in September 1954, a little more than a year after the war ended.

Much of my work was in rural evangelism, especially in Iri, Chulla Puk Do (North Chŏlla Province). I visited country churches and started a program of lay training. The Iri Christian Center became a focus of our work, with high school students coming from the surrounding area. I taught English to young people and adults, and occasionally did translation work.

In 1970 I began to work in Seoul at the All Korea Church Women's Association (CWA) of the Presbyterian Church in the Republic of Korea (PROK). I did meeting planning, handled English correspondence, assisted overseas visitors, and helped with CWA Mission Education Institute workshops throughout the country.

When people became active in the struggle for human rights and democracy, many women visited our office. They were wives of people in trouble with the authorities, as well as mothers of students and laborers. We became friends. We were connected with Korea Church Women United (KCWU) in World Day of Prayer activities; we worked with women laborers; and we sought and served Korean survivors of the atomic bomb blasts in Japan who had been shipped back to Korea. I also helped with the Telephone Life Line, begun by Rev. Lee Young Min (Yi Yongmin), and sometimes assisted in the National Council of Churches in Korea (NCCK) office.

Park Jung Hee took over the government by a coup d'état in 1962, beginning years of oppressive rule. His Yushin Constitution in November 1972 increased that oppression. Tanks and soldiers with guns were common sights on the streets. Student demonstrations were regular occurrences – and were roughly and cruelly put down by military riot-squads with clubs and tear gas. There were even occasional uprisings within the military. Because every young man had to serve at least three years in the military, there were many ex-university students in the ranks. News of these uprisings was usually suppressed. But at the office we met the mother of one former student, Lee Kwang Il (Yi Kwangil), a member of the PROK denomination, who had been imprisoned by the military. Lee later studied theology, became a minister, and was one of the first Korean missionaries to Canada. He served in Ontario in the early 1990's.

There were also uprisings among laborers who were tired of unbelievably long workdays and ridiculously low wages. There were strikes among women as well as men workers. Members of Korea Church Women United (KCWU) at times sat in with women laborers, then provided them sustenance when they were fired as a result of the sit-ins.

The Peace Market was not far from the Christian Building. It was a three-story building one block long with an aisle between small, crowded shops on both sides. On the bottom two floors, everything imaginable was sold, including shoes, clothing, fabrics, cheap jewelry, and lotions. The third floor housed sweatshops for making clothing. The conditions in those factories were unbearable: ceilings too low to stand upright; floors terribly crowded with people and machines; grossly inadequate heating or cooling systems; and unbelievably long hours and low pay.

Owners would not listen to complaints or requests for better conditions, and things seemed hopeless. Then one afternoon in November 1970, a young man working in a clothing factory set himself on fire on the street outside the Peace Market. He died in the hospital that night. Chun Tae Il (Chŏn T'aeil), a twenty-two-year old Roman Catholic, was protesting working conditions, seeking change in the only way he thought he could. His final plea to his mother, Lee So Sun (Yi Sŏsun), before he died was, "Mother, please continue my fight!" We came to know and work with her, and she faithfully did her part for the young laborers in the Peace Market. The self-immolation was tragic but also pivotal: it motivated many people with a passion for human rights to think about what they could do to bring about change for Korean workers.

〜 〜〜 〜

Not long after the Yushin Constitution was declared in November 1972, there was an incident in a PROK church in Chunju (Chŏnju), Chulla Puk Do (North Chŏlla Province). The Yushin Constitution made any action or speech in opposition to the government an offense, subject to arrest and imprisonment. Korean CIA agents were expected to keep an eye on anyone who might do such a thing. The Rev. Eun Myung Ki (Ŭn Myŏnggi), minister of Nam Moon (Namun) Church, was one of many church leaders who were being followed and watched. After completing a Wednesday evening service, the minister remained at the church and was arrested by KCIA agents while he knelt in prayer. Apparently he had said something unacceptable at the service.

I had come to know Rev. Eun and his wife when I lived in Iri near Chunju. So I decided to go to Chunju for the court hearing and verdict. But no decision was rendered until Rev. Eun had been in prison for nearly a year.

Rev. Eun later served a church in Kwangju, Chulla Nam Do (South Chulla Province). At the time of the Kwangju massacre in May 1980, he was again deeply suspect for standing with the people against the government. For fear of arrest he went into hiding and stayed in a United Church of Canada (UCC) missionary home for the whole winter of 1980-81. The home was that of the Rev. Walter and Lenore Beecham.

Lenore remembered that experience: "In September 1980, we

received a phone call from Marion Pope, a UCC [United Church of Canada] missionary nurse, to ask if we could give refuge to one of our ministers, whose life was in danger. He had first been hidden in the basement of the home of a church elder, but the family had two children and there was fear that they could be interrogated if they happened to say something to a young friend. Another UCC missionary couple had given sanctuary for two weeks but felt unable to keep him any longer. Fortunately, we had a home with an attic, and at the foot of the stairs to the attic there was a door that could be locked. We welcomed him into our home."

Rev. Eun's life *was* in danger. He had been given a death sentence. For "treason." What was his crime? It seems he had been asked to serve on a liaison committee to try to negotiate between the students who had taken part in demonstrations and the government. His crime was in agreeing to do this rather than just turning the young students over to the police. A one million *won* reward was posted for information leading to his arrest. Even his wife did not know that he was being hid in the Beecham's attic. Our friend, Marion, tried to assure her that he was safe. Eventually he was able to send brief letters to his wife by secret messenger.

By March of 1981, political tensions eased somewhat, and friends felt it was now safe for Rev. Eun to return to his family and congregation. Lenore Beecham wrote, "He was able to resume his faithful ministry, caring for his people and continuing to preach a social justice gospel of truth and love and justice for all."

The Rev. Pak Hyung Kyu (Pak Hyŏnggyu) was minister of Cheil Church (PROK), located not far from the Peace Market in Seoul. The 1973 Easter Sunrise Service on Nam San (South Mountain) was an annual celebration for Christians of all denominations, and it drew huge crowds. With the support of several other friends, including Rev. Kwon Ho Kyung (Kwŏn Hogyŏng), Rev. Pak passed around copies of a Declaration demanding changes in government policies. I learned of the incident after the ministers were arrested. I knew them both personally, and was also acquainted with Mrs. Pak, both as minister's wife and as an active member of the Church Women's Association.

When the trial began in August 1973, a number of missionaries attended. I remember the line-up outside the courthouse as we waited for the prison van to bring the men to trial. As soon as they appeared in their white prison garb, the crowd burst into applause. Rev. Pak, Rev. Kwon, and two other prisoners were all tied up (Korean version of handcuffs) and were untied only while testifying. At that first trial, the general consensus was that Rev. Pak and Rev. Kwon witnessed mightily to their faith and the church. A Korean woman friend said, "God really used them to witness to people that might never hear of Him!"

I got to know Louise Morris, Butch Durst, and Linda Jones – three members of the Monday Night Group – at that trial. I remember the crowd at the end of the trial, forming lines on either side of the road where the prisoners would be returned to the van and taken back to the prison. People applauded as the four men passed along. I can still see Rev. Pak acknowledging the people with a nod of his head and a smile to each and all. I also remember his wife and sons, and his elderly mother's strong voice as she urged him not to give in, to keep up the fight. We had no doubt where he got his strong character.

Cho Jung Ha (Cho Chŏngha) (Mrs. Pak), while completely sympathetic with her husband's stance, appeared totally unprepared for him to be imprisoned. She was very distraught over the whole affair. One of Rev. Pak's priorities upon being released was to prepare her for "the next time." I have no idea how he did that, but I do know that when the next time came, Mrs. Pak was the strong one who helped the others cope.

On the day the verdict was given, people lined up outside, but the courthouse doors were never opened. The men were taken in unseen, and at the end whisked away without anyone seeing them. What the authorities were afraid of was never known. The men were each sentenced to two years in prison, but a couple of days later they were released by a special decree of the President, called "*keum po suk* (kŭmposŏk)," similar to bail, except it came after the sentencing.

⁂

In the fall of 1973 a secret meeting of the signers of the Easter Declaration was to take place in the coffee shop of the YMCA Building. The purpose: to release another statement, this time opposing the Yushin Constitution. A previous meeting had been stopped by the KCIA, but these men were not to be stopped. Word was passed to Walter Beecham (United Church of Canada missionary) to get foreign reporters there and to come himself with a camera. Linda Jones had the reporter contacts and got the word out. Linda had only a Xeroxed copy of the declaration, which she feared would be found and confiscated. Because she knew little Korean and no Chinese characters, Linda put onion-skin paper over that original copy and *traced* the whole statement. Steve and Faye Moon and Lee Oo Jung (Yi Ujŏng) translated it the next night, and the following morning I typed it and made copies to send here and there.

Walter went to the Y coffee shop, where there was a big banner up on the wall with demands for a return to democracy. About 10 men were there, including Kim Chae Choon (Kim Chaejun) and Hahm Suk Hun (Ham Sŏkhŏn), a Quaker elder. One person read

246

the statement, and a couple of others made speeches. At that point a plainclothesman ordered them outside and into an open truck. The men went calmly, after three loud shouts of "*manse*" (hoorah!)

Linda and Walter then went to the Christian Building where Linda gave the news to the Korea Student Christian Federation (KSCF) and Walter to the PROK General Assembly office. When Rev. Kim Kwan Suk, General Secretary of the National Council of Churches in Korea (NCCK), got the news, he immediately went off "to do something about it."

The men were soon released but not until they had spent all day and into the night fighting with the authorities. The KCIA agents wanted them to sign a statement promising no more involvement in any such activities. Of course, the men refused. The authorities then pleaded with them, explaining that they were under orders to release the men. By not signing the men were messing up the plan. The men said they didn't want to be released. The KCIA kept insisting. Guess who won? The men didn't sign, and they were released. They were even given a good lunch and escorted home by car.

Dr. Kim Chae Choon played an important role in convincing PROK ministers that the struggles for democracy and human rights deserved their understanding if not outright support. Apparently, when it had been just Rev. Pak Hyung Kyu speaking out, other ministers were saying he was foolhardy, looking for martyrdom and such. Many clergy had criticized Rev. Pak's public actions. But with Dr. Kim also sticking his neck out, the ministers began to take Rev. Pak and public protest more seriously.

Dr. Kim was considered a long-time leader if not actual founder of the PROK. As a professor at and later president of Hankuk Theological Seminary in Seoul, his teaching was considered too liberal by the Presbyterian Church in Korea (PCK). For example, he taught that the Bible need not be taken absolutely literally, that even the Virgin Birth could be doubted by a Christian. He insisted that the church should be ecumenical, and recommended connection with the World Council of Churches and the Christian Conference of Asia. This was at a time when conservative church leaders in the U.S. contended that the WCC was communist.

Another bone of contention was Dr. Kim's teaching that the church should be involved in social issues. At its General Assembly in the spring of 1953, the PCK declared that persons who held such activist tenets of faith would no longer be welcome in the Presbyterian Church of Korea. This led to a split in the Presbyterian Church. Leaders considered no longer welcome in the PCK called a meeting and formed what became known as the Presbyterian Church in the Republic of Korea (PROK). From the beginning, Dr. Kim was one of the PROK's most recognized leaders.

꿈 꿈꿈 꿈

In 1974 we were confronted by a new case involving men allegedly connected with what authorities called the "People's Revolutionary Party" (see details in chapters by George Ogle and Jim Sinnott). What follows here are some of my personal involvements in and recollections of the PRP case.

Some of the wives of the arrested men living in Seoul began attending the Thursday Prayer Meetings at the Christian building as well as the Sunday afternoon services at Galilee Church. We got to know the "PRP" wives and, when possible, to help them. They also got together regularly on their own to support one another.

One of the wives was known as "the hat lady" because she always wore a hat. She was outspoken, telling anyone who would listen what was going on with the case. Another wife was a dressmaker with a teenage son who suffered from muscular dystrophy. I remember visiting her home, where the son lay on a mat on the floor. I also remember having a dress made by her. Her husband died in the Red Cross Hospital, where he was taken from West Gate Prison. We never knew for sure whether he died as a result of torture or from natural causes.

Mrs. Woo was another of the wives we came to know. She was tall, attractive and well educated. She was eager to introduce her handsome, well-educated husband to her new friends. Unfortunately, he was one of those eventually sentenced to die, so we never had the opportunity to meet him.

At one point we learned that a number of the wives had been taken to KCIA headquarters and forced to confess that their husbands were communists. The more timid the person, the more brutal the approach, and the shorter time it took to get a false confession. Such confessions were used as "proof" at the Supreme Court trials.

One woman held out for four days with no sleep. She finally gave in so she could get home to her children, whose father was under a life sentence. Another woman was afraid to go home after being released, for fear of being taken in again. She had been told that she, too, could be given a death sentence and that her children might die as well, to pay for their father's crime. The women felt that this desperate search for "evidence" proved that the authorities had no proof of their own.

Many political prisoners were not permitted visitors, even of close family members. The PRP men were among those were never permitted a visit. (In fact, their families had not even been informed officially of their arrests; they read it in the newspapers.)

Previously anyone could go to a prison and take money, books or other gifts for a particular prisoner. Then there was a ruling that only family members could do so. Identification cards had to be presented so the authorities could control who visited. This posed a tremendous problem for poor families and those who lived far from the particular prison. PRP families who lived in distant Taegu (South Kyung Sang Province) were a case in point. The men were in Seoul's West Gate prison. Their families, without breadwinners, had difficulty putting food on the table, let alone traveling to Seoul. Families residing in Seoul usually could obtain money to give to their imprisoned relatives.

Conditions in West Gate prison, especially the section where the PRP men were detained, were dreadful. One of the wives, who had talked to a prisoner released from the cell where some of the PRP were being held, said, "They are treated worse than pigs." She repeated several times, "They're treated like animals, not like human beings." She also said they were given nothing but boiled barley to eat. If they wanted even *kimchi* (pickled cabbage), they had to pay for it.

The Monday Night Group met the night before the Supreme Court decisions on the PRP and other cases were due to be handed down. We decided that as many of us as possible should try to show up at the Supreme Court. I went to that so-called "open trial" on April 8, 1975, and I can tell you it was neither open nor a trial. Judges filed in and read the names and the verdicts. It took them less than ten minutes to pass sentence on 37 men, eight of whom were sentenced to death. Those eight were the tragic victims of the government's fabricated "PRP plot."

The wives of the eight men, and the mother of one who was not married, were in various stages of shock, grief, anger and frustration when I finally managed to get into the courtroom. They were screaming and beating the seats with their parasols as they cried out, "It's all a fabrication! The death penalty with no evidence!" Several members of the Monday Night Group and other missionaries stayed in the room with the wives until all of them were dragged or carried out.

The next morning (April 9) at dawn, the death sentences were carried out.

That same day the government formally indicted the General Secretary of the NCCK, Rev. Kim Kwan Suk, on a ridiculous charge of embezzlement. Also indicted were Rev. Kwon Ho Kyung, assistant minister of Seoul Cheil Church, Rev. Pak Hyung Kyu, minister of Cheil Church, and Rev. Cho Seung Hyuk (Cho Sŭnghyŏk), a leader of the Urban Industrial Mission. Even the news media, controlled by the government, had reported that the embezzlement charge resulted at least indirectly from the four ministers' roles in helping the families of prisoners, especially the PRP. The government felt that the NCCK was a stronghold of opposition whose credibility had to be undermined. The timing was such as to undercut the NCCK's and the churches' expected strong protest of the PRP executions.

There was considerable apprehension among us about what would happen at the Thursday Prayer Meeting, two days after the executions. Stephen Moon preached at that service. He pulled no punches. Of course, the place was crawling with detectives and KCIA agents. The liturgist for the service, as well as those who led prayers, put their lives on the line. The authorities wanted to pin "communist" or "communist sympathizer" labels on them.

We had heard that the Taegu PRP wives were at the prison, so a group of us from the Prayer Meeting decided to join them there. We had heard rumors that they were not being allowed to take the bodies of their dead husbands.

When we arrived at the prison, we found no one, so we all left for an outlying Roman Catholic Church where we heard that arrangements had been made for a funeral service. On the way, traveling by bus, we saw a prison hearse surrounded by a crowd of people, many of whom we recognized. We got off the bus and joined them.

We learned that, on the way to the church, with the wife and daughter of the dead man aboard, the driver of the hearse had suddenly received orders to take the body directly to the crematorium. The family was not to be allowed even to have its own funeral service!

Our numbers weren't large, but we decided to protest this ultimate outrage to the limit of our strength. We held the vehicle up for several hours, but finally we were no match for the hundred or so riot police dispatched to remove us from in front of the vehicle.

The government was determined to cremate the body before anyone could examine it.

The wife had been dragged out of the front door of the vehicle. She then threw herself on the ground in front of it, clutching the bumper. The rest of the group held the police off as long as possible, but of course, it was just a matter of time. Eventually, while we were blocking the front of the vehicle, a tow truck was attached to the back of the hearse and dragged it away.

During our standoff with the riot squad there were a few superficial injuries among the protesters. Finally, minus the body, the group went on to the church, walking down the road singing "We Shall Overcome." We held a united Roman Catholic-Protestant funeral service for the murdered men.

Several of the bodies were cremated, but whether or not this was done forcibly against the wishes of the families, we didn't know at that point. The incident on the way to the funeral service caused more suspicion; speculation was rife. Why was it *that* important to get those bodies cremated? Were they so mutilated by torture that they dared not let them be seen? Was that also why they couldn't bring the charged men out to the trial? And, for that matter, was that why they had to execute them? Not once in all those months had any of the PRP men been seen by their families.

The next afternoon, the priests and ministers most involved in the Thursday Prayer Meeting were taken to KCIA headquarters. The priests were released the next day; the ministers were allowed to go home late each night and report back the next day. The next Thursday, those in charge of Thursday Prayer Meetings were forced to put out notices that the Prayer Meeting would not be held. Instead, a small, informal service was held in the hall outside the usual auditorium location. Three of the Taegu PRP wives were there in their mourning clothes, having come to Seoul specifically for the strength and comfort of that service, and to urge us to continue fighting for the restoration of democracy, that their husbands' deaths might not be in vain.

There were more agents than worshippers in the Christian Building that day, but we managed to complete a shortened service.

One special memory is of stories Rev. Pak Hyung Kyu told at Galilee Church after his release from prison in 1975 following a trial on charges of "embezzlement."

Rev. Pak became pastor to many of the prisoners he came to know. He told the story of two young men who were arrested in connection with break-ins. They had been living on the street with no way of making a living. They told Rev. Pak how they operated: "You climb up and sit on the wall," said one young man. "Before you jump down into the yard, you say to yourself, 'If I get caught, that's good; if I don't get caught, that's better.'" The reason for this attitude was that, in prison, you at least were out of the bitter cold of winter, even though the prisons weren't heated; and you would have something to eat, even if it wasn't much and tasted terrible.

Rev. Pak taught me, and lots of others, about Jesus' love for the poor and the outcast and the prisoner. Once, addressing a gathering of 3,000 Protestants, Rev. Pak whispered into the mike, "We learned a tremendous secret in prison." Then he shouted, "God is alive!"

～ ～～ ～

In January 1975 President Park announced there would be a February referendum on his rule, after which no more opposition would be allowed. The intent was as clear as it was scary: The president could announce the people's overwhelming support for his heavy-handed rule under the Yushin Constitution, giving himself even more license to crush all who opposed him and his tactics.

Leading up to the vote, the government said there must be no discussion – no speeches, billboards, leaflets, posters, loud speakers, tape recorders – nothing to influence voters for or against the referendum. Yet the streets were full of huge posters with the text of the president's referendum speech, including the need for people to vote as a matter of patriotic duty. When the opposition pointed out these contradictions, the government explained that it was not pressuring voters but simply "enlightening" them. Yet if the opposition leaders had dared to "enlighten" voters about the true meaning of the referendum, they faced arrest and imprisonment for up to five years.

The government claimed that eighty percent of eligible voters came to the polls on February 12, with seventy-three percent voting "affirmative." No one in the opposition believed the figures; but they knew the president could and would use the referendum tally to legitimize further crackdowns on dissent.

～ ～～ ～

All the media promoted the government propaganda concerning the referendum. All except the *Donga-A Ilbo*, one of the country's leading newspapers.

It wasn't the first time the *Dong-A Ilbo* refused to be a mouthpiece for the military dictatorship. And it wouldn't be the last. But by late 1974 the government began striking back, pressuring companies to withdraw their ads from the paper.

On December 26, 1974, the paper was published with blank spaces, and a public appeal was made for persons and groups to fill the ad spaces as a show of support for the *Dong-A* in its fight for freedom of the press.

The response was amazing. Here was a chance for even the "little guy" to have a voice. One day I counted more than 60 tiny ads on each of two pages, besides dozens more a bit larger on those and two other pages. The content of the ads not only supported *Dong-A* in its fight; it also gave hope to Koreans concerned about the future of the country. Many of the ads expressed sorrow, discouragement and frustration. One ad, signed by a university professor, said "I am quietly going mad!" But even these ads were encouraging, because they showed that people recognized what the government was up to.

In the early years of the dictatorship, perhaps only intellectuals would have responded to such an appeal. Now there were seemingly genuine ads from laborers, taxi drivers, small businessmen, and other ordinary people. Many were from local churches, church groups, and larger Christian bodies. These ads often simply quoted a verse of Scripture, perhaps about slavery, or justice. Many advertisers stated they had very little money, but wanted to give what they could to help the newspaper.

～ ～ ～ ～

"Freedom of religion" became more and more theoretical. "Goons" were sent to disrupt worship services at Rev. Pak Hyung Kyu's Cheil Church. An elder of that congregation was hauled in by the KCIA and told not to allow a "certain minister" to teach or preach at his church again.

For these and other reasons, Cheil Church moved its Sunday service into the street, where it worshipped for many months and gained a great deal of publicity in the process. When guests from other countries visited Seoul, many of them asked to be taken to worship at that church in its new outdoor location. The location just happened to be adjacent to the largest Presbyterian Church (PCK) in Korea, a church that tended to be more sympathetic to the government. But to get to Sunday worship now, its congregation had to pass by the Cheil Church's street service.

While the government felt it could not send riot police to chase worshippers out of the street, it did feel emboldened to arrest and torture Christian leaders. For example, the Acting General Secretary of the Korean Student Christian Federation was taken to KCIA headquarters and tortured for over twenty-four hours. Why? One of the KCIA's goals was to force an end to Thursday Prayer Meetings, particularly because of its support for the families of prisoners.

One of the heroes of the struggle was Professor Lee Oo Jung. She was in the center of action during most of the 1970s and beyond. I had the privilege of knowing her from the days when we were students together in Toronto (1951-53), and the honor of working closely with her, especially after I began working in Seoul in 1970.

When student Ms. Lee arrived in Canada in 1951, she was very shy, painfully sensitive about her lack of facility in English, and fearful of committing social errors. Korea was at war. She had suffered many privations, and she thought frequently of her family and friends back home as she lived and studied in the midst of plenty.

Born into a well-to-do family in Seoul on August 1, 1923, she had a traditional upbringing by her autocratic Confucian father and her docile Buddhist mother. Logically she should have become an obedient, conforming, gentle Korean woman. Korea was a harshly ruled colony of Japan until Ms. Lee was twenty-two years old. Her parents protected her from the Japanese military and its kidnapping of young girls to serve as prostitutes for its soldiers. Her parents accomplished this by removing her name from the family register and sending her into hiding with a Christian friend.

Oo Jung began to attend church, became a Christian, and decided to go to seminary. Her father was strongly opposed. During the Korean War, her father, a landlord, and her brothers, a factory owner and a judge, were in great danger. One brother was kidnapped by the communists and never seen again. Oo Jung convinced her parents that they should all leave their home and go stay with relatives in the country. That night, hours after they had left, their house was bombed. Her parents believed that God had saved them – and was protecting them in their long days as refugees.

After attending Hankuk Seminary in Korea, Ms. Lee spent two years in Toronto studying New Testament and Greek. On her return to Korea she joined the seminary staff. In 1974 she became Professor of Ethics and New Testament at Seoul Women's College. Her political consciousness grew during the late 1960's and early 1970's, and she joined other professors in signing petitions and protesting government policies.

In 1973 she was elected the President of Korea Church Women United. An ecumenical church women's organization, KCWU brought together women leaders from the major Protestant denominations. Under Oo Jung's leadership they courageously tackled a variety of social justice issues.

Prostitution tourism was one of the hot issues of the time, as the Park Jung Hee government was encouraging Japanese men to visit Korea to enrich the economy at the expense of Korean young women. Through press conferences, lectures, gatherings of women's groups, and public protest, Professor Lee and the KCWU made public these shameful practices. By 1978 the sex tourism industry had largely shifted away from Seoul to Cheju Island in the south, but KCWU kept up its campaign.

In March 1974 Ms. Lee visited Japan to meet with Church Women United members from the USA and other countries. The meetings broadened and deepened her commitment to justice. For example, she became aware of two concerns of Korean residents in Japan: the discriminatory treatment of Koreans residing in Japan and the sad plight of Korean victims of the atom bombs.

Many Koreans were unaware that more than twenty thousand Korean survivors of Hiroshima and Nagasaki had been quietly repatriated by Japan without compensation or health care. The KCWU began to seek out and meet with these *hibakusha*. They advocated for health care, accompanied them to hospitals, raised funds for their support, made public their situation, and appealed on their behalf to the Korean, Japanese, and American governments.

Oo Jung also helped pressure the Japanese Hitachi Company to hire a man it had publicly refused to hire because he was Korean. Publicity and boycott campaigns by the KCWU were so effective that the KCIA demanded that the women call off their appeal. They didn't, and they won.

As the Park Jung Hee government became more and more repressive, Korea Church Women United was involved in raising money to help support political prisoners and their families. It also backed a campaign to repeal the Yushin Constitution. Ms. Lee came under close surveillance and was frequently harassed by the police. In late April 1974 she was taken to KCIA headquarters and held for a week, accused of giving financial support to activist students. The government alleged that she was part of a communist plot linking south Korean students with north Korea. The fabrication was a typical government ploy to intimidate the democratic opposition.

Professor Lee increasingly invited the wrath of the authorities, in part because of her credibility with and her access to the foreign press. The government hated her for sharing stories of the struggle at international meetings, so they sought ways to quiet her voice.

The government pressured Seoul Women's College to dismiss her from the faculty by February 1976. She was given the choice of keeping her faculty position or resigning as president of Korea Church Women United. "There are plenty of people who would be glad to fill my job as professor," she said. "But there is no one who will take the job of Church Women United and do what needs to be done. Besides, there is no certainty that I will not be fired [from the college] anyway."

Quiet and shy in her youth, Lee Oo Jung had become a courageous, self-assured woman and a bold advocate for human rights and democracy. She once told her KCIA interrogators, "Now I know why I was never married. There's no one to suffer or worry about me. Go ahead! Give me fifteen years in prison!"

❧ ❦ ☙

Of all the issues I have written about, the March 1, 1976, incident was the one in which I was most directly involved.

It began innocently enough on a Sunday afternoon, February 29, at Galilee Church. I invited Elder Lee Oo Jung to join Marion Pope, Marion Current, and me – three United Church of Canada missionaries – for dinner to celebrate Marion Pope's birthday the next day (March 1st). Oo Jung accepted, came, enjoyed the dinner and asked if she might stay overnight. While surprised at the request, we immediately agreed.

She explained the reason for her unexpected request. She had with her a Declaration of Democracy, written by Rev. Moon Ik Hwan

(Timothy Moon) and signed by twelve persons of like mind. She was to read the Declaration at the ecumenical worship at Myung Dong Roman Catholic Cathedral in Seoul the next day.

March First is an annual holiday in Korea, commemorating a 1919 "Declaration of Independence" from imperial Japan. Back in 1919, amazingly, the word was spread secretly across the whole country that, at an agreed hour, crowds would gather in every town and city and shout their declaration of freedom: "*manse*!" (hoorah!).

Many people lost their lives over the incident, and independence was not realized. But Koreans still honor the spirit of the 1919 Declaration and annually recognize the courage and strength behind it.

The 1976 March First Declaration for Democratic National Salvation had to be kept secret until the moment of being read in the worship service. Aware of the KCIA's uncanny ability to obtain information, the signers of the Declaration had decided that the safest way to get the document to the service was for a woman to take it. Even so, there was a danger that someone would learn about it and confiscate the document before it could be read publicly.

Thus, Oo Jung's request to stay with us overnight. Surely the Declaration would not be traced to the home of some foreigners.

The next day, as one further precaution, the Declaration was carried to Myung Dong Cathedral in Marion Pope's purse. The signers of the Declaration included Rev. Moon Ik Hwan (Timothy Moon); Rev. Moon Tong Hwan (Stephen Moon); Rev. Suh Nam Dong (Sŏ Namdong), Yonsei professor; Dr. Ahn Byung Mu (An Pyŏngmu), Hankuk Seminary professor; Elder Lee Oo Jung (all of the above from the PROK Church); lawyer Lee Tae Young (Yi T'aeyŏng) (Methodist); Prof. Lee Moon Young (Yi Munyŏng) (Holiness), Korea University professor; Kim Dae Jung (Roman

Catholic), opposition political leader and later president of south Korea (1998-2003); and Fr. Ham (pronounced Hahm) Se Ung (Ham Sei Ung), who became head of the Korea Democracy Foundation in 2004.

As expected, there were KCIA agents at the service, and everyone knew that all the signers would be arrested. We asked Oo Jung if she would like to come back and stay with us again that night. She declined, saying it might put us in danger.

She phoned us quite late that night. Speaking in careful English (we didn't ordinarily communicate in English), she said, "The police are here, and I have to go with them. They have allowed me to phone you to let you know I won't be able to meet you tomorrow as I promised. I persuaded them that we don't want foreigners to think Koreans aren't dependable."

Because we had no arrangement to meet the next day, we realized this was Oo Jung's way of letting us know she was being taken to KCIA headquarters.

We hung up the phone and, after a few minutes of discussion, decided to telephone Dorothy Wagner, the General Secretary of Church Women United, in New York City. Dorothy knew Oo Jung well, and was knowledgeable about the struggles of the south Korean people for democracy and human rights. Several years earlier Ms. Wagner had led a group of U.S. Church Women United on a trip to six Asian nations, including south Korea. The U.S. women then invited two women from each of those nations to go to Tokyo to take part in a World Day of Prayer service prepared by Japanese women. Lee Oo Jung and Kong Duk Kwi (Kong Tŏkkwi) were invited as south Korea's representatives. Kong Duk Kwi was the wife of former south Korean President, Yun Po Sun (Yun Posŏn), who had served between the Student Revolution of 1960, which ousted President Syngman Rhee, and Park Jung Hee's coup d'état in 1962.

More than Witnesses

During the CWU visit to south Korea, we missionaries became acquainted with Dorothy Wagner, and we knew of her friendship with and high evaluation of Lee Oo Jung. So on that night of March 1, 1976, we called her in New York and told her what had happened at Myung Dong Cathedral, and what was happening at that moment to Oo Jung.

The next morning the KCIA was at a complete loss to understand how in the world the *New York Times* could so quickly report about the arrest of Lee Oo Jung.

The next two weeks were anxious ones, indeed. We soon learned that most if not all those who had signed the Declaration had been taken to KCIA headquarters that night. Ten days later we got word that Oo Jung had been released and was in Severance Hospital. It didn't take long for us to visit her. We were greatly relieved to know she had been released, and eager to learn what had happened to her and to the other detained signers. She told us she had not been tortured, except by being kept awake and interrogated constantly. She had been allowed no sleep for seven of the ten days of detention.

Among the signers of the Declaration, only the women and the elderly were released. The others were all charged and held in custody.

❧ ❧❧ ❧

The wives of the detained signers of the March First Declaration were each given a few tickets for family members to attend the trial. The families gave their tickets away and boycotted the 14 trial sessions, protesting that admission by ticket made this the first non-public trial in Korea's four-thousand-year history.

The wives dreamed up creative ways to support their husbands. For example, they all had mauve-colored Korean dresses made (mauve is the color of suffering and victory) and wore them on days of the trial, adding shawls on occasion. They would walk along together in front of the courthouse, often singing "We Shall Overcome." One day they each carried a parasol, letting it hang from their wrists. When they reached a spot that would attract attention, they would line up and on signal raise and open the parasols, on which they'd written a few words about the case or their protest of it. The next time, instead of parasols, it would be fold-up fans, which they would flip open all together, to display what was written on them.

The women were not young, and walking together along the street, all dressed alike, singing protest songs, followed by police or plainclothes agents – the sight drew a great deal of attention. They chose their exhibition sites carefully. One day it was the low step in front of the gate to the Royal Park, not far from the courthouse. More than once an official vehicle drew up, forced them all inside, drove them to some out-of-the-way place, and dumped them off, leaving them to make their own ways home or to the Christian Building.

The wives continued their prayer meetings and met regularly in the NCCK Human Rights Office in the Christian Building. Joining them were Lee Oo Jung and Dr. Lee Tae Young, the two women signers of the March First Declaration. Together they sought new ways to tell their story to the world. Soon they had an inspiration: Victory Shawls.

What began as a modest but deeply felt project soon grew larger and larger. The shawls were first sold locally, but the word spread, and soon they were being sold all over the world (see related story in Gene Matthews' chapter).

In the United States they were distributed by the North American Coalition for Human Rights in Korea in New York and by the Church Committee on Human Rights in Asia in Chicago for contributions of $15 each. In Canada, the shawls were sold in United

Church of Canada churches by United Church Women. Sometimes Canadian congregations paid for their shawls, then returned them to be re-sold for another $15. Funds raised in the U.S., Canada, and elsewhere were used to support imprisoned Korean men and women who had no families to provide for them.

I'm sure that every one of us involved in the project still proudly possesses a purple shawl. Because I worked in the building in which the women made the shawls, I not only greeted them daily; I also learned the stitch, and crocheted at least one shawl, sitting with the women in their special space.

Mrs. Kim Dae Jung (Lee Hee Ho) was very much a part of the group, and became friends with all of us. When I was leaving Korea, she presented me with a framed piece of calligraphy done by her husband. I hung it in a prominent place in my home with great pride. That pride increased more than two decades later when it became a piece of art created by the president of south Korea.

Each day prior to the trial of the March First Declaration signers, a worship service was held in Cheil Church, attended by the families and any interested friends. I attended these services regularly, and also attended the trial when given a ticket. One of those worship services was unforgettable for me. As usual, there were a number of plainclothes agents sitting at the back of the church. As it was time for the service to begin, Mrs. Lee Hae Dong (Yi Haedong), who was sitting near the front, stood up, turned toward the worshippers, and said, "I would like those men to leave!"

None of the agents moved.

So she turned directly toward them and shouted, "Please leave!"

At that point all the male worshippers quietly stood up and started moving toward the agents.

It Was Impossible to be Uninvolved

The agents quietly stood up and left the sanctuary.

That was the last time they appeared in church for a pre-trial worship service. No doubt, they were just outside the building, but at least they were out of sight.

At Galilee Church the following Sunday, the agent who regularly attended to keep tabs on the worship service was in his usual place toward the back of the church. As worship began, Elder Pak Yong Gil (Mrs. Timothy Moon) got up from her pew, walked back to where the agent was seated, and quietly asked him to leave. When he didn't do so, she reached over, took his hand, leaned back, and pulled on it. As a woman of small stature, she could not force him out. But the agent, recognizing her determination, stood up, went out, and from then on stayed outside the church during each week's service.

The Declaration signers were found guilty of violating the Constitution. They were sentenced to fifteen years in prison but ended up serving less than two years, with the exception of Kim Dae Jung (see below). The two women received five-year suspended sentences with additional three-year suspensions of civil rights.

⌇ ⌇⌇ ⌇

In addition to the women's gatherings in the office in the Christian Building, I regularly attended the Thursday Prayer Meetings and the Sunday afternoon services at Galilee Church. During the sharing time at one Galilee service I remember Faye and Steve Moon's teenage sons speaking about their imprisoned father in the proudest voices you could imagine. Mrs. Pak Young Sook (Pak Yŏngsŏk), wife of Prof. Ahn Byung Mu, told how their pre-teen son expressed pride in his father for taking a stand that landed him in prison. Such testimonies by members of prominent Christian families served to bond them with the families of other prisoners of conscience who attended Galilee Church and the Thursday Prayer Meetings.

Not long into his imprisonment, Rev. Moon Ik Hwan (Timothy Moon) began a hunger strike. He had planned to fast for forty days to follow the biblical example of Jesus' forty days in the wilderness. When his parents, then residing in Canada, heard about the fast, the mother decided to come to visit both sons (Timothy and Steve) in prison, and to bring Timothy a special message from his father. The father, Rev. Moon Chai Rin, an outspoken critic of the south Korean government, felt he couldn't risk going to Korea himself at the time. The message he asked his wife to take to Timothy concerned the purpose of Timothy's fast: was it for God's glory? Or was it to bring honor to himself?

We heard that Moon Ik Hwan had listened seriously to his father's message and realized that perhaps his father was right. He decided to end his fast.

When Timothy's wife, Elder Pak Yong Gil, shared this story, she encouraged each of us to take over her husband's fast, one day at a time, making that day a time for special prayer for the country and especially for human rights.

To this day I have in my Bible a bookmark given me by Elder Pak to commemorate the fast. The bookmark, appropriately, is purple. On the front at the top in her writing in white ink is "Save the Country." Below that on either side of a small gold cross is written "Fasting Prayer." Under that are the words: "Seek ye first the Kingdom of God and His righteousness" (Matt. 6:33). On the back of the bookmark she wrote my Korean name and two dates – 1977. 11. 3 and 1978. 1. 27 – the two days on which I took my turn at fasting and praying.

⁓ ⧉⧉ ⧉

Except for Kim Dae Jung (not released until December 22, 1978), all of the March First Declaration signers, along with other human rights activists, were released from prison under a special amnesty declared on New Year's Day 1978. There was great rejoicing and celebration.

Soon after their release, I remember an incident as worshippers left a Thursday Prayer Meeting. Elder Pak Yong Gil, with husband Timothy by her side, tangled with an agent at the bottom of the stairs. Usually Korean women were quiet and subservient. I can still see the amazement, amusement, and great pride on Rev. Moon's face as he watched his wife, who barely reached his shoulder, stand her ground with the burly agent. We outside the prison walls had observed the changes that were taking place in all those strong, proud, faith-filled women. But their husbands, whose imprisonment had been the impetus for those changes, had not seen it happening, Suddenly they came upon it in its full-blown maturity. You can imagine their surprise!

Lee Oo Jung had worked tirelessly to free the prisoners, get adequate medical care for those who were ill, and join prisoners' wives in their protests. She summed up her involvement in the March First Incident this way: "With all the help I have had from the families and prisoners, and being a defendant, but at the same time one with the families of the others in the same incident, I received a sort of blessing; it could almost be called a joy. Through my involvement, I learned the trust of Christian solidarity and Christian love, both with other Koreans and with Christians around the world. This is no longer just an expression; I came to know it as a fact. I will never forget the closeness of our love for each other in our mutual suffering, and the support we were to each other."

        ❦ ❦ ❦ ❦

There is probably no work I could have done anywhere in the world that would have given me the opportunities I encountered and embraced in Korea. Working in the PROK General Assembly Office during south Korea's struggle for human rights, democratization, and more recently, for the reunification of the nation, I was challenged to grow as a person, as a woman, and as a Christian. As a bonus, I got to know and work with people from the worldwide church.

What a privilege it was to know and journey with the Korean heroes of the human rights struggle. What an honor it was to work with men and women who consciously and faithfully did things that they knew would lead to their arrest and imprisonment. I witnessed their faith and their conviction as they courageously spoke out about human rights and democracy during their trials.

To those who claim that the church should not be involved in politics, I believe I have learned that to say nothing is, in fact, to support the status quo. In other words, it is not possible to be uninvolved.

It was my privilege to work alongside people who were taking great risks. It was an education to be with the wives of the prisoners, and with other brave women like Prof. Elder Lee Oo Jung, as they worked for a better day for their country.

Many of the persons we have written about in this book have suffered for "maligning the government." They have been called "traitors" by that government.

In fact, they were the true patriots.

Because of their courage and sacrifice, south Korea is a functioning democracy. One of the signers of the March First Declaration became its president.

Perhaps the next chapter in Korea's history will be about the reunification of south and north Korea. If it is, much of the credit should go to these same heroes and patriots.

MNG Photos

By the mid-1970s, worship services such as this outdoor one in Seoul included calls for democracy and human rights.

While Faye Moon's husband, Moon Tonghwan, was in prison, their children joined in this appeal for his freedom: Release Our Dad. From left: Faye, Younghae, Changkun, Taegun, Choe Hyosong (family friend), and Youngme Moon.

December 14, 1974. George Ogle is escorted from a police van to a Korean Air Lines 747 at Kimpo Airport during his deportation.

Seoul, 1974. Riot police surround Korean Christians marching for democracy and human rights. The signs urge Bishop Chi's release from prison.

Kim Dae Jung, the future democratically elected president of south Korea (1998-2003), hosts a dinner at his Seoul residence in this undated photo. Seated (from left): Yi Hiho (wife of Kim Dae Jung), Rev. Kim Sangkun, Rev. Yi Sangchol, Kim Dae Jung, Ann Squire and Monday Night Group member Willa Kernen.

April 9, 1975. Wives of alleged People's Revolutionary Party members are overcome with grief outside Seoul's West gate Prison following their husbands' executions. Two Monday Night Group members comfort the widows: the tall man on the left is Gene Matthews; near the prison wall with her back to the camera is Willa Kernen. Photo by Roy Whang.

Photo 7

After worship at Galilee Church, Lee Hee Ho, (lower left, wife of Kim Dae Jung), Lee Oo Jung (front row, second from left and Monday Nighter Sue Rice (second row second from left) pose with wives of political prisoners and their supporters.

Photo 8

Willa Kernen congratulates Choe Yunghi and Chang Myongguk at their wedding. Both the bride and the groom spent time hiding in Monday Night Group member's homes to avoid arrest. The woman on the left is the mother of Kim Yun, another person who hid in MNG homes for many weeks.

Photo 9

June 1974. Pictured at a Monday Night Group retreat held in Suwon south of Seoul are (from left): David Jones, Butch Durst, Louise Morris, George Ogle, Linda Jones, Randy Rice, Sue Rice and Willa Kernen.

Photo 10

April 9, 1975. Maryknoll missionary Jim Sinnott is dragged off by police while protesting the handing of the alleged members of the People's Revolutionary Party at West Gate Prison. Photo by Roy Whang.

Marty Lowery, Maryknoll priest and Monday Night Group member, stands tall during this 1974 demonstration by Christians demanding democracy and human rights.

Photo 12

July 1975. Pro-democracy advocates (from left) Rev. Cho Seung Hyuk, Rev. Pak Hyung Kyu, and Rev. Kim Kwan Suk appear in Seoul District Court on trumped up charges of embezzling church funds.

Photo 13

Rev. Moon Tonghwan (Steve Moon) holds Reed Durst at Reed's Easter Sunday 1978 baptism at Galilee Church. The proud parents are Louise (left) and Butch Durst. Faye Moon is second from right. The sign says Resurrection is the "Fruit of the Cross."

Jim Sinnott (seated) meets with Dong-A Ilbo reporters during their 1975 struggles for freedom of the press. (Photo provided by The Dong-A Struggle Committee for Free Press).

Chapter 8

Missionaries, Cows and Monday Nights

Butch Durst

Even today it's a mystery to me how I ended up in Korea.

During my college years in the early 1960's, a pivotal event changed my life. I had joined ROTC (Reserved Officers Training Corps) – a requirement for graduation in those days. I hadn't thought too seriously about the military, but in 1962, the year of the Cuban Missile Crisis, it became crystal clear to me. President John F. Kennedy demanded that the Soviet Union pull its missiles out of Cuba or face a full nuclear response from the U.S. The deadline was fast approaching and, to me, it meant that civilization as we knew it could literally end. I spent many fearful nights praying that the crisis could be averted. It was then that I decided to work for peace, not war.

More than Witnesses

First I considered joining the Peace Corps, a new program established by President Kennedy. Then my campus minister introduced me to a similar program of the United Methodist Church: the short-term mission program. I learned later that the Peace Corps had been modeled after that Methodist program. Being an active Methodist, I decided to throw my lot in with the church.

When I was accepted as a "short-termer," I had never been west of Colorado, my home state. Seven of us short-termers boarded the U.S.S. President Monroe in San Francisco, a freighter that would take us halfway around the world. Accompanying us and the ship's crew were thirty cows being sent to Korea by the Heifer Project. The Heifer Project, an anti-hunger organization that provides farm animals to people in poor countries, certainly knows how to get the most bang for its buck. All the animals it donates are female and pregnant. The first-born calves are donated to other farmers so that the program perpetuates itself and the wealth is spread. These thirty pregnant cows would soon multiply – two for the price of one – a great boon to the farmers who would receive them.

After ten days on the ocean, we arrived at the southern city of Pusan. I'll never forget waking up that morning and seeing the sun glistening over the rolling hillsides as we pulled into the harbor. We were so excited to be finally arriving in Korea. Off in the distance we could see some people holding up a huge welcome sign. As we got closer, squinting at the sign, we realized that it was *not* for us, but for ... the cows! Then over to the side, we noticed another smaller sign – this one welcoming the new missionaries. It occurred to me that Koreans must be a very pragmatic people. I hoped we would prove as useful to them as the cows.

The first assignment in Korea for us seven short-termers was six months of language school. Along with learning the rudiments of the Korean language, we heard many funny stories of missionary attempts to learn the language. One that I will never forget was told by Kate Cooper, one of the early missionaries, about herself. In those days there were no formal language schools, but Kate was quite determined to learn. She would often go down to the market and listen to the vendors hawking their wares. One day she heard someone shouting, "So yo! So yo!" and noticed that the crowd immediately opened up a wide berth, letting a farmer make his way through the market unimpeded, with his cow following along behind. Here was an easy-to-remember phrase that must mean something like, "move out of the way." The next time five-foot Kate was at the market, she decided to try out her new Korean phrase, "So yo! So yo!" Immediately, everyone broke into gales of laughter. Then she learned what the phrase actually meant: "Here comes the cow!" What was it, I wondered, about missionaries and cows?!

I was assigned to teach English at Paejae Boys High School, and later at the Elementary Demonstration Laboratory School associated with Ewha Women's University. Having majored in education in college, I found teaching to be great fun. Furthermore, I fell completely in love with the Koreans and their beautiful country. After class, I would occasionally go with the students to a nearby coffee shop – a good way both for me to socialize and for the students to practice English. We would discuss silly topics like "how to beat the heat during the summer." Sometimes, though, we would discuss more serious topics, like the future of Korea.

Even though Korea was poor, the industriousness and ingenuity of the Korean people amazed me. By the mid 1960's signs of development were evident. New buildings were going up, roads were being improved, and "luxuries" such as fruit began to appear in the market. For the most part, however, most of the development seemed to be in the industrial sector. This resulted in mass migrations of people from the countryside into the cities to find work – in fact, scrambling to find work – anything to earn a little money. This population explosion was happening in all the major cities of Korea. For example, when I first arrived, the population of Seoul was 3,000,000. When I returned, only six years later, the population had doubled to 6,000,000. Nevertheless, many Koreans had a sense that the country was progressing. I mentioned this to a young man at church one day. He said "Yeah, but in the back of our minds we wonder what is going to happen when this administration has served its full two terms. Are they going to turn over power, or is something else going to happen?" That conversation was in 1966. I pondered what it might mean.

After three years as a short-termer, I returned to the U.S., completed graduate school, married Louise Morris (see her chapter), and returned to Korea in the fall of 1972. Within just a few weeks of our arrival, the Park regime's new "Yushin" Constitution was rammed through the National Assembly. From then on, I think Koreans knew what the intentions of the Park administration were. This change in the Constitution was a dark cloud on the horizon – an ominous sign for the future of democracy. The young man I had talked to at church six years earlier had been worried about such a thing. He – and probably others – had a premonition, even then.

≈ ⊗❧ ℘

I loved teaching, but I also wanted to contribute to Korea in some other way. I kept remembering a conversation I'd had in my earlier term with Maud Jensen, the first woman whose ordination in the Methodist Church was recognized across the entire denomination – and one of Korea's long-term missionaries. Maud sat me down and talked to me about mission work. Her instructions were very clear:

"Teaching English is only your excuse to be here. The real reason you are here is the Gospel."

Urban Industrial Mission (UIM) was an organization that took Jesus' teachings seriously. It was a program run by Korean ministers to help factory workers and slum-dwellers who had migrated from the countryside to the city to find work. One of the basic tenets of Christianity is social justice – fairness for everybody – and it seemed to me that UIM was headed in that direction. It sought to empower some of the poorest people in society. I felt drawn to this work, maybe because my family had been poor; my father worked six days a week at hard physical labor all his life to provide for his family.

The UIM leaders had to struggle to get funding for their ministry. Sometimes they would solicit help from overseas – especially from some of the major church agencies in the U.S. or Europe. Reports to these agencies had to be written in English, and the UIM ministers began asking me to help with the translating. This was a way I could be of service to those who were truly living out the Gospel on the front lines. Now I had found the meaningful work I had hoped for. I was happy to be of some help to these dedicated ministers.

The more translating I did, the more I learned about the UIM ministry and the factory workers' situations. They were often forced to work twelve to fourteen hours – sometimes twenty-four hours around the clock – in order to fulfill an export order. There were no health benefits, just straight hourly wages, but sometimes the young bosses would even renege on that, so there was always some kind of struggle going on.

At first, management gave the UIM ministers full permission to teach the workers about the Bible during their lunchtime at the factory. Management thought this would give the workers some solace and make them more willing to endure their plight. But when the ministers began telling the workers, "God loves you; you are worth something," this was unacceptable to management. Feelings of self-worth in a laborer can lead to demands – for safer working conditions, a just wage, or other troublesome demands. This evangelism was not contributing to a docile (and underpaid) labor force, conditions needed for a "good investment climate." Soon, permission to evangelize at the factory was revoked.

Not to be deterred, the UIM leaders continued meeting with the laborers off-site. What management did not realize was that, in addition to teaching about Christianity, the ministers were also teaching about south Korea's labor laws, which were not being enforced. In this and other ways UIM was helping workers figure out how to improve their situation.

One of the factory areas was Youngdungpo (Yŏngdŭngp'o), the location of many textile mills and assembly plants for toys, small metal goods, computer parts, and electronic parts – eight hundred factories in all. To get to the factories, you had to follow through a maze of narrow alleys and high walls, passing the many one-room dwellings rented by the workers, where six or more shared the expense of the rent, and where they had to eat and sleep in shifts.

I remember the day Rev. Cho Chi Song (Cho Chisong), director of the Youngdungpo UIM, took us to see the living quarters of the young women factory workers. Most of the rooms they rented were about six-feet square with eight-foot ceilings and one lone fluorescent light. On the walls were some shelves where the girls kept their clothes, bedding, toiletries, a pot to cook in, a plate, and eating utensils. It was clean but very sparse. They had to share an outdoor communal bathroom, and they sometimes complained about having to stand in long lines for the bathrooms or to get water, since there were only one or two spigots for everybody in the area to use. Sometimes it took so long that they couldn't get washed up and dressed fast enough to make it to their work shifts on time.

Missionaries, Cows and Monday Nights

I couldn't imagine such a life – working such long hours, coming home just as your roommates were getting up to leave for their shift at the factory, quickly cooking something to eat, immediately going to bed for a few hours of sleep before the next group of roommates returned, then back to the factory for another shift. Life for these young women was so different from the family lives they had left behind in the countryside. Yet they did the best they could to earn money, spending some for their basic needs and sending back home to their families what little was left over.

Association with the UIM ministry had a very important influence on me. It served to deepen my faith significantly. I felt beyond a doubt that God was on the side of the poor and the oppressed and would not abandon them. While other Christians shunned factory workers and slum-dwellers, the Christians who worked in Urban Industrial Mission were there with them, day after day, teaching, comforting, and taking action on their behalf, even at great personal risk. To me it was a true manifestation of Christ among us.

⁂

Just a few days after my return to Korea in September of 1972, President Park declared martial law. Tanks and soldiers seemed to be everywhere.

At language school Louise and I met another new missionary couple, Linda and Dave Jones, Presbyterians from Illinois. They introduced us to what later became known as the Monday Night Group. We expatriates needed to figure out what our role was in this state of emergency the country was experiencing. Our Korean friends were asking us questions about the tanks used to barricade the gates of the universities and government buildings, and the tear gas canisters being used to put down the student demonstrations. The tanks had the American aid logo all over them – two hands shaking – a symbol of the relationship between the Koreans and the U.S. But why was U.S. aid being allowed to be used by the Korean government in a crackdown against its own citizenry? The Monday Night Group meetings gave us a place to discuss these questions, share bits and pieces of information we gleaned from other sources, and figure out what if anything we could do.

One of the things a dictatorship needs in order to stay in power is control over information, especially information from the outside world. Articles in *Time, Newsweek,* and other international media concerning martial law and the erosion of democracy in Korea did not make the Korean government happy. To prevent such articles from getting to the Korean public, the government censored them before they ever hit the streets. You might buy the latest issue of *Newsweek* with an article on Korea listed in the contents, but when you turned to that page, the whole article would be missing. Or sometimes the article would be blacked out, making it even more obvious, and causing the reader to think, "I wonder what was in *that* article?"

Fortunately, the Monday Night Group had other sources of information, especially our Christian friends in Japan, who would send the articles to us. Of course, they could not use ordinary channels, but they would ask visitors to take the articles to Korea hidden in their pockets or suitcases. Once in Korea, the visitor would contact us and we would arrange to meet and collect the smuggled materials. We would then try to deliver them to our Korean friends. Linda Jones was one of the primary persons who helped with this distribution of information. She would deliver them to specifically designated key leaders – the head of the Korean Student Christian Federation, Ahn Jae Woong (An Chaeŭng); head of the YMCA, Rev. Kang Moon Kyu (Kang Mun'kyu) ; General Secretary of the Korea National Council of Churches, Rev. Kim Kwan Suk, and others.

These leaders needed to know what the outside world knew and how the news about Korea was being reported.

The articles sometimes had to be duplicated before being distributed. That was another way we foreigners could help. Xerox machines were rare in those days, but there was a little copy shop in my Seoul neighborhood. Sometimes I would walk in and request a certain number of copies, hoping that the person making the copies wouldn't be able to read English very easily. I would say, "Oh, I'm an English teacher, and I need these materials for lessons and homework." Which was very true – they certainly *were* materials for lessons and homework – for the Koreans who needed them.

I remember one copy shop in particular. As my material was being copied, the owner came by and took a look. He seemed pretty well educated and, after glancing at the materials, he commented to one of his employees, "It may be leftist material." My heart sank when I heard him say that, so I tried to divert his attention. I looked straight at him and said, smiling, "It's such nice weather we're having today, isn't it?" I got him into a conversation about the weather, and as soon as my materials were copied, I paid for them, got out of there as fast as I could, and never went back to that shop again.

UIM work was not limited just to factory workers. It extended also to slum-dwellers and other vulnerable, marginalized people. There were slum areas all over Seoul, usually up high on the surrounding mountains, away from the middle-class residential areas. I had first-hand knowledge of the slums: a large number of people were living in shacks up on the mountainside just behind the Methodist Seminary where I taught.

Rev. Lee Kyu Sang (Yi Kyusang), a UIM minister, had started a day-care center in one of the slum areas, so that during the day mothers could work and earn a little money. I learned about Rev. Lee from Faye Moon at the Monday Night Group. She knew ministers like him who were organizing people in the slums on the eastern side of Seoul. Louise and I went out to visit the area to learn more about how Rev. Lee was organizing the people and encouraging the people to collaborate.

These were poor people from the rural area, people who could no longer make it on the farm because the price of rice and farm produce had been intentionally depressed by the government in order to provide cheap food for the urban areas. These rural people had to make a living somehow, so they came to the city and scraped by as best they could. They first had to scavenge a few boards here and there to build a shelter in which to live. On the outside, the shacks seemed hastily thrown together – probably because they didn't know how long they were going to be able to stay there. But inside the shacks things were very neatly arranged. Clearly these people were trying to do the best they could for their families.

The problem was that the government would periodically come in and remove them. It would tear-gas the squatters, knock their heads together, bulldoze their houses down, carry them off, and dump them in another area. Left with nothing, these once-again-displaced families would have to scramble to find something with which to start over. Then, as the government came in to develop another area, it would again move the squatters out. Sometimes the excuse was to "beautify" the city, as was the case when President Jimmy Carter came in 1979. Rev. Lee's role was to help the squatters organize themselves so they could resist being treated this way.

We invited Rev. Lee to dinner to tell us more about his work. After dinner he mentioned that he and some other UIM ministers were going to the Christian Building in downtown Seoul to have a little demonstration against the government's repressive policies. This was less than two weeks after an Emergency Decree which declared that anyone criticizing government policies would be sent to prison for up to fifteen years. These ministers were really brave, willing to risk going to prison for their belief in democracy. I decided to take my camera and go downtown to witness the event. This could be history in the making, I thought.

At the Christian Building, after reading their statement, the ministers unfolded an eight-foot paper banner that read, "Restore democracy! Repeal the Emergency Decrees!" Here was my photo op. In the back of my mind I thought that someone in the press might be interested in the pictures.

It never occurred to me that the Korean government would be even more interested in those pictures.

❧ ❧❧ ❧

I'd lived in relative freedom in Korea from 1966 to 1970, during my first missionary term. In those years, there were no repressive measures, even in 1968 when north Korean communist guerillas came all the way to the Blue House in an attempt to assassinate President Park. Nor were there any Emergency Decrees that same year (1968) when a U.S. Navy spy ship got too close to north Korean territorial waters and was captured. Tensions rose when north Korea detained the crew, but nothing out of the ordinary was done about it by south Korea. Perhaps the legitimately elected Park government felt secure in 1968. As that legitimacy declined, authoritarianism grew. By 1973, the regime found few repressive measures it didn't like.

I got home from the Christian Building demonstration and, just as Louise and I were finishing lunch, there was a knock at the front gate. When I opened the gate, two men nicely dressed in suits were standing there. They said they were from the KCIA and, because I had been at the demonstration downtown, I would have to go with them for questioning – right then and there. Naively, I got in the car with them and was driven to Nam San (South Mountain, the KCIA headquarters). I had heard many stories about people being taken there for questioning and, I must admit, I was really scared – not so much that they would hurt me physically, even though I guess that was possible. What really scared me was, "would I be getting someone else in trouble?" and "would I get kicked out of Korea?" I certainly didn't want to be the cause of trouble for any Koreans, and of course, I didn't want to have to leave the country I had come to love.

The KCIA agents drove me right up to the foot of the mountain, took me up in an elevator, and guided me into an interrogation room. There was a main desk at the front of the room and several other desks lined up along the length of the room. They led me to the back, to a room in the corner. One of the men was a friendly sort who tried to reassure me, saying, "Oh Mr. Durst, don't worry. This will be all over soon." He seemed to be the translator. Another man was the note-taker. There was only one other man in the room. He was in his late forties or early fifties – older than the others – and had on a leather jacket with some stars on his shoulder – indicating that he was a higher rank than the others. He was apparently the head of that department, and it was he who asked all the questions.

He immediately began yelling at me: "Why were you there?" "Why did you attend?" "How did you know about it?" "What were you doing there?" "Who invited you?" So I told them: I had heard there was going to be a demonstration and I knew Rev. Lee Kyu Sang, one of those who attended. "How did you know Lee Kyu Sang?" I told them I had met him through Faye Moon, an American friend of mine. They wanted to know if I knew any of the other ministers, and actually, I didn't really know many of them. Then they brought another man in the room and asked if I'd ever seen him before. I said, "No." (I still don't know who the man was, but it could have been someone else they were trying to implicate.)

I don't think they intended to keep me there very long, but everything had to be translated – both the questions and my answers – so it took four or five hours longer than expected. Fortunately, as the questions were being asked in Korean, I could usually get the gist of what was being said. So I had the advantage of hearing the question twice – first in Korean and then in English translation. That gave me a little more time to prepare my answer.

I was brought up to never get in trouble with the law, but to always obey it. I had never been picked up or arrested for anything in my life before that day. But there I was, being interrogated by the Korean authorities for breaking their Emergency Decree, for aiding and abetting those who were criticizing the government. Sometime during the interrogation, it hit me that the UIM really *must* be doing something right if this repressive government was as concerned about someone as insignificant as me – an ignorant, bumbling missionary.

It also made me realize that the authorities were dead serious about not being criticized, though it was hard for me to imagine Koreans ever being hesitant to speak their minds – an openness that I love.

Finally, I was taken home around 9:00 pm and, removing my shoes to enter the house, I breathed a sigh of relief – relief which turned out to be a bit premature. The next day the two men returned to our house. This time they said, "We heard that you took pictures yesterday at the demonstration. We need that film." I said, "Oh, sure." I walked into my bedroom, picked up the camera, and pulled out the film with the pictures I had taken. Then I put blank film in the camera and took it back to the living room where the agents were waiting. I handed them the film, and they left, seemingly satisfied.

Of course, as we expected, they came back again later that day. Anticipating their return, Louise had called two Methodist missionaries, Gene Matthews and George Ogle, and asked if they would mind coming over for a "visit" that afternoon. When the agents arrived, Louise served everyone cookies and coffee. We sat around drinking coffee and making small talk, and then the men got down to business. "There were no pictures on the film. Why was there nothing on the film?" I said, "Maybe the film was bad." But they weren't buying it: "No, we think we heard you take the film out of the camera when you were in the other room." I replied, "Oh, I was just rewinding the film in the camera. It's a new camera and I don't really know how to work it very well yet. Maybe I just didn't get any pictures."

Of course that was not true, which I'm sure they knew, but they didn't press the matter. Maybe they just didn't want to deal any longer with an ignorant foreigner who didn't know enough to stay out of trouble. Before leaving, however, they issued a warning, "We don't want to see any of that film appearing anywhere. If those pictures show up anywhere outside of Korea, you are going to be in serious trouble!" That probably meant that I would be kicked out of Korea, and to me that would be the most terrible thing they could do to me.

Worse than getting kicked out of Korea, however, was the fear that I might have caused harm to other Koreans. I worried a lot about that, especially about Lee Kyu Sang. As it turned out, his involvement with me did cause him some problems. They interrogated him longer than the others because of his inviting me to the demonstration. (Every additional hour that you are under interrogation by the KCIA means that the interrogation gets worse, especially if you are a Korean.) He told me later that one thing they said to him was, "Durst doesn't speak Korean very well. Do you speak English?" When he said no, they asked, "Then how did you communicate?" He replied, "Well, we just kind of nod at each other, blink our eyes, and shake our heads – that kind of thing." I don't think the interrogators were that dumb, and I would have thought that they'd be back on my doorstep asking me about it, but maybe they just wanted to scare me, and, indeed, they did a pretty good job of that. The whole experience cast a kind of dark shadow of depression over me for a while.

Then the harassment started. Louise and I would get strange phone calls in the middle of the night – an unidentified person on the other end of the line would ask, "Where are you going?" After a while when the phone rang I would pick it up and just listen – not saying anything. When the person spoke, if I could tell that they were from the KCIA or the police, I would just hang up. When my friends would call, they would have the strange experience of hearing the phone picked up and then nothing at the other end. All they could hear was breathing and they would say "Butch?" or "Louise?" Then I would know who it was and would answer. During our conversation, however, you could hear a series of clicks on the phone – probably the conversation being recorded. Sometimes these harassing phone calls were so frequent I would just unplug the phone for a while.

Another form of harassment was being followed by plainclothesmen. It seemed I was always being tailed – though this probably wasn't unusual. It was one way the government kept an eye on suspicious persons. Occasionally, I would be able to shake them. I would be walking down the street and, without warning I would do a hundred-eighty-degree turn and walk back, right past them. I could usually tell who they were, because all of sudden they would get real busy, pretending to look at a magazine or at something in one of the shop windows. I would dodge into a side street and wait for them to go by. Then I would continue on my way.

One man was always standing nonchalantly in the alley across from our house, watching our comings and goings. He was usually reading a newspaper. Did he really think we wouldn't notice? How normal is it for someone dressed in a suit to be standing in an alley reading a newspaper hour after hour? Not to mention the fact that the antenna of his walkie-talkie was sticking up in plain sight from behind the paper.

Once, when a friend from the U.S. had come to visit, we left the house one afternoon to do some errands. We were obviously being followed. My tail stayed back a distance, far enough to let me know he was there, just to keep me off-guard. We went down to the bus stop and got on a bus. Mr. Tail got in his car and followed the bus. On the bus, my friend and I conspired together and decided we would try to lose him.

At the next stop we quickly got off the bus, hailed a taxi and hurried off to the Shinchon (Shinch'on) Market area. At the entrance to the market we got out of the taxi, went all the way through the market to the other side, got another taxi and headed downtown. Success! Our tail was nowhere to be seen! We finished our business downtown and smugly returned home later that afternoon. There, standing in the alley, across from our gate, was our man – smiling. We smiled back. Even though he was working for the authorities – politically on opposite sides from us – that smile, that natural jovialness of the Korean people, came through. He was probably just an ordinary fellow making a living; at that moment he was more than just a police detective or KCIA agent. It was hard not to like him.

Even though it was somewhat unnerving to be followed everywhere, it seemed to be just normal procedure. When I would mention it to other Koreans, they would say, "Oh yeah, that's just what happens." I even got a note from Rev. Ahn Jae Woong, executive director of the Korean Christian Student Federation, telling me not to be depressed, that it happens to all of us. I knew that he, himself, had been arrested and taken in for questioning numerous times, and had even been tortured for several weeks at the Nam San KCIA headquarters. Such a message coming from him really meant a lot to me – letting me know that he appreciated what I did, or what I was trying to do, in my own clumsy way. It made the whole ordeal more bearable.

⁓ ⁓⁓ ⁓

At the Monday Night Group meetings, we struggled with what we could do as expatriates to support our Korean friends and colleagues, especially Korean Christians. We found that one thing we could do was to be witnesses. We could go to the trials of those charged under the Emergency Decrees for criticizing the government – that is, for speaking out for justice and democracy. We could be outside observers.

The first trial I attended was that of Rev. Pak Hyung Kyu, a prominent Presbyterian minister in Seoul. When they brought him into the courtroom, he was handcuffed and wearing white prison garb. I remember feeling really proud of him, the way he stood so tall. The first question they asked him was, "What is your occupation?" and proudly he said, "*Moksa imnida*" ("I am a minister"). Here was a Christian minister speaking out on behalf of democracy and being tried as if that were a crime. And we – a small part of the outside world – were there to watch, to be a Christian witness.

Another trial we attended, though we were not allowed inside the courtroom, was that of opposition politician Kim Dae Jung. Standing next to me outside the courtroom was Belgian priest, Didier Terstevens, known to all of us Monday Nighters as the "cheese priest." Even his Korean surname – Father Chi – sounds like "cheese," but the real reason for the nickname was because he ran a cheese factory in the country where his parish was located. There wasn't a very big market for cheese among Koreans – a foreign food that, to them, smelled like dirty feet – so he often made trips to Seoul to supply cheese to some of the tourist hotels. This bearded fellow with wild eyes and a ready laugh was quite a character. In fact, once he brought to the Monday Night Group his edition of underground literature – sermons, statements, and declarations of conscience that had been made by various groups of people against the government. He'd printed up a thousand copies and was distributing them wherever he could. On the cover was a quote from the Beatitudes in the Gospel of Matthew: "Blessed are they who suffer persecution for the sake of justice."

As the cheese priest and I were standing outside Kim Dae Jung's courtroom, all of a sudden there was a ruckus. The trial had ended abruptly for some reason, and the police were trying to disperse the crowd. In the midst of the jostling and pushing, my shoe came off; the cheese priest grabbed it and angrily whacked one of the policemen on his helmeted head. The police threw us both on their bus, then picked up the shoe and threw it in after us. It was then that I learned why the priest had whacked the guy on the head – as Didier was being thrown on the bus, the policeman had grabbed him by the "privates."

The police bus took us to Yongdungpo, one of the industrial areas on the outskirts of Seoul, and dropped us off, leaving us to make our way back into the city however we could. But the cheese priest, ever resourceful, just stuck out his thumb and in no time a Korean driver picked us up. On our way back downtown, Didier told the driver all about what had happened, including the part about being grabbed by the police. I thought the driver was going to run off the road, he was laughing so hard.

≈ ≋≋ ≈

In the spring of 1974, the Korean government fabricated a case called the People's Revolutionary Party (PRP). They picked up some men and arrested them, accusing them of being the ringleaders of a communist group that was supposedly instigating the widespread student demonstrations.

The wives of some of the accused came to George Ogle and asked for his help. George remembered that there was a similar case in 1964 and he asked me to look back through old issues of the English-language *Korea Times* and *Korea Herald* to see if I could find anything about it. I went down to the U.S. Information Service (USIS), near the U.S. Embassy, and started going through the 1964 back issues of the newspapers. Sure enough, I found articles about an earlier People's Revolutionary Party. Not only that, but lo and behold, the man who was the KCIA director *then* was the very same man who was the *current* KCIA director.

Of course, 1964 was long before the Yushin Constitution, so the court system was still relatively independent of the Park administration. Now, however, the court system and the legislative system were both consolidated under the thumb of President Park. It seemed pretty obvious that Park was once again trying to make the PRP look like a communist conspiracy, linking it to the student demonstrations in order to discredit them. It was the same ploy that had been tried back in 1964-65 to stop the students who, at that time, were protesting the normalization of relations with Japan. When I read those articles, I had a sinking feeling in my stomach that there was going to be trouble. I made copies and headed back to George's house. Riding along on the bus, I had a foreboding feeling that the men, their families, and even George, were probably headed down a difficult path.

The 1964 articles convinced me that this new PRP case was also fabricated – that, and George's interpretation of the case. George was a person of impeccable character, so I trusted him completely. Unfortunately, my premonition about this dangerous path he might have to tread did come to pass. The result of George's efforts to help the wives and their husbands – almost exactly ten years after the first PRP case – led to his deportation from Korea, the country he loved so much, the country where his children were raised, and where he had spent the majority of his adult life. It was sad to see this pillar of our missionary community be forced out of Korea – the man who, along with some Korean Christians, had started the UIM, a man who was concerned about the poor and the oppressed. It was very bleak that day in December 1974 when we said goodbye to George.

The following April, at the final Supreme Court trial of the PRP men, Louise and I and a few others somehow managed to get into the courthouse. Others tried to get in but were having trouble getting past security. Inside the courtroom were the wives of the PRP men. The judges all filed in and sat down. Then the chief justice announced, "The sentences have been upheld." With that, the judges stood up and walked out. It happened so fast we were stunned. The women started shouting and crying. I still remember Mrs. Woo beating her umbrella on the back of the chair, sending its ribs flying all over the courtroom. She must have known, as did the other women, what that verdict meant – that she had lost her husband.

We stood there in shock, not knowing what to do. Soon, a very angry Jim Sinnott began protesting and yelling out, "It's a lie! It's a lie!" About that time Brian Wroble, a lawyer from Amnesty International, came bounding up the stairs to the courtroom. Brian had come to Korea a few weeks earlier to document the situation of political prisoners, as well as the PRP case. He had tried to get to the courtroom for the "hearing" but was kept outside by the plainclothesmen until the charade of justice was over. Finally getting to the courtroom and seeing the chaos, he asked, "Where are the judges?" When we told him what had happened, he thrust his briefcase at me, asked me to safeguard it, and hurried off to find the judges to protest the so-called hearing.

I found myself standing there with Brian's briefcase containing all the research, data, and important documents he'd gathered in Korea regarding political prisoners and human rights abuses. "What will happen to it, if they arrest us?" I thought. It gave me a dreadful feeling of responsibility, and I was determined to protect it, no matter what.

Soon, after everyone else was out of the courtroom, one of the court guards looked at his watch and said to us, "It's lunch time; we all need to go now." But Louise had the idea of sitting down and not leaving – causing a spontaneous mini sit-in protest. The three of us – Louise, Jim Sinnott, and I – sat down on the floor, me with Brian's precious briefcase on my lap. Eventually, some plainclothesmen showed up and ordered us to get out. Two guys grabbed me under the shoulders and the knees, picked me up, and carried me down the stairs, just like I was riding in a chariot or something. I held on to the briefcase as tightly as I could. The men put me down on the concrete plaza area just outside the back of the courthouse. Luckily, the briefcase was still intact. When I looked up, there, looking over the wall was a policeman taking pictures of the whole event. I smiled weakly and waved. He smiled and waved back.

The next Monday Night Group meeting was at Randy and Sue Rice's house, and it was a gloomy gathering. Sitting there talking about the courtroom experience and the horror of the next day's executions of the eight PRP men, all of us felt angry and helpless, but we also felt a strong need to respond in some way to this travesty of justice. "You know, I think we need to do something," Randy said. "Maybe put some black hoods over our heads and do some kind of public witness, some kind of symbolic gesture of our outrage." I picked up on the idea and said, "Yeah, let's get some black hoods and maybe tie a rope or something around our necks and demonstrate in front of the American Embassy!" It would be a way to protest what we felt was U.S. complicity in this tragedy; embassy officials knew the men were innocent but did not speak out against it. Repeated attempts on our part to get the U.S. to intervene with the Park government on behalf of the men had resulted only in weak excuses: "We're working behind the scenes," they said. "We're engaged in quiet diplomacy."

Our decision was made: eight of us men – representing the eight men who had been hanged – would demonstrate. Some of the Maryknoll sisters and other Monday Night Group women found some black material and sewed the hoods together. I went down to Shinchon market and got some very thick straw rope to make the nooses.

Jim Sinnott was to be one of the eight, and he had been given one of the hoods, but he had come under such suspicion that the authorities put him under house arrest. On the day before the demonstration, we met at Gene Matthews' house near Ducksoo (Tŏksu) Palace. I called Jim to ask if he would be able to meet with us, but he said he couldn't leave his house. We knew his phone was tapped, and I tried to think of some cryptic language to use to communicate with him. I said, "Well, it sure would be nice to have you at the 'party.' We're so sorry you won't be able to make it. Do you know . . . of . . . of . . . ." I was stumbling around looking for the right words, when Jim said, "Oh, do you mean another person of my persuasion?" "Yes, someone else of your persuasion." Jim replied, "Yes, someone will be there."

The day of the demonstration we all met at one of the houses on the missionary compound not far from the U.S. Embassy. Father Tynan, a priest from Pusan, had come up to Seoul to take Jim's place. We got our stuff together and walked the fifteen minutes to the embassy. Taking our places in front of the embassy, we silently put the hoods over our heads and the ropes around our necks. Then we pulled out a long banner and held it up: "Is this the result of quiet diplomacy?" This was our way of expressing what we thought of the U.S. Embassy's behind-the-scenes, so-called quiet (and very ineffective) diplomacy.

The Korean authorities were not very happy about our little demo. It wasn't long, after going back to our respective homes that a call came from Fran Nelson Krauth, a Presbyterian missionary. Some men had come and taken her husband, one of the eight demonstrators. I called around and found that Charlie Krauth and Gene Matthews had been taken to the Immigration office for questioning.

I knew it was just a matter of time before they would be coming for me. Soon there was a knock at our gate. I assumed it might be the police and didn't open it. They shouted that they needed to talk to Mr. Durst. "Who is it?" I asked. "We are the police. You must come with us," they replied. "I don't know you. How do I know that you are the police? Do you have a warrant? I won't go anywhere with you," I yelled back. After a half hour of shouting, they left.

We knew they would be back, but we decided not to make it easy for them. It was getting dark, so Louise and I turned off all the lights, unplugged the phone, and refused to talk to anyone. After a while, the police returned. They banged on the gate and demanded entry. We didn't answer. They shouted, "We know you are in there! Let us in!" Still we didn't answer. They even sent a female police officer up to the gate, pretending to be a mother looking for her lost child, *Suni*. She'd call out to us asking if her little *Suni* was there. It was an obvious trick, and I wasn't about to go to the door.

The police then went into our neighbor's yard and, peering over the concrete block wall between our two homes, shouted in our direction, "Mr. Durst, you must come with us. We have a subpoena!"

I let them continue shouting for a while, but finally I relented. I didn't want them bothering our neighbors, so I agreed to go with them. At least I had the satisfaction of having kept them at bay for several hours.

The questioning at the Immigration Office was much different from the KCIA interrogation at Nam San. This time, an observer from the U.S. Embassy was present the whole time; that seemed an ironic twist, considering that our protest was at the embassy. Of course, the immigration authorities wanted us to sign a statement promising never do anything like that again. I refused to sign anything, saying that it was strictly a matter between myself and my government. I wouldn't tell them anything about what I had done and I wouldn't acknowledge that I had done anything illegal, because in my eyes I hadn't. I was on U.S. Embassy grounds, and I was communicating with *my* government about *its* actions (or lack thereof). I continued to stick with that story. The evening wore on, and it got to be late. Everyone else had already been released, so they finally let me go. It felt good that I had managed to get out of there without signing anything.

～ ✕ ～

I guess we missionaries were somewhat of a problem for the Korean authorities, especially for a dictatorship that needed secrecy and isolation. Unfortunately for them, however, missionaries are not isolated people, and neither are Korean intellectuals, especially those who have studied and lived abroad. They have connections all over the outside world. Maybe that's one of the reasons why the authorities didn't do much to us Western missionaries. They may have been afraid that if they seriously abused missionaries, it could have negative consequences. Or maybe they just had bigger fish to fry. Whether extreme actions against us would have caused trouble for the Park regime or not, we'll never know. But we do now know of cases in other countries where Americans have been tortured and even killed, and the U.S. has said or done very little about it. Luckily for us, the Korean authorities were not that brazen.

At the Monday Night Group meeting that followed the embassy demonstration, Father Tynan, who had stood in for Jim Sinnott, came up from Pusan and met with us. He was a well-known and highly respected priest in Pusan. The local authorities there knew him too and respected his work.

At the Monday Night meeting, we shared stories about our investigations by the immigration authorities. We learned that Father Tynan had also been picked up and questioned when he returned to Pusan. He told us that the local chief of police had called him in and said, "I can't believe this – that you, our local priest, went up to Seoul and were causing trouble." Father Tynan looked him straight in the eye and said, "Well then, don't believe it."

One of the side effects of our activism and public witnessing was that our residency permits were shortened. Usually these permits were renewed annually; an innocuous reminder that we were guests in a foreign country – even though that was easy to forget, living among the gentle, friendly, accepting Koreans. Permit renewal was a routine that we never gave much thought. We would submit our papers, pay the fee, and when the official stamp of approval was given, go down to the Immigration Office, pick up the permit, and enjoy another year as a legally-registered alien in this "land of the morning calm."

This process, however, soon became anything but routine. Our permits were approved for only three months at a time, and for one short period, they were cut down to even less than that. Now, almost as soon as the permits were approved, we'd have to start the process all over again. It was another example of government harassment.

More than Witnesses

After the execution of the PRP men, our attempts to protest it, and our subsequent investigations, we continued to try to support the PRP families in whatever ways we could. I remember a particular visit to Mrs. Woo's house. Her husband, whom she loved so dearly, had been executed – not for a crime he committed, but as a scapegoat of bigger political interests. It was the first time I heard the Korean expression, "When the whales fight, the shrimp get crushed." She went on to explain how in the struggle between bigger nations, Korea has often been caught in between and crushed, just like her husband and the other men had been. I thought that pretty much explained it – throughout Korea's history, wars have been fought between Russia and China, between China and Japan, between Japan and Russia, and in the process Korea has been trampled. Now, because of American interests, Japanese interests, the Park government's interest in staying in power, ordinary south Korean people had become the shrimp. They were the ones being caught and crushed.

I think there's a very deep hurt that occurs in the psyche of people who have experienced the violence of war, or in this case, government violence against its own people. But it amazes me how resilient the Koreans are. Fortunately, Korea has been free of war from outside forces for more than fifty years now, and it continues to thrive. It can only be because of their dynamic spirit and their strong desire to live in freedom. They are determined to maintain their own culture, to be the people God created them to be: wonderful, strong, loving people, with an abundant sense of good humor.

Living and working in Korea for twelve years was an eye-opening experience for me, to say the least. Growing up, I had been taught how Americans are such a hardworking, creative, and innovative people, and what a great country the U.S. is. All that is true to some extent but the U.S. is only one great country. Korea is also a great country; Japan is a great country, and other countries are great, too. So when I hear my fellow U.S. citizens say that our country is better than other countries, it makes me sad. When Americans feel that we always have to be on top, it makes us less able to appreciate or benefit from the good in other countries; we miss out on the diverse gifts and wonderful contributions of others. Perhaps more dangerously, it makes us a nation less able to cooperate with the rest of the world; we cooperate only when it's in our own interest. This, unfortunately, breeds a kind of arrogance, something the U.S. seems to be becoming more and more widely known for around the world today.

I feel fortunate to have lived in another country long enough to get a different perspective. It has helped me realize that to be a good American, I need to be a good citizen of the world. I like feeling part of the wider world, instead of being so "culturally exclusive," restricted to just one country or one culture. It helps me see our common humanity, the God-given worth of all people, no matter where they are from, or what their language is, what their customs are, or even what their professed religion may be. God is larger than any human-made institution, any rule of law, any culture or tradition, including our own, and does not discriminate among the children of the earth – all are loved equally.

In Korea I also learned that, in the global village we all now live in, what affects one country affects all others too. For example, actions of the powerful have consequences for the less powerful. A prime example is U.S. consumerism. I remember returning to the U.S. and being appalled at how many grocery shelves were devoted just to pet food. Our consumerism has reached an almost obscene level. We have too much, and it fools us into thinking that our value is proportional to the things we own. But it hurts the rest of the world in ways we may not realize.

Our economic policies export our consumer lifestyle to other countries, often to their detriment. I saw the direct effect of that in Korea. A small example will illustrate: when our son was born at Yonsei University Hospital in Seoul, Louise was the only one among all the new mothers there who chose to breastfeed. The Korean women were using infant formula – an expensive and less healthy way to start their children's young lives – and all because of the massive marketing job being done in poor countries by U.S. and European companies. Another example: in the markets, more and more high-priced, canned vegetables from the U.S. line the shelves, right next to the cheaper, healthier, locally-grown fresh produce.

The U.S. has also become sort of a sponge, absorbing the world's resources, in order to support our high-end lifestyle; this, in turn, becomes the backbone of our foreign and military policy. I saw this first-hand in Korea. The largest department at the U.S. Embassy in Seoul was not devoted to helping the Koreans have a better life, or to supporting freedom, democracy, or human rights. The Department of Commerce is the biggest section of the Embassy – getting better deals for American business at the expense of hard-working, low-wage Korean laborers. Seeing the effects of that policy in those cheek-by-jowl hovels shared by the young Korean factory workers pains me to this day.

I am less trustful of government leaders, because they so often seem to act and speak on behalf of business or the military, not on behalf of the people, even their own citizens.

Backing up U.S. business interests is the U.S. military, the other biggest factor in our policies toward other nations. It seems that in every conflict, in every war in which the U.S. gets involved, we have to dig beneath all the rhetoric about freedom and democracy to find the actual motive. Usually that deeper motive is our strong interest in that country's resources.

The U.S. has maintained up to 50,000 troops in Korea since the end of the war there in the early 1950's. To this day, there are tens of thousands of U.S. troops still in Korea. On September 11, 2001, the U.S. World Trade Center, the symbol of commerce, and the Pentagon, the U.S. military center, were attacked. Do Americans really understand the symbolism of those attacks? It seemed clear to me then that elements of the Third World were striking back against the major commercial empire, against the biggest military empire in the world today. I do not condone the actions of the 9/11 terrorists, but I think most Americans fail to realize how much hardship our policies have caused people in other parts of the world. We need a world where peace based on social justice isn't just rhetoric but is reflected in our policies and our actions. Unfortunately, we seem to have a long way to go.

I will always be grateful for the unique opportunity I was given to work with Christians of another land who were trying to do just that – bring peace and justice to their homeland. They stood bold in the face of incredible hardship and oppression, just as Christ and his disciples did many years ago. Having the opportunity to support them in some small way deepened my faith and taught me how to be a better Christian. I pray that the time I spent there was as beneficial to the Koreans as it was to me – perhaps even as beneficial as those thirty Heifer Project cows were to the rural farmers who received them.

Chapter 9

Acting on Our Convictions

Sue Rice

In late 1965 my husband and I were appointed missionaries to Korea by the Commission on Ecumenical Mission and Relations (COEMAR) of the United Presbyterian Church. We had been living in Bridgeport, Conn., with our four children, from newborn to age 8. My husband, Rev. W. Ransom Rice, Jr. (Randy), was assistant pastor of the First Presbyterian Church.

I had grown up in Niagara Falls and Lewiston, N.Y., bordering Canada. My high school was a rich mixture of ethnic groups: eastern European, Jewish, Italian, Polish, and African-American. I attended St. Lawrence University in upstate New York. The university chaplain steered me into the Student Christian Movement, which was active in local and international issues. A summer conference led by Rev.

Acting on Our Convictions

James Robinson, an African-American pastor from New York City, and Dr. Richard Shaull, a missionary to Brazil, sharpened my interest in the worldwide work of the church. Except for a Japanese student pen pal, however, I had no relationship with Asia.

In 1965 I was appointed a fraternal worker with the United Presbyterian Church (now Presbyterian Church USA, or PCUSA). After six months of training at the Missionary Orientation Center at Stony Point, New York, our family arrived in Seoul on September 6, 1966. Randy and I began two years of intensive language study at the Korean Language Institute of Yonsei University. We were then appointed to teach English conversation at Kyunghee University. Randy was also asked to work with the Korean Student Christian Federation (KSCF) on campus.

～ ☙❧ ～

What first drew me into the tragic side of 1960's south Korea was the plight of young Korean girls from poor rural families who had come to Seoul seeking work. Living in poverty, with few options for employment, they were often lured into prostitution. I became involved in the ministry of a residential program for these young women. The program had been started by a former PCUSA missionary and social worker, Eleanor Van Lierop, along with several Yonsei University faculty wives. They called the program the Eun Hae Won (Ŭnhyewŏn) (House of Grace). I discovered that my hobbies of sewing and knitting could be put to good use there teaching crafts. Later I became a staff person and served as director during 1972.

House of Grace reached out to girls ages thirteen and up. Most of these young women had left their homes in rural areas after graduating from primary school (free public education in south Korea was provided only through elementary school). They sought jobs because their families could not afford their school fees. In many cases, the young women sent money home so that their brothers could go to school. Education was considered more important for male members of the family.

The girls thought they were to be employed in shops or restaurants in Seoul. But many of them ended up in downtown brothels or near the U.S. 8th Army base at Yongsan in Seoul. Then they were trapped. The brothel owners took their national ID cards, forced them into debt, and told them that the only way out was to serve as sex workers.

Because my Korean language skill was still developing, I wasn't able to comprehend fully what these young women's lives had been like before they came to House of Grace. I came to know their situation and their need for protection under Korean law, in weekly meetings with House of Grace staff, in case conferences, and through visits to the countryside.

The yearly Christmas pageant at the House of Grace brought tears to my eyes as I watched the angelic faces of the young girls portraying Mary and Joseph in the manger scene. It was particularly poignant after the residential program became a temporary home for unwed mothers and children.

As a Christian and American wife and mother, I arrived in Korea understanding little of the Confucian system of hierarchy within the Korean government and family system. I couldn't really know what Korean women face, and I couldn't put my own feelings into words. That changed when I heard lectures by Dr. Lee Hyo Chai (Yi Hyojae), noted professor of sociology at Ewha Women's University and author of *The Status of Women in Korea*. She taught me how women were under the control of their fathers, husbands, and oldest sons. She explained how a woman was considered a nonperson until she married and bore a son. She used the word *han* – that intense mixture of profound pain and burning resentment felt by the Korean people, especially the women, because of a long history of injustice and discrimination.

I was particularly shocked by the harsh treatment that I later witnessed toward low-income and working-class young women in the industrial zones of Seoul, the capital city of then 10 million people. I faced some of these realities while counseling girls at House of Grace and at the Ewha Women's University Social Service Center. Realizing I needed more training in social work, I enrolled in the Social Work Department of Ewha Women's University for a year and worked at their Social Service Center in a low-income neighborhood adjacent to the campus.

I had been a member of the "Group of 50" in the 1960's (see Randy Rice chapter), and I began attending the Monday Night Group when that started in the early 1970's. In the Monday Night Group, I discovered that I could discuss my thoughts and feelings of sadness and anger and channel them into action. Because the MNG was formed to educate, inform, and take action as expatriates, the members helped me to understand and put into practice what it meant to be a responsible American citizen living abroad – including communicating with my government regarding matters of human rights and justice.

❧ ❧❧ ❧

I had lots to learn about Korean factory life, especially for young Korean women. Industrialization was rapidly transforming south Korea from rural to urban and from agricultural to industrial. Young women were seen as compliant and skillful components of the workforce.

During long MNG meetings we heard what was not being

reported in the media concerning exploitation of labor. We learned about working conditions that ranged from the poor to the inhumane and about severe curtailment of union activity. As MNG members delved into these matters, we discovered that many of the factories with oppressive conditions were directly or indirectly tied to U.S. corporations.

Rev. Cho Chi Song (Cho Chisong), a minister and staff member of the Urban Industrial Mission (UIM), met with the Monday Night Group twice during April 1971. The UIM and its Roman Catholic counterpart, Young Christian Workers (JOC), offered support for laborers who were working in oppressive conditions. Rev. Cho was one of the pastors working with UIM in the Youngdong Po industrial area.

He explained to us the plight of young women workers in their teens and early twenties who were losing their normal vision after looking at computer chips eight hours a day through high-powered microscopes. The workers had no rest periods except for a 30-minute lunch break. Complaints of eye disease were received from female workers in seven companies, including Control Data, Motorola, Sygnetics, and Fairchild Semiconductor International.

Factory owners and managers were not providing eye tests nor were they giving appropriate attention to working conditions. With UIM help, approximately 150 workers decided to undergo eye examinations and get treatment as needed. The examinations showed that the women were indeed losing their 20-20 vision due to the long hours of stressful, eye-straining work with no breaks and no provision for cleaning and repairing the microscope lenses.

I was deeply troubled by what was happening to the young women. And I felt compelled to try to do something to help them. With other Monday Nighters I met with some of the women at the UIM headquarters in Youngdong Po. The young workers were intelligent and cheerful; they appeared capable of benefiting from further education had that been an option.

They told us stories of their oppressive working conditions. The room we met in was stark, with desks squared against the walls. But the young women brightened the room as they spoke boldly and courageously about themselves and their work. I realized that each of them would be fired if seen in the UIM office. What other opportunities would they then have?

I feared for them as they talked. Who might be listening through the cracks in the thin walls and doors or on the phones that were probably tapped? Rev. Cho had picked up the phone one day and heard one of his previous phone conversations being played back to him on tape. Were there other company workers who had decided it was too risky to come and tell us their stories? I wondered what made these women so brave. And I wondered how they felt about their damaged eyesight.

We left the meeting feeling empowered. If these workers could take what little rest time they had on their day off to meet with us, surely we could gather the strength to listen – and the courage to act. I could worry later about what repercussions I might encounter as I returned home to my husband and children in the safe western section of Seoul.

Tests conducted at Paek Hospital proved conclusively that women who had been employed for two years or more were indeed losing their good eyesight. Rev. Cho asked some MNG members if we would be willing to meet with managers of one of the American companies, Fairchild Semiconductor. I vividly remember being taken into the plant's main open working space. Women were seated in long rows, heads bowed over the microscopes, not allowed to look up at any time from what they were doing. Behind them, young male supervisors were keeping track of whose heads might bob up and down.

It was chilling. The workers were almost like robots, unable to see even the foreign strangers who had come to observe.

The American manager of the Korean-run company took us into his office. We began telling him about the eye testing that had been done and how the results showed that workers' eyes were being damaged. He acknowledged that the work was a strain on their eyes. When confronted about the company's lack of arrangements for testing workers' vision, and the long working hours without morning or afternoon breaks, he interrupted us to ask who we were.

We explained our jobs with our various church-related missions. And we explained that, as concerned Americans, we felt compelled to let American company managers know of our concerns for the physical and mental well-being of the workers. The manager said, "You came here to work in Korea as missionaries. I didn't. My company came here to make a profit."

I was floored. Of course, to make a profit! Weren't we innocent and naïve! A company that comes half way around the world to set up a plant must have some incentive, and there it was, loud and clear. It was a revelation to me.

He was telling it like it was; no qualms about it. I admired his candor and forthrightness, and I thanked him for it.

Not long afterward, women at the Fairchild plant did start getting morning and afternoon breaks, and a machine was brought in to test their eyes.

We approached other companies and requested meetings, but none responded. According to Rev. Cho, however, other companies did eventually meet union and UIM demands to repair broken and unfocused microscopes and to provide enough of the expensive tissues needed to clean them.

Control Data and Sygnetics met with UIM staff through the labor unions at the plants. The companies were reminded that, under

Acting on Our Convictions

Korean labor law, factory workers had the right to five to ten minute breaks every four hours. They knew the law, of course, but often did not comply, especially when the government, so eager for rapid development, often looked the other way.

The impact that the eyesight testing had on the Monday Night Group was huge. We felt part of an important process. As Christian expatriates, we were able to educate ourselves on the workings of multinational corporations. We realized that, working with Korean Christian labor advocates, we could play a role in improving conditions for workers. This brought us in touch with other sources of empowerment for workers, especially Korean women workers.

Even though I grew up in the industrial city of Niagara Falls, New York, I knew little about trade unions. My hometown was a boomtown in the 1940's and 1950's, with many major chemical plants that relied on the Niagara Power Company's cheap energy.

I was a chemistry major the first two years of college, and during one of my summer vacations, I decided to look for a job at one of the chemical plants. The personnel manager took one look at me and said, "We really don't have any jobs for women at this time. These are high-risk jobs working with chemicals, and we don't allow women to do them. Why don't you study to be a teacher instead?"

I was stunned by his remarks. I never felt inferior as a girl. I remember thinking I could be a Madame Curie and discover a cure for cancer. So I resented his stereotyping me, but I didn't let him know how I felt. I repressed my feelings until I saw those women in Seoul, Korea, bent over their tables day in and day out, manipulating microchip parts beneath the microscopes.

I had to ask, what kind of American companies would take their plants overseas to make big profits by exploiting workers, avoiding government regulation and scrutiny, and ignoring the demands of workers and their unions? Were they totally blind to the incredible situation of young Korean textile workers laboring in cramped quarters like the "Peace Market" in Chungyechun, downtown Seoul?

To imagine the Peace Market, picture long city blocks of cement buildings, six stories high, along a wide underpass of what used to be an open sewer. The first few floors were the open retail stalls with all kinds of garments. On the upper floors were the sweatshops for the garment workers. Here hundreds of mostly young teenagers did piecework, sewing garments primarily for export, in quarters so cramped they could not stand up. They breathed stale air mixed with the toxic smell of the textile goods. In the summer it was sweltering hot. In the winter their fingers were so cold it slowed their output. They were cogs in a machine that would soon export $10 billion in textiles, mainly to Japan and the United States.

It took the dramatic suicide of one of the three thousand workers in the Peace Market to draw attention to the miserable conditions of the workers. Chun Tae Il (Chŏn T'aeil), himself a young worker in the Peace Market, agonized over the wasted youth of these young workers and the inhumane conditions in which they labored. He had attempted everything – research, organizing, and protest – to bring public attention to his cruelly exploited fellow workers. Finally he burned himself to death on the street in front of the market. His death, and the suicide note he left, had a powerful and lasting impact. For many years his mother, Lee So Sun (Yi Sosŏn), and his sister carried on his work. Others joined them in seeking justice for workers not only in the Peace Market but elsewhere in the country through the Chungyechun (Ch'ŏnggyech'ŏn) Labor Union. In 2005 Lee So Sun was still actively engaged in the work her son started.

Acting on Our Convictions

The Monday Night Group decided to tell the story of the Peace Market workers and their working conditions on national radio in the United States. Sometime in 1973 three MNG members – David Jones, Linda Jones, and I – linked up with Bernie Wideman, a Fulbright Scholar, and together we boldly entered one of the Peace Market buildings. We were pretty low-tech. Lacking a small handheld transistor recorder such as one might carry today, we instead strapped to David's back one of the first taping systems made. It was as big as a present-day commercial movie camera!

We couldn't have been more conspicuous as we began to interview some of the workers. They were surprised that some Americans really cared about their conditions. They talked as they worked, bent over their sewing and serging machines, looking up only to marvel at our interest. They said they were working at least 10 hours a day, making an average of $60 a month.

Linda succeeded in keeping the national police at bay downstairs. But it wasn't long before the foreman, attracted by the flashing of cameras to document our interviews, stuck his head in to see what was going on. It was time to leave quickly.

The story became a five-minute piece on National Public Radio in the U.S. I had no idea that our taping of workers in oppressive Korean sweatshops might be newsworthy back home. But it was, because most of the garments were headed for U.S. markets. I felt good that we were able to do something to educate Americans about the abusive conditions that produced inexpensive garments for their consumption. We all need to think twice before we buy our clothes, remembering where they are made and by whom – often young, innocent children laboring long hours in harsh conditions for low wages.

More than Witnesses

Through the Monday Night Group I learned how we from other countries might, in our small ways, contribute to the restoration of democracy in Korea. But I knew first and foremost that it was the Korean people's struggle. We MNG members were surrounded by inspired and inspiring Korean activists, and by ordinary but outraged Koreans who eventually joined them in the democratization movement.

The most significant places of inspiration for me were the Thursday morning prayer meetings at the Christian Building in central Seoul and the Sunday afternoon worship at Galilee Church on the outskirts of the city. Galilee Church was established by the wives and mothers of political prisoners – people who had received harsh prison terms for supporting movements for democracy, labor rights, and human rights. The service provided a special time for the wives and mothers to pray, reflect on Scripture, share about their loved ones, and support one another.

Other Koreans, and MNG members and other foreigners, attended not only to support the women but also to hear their news – and to admire their faith. These were women in extreme anguish, often sharing distressing news about husbands in poor health in prison, or sons in solitary confinement, or anxieties about upcoming court trials. The women visibly drew strength from one another and from God, and they strengthened us worshippers in the process.

On occasional Sundays when I could leave our four children in good hands, I took the long, crowded bus ride to the eastern outskirts of Seoul and drew upon that strength. I was encouraged by the wives and mothers and Christian supporters of political prisoners who religiously came to Galilee Church Sunday after Sunday. They had such faith and fortitude. They shared a profound bond of suffering in the temporary loss of their husbands, sons, and daughters. They vowed to continue their loved ones' struggles: fighting for restoration of democracy, labor rights, and freedoms of assembly, speech, and press.

We sang not only Christian hymns but also American songs of freedom, peace, and justice such as "We Shall Overcome." Through laughter and tears, these women found the courage to confront whatever and whoever awaited them outside – including the plainclothes KCIA agents who followed the women everywhere, even to church.

Galilee Church embodied for me a safe haven for women, where weak and strong could meet to console one another and gain the strength needed to stand up and continue their loved ones' work. Galilee was God's gift to them, and to me: there I found the faith and courage I needed to sustain me in my small contribution to their large struggle.

I never felt that my government fully understood or really cared about the dark side of the Korean economic miracle – the oppression, the arrests and torture, the exploitation of workers, the denial of freedoms of assembly, speech, and press. The U.S. State Department didn't seem particularly interested in what I and other concerned Americans thought about our foreign policy, let alone the views of the Korean opposition. The largest section of the American Embassy in Seoul, the Economic Division, appeared to do most of the intelligence gathering. But if they indeed did know what was going on in south Korea economically and politically, they showed little sign of it to us or to the Korean people.

Returning to Seoul from a one-year furlough in Lewiston, New York, in 1971, Randy and I moved our family into the Yonsei University faculty neighborhood in Yonhee Dong (Yŏnhŭidong).

More than Witnesses

Among the first persons to visit us were a Yonsei professor, Rev. Kim Chan Kook (Kim Ch'an'guk), and his wife, Sung Yoon Soon (Sŏng Yunsun). She made us feel at home, bringing over a gift of food and inviting us to their home. Our family felt most welcome in their home, and we enjoyed exchanging thoughts about daily life in Korea. Rev. Kim always had such a lovely, bright smile as he talked about his work as dean of the Theology Department at Yonsei University. Their daughter, Min Soung Hae (Min Sŭnghae), tried to teach our daughter Liz to play the piano.

One frosty mid-winter morning we called Rev. Kim's family to see if anyone wanted to go skating with us. Their youngest son, Eun Kyu (Ŭn'gyu), wanted to go, so we all bundled ourselves up, jumped into the blue Datsun station wagon, and drove to the huge speed-skating stadium on the outskirts of Seoul. Our friendly relationship meant that, in time of trouble, we could share easily with each other.

On May 7, 1974, the Korean CIA took Rev. Kim from his university office. His family did not know his whereabouts for five weeks. Gathering information from a variety of sources, his wife guessed that he was being held at the KCIA headquarters at Namsan (South Mountain). He was accused of encouraging a student alliance in its alleged plot to overthrow the government, and he was sentenced to ten years in prison. He was released from prison after nine months. Throughout this time we prayed for Rev. Kim and visited his wife to console and encourage her.

We admired his bravery in speaking out for democracy and human rights, and we saw the strength of Sung Yoon Soon as she stood firmly behind her husband and carried on the family responsibilities. The children, too, helped their mother and made sure her needs were met.

The arrest, imprisonment, and all that followed brought home to me the testing and the grief that Korean activists and their families experienced. We in the Monday Night Group were further confirmed in our solidarity with these Christians – and in our commitment to protest what could only be perceived as U.S. support for the Korean government's increasingly draconian measures.

Min Soung Hae, Rev. Kim's daughter, helped me remember a story about her father's imprisonment. While he was in solitary confinement, he was not allowed visitors, even his wife. He could not receive any news from his three sons and daughter. But each prisoner's family was responsible for that prisoner's laundry, so Sung Yoon Soon each week wrote short messages on flat elastic bands that she then stuffed into her husband's loosely packed underwear. Much later this story was told on Korean TV as an example of the creativity and caring that emerged in most difficult times.

And it was most difficult: under government pressure, Rev. Kim was expelled from Yonsei University for six years. Briefly reappointed in the spring of 1980, he was finally allowed to return as full professor and permanent faculty member in 1984.

Another extraordinary human being was Lee Tai Young (Yi T'aeyŏng), the first woman lawyer in Korea. She was exemplary in her fight for human rights and justice for women. Dr. Lee helped organize the One Hundred Women's Building Project, named in honor of two groups of Korean women – one hundred in south Korea and one hundred living in or working in the United States – who contributed substantially to the project. Working under adverse conditions, the building was completed and became the home of the Korea Legal Aid Center for Family Relations, which Lee Tai Young had founded to empower women seeking equal rights under Korean Family Law. The center launched the country's first free legal aid program especially for women and families. For seventeen years Dr. Lee worked to revise Korean Family Law, achieving modifications step by gradual step. For a short time I worked in the office at the One Hundred Women's Building in central Seoul. I saw daily how the women counselors dealt with a wide variety of individual, family, and societal problems.

Dr. Lee had a strong influence on the movement for human rights and the restoration of democracy. She became a symbol and inspiration for other Korean women. She was one of the two women who signed the March 1, 1976, "Charter for Democratic Salvation of the Nation." Even though she was disbarred, she was always available for legal assistance and was aggressive in protesting policies and actions of the dictatorial regime. She was also a skillful international networker. She knew well the oppressive conditions faced daily by her Korean sisters and brothers, and she communicated these realities clearly and boldly in numerous trips abroad.

My years in south Korea – especially my relationships with so many remarkable south Koreans – changed my life forever. I grew tremendously. My mind and heart were stretched by the economic and political realities in Korea. I was empowered to act upon my convictions. I felt blessed to find, know, and work with other expatriates who were willing to learn what was happening and then act on those learnings.

We in the Monday Night Group were leaderless, sharing the work, meeting in each other's homes, learning new things, and deciding how we might influence our governments and our churches and church members back home. As we became more aware and knowledgeable, we in turn could educate others. For example, we met with delegations from the Young Women's Christian Association

(YWCA) and U.S. Church Women United when they visited Seoul. We understood that part of our mission in the MNG was to educate these traveling ambassadors, to remove blinders just as our blinders had been removed, and to help them see and understand the glaring inequities that so many marginalized Koreans were experiencing.

The Monday Night Group also had some special visitors. U.S. Rep. Donald Fraser (D-Minnesota.) was one of them. In the mid-1970's he headed a congressional subcommittee investigating human rights abuses in Asia. He came to the Monday Night Group on a night when the meeting was held in our home. Expatriates came from all over Seoul and from elsewhere, filling our living room and spilling over into the kitchen, sitting and kneeling on the floor. As was the custom, shoes were removed (and that night piled high) at the door.

Rep. Fraser arrived late. Not knowing the custom of taking shoes off at the door, he proceeded to walk into the middle of the meeting in his black dress shoes. He looked awkward as he careened into the room, trying not to step on hands or feet. He had heard that we could help enlighten him on human rights abuses in south Korea. He listened carefully as we told our stories – news about factory workers, college students, and mothers and wives of political prisoners. He didn't stay long, perhaps because of the crowded, stifling room, but we felt gratitude that a person of his stature would meet with us.

Occasionally the Monday Night Group invited key embassy personnel from countries that we thought might be interested in our issues and causes. For example, when Canada appointed a new ambassador to south Korea, we invited him and his wife to join us for dinner. We had a simple dinner on our comfortable *ondol* (radiated-heat floor), followed by a good discussion.

When we walked the ambassador and his wife to the front gate, we saw a uniformed man up the telephone pole listening through the line. We knew he had been snooping in on our living room conversation. But maybe the reception wasn't very good, because a few days later a "telephone man" came to "repair" the phone in the living room. He opened the mouthpiece, placed some kind of device into it, screwed it shut and said, "Okay, it should work now." I smiled and thanked him for the good service. From then on, when we had conversations in our living room, we entertained the snoopers with music from the radio we placed next to the phone.

Following the government's execution of the eight "PRP" men and the deportation of Fr. Jim Sinnott in April 1975, the Monday Night Group decided to have a retreat. We felt we needed to learn about methods of nonviolent resistance, and we had a good person to teach us: Rev. Richard Deats from the U.S. Fellowship of Reconciliation. We met at a Christian campground outside Seoul. The weekend was intense, because we were still dealing with our powerful emotions over the hangings of the eight men. One of the things we did was reenact the scene in the Supreme Court the day that the eight men were condemned to death. We talked about our shock, anger, despair, and sense of powerlessness. And we reminded one another that, even as we came to understand our own emotions at that time, we would never be able to comprehend the shock, anger, despair, and powerlessness experienced by the wives of the hanged men.

In 1981 Eleanor Gregory, then U.S. national president of Presbyterian Women, came to Korea for the 25th anniversary of the Legal Aid Center for Family Relations, which American women had supported through donations to the One Hundred Women's Building. Eleanor and I met at the Yonsei University campus, and I told her about my work. She wanted to see firsthand the oppressive conditions for garment workers in the Peace Market in downtown Seoul. So we went to the garment district. We saw the shops where the garments were sold, and we climbed up the dark, dingy stairs to the fourth- and fifth-floor sweatshops where the garments were made. We saw the young women bent over their work in their cramped quarters.

Twenty-three years later, in December 2004, I received a Christmas greeting from Eleanor, now a member of a Presbyterian Church in East Aurora, New York. She wrote, "I still remember my visit with you in Korea. You opened my mind and eyes to so many things. I particularly recall visiting that old warehouse with the young kids working away inside. My heart ached and still does so when I read of sweatshops around the world, including here in the U.S.A."

Korea and Koreans taught me so much. Witnessing and walking alongside Koreans in their struggle, I learned how critically important it was for my own development and for the betterment of society to *work locally and globally, one person or one group at a time,* as in the Monday Night Group.

It was and is sobering and liberating to continue to educate, inform, and act on our convictions, wherever we witness society's contradictions and disconnects. That's what inspires me today in the U.S. in my work with immigrants and survivors of mental illness. Seeing and learning isn't enough; we have to act on what we are seeing and learning. Korea and Koreans taught me that.

They taught me the powerful truth of Isaiah 61:1-2: "With God's help, we can all become ambassadors of justice and peace on this earth."

Chapter 10

Let It Be an Experience

Jean Basinger

Growing up on a farm in Goldfield, Iowa, in the 1930's and 1940's, I certainly had no idea that I would have the opportunity to live in Asia and to share the joys and the heartache of the people there. Perhaps I did catch a vision of what was in my future when as a young child I would walk through the fields at sunset bringing home the cattle. Often I would be filled with a sense of the inter-connectedness of God's entire universe.

For eight years I attended a country school that was one and a half miles from my home. As I walked to and from school each day, I thought about the children I learned about in my geography books. I felt that that they too were God's children, and therefore my brothers and sisters. Perhaps being an only child made this more meaningful to me.

Let It Be an Experience

From the time I was a toddler, I always attended Sunday School and worship at the Methodist Church. God was the center of my life. I went to church camp from the time I was in sixth grade. By eighth grade I felt God was calling me to become a missionary. I imagined going to Africa or China, probably because most Methodist missionaries seemed to go there. During high school there was a miserable time when I doubted the call to become a missionary. Then one Sunday morning a friend told me about the nursing school at Iowa Methodist Hospital in Des Moines. Suddenly it was clear what I was supposed to do next. I was sure I was moving in the direction God wanted for my life.

I met future husband Bill Basinger when we were both students at Drake University. He too was from Goldfield; his father, the town doctor, had delivered me as a baby. Bill and I didn't really know each other growing up because of the seven-year difference in our ages. We were married in 1955, and soon thereafter joined Knox Presbyterian Church in Des Moines. Bill got his master's degree in rehabilitation counseling from the University of Iowa

Since the time we were married, Bill and I shared a dream of church mission work overseas. He wanted to go back to Japan, where he had served in the Navy. Every summer our family attended Presbyterian Synod School. One year a Christian Education teacher asked me to help her lead a synod workshop for preschool teachers. I told her that I had never actually taught a preschool class. She said, "Well, let it be an experience!" From that time on, whenever I was asked to do something that I really wanted to do, but for which I lacked experience, that became my mantra: "Let it be an experience!"

❧ ❧❧ ❧

In February 1967 our family – Lori, 9; Brian, 8; Denise, 7; Chris, 3; and Bill and I – participated in the annual Foreign Student Weekend sponsored by the Council for International Understanding. Two students from Indonesia who were attending Dubuque Theological Seminary stayed in our home. They had been with us for only a few hours when they told us that we should go and work in Asia. The U.S. had many health professionals, they said, while countries like Indonesia had so few. They thought it would be wonderful if we would go where we could be of greater service. Bill and I decided this must be God's way of telling us that the time had come for us to make a decision about our long-standing call to mission.

We called the Presbyterian Mission Service, which sent a person to interview us. We took tests, filled out applications, and before we knew it we were at the Stony Point (New York) Missionary Orientation Center. After six months of intensive orientation we were on our way to Tokyo, Japan, in February 1968.

It was a unique time for Bill to arrive in Japan. A new state-of-the-art center for mentally and physically handicapped children and adults was being opened in Tokyo. The facility was to be a model for other such centers across Japan. The Japanese had the money and the desire to move ahead in services to handicapped persons. Bill saw this opportunity as a way not only to develop programs for mentally and physically handicapped persons in Japan, but also to establish Japan as a training center for professionals in the field from throughout Asia.

During the six years we were in Japan, Bill brought in staff from Holt Adoption Services in Korea to be trained in Tokyo. He made several trips to Korea to serve as a consultant on rehabilitation to various programs there. In 1973 the Koreans asked him to come there to work full-time. In Bill's response to their request he wrote that, as a Korean War veteran, he always knew that he would someday return to Korea. He said that as an American he also felt some responsibility for the U.S. role in the division of Korea in 1945, for the Korean War that resulted, and for the devastation caused by the war.

Let It Be an Experience

꩜

We arrived in Korea in August 1974 with some understanding of the struggles going on for democracy and human rights. During our years in Japan we had become aware of the some of the realities of conditions in south Korea under the Park Chung Hee dictatorship. But hearing about these things abroad was not the same as seeing them first-hand. The Monday Night Group introduced us to the harsh reality of the dictatorship and how it affected every aspect of the Korean people's lives.

We met with the Monday Night Group just one week after our arrival in Seoul. We had attended a meeting of the Seoul Station Presbyterian Mission, where we met Linda Jones. We were deeply moved by her prayers for Koreans involved in the struggle for human rights and justice and for those in prison. We accepted her invitation to attend a meeting of the Monday Night Group. We will always remember that when we arrived at the meeting, Linda met us outside the door and told us not to feel pressured to do anything we were not comfortable doing. Little did we realize then all the choices and experiences that lay ahead of us.

That first MNG night we were among those who signed a letter asking President Ford not to come to Korea, because the Park Government would exploit it as U.S. approval of the regime. We also met Father Jim Sinnott and George Ogle, two MNG members who would be deported within a year.

Professionally, Bill and I witnessed the denial of basic human rights in our work for Yonsei University Medical School and for Severance Hospital. Both institutions were diligently attempting to deliver medical services to the poorest people in Seoul and to those who were marginalized due to disabilities.

One of our friends commented that Bill must have found working at the Tokyo Center for the Mentally and Physically

More than Witnesses

Handicapped in the 1960's and 1970's like a preview of rehabilitation in the 21st century – and that doing rehab work in south Korea in the 1970's was like being thrown back into the 19th century. To some extent this was true. South Korea's only government rehab center was shut down just before we arrived. Rehabilitation of the disabled was left to non-governmental organizations (NGOs).

～ ～～ ～

The first act of a totalitarian regime, of course, is to suppress the individual rights of the people – and this unfortunately includes even the right to basic health care. Under Park Chung Hee, even minimal health care was denied to those who could not pay for it. This was further complicated by the fact that so many people were displaced by the mass migrations of people from rural areas into the cities. The government, in its effort to force people off the land and into the cities, failed to provide support for agriculture. The policy provided an unending surplus of cheap labor for Korea's factories – the human fuel for what became known as south Korea's "economic miracle." The policy had tragic effects in city and countryside. The people served by the Yonhee (Yŏnhŭi) Primary Health Center in Seoul are a good example of the human tragedy that occurred as people were first displaced then, once in the city, denied basic human services. It also illustrates how a Christian-based organization tried to reach out and respond to those needs.

The people served by the Yonhee (Yŏnhŭi) Community Health Center lived on the mountain sides of Yonhee Dong, between the Seoul Foreign School and Yonsei University, on the outskirts of Seoul. They were discovered by students of Yonsei University Urban Studies Program while they were surveying the needs of the people living in the area immediately surrounding Yonsei University. The students found that the number one need of the people was basic health care services. The city of Seoul agreed to provide space in the bottom floor of one of the Yonhee apartment buildings, a substandard city housing development where there was one sink and one toilet on the entire floor. This was the only contribution ever made to the health center's work by any level of the Korean government. One time, in fact, the city shut off our water supply when it discovered we weren't paying the water bill. A newspaper account of how the city had cut off water at a clinic providing free medical services to the poor of Yonhee Dong was all that was needed for the water to be turned back on.

Yonsei University Medical College agreed to provide the health center with $50,000 to cover the cost of staff, meds, and equipment. There was a pharmacy formulary consisting of fifty basic drugs. The pediatric clinic and general clinics were staffed with residents from the Yonsei Medical School. The tuberculosis clinic was held once a week and was staffed by a TB specialist from Severance Hospital. A medical director, public health nurse, social worker, midwife, pharmacy tech, x-ray tech, several registered nurses, and a custodian were also on the staff.

I worked in the pediatric clinic two days a week and in the TB clinic on the day that the TB doctor was there. In the afternoon I often went on home visits with the staff. I had no training in primary health care, but my dream since I entered nursing had been to work in the field of public health. Once again I had to remember my friend's charge, "Let it be an experience!" It certainly was.

The health center attempted to bring primary health care services to the approximately five thousand low-income families living there. Many were squatters living in shacks made of whatever materials they could find. The poor were pushed higher and higher up the sides of the mountains, increasingly far from what few services there were. People had to carry water long distances, and rig up illegal lines to get electricity. Things like garbage pickup, coal and food delivery, and transportation were nonexistent. People who lived on the opposite side of the mountain had to travel hours to get to our clinic, often carrying their babies and/or small children. People barely managed to survive from day to day.

These poor people were drawn to the city by promises of work in the factories, but those jobs, when they did exist, were usually for the girls and women who would work for lower wages in miserable conditions with less complaining. The unemployed men were left to pick through garbage in hopes of finding something they could sell for a few *won*. Alcoholism was a big problem among the men, who often turned to cheap liquor to dull the pain of not being able to provide for their families. Many people who came to our general adult clinic suffered from stomach ulcers and hypertension, symptoms of the stress of their daily lives.

The number one problem we faced at the health center was the high incidence of tuberculosis among the 25,000 slum residents we served. Many of them had strains of TB that proved resistant to the primary drugs normally used to treat the disease. These primary TB drugs were available free through the government, but many people did not take them long enough to fully recover; they either didn't understand how important this was and/or they didn't like the side effects. Lack of education about the disease also played a role.

Many persons whose TB was resistant to the primary drug could be cured with the secondary drugs – if we could purchase them. I set up a sponsorship program so that churches and individuals from the U.S. and other countries could send funds to purchase the drugs for an individual patient. I sent donors information and updates about their particular patient. Because of this program a number of people who would have died were able to recover. Another positive outcome was that Yonsei University noted the results and agreed to provide the secondary medications free of charge to anyone needing them. Thus the funds from outside the country became unnecessary.

We also realized that among the 25,000 residents in our target community there were probably many more people with active TB than the five hundred with whom we were already working. We hired five new TB workers who went door-to-door interviewing people, taking sputum samples, and urging people to come to the center. The campaign was successful, not only in identifying a number of new TB cases, but also in making many more people aware of our basic health-care services, including our well-baby clinics, prenatal care, and immunization clinics.

～ ～ ～ ～

In 1977 the south Korean government came up with a motto for its new medical care programs, "Let's Give Help in Illness When We Are Healthy." For many low-income citizens, however, "getting help in illness" remained difficult if not impossible. There was much fanfare and publicity in the English press about the government's new Medical Insurance System, but the results were far less impressive. The experiences of low-income people seeking care in time of dire need were often heartbreaking.

A second program – often incorrectly reported as the "free" medical care system – was the "Yellow Card" and "Green Card" program. If an individual had no income whatsoever, and no relative who contributed to his or her support or could help with medical emergencies, then that person would be eligible for a "Green Card." Then when someone required medical treatment, he or she would be required to pay only thirty percent of the admission fee and the hospital charges; the government would pay the other seventy percent. One cannot help but wonder where such a person would get the money to pay thirty percent of the bill, since the fact had already been established that he or she had no income and no family to help pay expenses.

The "Yellow Card" system was for those who were employed in low-wage or part-time jobs. In those cases the individual was required to pay seventy percent of inpatient medical costs, and the government would pay thirty percent. To qualify for a "Yellow Card" a family of five had to have monthly income below $100. Here again, there was little chance that a family with such low income would be able to come up with seventy percent of the cost of admission and hospitalization.

One experience illustrates the suffering of the poor under the Park Chung Hee regime, and the emptiness of its claims that it was providing health care through the Medical Care Programs. Thursday was our day to visit TB patients enrolled in our secondary TB drug program. On one particular Thursday we visited Mr. Hwang, a patient who had made a very deep impression on me. He was such a gentle person; he seemed to have such faith in our services, and such appreciation for the help which we gave him.

The public health nurse started into the room where Mr. Hwang, his wife, and two small daughters made their home. Then I heard the nurse gasp and step back in shock. I looked into the room and saw Mr. Hwang lying on the floor, his face drained of color, his eyes darting wildly, apparently seeing nothing. He coughed frequently, bringing up bloody sputum from his disease-wracked lungs. We recognized immediately that he was having a hemorrhage and must be admitted to a hospital as soon as possible

Mr. Hwang's two small daughters were at home, and his wife soon returned home. She began to tell us how Mr. Hwang's condition had grown steadily worse during the past week: He couldn't eat, had become increasingly weak, and was constantly coughing and bringing up bloody sputum. She told us how, just the evening before, she had taken him to the Red Cross hospital for treatment. Even though he had a Yellow Card, he was refused admission because he could not pay the $90 admission fee.

Mrs. Hwang began to cry. Her daughter stood with her arm around her mother and silently wiped away the tears. She was only four years old, but she understood her mother's grief and agony.

We knew no hospital would take Mr. Hwang unless it was ruled an emergency; so we had to create an emergency. Even the city hospital did not take non-paying patients unless they absolutely had to. Our social worker called the police and told them that she had found a critically ill man and she requested that an ambulance be sent. Then she contacted the village leader and explained the situation. He came with a two-wheeled cart. This type of cart is used for many things in Korea – hauling supplies, selling fruit, moving garbage. Today it was to be used to transport a critically ill slum-dweller down bumpy streets in search of help.

We got Mr. Hwang into the cart, his head resting on the sharp edge of the side of the cart (he didn't have the strength to hold it up.) Drops of blood were on his lips and chin, bearing witness to the disease tearing at his lungs. A neighbor pushed the cart up to the main road and across to the other side to wait for the ambulance. We were told not to go near because, if the city police discovered that this man had friends and family to help him, they might refuse to take him. Even Mr. Hwang's wife was cautioned to stay away. We watched from across the road. The June sun beat down on the patient, and his face convulsed with pain. The minutes seemed endless. As I looked at him and saw his anguish, I began to feel faint; my stomach churned. I scolded myself; I didn't want to be distracted by my own physical reaction. I wanted to concentrate on Mr. Hwang and his suffering. But my mind and heart churned with questions: Why do we tolerate such madness as this? Why don't we cry out against this obscenity forced upon fellow human beings? Perhaps because experience has taught us that the only alternative is to do the best we can.

We waited for help to come. People waiting for the bus milled around. I wondered how many times the residents of this slum area had witnessed such a scene. Twice the city police came, but they did not go near Mr. Hwang; it seemed clear that there would be no ambulance. They told the social worker to take him to the city hospital in a taxi.

The next day I learned that she had finally managed to get him to the hospital and he had been admitted and taken directly to surgery. But it was too late. He died on the operating table. Unless you had the money in hand, "Help in Time of Illness" was a myth, not a reality, under the regime of Park Chung Hee.

July 5, 1976, was moving day for thousands of people living on the mountain sides of Yonhee Dong. Most of them were squatters living in makeshift shacks. They were given less than two weeks' notice to move out due to "city land development." It seemed that there was a prestigious university located on the mountain overlooking the slum area, and many foreign visitors came to visit the campus. Those honored guests often asked embarrassing questions concerning the slum area. Because of this, the university gave the city a large amount of money and asked it to eliminate the slum area and build a lovely park on the site.

The majority of these people had come from the rural areas seeking work and hoping for a better life for their families; instead they had found poverty, disease, and loneliness. All of them lived in the target area served by our health center, and we had a deep concern for each of them. We knew they were squatters with no legal right to the land on which they were living. But we also knew that those who had the power and the money to help these people were not doing so.

Instead, they were denying the slum-dwellers the right to have some place to live and raise their families without fear of eviction.

I could not imagine that such a thing could happen to my own neighbors. I walked across the road and up the mountain to see if what I had heard was really true. I had never been in a war zone, but the devastation I saw that day looked like one. Families were standing around with their belongings in piles in front of them. I tried to imagine what it would look like if Bill and I tried to put all of our belongings in one pile. I think it would form a small mountain; perhaps it might even topple over and crush us beneath its weight. That might be a just reward for those of us who own so much more than our share of the material goods of this world.

Some of the families had gotten together and hired a small truck to haul their belongings away. A few persons were lucky enough to have some place to go. As everyone attempted to move out, city workers were already breaking down their homes with sledge hammers. I saw one house that I had visited several months ago. At that time white streamers had hung from the top of the door frame to announce the birth of a child. The mother had been filled with hopes and dreams for her new child. Now I watched as a worker ripped the door off of the house; I felt as if he had ripped off my arm.

Probably like others in such a situation, I expected to see pain and agony in the faces of the evicted as they watched their homes being destroyed. But what I saw reflected in their faces was sadness and weariness, for they had experienced this moment too many times before. The poor people of Seoul moved every six months on average, chased from place to place, crushed into smaller areas and tinier shacks. Always there were promises of low-income housing, of a place of their own ... someday.

Within a month most of the houses were gone, the debris was hauled away, and a tall fence was put up to hide the remains. As we health center workers made our rounds, we found many of the people who had been evicted. They were living in drain pipes, boxes, tents, and any kind of shelter they could erect. Many told us they didn't want to move out of the area because they wanted to be able to come to our center for health-care services.

During this time I collected coats and sleeping bags from members of Seoul Union Church to be distributed to the people who were displaced. One person who received a coat came back the next day to give me money that he had found in the coat pocket. I was touched by his honesty, especially at a time of such great need.

※ ※※ ※

We had a full time mid-wife at the center, and we did everything we could to try to find pregnant women and provide them with prenatal care early in their pregnancies. Despite our best efforts, we often didn't see them until the seventh or eighth month. Often the mothers were very anemic.

We also tried to encourage women to use birth control. They did not want to keep having children they could not afford, but their husbands insisted on having sex. Even though we offered free vasectomies, men rarely agreed to this procedure. They were convinced that vasectomies would make it impossible for them to perform sexually. Mothers-in-law also tended to discourage birth control; they wanted grandsons who would provide for them in their old age. They considered this a matter of survival, because there was no Social Security system in south Korea.

I had been an obstetrics nurse for 10 years before going into mission work, so I was eager to accompany our health center's midwife for a home delivery. The women in our area could not go to the hospital for deliveries, so they often had the local midwife come to their house to assist with the birthing process. Because the center's midwife did not live in the neighborhood, and because of the midnight curfew, she could not go to homes for deliveries after midnight. When she finally got a call to attend a birth during the day, I went with her.

The woman lived up on the mountain, and we had to walk across a ravine on a long narrow plank to get to her house. I was very surprised when the nurse midwife showed me the "sterile home delivery kit." Inside the sterile wrapper was a razor blade and piece of string. I expected the midwife to start boiling water, like they do in the movies, but instead she asked where the cooking oil was kept. She explained that she would rub the oil on the skin of the newborn. She expressed surprise that labor had started so soon after the mother had visited the center. The mother was embarrassed, and she admitted that she had visited the Chinese medicine store where she picked up something to induce labor. The midwife gently scolded her. Our patients often used Chinese medicine. Others visited the local shaman, often due to advice from domineering mothers-in-law who believed they should be in charge of the family's medical care.

A beautiful healthy baby boy soon arrived. We rubbed him down with oil, cut the cord, and placed him in his mother's waiting arms. After making sure that the mother and baby were doing well – and urging the mother to come to the health center soon for a check up and birth control instructions – we headed back to the health center. There would be joy in the household for a time, until reality set in regarding one more mouth to feed.

Sometimes the burden of the cost of children did not become overwhelming until a child reached middle school. The government provided free education only through sixth grade; then there were school fees and the cost of school uniforms. There were several alternatives. One was for the child to drop out of school and go to work. Another was for the family to put the child up for foreign adoption.

More than Witnesses

Along with our center's social worker, I went to the home of one the families in our neighborhood to help make arrangements for such an adoption. The oldest girl in the family was entering junior high, and the family had no money to pay the fees. They had decided that she would have a better life in the U.S. Everyone in the family was crying except the girl. "I will be the one to go," she said, in a very matter of fact way.

~ ⋙⋘ ⸰

The Monday Night Group got weekly updates on conditions in Yonhee Dong. I also wrote several of the MNG "Fact Sheets" using information I got from the health center staff. And I arranged for MNG members to meet and talk with the residents of Yonhee Dong. For some of them, this was their first introduction to health care (or the lack of it) among Seoul's slum dwellers.

Regarding my years in Korea, people often ask, "What was it that moved you the most?" How can I make a choice from such a rich tapestry of experiences? For me I think it was the fact that no matter how poor in material things people were, no matter how they were suffering, when you reached out to help them in some way, they always gave you something back – and they did so in ways that enriched my life in a very deep and precious way.

A young couple with a baby came to the health center. He had far advanced tuberculosis that was resistant to the primary TB drugs. We got a sponsor for him and put him on secondary drugs, but he lived in such poor conditions and the disease was so far advanced that he simply couldn't recover. The couple was not married, so chances were that his parents would take the baby, and the woman would be on her own. One morning shortly after he died the social worker asked me to come to her office. The young woman was there. She had a gift for me. It was a bag of sugar which she held out with both hands in the Korean way of presenting a gift. This was to thank me for arranging for the money for the medicine. The medicine didn't help; she would be left alone; still she brought the gift.

One of the men accused of being a communist in the People's Revolutionary Party case died of a heart attack after being tortured. Some of us helped his wife start a dressmaking shop. One day when we went to the shop, Bill noticed that a young woman working in the shop had a deformity quite common in post-polio patients. He knew that it could be corrected quite easily, but if left uncorrected it could cause permanent damage to the heart.

Bill talked to her about it, but she had no resources to get the surgery done. He spoke with colleagues at Severance Hospital, and they found the money and arranged for the surgery and therapy. The girl's mother was overjoyed and brought Bill a bouquet of crocheted, starched flowers in a glass case. This gift of appreciation had taken many days to make, but she just had to have some way to say thank you to Bill for noticing her daughter's condition and caring enough to help get it corrected.

❦ ❧❧ ❦

When the plans were made to open the Yonhee health center, the Yonsei faculty decided it was important that the hired staff be Christian. They felt that the work required people of deep faith who were willing to work long hours for small salaries in a very challenging situation. I imagine that people of other faiths who had the necessary skills could have done as well in delivering health services to the slum-dwellers. But they could not possibly have been more committed than the remarkable group of Christians I worked with in a very difficult mission. The staff had a deep and sustaining sense of community that carried us through even the worst of times.

More than Witnesses

Because of the National Security Law we dared not speak out about the terrible things that the government was doing, but I knew that loved ones of some of the staff members were involved in the human rights struggle. And they knew that I was a part of the Monday Night Group, and that it supported the movement. We had ways of communicating that we hoped would seem quite benign to anyone overhearing our conversations. We also had nonverbal ways of showing our support.

Our whole family was involved with the work that Bill and I each did. One night the health center midwife, Mrs. Kim, was going home from work very late. There were few street lights and often there were obstacles in the streets with no barriers to block them off. Protecting citizens was low on the government priority list. Mrs. Kim fell down an open manhole and was badly injured. Our 6-year-old son, Miki, was very upset. He often went to the health center with me, and he loved Mrs. Kim. He couldn't rest until his dad took him to the store to buy a flashlight that he could take to Mrs. Kim in the hospital. She was very moved by his concern.

As a staff we did many things together to build community. Every morning there were devotions before the workday began. At one time we all took guitar lessons. I failed miserably at this, so the staff decided that if I couldn't play I at least could sing along. One day the Vietnamese women who lived in one of the apartment buildings and received medical care at the health center came and taught us to make Vietnamese steamed buns. After we ate lunch each day I taught English and I also taught American cooking. My one regret was that I never learned to speak Korean well.

One December we had a Christmas party at our home for the center staff. Our youngest daughter helped me make Christmas cookies and candy. We sang carols and played games. The staff gave me a complete Korean outfit in shades of blue. I finally understood why in previous weeks the staff had been asking lots of questions about my measurements. One day they even sat me down and measured my feet. This caused them great consternation, because my feet are huge compared to Korean women's feet. But, after a long search, they were able to locate some *really big* blue shoes!

The staff shared the suffering, pain, and death of people living in poverty – unnecessary poverty created and sustained by a ruthless, totalitarian government. They got through it by coming together, sustained by their mutual faith, commitment, humor, and stubbornness. I felt blessed to be so warmly welcomed into their midst, even though the gifts I brought were so small.

One of my worst memories of my personal behavior in Korea came just before we were to return to Iowa in June 1980. We had a garage sale at our house and many people from the neighborhood came. Koreans are great bargainers; they pride themselves on "buying well." I, however, really dislike the bargaining process and avoid it whenever I can. After a whole day of intense bargaining, my nerves were raw. The following day one of the buying women came to my door. She said she had bought a comforter for 100 *won* (25 cents). Her husband had told her to give it back and get her money back. I refused her request – maybe because the comforter had been my youngest daughter's and was almost new, maybe because I was just tired from the whole process of moving.

I have always regretted that decision. To this day I can't forget it. I relive the moment, mulling it over in my mind, trying to make it come out right. I imagine giving her back her 100 *won* and telling her to keep the comforter. I try not to think what 100 *won* meant in her life. I try not to wonder if her husband might have abused her verbally and/or physically when she went home. It is a burden on my heart.

More than Witnesses

The people involved in the struggle for human rights and democracy had an impact on the lives of everyone in our family. The Monday Night Group often met at our house. The children realized, without us even telling them, that they shouldn't talk about who came to those meetings, or discuss anything they heard, with anyone outside our home. They were very aware of the deportations of George Ogle and Jim Sinnott. I bought a pair of George Ogle's long johns when Dorothy had a garage sale before she left Korea. Our oldest son wore them with pride for years. He firmly believes that someday he'll be asked to donate them to a museum!

The children knew that some of our activities led to our being watched by the KCIA and also put our alien registrations at risk, but they never complained. When we returned to Des Moines and had gatherings in our living room there, one child or another would whisper in my ear, "Is this the Monday Night Group?"

Emotions such as anger and humor sometimes reduced the fear we felt in difficult situations. Bill was one of the men who participated in the demonstration at the U.S. Embassy after the hanging of the members of the so-called PRP. When the men from the KCIA came to our door to take him in for interrogation, they had the *Korea Mission Yearbook* in their hands. The idea that they were using that book to look up our addresses made me so mad that I forgot to be scared about Bill's arrest!

One day Butch Durst called and asked if Bill could come right away and pick up the Monday Night Group's files. He had been warned by the KCIA not to do any more work with the Urban Industrial Mission. Butch not only had attended UIM meetings but also had discussed UIM work with a Japanese TV station reporter – and the report, with Butch's face, was then seen on TV in Korea thanks to the U.S. Armed Forces network. Butch was sure the KCIA would be at his door any minute. Bill rushed to his house, grabbed the MNG files, and hid them in our bedroom under a scarf.

Shortly after that our second son, Chris, had a Korean friend over for dinner, and I asked him what his father did. He said, "Oh, he works for the KCIA." We all gulped, wondering what his father might know about our family – and thinking about the box in the bedroom. Later Chris's friend asked him why everyone looked so strange when he said his father worked for the KCIA. To our complete amazement, Chris told him that the KCIA had taken Bill in and interrogated him for nine hours. His friend said, "Gee, Chris, I'm really sorry."

The Kwangju Massacre took place in May 1980, one month before we left Korea. One night about 11:30 pm. we received a call from Kim Yun, a college student leader in the student Christian movement. Because of her activism in the struggles for democracy and human rights, she had been imprisoned several times. She managed to convey to us that she, her mother, Kim Hallim, and her friend, the executive secretary of Amnesty International in Korea, needed a place to stay; they were not safe where they were. Without even discussing it, Bill and I agreed that the three should immediately come and stay with us.

They stayed with us until just one hour before we left for the U.S. They kept saying they would leave earlier so they wouldn't disrupt our packing, but we told them to stay; it was important to us to know they were safe. Mrs. Kim crocheted doilies which she gave to every member of our family. She told us that, as she crocheted, she prayed for those in the movement who had given their lives, those in prison, and those in hiding.

When our family was out of the house, they would answer the phone in English or Japanese, telling callers that they couldn't speak

Korean! They were able to remain in hiding for many more months, until an amnesty was offered. We were very relieved that they were not punished for their human rights activities.

⌁ ⌇⌇ ⌁

The impact of my Korea experience on my life after returning to the U.S. has been enormous. I continued to work for human rights and democracy in Korea, including educating Americans about the situation. I believe I was given a mandate to do this work during a worship service at Galilee Church in Seoul at the time of the Kwangju Massacre. During the service the mother of Timothy and Steven Moon talked about how, at the time of the Japanese occupation of Korea (1905-1945), American missionaries took back to the U.S. painful stories of the suffering of the Korean people under harsh Japanese rule. She said, "Where are the American missionaries now who will go back to the U.S. and tell our stories?"

We were the only U.S. missionaries present at that particular worship service, so we felt a special call to this mission. We also came to believe that it is not enough to give lip service to our faith – we have to live it out, no matter what the cost. We saw that over and over in Korea as our Korean friends put their lives on the line for the cause of peace and freedom. We saw what it really means to love your neighbor as yourself and to do nonviolent civil disobedience. Although my own witness to this day pales compared to my Korean models, I gained from them the courage I needed to do civil disobedience, to be arrested, to stand trial, and to risk going to prison myself.

In late 2004 our 8-year-old grandson, Ryan, saw a picture of me on our refrigerator door. It showed me being arrested at the Iowa National Guard Headquarters for protesting the involvement of the Iowa Guard in the war in Iraq. When the picture was taken a sheriff's deputy was putting handcuffs on me. Ryan said, "Grandma was this when you got arrested for crossing the line to protest the war?"

Let It Be an Experience

Surprised, I had to pause for just a moment. He asked the question so naturally, as if this was just exactly what he would expect me to be doing. I'm happy about that, but I know that it never would have been that way were it not for the powerful witness of the people of south Korea.

I glanced at my picture on the refrigerator and noticed a slight smile on my face. I must have been thinking, "Let it be an experience."

Chapter 11

We All Know More Bible than We Live by

Fran Nelson

I didn't always recognize or appreciate it at the time, but it seems that since childhood God was always conspiring to open my eyes and my heart to the larger world, both in its harshness and its beauty.

Growing up in a pastor's home, I sometimes sat on the laps of returned missionaries who visited our home. I listened to their stories in awe.

Throughout my early school years (during World War II) my pen pal was a Japanese-American girl who lived with her family in an internment camp. Today I can't remember her name or the details of our letters, but I know she expanded the boundaries of my world.

Soon after I married Charlie Krauth, we joined a United Presbyterian church. The denominational study focus one year was the

Sermon on the Mount and the United Nations. My global horizons expanded, and my awareness and compassion were heightened as I learned about conditions of people around the world. And I will never forget one thing the Bible teacher said during our study: "We all know more Bible than we live by."

I was also introduced to new and larger worlds in 1957 when we moved from small-town America (Oak Ridge, Tennessee) to Birmingham, Alabama, known then as "the most segregated city in the United States." I had never ridden on a city bus. The first bus I took in Birmingham was packed with African-American women, maids going to their jobs in the suburbs. The bus driver, surprised to see a white woman get on the bus, told the black women in the front two seats to stand up so that I could sit. They stood, but I refused to sit. I encouraged them to reclaim their seats, but we all remained standing for the whole trip.

Charlie and I became discouraged about the racial problems in Birmingham, especially when our church congregation voted not to seat African-Americans if they came to a "pray-in". Not long after that we went to Montreat, North Carolina, to attend the commissioning of missionary friends headed to Africa. During the gathering various missionaries encouraged us to consider becoming missionaries to Africa ourselves. Something began to buzz in our heads, and we decided to volunteer to go to Africa. As Charlie was composing our letter to the Presbyterian Mission Board, I was reading *Presbyterian Survey* magazine. An ad caught my eye: "NEEDED: Chemistry professor for Taejon College, Korea." I called out to my chemist husband, "Look at this!"

Charlie changed the application letter from Africa to Korea and, less than one year later, in 1965; we arrived in Taejon, south Korea, with our three-year-old daughter (the first of our three sons would be born three months after our arrival in Korea). Charlie began teaching chemistry at the university, and I taught piano to Taejon college students and missionary children. I also experienced a "dark night of the soul" as I struggled with culture shock, post-partum depression, missionary community adjustments, and physical illness.

My lack of Korean language skill, and living with other Americans in a missionary compound, contributed to my crisis of faith. So Charlie and I dealt with those factors in our second terms as missionaries to Korea (1969-73). We took full-time language study for half of that term, and we gradually worked our way out of the compound and into the Korean community in Seoul. Charlie worked at Soongjon (Sungjŏn) University (later renamed Soongsil University) and I served as a music therapist at Holt Orphanage.

Those were happy, exciting, and hopeful times. I loved singing and playing with the children and Charlie enjoyed his teaching. But there were clouds on the political horizon. Turmoil was brewing as President Park Chung Hee began his march toward dictatorship. As he tightened his grip, and as people's suffering grew, we knew we had to get involved.

~ ~~~ ~

The Monday Night Group was our bridge between knowing we had to do something and not knowing what to do. The group also became our extended family. Charlie and I felt comfortable and secure in the group, and we bonded quickly with the members. The group became not only a source of information, ideas, and actions but also of personal sharing, therapeutic healing, and *laughter*. Sometimes I think humor was as important as faith in getting us through those times when the government was arresting and brutalizing our Korean friends. I was always amazed how the Koreans maintained marvelous senses of humor during even the direst times.

I was both inspired and amazed by the witness of Korean Christians, from church leaders and preachers to students and parishioners. I remembered what that Christian educator had said – "We all know more Bible than we live by" – and I realized that these Korean Christians were daily teaching me how to narrow the gap between biblical knowledge and faithful action.

Charlie's and my lives were changed forever in early 1975 when we got to know Kim Yun, a well-known and highly respected leader of the student movement against the Park Chung Hee dictatorship. The connection began with a chance meeting Charlie had while riding on a train. My husband's seat partner introduced himself as a local church pastor. When he learned that Charlie was a Presbyterian missionary he invited Charlie to his church, which happened to be near our house in the Yunhee Dong section of Seoul. The next Sunday, Charlie went to the Pong Won Church and saw in the church bulletin, "Please pray for Kim Yun who is in prison." When we heard her story – including that she was the only woman among many students arrested following a demonstration – we knew we had to become involved. But we didn't want to create new difficulties for the Pong Won Church or for Pastor Lee and his wife. We asked Rev. Lee for guidance, and he encouraged us to act according to our consciences.

Between her prison incarcerations, Yun and her brother In Bom (Inbŏm) became close to our family, especially to our youngest son, Tom. Yun and In Bom visited us occasionally in our home. When Yun was back in prison, we joined our second extended family – the "Pong Won Church Family" – in sitting together as a group at her trials. Yun's mother, Kim Hallim, took me under her wing at trials, prayer meetings, and other events. I always felt that Yun's family gave me more support than I ever gave them. More than anyone, they showed me how to "live by the Bible."

Because I didn't have a regular work assignment or a place I had to be every morning, I was able to attend more trials and Thursday

More than Witnesses

Morning Prayer Meetings than some of the other Pong Won Church or Monday Night Group members. In Bom kept me informed about Yun's trial dates. On several occasions we'd get to the courthouse only to hear that the trial was postponed – another form of harassment, I thought.

At one of Yun's trials a crowd was standing outside. The police pushed us back as three busloads of prisoners were brought in. When Yun got off the bus she, as always, was mindful of her manners and bowed slightly to the crowd. One policeman laughed at her. During the trial I sat between MNG member Benny Zweber and Yun's mother. Many priests from Sogang University also attended. The prosecutor asked for three years imprisonment for Yun.

At the sentencing a couple of weeks later, I managed to take a good photo of Yun as she got off the prison bus. She looked at me and smiled. I saw the police taking notice of me and my camera, and I knew it would come to no good. Sure enough, after I got seated in court, I was tapped on the shoulder and asked if I was the person who had taken a picture. The policeman asked for the film. I tried to argue, saying the film was expensive and that he first would have to pay me for it. He was unimpressed, and I lost my appeal.

Yun was sentenced to one and a half years in prison. (For more about Kim Yun, see story toward the end of Jean Basinger's chapter.)

⌁ ⊷⊶ ⌁

Inside and outside the Monday Night Group, it seemed that the more our hearts cried out, the more sustenance we found for our souls.

Prayer was important in those days. I had never before prayed as fervently as I did for Yun and other imprisoned Koreans. A *sense of humor* became a survival mechanism. I remember Steve Moon at a prayer meeting one day discussing a new law declaring that Koreans could no longer talk to foreigners. "I guess I can't talk to my wife, then," he said. *Food and fellowship* became more important, especially in groups that included wives of imprisoned church leaders and alleged "People's Revolutionary Party" members. Lunches following the Thursday Morning Prayer Meetings were often settings for the healing power of jokes and laughter.

But I was sustained perhaps most of all by *music,* especially hymn singing. At the Thursday Morning Prayer Meetings and other settings we often sang "Once to Every Man and Nation," "Not in Dumb Resignation," "We Shall Overcome," and "Are Ye Able." Perhaps it was only appropriate that I, a music therapist, found hymn singing so therapeutic! The singing not only joined Korean and foreign voices into one; it also invited us to breathe in God's amazing grace and breathe out God's healing love.

Prayer, humor, fellowship, and music were needed during the "People's Revolutionary Party" case. Never have I experienced a more intense emotional rollercoaster than from April 1974 (the arrests of alleged PRP members) to April 1975 (through the days that followed the executions of eight of the alleged PRP men).

One of Charlie's most meaningful experiences in Korea was "adopting" one of the PRP men. Among other things, this meant taking a sleeping bag to the prison and visiting the man's family down country. Charlie found a job for the man's daughter in the chemistry department at Soongjon University, but she was fired when authorities discovered her family connection to the PRP. Charlie then helped her to enroll in and graduate from acupuncture school and to get a job.

The day the eight alleged PRP men were executed was also our daughter Elizabeth's birthday. Because she too was deeply concerned about the PRP men, Charlie and I decided not to ruin her special day by telling her of the hangings. Of course, she found out later, and the news had a powerful effect on her. The two of us, mother and daughter, shed many tears on each other's shoulders. To this day Elizabeth remembers the horrible tragedy that occurred on her birthday, and it continues to influence her worldview.

The Monday Night Group decided to protest the executions in front of the U.S. Embassy in Seoul. I helped Marion Current and Marion Pope cut and sew the black hoods that eight of the MNG men would wear over their heads.

On the day of the demonstration I went about my activities as usual. It was my day to go to Ilsan where I did music therapy at Holt Orphanage. When I arrived home in late afternoon Insook, the baby sitter, opened the gate for me.

"Why are you still here?" I asked her, "Where is Daddy?"

"He went away with some bad men," she said.

My heart sank. Charlie and the seven other Monday Night Group demonstrators must have been arrested and/or incarcerated. Our children didn't seem frightened, but I probably made them so. At the Seoul Foreign School the next morning, our children joined other children of detained fathers in the hallway to compare notes and share anxieties.

I didn't hear any news about Charlie until early that next morning. I was frightened for him – and somewhat concerned for myself. I didn't know whether Charlie's interrogator was insisting on knowing who made the hoods. When Bill Basinger told me that his interrogator had asked him to name the hood makers, I became even more anxious.

Fellow missionary Homer Rickabaugh helped relieve my fears until Charlie returned home safely. I am grateful to Homer also for his moral support of Charlie at that time and again a few months later when Charlie was one of two foreigners arrested while attending a trial.

≈ ☙❧ ≈

In 1976 Charlie received a grant from the Presbyterian Church's "Halt Hunger Program" for a rural development project in one of the poorest regions of southwest Korea. The projects, sponsored by Soongjon University, focused on working with the rural villagers to research and develop alternative energy sources.

We chose a small mountain village that had an empty house waiting for us, and in the summer of 1976 our family moved to Ma Dong, in the deep country far from bustling Seoul. We quickly settled in and began trying to "go about doing good" wherever we saw a need. We enjoyed the serenity of a snow-laden landscape in winter; the green fields, frogs, and crickets in summer; and the drying rice and red peppers, plus persimmons and cosmos in autumn. At Christmas we had a real live cow and manger at our back door.

What a contrast it was with everything that was going on in Seoul. We had every intention of leading a quiet life and not causing trouble, but we soon discovered that we could not escape the watchful eyes of the government: our KCIA "tail" in Seoul followed us even to our mountain village! We could never come or go without it being known. If Charlie and I went to a *tabang* for a cup of tea, I might lose my conversation partner to a "stranger" who would then accompany us to the bus to make sure we got on the bus we said we would take. Charlie was "invited" to stop into the police station every time he was in the county seat. Among the many curious onlookers of Charlie's work were most certainly some of his dutiful "watchers".

Despite this surveillance, we continued our contacts with the Monday Night Group. We even had unofficial satellite meetings in our Ma Dong home on weekends when the Basingers, Dursts, or others would visit us. I also occasionally went to Seoul to attend regular MNG meetings. These ongoing contacts with the MNG are probably what convinced our "watchers" that we were up to no good. Charlie once found great satisfaction in managing to lose his "tail" by crossing the mountain in the opposite direction from usual and taking a different bus.

❦

Our work in south Korea ended in July 1978 when we returned to the U.S. for missionary furlough. But we stayed in touch with our friends in Korea and never stopped being part of the MNG.

Other contributors to this book did so much more than I did in Korea, even to the point of being deported. I lacked their initiative and their courage. But I am forever thankful for their witness in support of the Korean people – and for reminding me that the Bible is to be lived, not just known.

Chapter 12

A New Day Had Dawned

Marion Current

In August 1956 I was one month away from leaving Canada to take a job in New Zealand as a physical therapist. I was 26 years old, single, and off to see the world. But an encounter changed the direction of my life.

That August I was a leader in a summer church camp. The director of the camp, Rev. Laura Butler, called each of the leaders in for a brief chat. Her question to me was, "Where are you going?" I knew that wasn't meant as a geographical question but as a question of faith. It happens that I had spent the previous night tossing and turning, like Jacob wrestling with God. I was pondering whether taking a job in some exotic country where I could sightsee "on the job" was a sufficient objective for my life?

So my reply to Rev. Butler's question was simply, "I don't know." Her next question was, "Have you ever considered attending the United Church of Canada Training School" (now called the Centre for Christian Studies)? I had never heard of the school, so she explained that it was a program for people who wanted to become diaconal ministers or missionaries. I told her it sounded interesting and that I would think about it.

That was the end of the interview and the beginning of a new and exciting life journey, and one with a much more satisfying objective. After considerable soul-searching I returned my boat ticket to New Zealand and wrote to the hospital there about my change of plans. That decision, the subsequent two years of study, and my choice of a new vocation, would literally change my life.

I became a diaconal minister of the United Church of Canada and made plans to become a medical missionary. In south Korea physical therapy was beginning on a small scale, but there was not yet a professional school established. It seemed that this opportunity best suited my background and skill level. At the training school, my eyes were opened to matters of faith and politics and a great deal more – all of it mind-stretching.

One of the things I was challenged to do at the training school was to clip newspaper articles of world events, something I continue to this day. I was also stretched in mind and spirit by my mentor, Katharine Hockin, a well-known missiologist and former missionary to China. She experienced the communist revolution in 1949 in China and the conflict between the communists and the Christians there. Those experiences, and her subsequent deportation from China, formed the basis for much of her thinking and lecture material which, in turn, stretched my parochial ways of thinking and prepared me for my Korea experience.

A New Day Had Dawned

Before going to Korea I attended missionary orientation that stressed the concept of "partnership in mission." We learned the importance of mutual respect for the people of other countries. Even if we had more education than persons we were serving among, a top-down attitude was discouraged. This conviction served me well, allowing me to defer to the wisdom of Koreans, even in the face of opposition from missionary colleagues who sometimes wanted me to exercise my "authority" in certain situations.

I arrived in Korea in September of 1959 and was appointed to work at Severance Hospital (now Yonsei University Medical Center). For the next twenty years I served as a physical therapist at that teaching hospital. I was also associated with the Presbyterian Church in the Republic of Korea (PROK). Founded in 1953, it was one of several autonomous Korean denominations with which the United Church of Canada maintained a close partnership. From the 1970's on, the PROK was one of the front-runners in the human rights movement in Korea, with many of its pastors active in the movement. This church had a very big influence on me personally.

I learned of and began attending meetings of the Monday Night Group in the early 1970's. Until then I was a relatively naïve person, especially politically. In fact, I had never been very interested in politics, in Canada or elsewhere. My initial motivation regarding human rights was sparked by my thirst for knowledge about what was happening at that time in Korea. Information was not readily available within the country, and there was strict censorship of outside information. For example, if *Time* or *Newsweek* magazines reported on human rights violations by the Korean government, the government blacked out those articles.

Koreans knew not to discuss the political situation unless they were perfectly sure no one could be listening. Because we suspected our telephones were being tapped, eventually we began using a kind of code language on the phone.

Heavy control of the news meant that very few people actually knew what was going on within Korea, and they were anxious to get reports from abroad. The Monday Night Group meetings were one key way we could get access to some of this censored information and learn more about what was really happening.

My interest in the human rights movement was inspired mostly by the Korean ministers and professors of the PROK denomination. I became inspired by the beliefs and actions of persons like the Rev. Moon Ik-Hwan (Timothy Moon), his wife, parents, and brother Moon Tong-whan (Stephen Moon), plus Steve's wife, Faye. I saw the change that came over them as their involvement in the struggle deepened. I also knew the Rev. Suh Nam-dong and his wife, and Professor and Elder Lee Oo-jung, president of Korea Church Women United and a wonderful woman activist. Like so many other Korean Christians mentioned in this book, their concern and activism inspired me to do something about the rapidly deteriorating situation. The Monday Night Group was a prime vehicle for figuring out ways to support our Korean colleagues.

⁂

Involvement in political activism was quite a change for me. Growing up in northeastern Ontario, I was too naïve to wonder why the English-speaking minority held the power even though French-speaking Canadians were in the majority there. I grew up never knowing any aboriginal, native Canadians, many of whom lived in the area.

In Korea, in retrospect, I realize that I had been completely brainwashed by the dominant culture; it never occurred to me to ask why the society was so skewed in favor of white protestant/catholic English-speakers. I was unaware of my prejudice, and it took quite a bit to change my attitudes. Even the Korean student revolution of April 1960, which toppled President Syngman Rhee, did not trigger a strong change toward activism on my part. Instead, the change occurred gradually during the 1960's as the Park Chung-Hee government became increasingly repressive and anti-democratic. The capstone of the military-style dictatorship was its Yushin Constitution in 1972. What finally woke me up was the conscientization I received at the hands of the Korean human rights activists. I am eternally grateful to them and to members of the Monday Night Group for deepening my reeducation process.

When I was on home assignment in Canada in 1974, I served as interpreter for two Korean physiotherapist colleagues who were critical of my speaking to church groups about the human rights oppression in Korea. They accused me of "hanging out the dirty laundry of their country," and they questioned my motivation for doing that.

I tried to explain that it was better to be up-front about these problems and help Canadians, especially our church denomination, become aware of the price the working people of Korea were paying for their so-called economic development.

Galilee Church was born in July 1974 during a period of severe crackdown on dissidents by the Park Chung Hee government. Its first worship service was held in a restaurant in downtown Seoul, with about thirty worshippers (and nine plainclothes KCIA police) in attendance. The purpose of this new congregation was to provide a place where Christians active in the movement for democracy could worship together, and where the love and compassion of God could be openly shown to those suffering under the Park dictatorship.

More than Witnesses

On the second Sunday, when we arrived at the restaurant, we found a sign taped to the door, saying that the service would be held at a different location that day. It seems that the "authorities" had pressured the restaurant owner not to allow us to meet there. So much for freedom of assembly, we thought. A church that welcomed the "rejected" of society had itself became one of the rejected, much like those who had been rejected and chased out of Jerusalem after the death of Jesus.

Eventually, Galilee Church was invited to hold its afternoon services at Hanbit ("Great Light") PROK Church, a congregation brave enough to risk the displeasure of the authorities. But constant government surveillance became a fact of life for Galilee Church.

The name "Galilee" was based on Mark 16:7b. After Jesus was crucified and buried, Mary Magdalene went to the tomb and found it empty, and then encountered the risen Jesus in the garden. She told the other disciples, "He is going to Galilee ahead of you; there you will see him, just as he told you." The disciples were to leave Jerusalem (the capital) and return to Galilee, where the people were downtrodden and oppressed. There the disciples would have to regroup and decide what they were going to do next.

While Galilee Church fit the definition of "church" – that is, a group of believers – it was different from most traditional churches. It did not have a regular minister or a building of its own. Its services were held on Sunday afternoons so that members of other churches could attend. Those who attended Galilee Church (in addition to a handful of us foreigners) were the wives, mothers, and other family members of prisoners of conscience; factory workers treated harshly for standing up for their rights; fired professors; ministers who were periodically imprisoned for their actions; and the ever-present, ubiquitous KCIA plainclothesmen.

Outside of Galilee Church, persons who were suffering unjustly often could not talk about their experiences, even with their close friends. They knew various kinds of fear, including the fear of not being understood. Friends who had not shared the same experience simply could not understand their pain. Inside Galilee these persons could find understanding and comfort. It was a place where they could express their outrage about the injustices to which they had been subjected. Just as important, it was a place where Christians could reflect on the meaning of their faith at a time when injustice and oppression were rampant. Everyone who came – usually twenty to thirty worshippers – knew the meaning of "suffering for my namesake."

For such a small congregation, its witness reached far and wide. It stood out among other larger, more socially prominent Korean churches. There were many Sundays when foreign visitors came – church leaders from other countries, journalists, and other interested foreigners. For example, Dr. George Tuttle, moderator of the United Church of Canada, came one Sunday, as did the moderator of the Presbyterian Church of New Zealand. Alan Boesak, the South African Reformed Church theologian famous for his ministry with the "Colored" during the apartheid era, visited Galilee Church. I had to pinch myself to realize I was actually sitting with such a world-renowned church leader, a fighter for the human rights in his country and a supporter of Korean brothers and sisters in that same struggle.

The story of Galilee Church reached far beyond the Korean shores. For example, the United Church of Canada published several articles on Korea in its *Observer* magazine. A photo accompanying one of the articles showed United Church of Christ missionary Willa Kernen taking notes during a Galilee sermon – while a KCIA agent sitting behind her is taking his own notes.

Some *Observer* readers wanted to know why the church was "meddling in politics." The magazine responded, "The missionaries...

are neither making political statements nor walking picket lines of dissent. They are simply exercising loving pastoral care for the dissenters' families and sitting with them as they pray together."

Of course, the Korean government didn't quite see it that way. KCIA agents staked themselves out along the alley that led up to the church, noting everyone who walked up the hill to attend the services. The agents also attended the services, taking notes on the content of the sermons and prayers, as well as recording who was attending. Even the pastor of Hanbit Church, where Galilee services were held, was jailed. His crime: mimeographing the order of worship for the March 1, 1976, service at which a "Declaration to Save the Nation for Democracy" was issued, signed by prominent Korean leaders.

Both Willa Kernen and I were called into the Korean Immigration Office and virtually threatened with having our residence permits withdrawn if we continued to attend Galilee's worship services. Naturally, that was a very frightening prospect. I invited some trusted Korean friends to my home to ask what they thought I should do. They were very supportive, so I continued to attend, but it was a very emotional time for me.

I announced my decision at one of our United Church of Canada missionary meetings, explaining that I sincerely felt that I could not continue as a missionary if I had to stop standing on the side of the oppressed; I had to stand with those who were risking their very lives for freedom and democracy. Also, I could not allow the Korean Government to define my role as a missionary. So I continued to attend Galilee Church – and my residence permit was not revoked.

I was very proud of the position the United Church of Canada took in relation to its Korea missionaries:

"The expatriate missionary enters a sovereign state not
by right but by the suffering of the duly constituted authority

of that country. It is expected of the missionary that he [sic]
will render appropriate respect and obedience to the laws of
the land. However, prophetic utterance by the missionary
and his [sic] sending Church, even though they may have
political connotations and be regarded by the government as
subversive, are always required by the Christian conscience.
This is particularly true if the missionary is confronted by a
situation in which basic human rights are violated, social
injustices perpetrated or tolerated.... The compulsion to
proclaim the word of God under such conditions, even
though it may incur the displeasure of the government,
is inherent in the Christian's duty to God and his [sic]
responsibility for his [sic] fellowman."

I felt strongly supported by this position of my church, and it
enabled me to continue in my "dissident" activities, such as attending
worship at Galilee. So many of the now famous torchbearers of the
march towards democracy in Korea were a part of Galilee Church;
I feel very blessed to have been able to participate with them in this
small but powerful community of faith.

❧ ❦ ❧

"The pen is mightier than the sword," the saying goes, and this
was very true in the days of the south Korea's military dictators. The
military had the swords, and all the people had was the pen. But
what a powerful tool it was! Almost daily some group of students,
laborers, church leaders, or journalists would write a statement
about the political situation. Poet Kim Chi-Ha and other poets
wrote prolifically about the injustices being perpetrated by the Park
regime.

Those who dared to write such things paid a high price. Their
homes would be ransacked by "investigators." They might be hauled

off to Namsan (South Mountain, KCIA headquarters), where they would be held for days or weeks – questioned, tortured, then imprisoned. Family members would be harassed, threatened with being fired from their jobs or expelled from school. So wielding the pen was not something to be done lightly. Yet, time after time, people willingly took these risks for their beliefs and for the future of their country.

By the latter part of 1974 reporters for the daily newspapers had become very vulnerable. One newspaper, in particular, – the *Dong-A Ilbo* – underwent a tremendous struggle. The *Dong-A* was Korea's largest and most widely read newspaper in the 1970's. Its reporters exposed government corruption, business scandals, and even the injustices suffered by those in the growing movement for democracy. They even reported about the torture inflicted on those taken in for interrogation by the authorities. This reporting was done despite heavy government surveillance, censorship, and pressure on the editors not to publish such articles. However, the reporters at the *Dong-A* believed in freedom of speech and refused to shut up.

When it became obvious to the authorities that the threats were having no effect, the government pressured advertisers to withdraw their ads, the newspaper's main source of revenue. Business sources reported that they had to sign statements promising not to buy ads in the newspaper. Schoolteachers were warned (on threat of dismissal) neither to read, nor to let their students read, the *Dong-A*. Distribution in outlying towns and villages was banned. This was serious because at that time television and radio were commonly available only in large cities; most people depended on newspapers for their news.

When all advertisements had been successfully pulled, the *Dong-A* reporters began to demonstrate outside the headquarters building, located in the center of the capital city of Seoul. Daily, from 10:00 a.m. to noon, they stood in a long line holding placards stating their case. With no income, the newspaper had no money for their salaries, but the reporters came every day nevertheless. Other sympathetic Koreans, as well as a few of us foreigners, joined their vigil whenever we could.

Then a most remarkable thing happened. Ordinary Korean citizens and even people in other countries, rallied to the cause by buying ads in the newspaper, which continued to publish despite no income stream. Some of the "ads" were less than an inch square; others, from individuals or organizations of greater means, were as much as a half page.

The "ads" might be just a person's name, or an expression of encouragement, or a statement about the situation. "Freedom and justice will win!" "Keep up the good fight!" Some said, "Spring is coming," a not-so-subtle reference to the April 19, 1960, revolution that toppled the Syngman Rhee government. People would line up for hours to pay for their ads. To the government's consternation, the daily circulation of the paper quickly increased from 600,000 to 800,000.

Despite this outpouring of support and financial donations, the newspaper was losing money – some said up to US$75,000 per day. Charitable contributions to the *Dong-A* were outlawed. And it wasn't entirely safe to purchase an individual ad. On January 14, 1975, a 1-inch by ½-inch ad was purchased by a lowly Korean Army lieutenant. The ad stated simply his rank – no name or any other information. Among the hundreds of other ads, it took a Korean schoolteacher friend of mine half an hour even to find the ad. But the government considered it such a threat that it arrested three *Dong-A* staff members on charges of "disrupting the unity and morale of the army." The three were eventually released, but this flap caused the National Council for the Restoration of Democracy (established in

1973 by key clergy and leaders in the struggle for democracy) to issue a public appeal to the nation for protection of freedom of the press.

The courageous response of ordinary citizens – all those who lined up to buy ads, or just stood in solidarity with the reporters in front of the headquarters during their daily silent vigil – was a great witness. And it affected me greatly. I credit the *Dong*-A protest for my subsequent willingness to join other such protests in following years: silent vigils, nonviolent protests and marches, letter-writing campaigns, etc. – many in Korea, but also in Canada when I retired. I will always be grateful to those brave *Dong-A Ilbo* reporters for their courageous actions, and for what they taught me about standing up for justice and freedom of speech.

❦ ❧❦ ❧

Ordinarily, a church is assumed to be a building where people worship, waiting for others to join them. Sarangbang Church in Seoul was just the opposite. This was a group of suffering people who had no church building. In fact, they had no homes either. They were slum-dwellers in Seoul, persons more in need of social services than worship services. They needed someone to hear their stories of suffering, someone who would stand in solidarity with them in their struggle just to live.

Who were these slum-dwellers? Why were they living in slums? What kind of conditions brought them there? They were the poorest of the poor, persons pushed to the edge of the city – and to the edges of existence – during south Korea's "economic miracle". Some of them had come to Seoul from the countryside, no longer able to make a living there. They were the victims of Park Chung Hee's policy to develop the economy no matter the human cost. The poor people at Sarangbang Church had become sacrificial lambs.

I became aware of the needs of these people at the Thursday Morning Prayer Meetings, held at the Christian Building in Seoul.

A New Day Had Dawned

The slum-dwellers lived in cardboard shacks in Imun-dong, in southeastern Seoul; they had only plastic sheets to keep the rain out. And now they were being evicted. The land they were living on had been designated by city planners for construction of apartment complexes – places where these poverty-stricken people could never dream of living. What few possessions they had were being taken away from them, and their future looked bleak indeed.

Evicted from their shacks, with no place else to go, they secured a few tents in which to sleep. Each day they went into the city to try to find work, mostly day-labor jobs. But when they came back to the slum at night, they would often find the tents torn down by the authorities. The "authorities" in this case were not government officials but bullies and goons hired to do the dirty work.

Some of the Thursday Morning Prayer Meeting worshippers wanted to help, so we met with the slum-dwellers to learn more about their plight. I clearly remember standing beside Rev. Suh Nam-Dong and listening as the people explained their sad situation. It was very emotional.

Looking back, I can see how situations like this influenced Rev. Suh; he was one of the developers of an indigenous theology which came to be known as Minjung Theology, theology of the poor and oppressed. The slum-dwellers became his teachers.

Concerned Christians and evangelists continued to work with the slum-dwellers, and the nucleus of a "church without walls" was formed. On January 30, 1975, a worship service was held to celebrate the establishment of the Sarangbang Church. In Korea the *sarangbang* is a detached living room used for entertaining guests. But this worship "room" had no walls. It was simply a gathering space among the slum-dwellers' tents. Many supporters attended the church's first worship service, including Mrs. Kong Duk-Kui, wife of a former south Korean president; Ms. Lee Oo-Jung, church elder and president of Korea Church Women United; and several ministers and human rights activists who were members of the Seoul Metropolitan Community Organization, sponsored by the National Council of Churches of Korea.

A photo taken on the church's opening day shows many happy faces as a white cross was set up and worship was held in those very humble circumstances.

The next week, however, all of that was destroyed. On February 9, 1975, a bulldozer came in and destroyed the tents and the flooring that had been added under them. Why such destruction? Because, we were told, the slum-dwellers had refused to heed warnings to stop attending the Thursday Prayer Meetings.

When the bulldozers were done, the people's belongings were scattered everywhere, and their rice and flour were dumped on the ground. Thirty people – men, women, and children – were carted off to the police station. A summary court sentenced six of the women to five days in prison, and four men to ten days in prison – presumably for making a fuss when their tents were being destroyed.

When I heard this news, I became extremely angry. How could such a thing be done to these poor people? Were they a threat to the stability of the country or to the government? Hadn't they suffered enough?

I made sure to attend the worship service held at the site on the following Sunday. I brought my camera and took photos of the destruction. Normally, I am a fairly respectable photographer, but the photos I took that day came out blurred. I realized later that it was due to my strong emotions. I was filled with so much outrage that my hands were shaking as I took the photos.

One photo became quite in demand afterwards. It was of Rev. Moon Ik-hwan (Timothy Moon), head bowed, holding the now-smashed white-plywood cross on his shoulder. The cross had been trampled on, broken, and splattered with excrement. That image is forever burned in my memory.

The Sarangbang persons who were not imprisoned, temporarily moved in with their organizer, Lee Chul-yong (Yi Ch'ŏyong). How 40 or so people managed to live, even for a few days, in two small rooms, I cannot imagine. Mr. Lee truly understood the slum-dwellers. He was a "worker-in-training" supported by the Seoul Metropolitan Community Organization. He had very little formal education, but he had all the qualifications of a fine leader, including a warm personality and a sincere concern for the people with whom he was working. He also had a prison record: he served eight months for reporting irregularities by officials in charge of voting in the 1975 National Referendum.

A committee of concerned individuals and representatives of churches and other groups was organized to raise money to buy a small piece of land for the Sarangbang people, so they could not be evicted again. SarangBang Church was still alive and well, but facing continued harassment. As we witnessed the struggle of this small group of people, we were reminded of Jesus' words to the authorities of his day, "Destroy this body and in three days I will raise it up."

While many of us in the Monday Night Group knew that our telephones were tapped and that our activities were under surveillance, I initially didn't feel that I was being watched very closely. There was just the one incident that I mentioned earlier: when Willa Kernen and I were warned by the Immigration Office not to attend Galilee Church. Gradually, however, there were other indications that my activities were being tracked by government agents.

For example, in 1976 I was informed by the Korean government that I would no longer be permitted to teach therapeutic exercise (a definitely nonpolitical subject) to students of physiotherapy at Korea

University. Why? Because of my pro-human rights activities outside the university.

Another time, the director of our Rehabilitation Medicine Department at Severance Hospital (where I worked) called me into his office and requested that I stop associating with activists like the Rev. Moon Ik-whan and the Rev. Suh Nam-dong. The director said he had received phone calls from "the authorities" suggesting that I should curtail my relationships with these dissidents and their related activities.

I ignored these directives. I had already decided that I would not let the Korean government define my "missionary activities." Officials used the argument that my actions on behalf of human rights and democracy were not allowed under my visa status as a medical missionary. But there was a strange disconnect: They were threatening to disallow my contact with students, even though I had never mentioned anything about human rights in my classes.

I continued to associate with the activists in question, more determined than ever to support activities for justice and human rights. But the authorities never stopped me from working at Severance Hospital, a Yonsei University institution with great political influence. I wonder today what might have happened if I had gone to the president of Yonsei and complained about my harassment. At that time, however, I wasn't so politically alert. And some of my activist friends might have argued that my work was too important to risk being deported over such a minor matter.

Another incident took place when the Japanese foreign minister made his first visit to Korea in late 1979. It was a very big event. I was surprised by a phone call from someone asking where I would be on the evening of the diplomat's arrival. I suppose the police were trying to make sure that none of us "troublemakers" would cause any upset during the visit. I assured the caller that I would be home that evening.

A New Day Had Dawned

When I received an invitation to go out for dinner, I had no way to contact the person who had phoned me to tell him my change of plans. The next day I received another phone call asking why I had not been at home after saying I would be. Thankfully, nothing untoward had happened during the diplomat's visit, so I assume the man whose job it was to check on me didn't get into any trouble.

❧ ☙☙ ❧

I was on home assignment in Canada in 1980. When I returned in 1981 my work assignment was changed to the College of Health Science, a branch of Yonsei University located in Wonju City, nearly three hours south of Seoul by bus. That meant I was unable to attend Monday Night Group meetings except for winter and summer school breaks. But I did attend when I could. I don't know whether this new assignment resulted from the authorities' desire to curtail my human rights activities in Seoul.

I wrote a small book (published in 1983) contrasting Western and Korean cultures. There was nothing political about the book, and the book was so little publicized that not even some of my friends knew about it. So it was interesting that the first person to phone and congratulate me on the book's publication was a man I did not know. I knew the man had to be the agent assigned to keep track of my activities.

I felt sorry for these people who were only doing what must have been a very boring job, but who would have been in great difficulty if anything happened during their "watch."

❧ ☙☙ ❧

The Monday Night Group was a very significant part of the texture of my life from the early 1970's through the 1980's, though by then most of the early members of the group had left Korea. During the 1980's and 1990's MNG meetings were held irregularly, only when there was a need. Fewer people attended, but it was amazing how the meetings fulfilled the group's original purpose: to inform and guide people in keeping alive the concern for human rights in Korea, and to share what was going on in one another's lives.

Eventually it was safe even for Koreans to attend Monday Night Group meetings, although it was usually limited to Koreans who spoke English well. Even though the political climate and the group membership had changed, the group had a continuing sense of solidarity and unity of purpose. The MNG meetings helped us keep things in perspective as Korea gradually moved from militaristic rule to democratic rule in the 1990's. As the democratic spirit grew, more information and news became available, and there was less fear of reprisals. Koreans who had been imprisoned and often tortured for their human rights activities began to accept positions of authority in the government.

We knew a new day had dawned when Kim Dae Jung – the opposition leader who nearly defeated Park Chung-Hee in the 1971 election – was elected president of south Korea and later received the Nobel Peace Prize; Rev. Moon Dong-Whan was appointed to serve in the National Assembly; first Rev. Pak Hyung-Kyu then Father Ham Sei Ung became presidents of the Korea Democracy Foundation; the National Security Bureau, where many activists had been tortured, was turned into a Human Rights Memorial Hall; and so many other dreams became realities for Koreans who had struggled so long and so valiantly.

Monday Night Group members after 1980 have a hard time even imagining the struggles of the south Korean people in the 1970's. That's why we, who did live through it, must tell our stories. I thank MNG members and all those who supported, guided, and shared in the heartaches, tears, and struggles of those years. And I thank God.

Chapter 13

Now You Are Free to Speak Out

Father Jim Sinnot

In the cold snowy late January days of 1974, seated in my rural island parish rectory, I pondered Christian Korea where Korean pastors, young husbands, and fathers spoke out in protest against the latest "Emergency Decree" and went to jail, while I, fat, happy, 44, and celibate, sat and watched from a safe distance as the dictatorship tightened its grip.

Spring came and things got worse. Students – many Protestants, some Catholics – were hit with Emergency Decree #4, threatening fifteen-year jail sentences for the mildest kind of protest, death for more serious "treason." My reaction: "Why doesn't somebody (else) do something?!" In frustration, I wrote to our highest church man, Cardinal Stephen Kim, impertinently telling him to "get with it."

My letter to Cardinal Kim was not out of the blue. I knew of his concern for human rights. Cardinal Kim had addressed a group of western missionaries in 1971: "You missionaries can help our Korean Catholics overcome one great defect in their training. They do not realize the dignity of each person in this world. If an army climbed the hill to break the stained glass windows and destroy the cathedral, Catholics would throw their bodies down and die to protect the house of God. But today fellow Koreans are being deprived of their basic dignity, falsely imprisoned, tortured for their beliefs, and our Catholics do not react. You westerners must teach them to care for others who are in danger of oppression, as well."

In hindsight, I see my letter as an attempt to throw the ball back into his court. "If you ask where is the Holy Spirit," I wrote, "it is hovering over the jails and police stations where Protestant pastors and students are being tortured.... Why aren't we Catholics doing something?"

I received no reply to this impudence, but when I visited our Seoul Center House a week or so later I was told Cardinal Kim had asked for me. Alarmed, I closely questioned my informant only to find that the Cardinal did no more than ask that question; he did not breathe fire or threaten excommunication. Though he did not actually request my appearance, I figured it was the right thing to go see him and apologize for my hasty letter.

Like the Irish Catholic New York parochial schoolboy I was, I felt no happy anticipation at the prospect of a lecture from a high churchperson, but I screwed up my courage and called at his Seoul Cathedral residence. Kim, Korea's only Cardinal, head of the Catholic Church in Korea, was far from a frightening figure, but I'd been well trained to respect authority and preferred doing it from a distance. I was ushered up the creaky wooden stairs in his old, drafty manse. Then I was left to find his door and knock on it myself, which after a few deep breaths, I did. He opened the door and I introduced myself as the writer of the letter. "Oh, it's you," he said with surprise. We'd met before, but I'd never dared to say two words, much less preach to him as I had in my letter. He stepped back and let me in.

Of middle height and slight build, wearing a white summer cassock with red piping, he looked more than usually saintly; not ascetic and other-worldly, but open and friendly with an attractive touch of good humor about his features. Still, I felt like the altar boy caught swigging the wine. Before sitting down, I began excusing my letter: "My words were a little strong, maybe, but I...." "No. No. No. No," he said in English, putting up his hands and raising his palms toward me, to stop my apology. Then he said, also in English, words that to this day still bring tears to my eyes: "The things you said in your letter, these are the daily problems of my heart."

Open-mouthed, I backed into a chair and listened as he told me from his heart the things I most wanted to hear. His perceptions and frustrations were very much like mine, and here he was sharing them with me. For more than half an hour we talked. I left him immensely encouraged. He sent me off with one word of caution: "Don't get too far out in front of everybody else." (I, the "obedient schoolboy?" I couldn't imagine what he meant.) I floated down the hill from the Cathedral, feeling as if I were with a crowd at the head of a parade, maybe a parade being held in my honor.

⌘ ⌘⌘ ⌘

On the morning of July 23, 1974, I set out in plenty of time to be at St. Mary's Hospital in the MyungDong (Myŏngdong) area of downtown Seoul by 9 a.m. Don Oberdorfer, Tokyo bureau chief for the *Washington Post*, was in Seoul that week. The night before, he had received an anonymous phone call: "Bishop Chi wants you at St. Mary's by nine."

More than Witnesses

Don had written me that he was coming to Korea. Now he was there: a Bishop under arrest was the "handle" he wanted for a news story on Korea.

The Most Reverend Daniel Chi, Bishop of the Catholic Diocese of Wonju, grew up in what is now called north Korea during the time that Japan occupied the whole Korean peninsula. At age twelve he converted to the Catholic faith, and in his fervor refused to face east and bow down to the Divine Emperor of Japan. Danny was punished and threatened with expulsion from school. In 1945, the Japanese were suddenly gone, but now the Soviets were in charge in the north. Danny, one year short of ordination to the priesthood, was ordered by the new authorities to break the Rome connection and join a newly organized National Church. The handsome young Daniel refused and was beaten and jailed. Eventually he escaped to the south, the Soviets probably glad to see him go. Now two decades had passed.

Bishop Chi had been the center of attention for two weeks. He had been arrested by the KCIA at Seoul's Kimpo Airport on his return from Germany and Austria, where he had publicly criticized the Park regime. Thanks to efforts by the Vatican ambassador, Chi was released into house custody at his brother's home. "Too many cops around," he complained. "My brother's family can't function." So, he was allowed to move to a Catholic nun's convent guesthouse, but again, "Too many cops. The sisters can't pray." Finally he was put on the 6th floor of St. Mary's Hospital.

At 8:30 a.m. the yard below his hospital window was half filled with nuns praying and well-wishers looking up to the 6th floor. July 23 was Bishop Daniel Chi's "Name Day." Don Oberdorfer and I, his volunteer stringer-translator, met in the foyer at 8:45. I had arranged for Don to interview the bishop at the hospital the week before. He had accompanied me into the bishop's room then disguised as a

378

colleague from the Washington diocese. All it took was the loan of a black shirt and Roman collar. (Jewish by birth, Don still talks of his twenty minutes as a Catholic priest.) At that interview Don had chatted with the bishop while another priest and I talked loudly to foul the bugging system. KCIA agents, of course, had also been there all through our supervised visit. Don never told me what passed between them, but the bishop must have been impressed to invite him back this morning.

In the hospital lobby I was trying to get permission to take Don to the 6th floor when a commotion arose. Who should appear marching down the stairs in full Episcopal dress but the Most Rev. Daniel Chi. He had broken out of custody. The agent on duty hung about him, telling him, "You can't do this," but never daring to stop him forcibly. When the bishop reached the ground floor, however, many plainclothesmen rushed to stop His Excellency's forward motion – and many of the "other team" of supporters, including the *Washington Post* and I, also moved to surround him. We outnumbered the forces of law and order.

From his full black red-rimmed clerical sleeve, the bishop pulled out three or four letter-sized plain brown envelopes. He handed one to Don Oberdorfer who tore it open, saw that it was in Korean, and handed it to me, shouting over the din: "Get this translated." With all the pushing and shoving, I could barely keep my feet, much less find a capable translator. At Chi's direction, the circle around him, still including cops, shoved its way out of the hospital lobby and into the yard where the nuns were still praying. The yard was full now with friends and foes, bathed in the hot July sunlight.

In these less than ideal conditions, the *Washington Post* interview began. "Are you free, Bishop?" "I am free in no way, not free physically as you can see, nor free as pastor of my people, even to pray with them." Elbows were flying, hips were flung as the police tried to force their way to the bishop. TV cameras ground on, inhibiting overt action. "Let us join the nuns in prayer," Bishop Chi said, looking toward the end of the yard where they were gathered for another rosary. The mass of us around him started in that direction, the bishop like a fumbled football in our midst, the police trying for recovery.

We all knew the cops had orders to fall back when nuns were present. (The Filipinos learned this from us and helped overcome Philippine dictator Marcos by giving high visibility to nuns at their demonstrations.) After prayer, as Daniel Chi spoke of the injustices in Korea, I had time to seek out a capable translator in the crowd. Fr. Ham (pronounced Hahm) Sei Ung (current president of the Korea Democracy Foundation) hurried off to find a typewriter, with "The Declaration of Conscience" in hand that Bishop Chi had given to Oberdorfer. It blasted the regime.

Homily ended, Chi said, "Now let us all go up the hill to the Cathedral and offer Mass." "What daring," I thought, and was thrilled to hear the sisters break into song and lead the way. I looked up the hill just in time to see Cardinal Kim arrive at its brow and look down at our gathering. His jaw dropped unceremoniously and he gaped in sheer surprise.

Our motley procession climbed the cement driveway, passing the rambling old wooden rectory. Sisters, priests, parishioners, KCIA men, press, cameras, all entered the main door, the same door we had so solemnly entered to pray for Bishop Chi's release two weeks before. Accompanied by a cohort of priests, he went forward to the sacristy to vest for Mass. I stayed behind with Don. Three hundred people filled the front pews. I was doing my job for Don as cleric-technical-advisor on things Catholic when the little bell rang and Bishop Chi came out of the sacristy and to the altar to begin Mass. At his side, also vested for Mass, was Cardinal Kim (a political statement if there ever was one). "Now you know where our Cardinal stands," I told Don, in case he missed the significance.

As I launched into an explanation of Mass as the re-enactment of Jesus' suffering, and a description of the trials of Korean martyrs 200 years ago – a KCIA man right behind us taking in every word – Chi approached the pulpit to read the Gospel. He chose the passage, "And Jesus said to his disciples, 'I must go up to Jerusalem and suffer many things....'" My translation for Don caught in my throat.

When Mass ended, Daniel Chi's re-enactment of Christ's suffering began. He left the Cathedral, back in the custody of the KCIA, and was taken from the crowd and the cameras to a real prison. When he was released – six months later – the Korean Catholic Church had become a formidable force for peace and justice.

❧ ❧❧ ❧

In April 1974 – having finally opened my eyes and ears to the repression in south Korea by the supposedly democratic regime, fast turning into a military dictatorship – I looked around for somebody I could trust to listen to my concerns. Marty Lowery, a tall, quiet 35-year-old Chicagoan, was the best bet. A fellow Maryknoll priest 10 years my junior, Marty had dared attend the trial of the Presbyterian activist-minister Pak Hyung Gyu. ("I'll send you a 'care package,' Marty, when they throw *you* in jail!" I had joked.)

I took the twenty-minute ferry from my island parish to Inchon and called Marty: "Meet me in a tea room," I demanded, sure his house was bugged. After I'd poured out my concerns (in a low voice, at a table away from eavesdroppers), Marty smiled and said, "Welcome to the club! Come with me on Monday night to Seoul where a bunch of people meet to talk about these things." Because I was steeped in anti-communism during the 1950's, including a short stint in the U.S. Army during the Korean War (though my assignment kept me safe

381

in Oklahoma), I reacted immediately: "I don't go to cell meetings!" But after another anxious week of more government crackdowns on church people, I agreed to go.

The Monday Night Group, which had been gathering weekly for several years, had a fluid membership and a floating location. Marty and I arrived in the middle of a debate about the proper grammar to be used in a letter to a U.S. congressman named Don Fraser, who apparently was interested in the lack of human rights in U.S. foreign policy. This didn't sound very subversive to me. After a rather too extensive discussion and final agreement, the next agenda item was another lengthy debate on how to get warm underwear to some student prisoners. Was I being purposely bored into dropping my guard against these "dangerous people"? There were about a dozen of them, Americans and Canadians, Presbyterians and Methodists, ordained ministers, lay missioners and interns, mostly married couples.

The hosts that evening were Randy Rice, a soft-bearded, soft-spoken Presbyterian minister from western New York State, and his wife Sue, social worker and mother of their four school-aged children who were in and out of our meeting room. Sue told us about their neighbors, a Korean couple now separated by a jail sentence incurred by the husband. He was a seminary professor who had answered a question raised by one of his students about the theoretical morality of dissent. His answer, "it sometimes could be done," got him a two-year prison sentence.

The talk turned to requests that had come from those in jail: the collected works of Shakespeare and T.S. Eliot were the two that hooked me. What kind of criminals were these people that the Monday Nighters were trying to help? For Christmas 1950 my sister Gloria had given me the collected works of T. S. Eliot. I had brought it to Korea and still prized it. I also prized her inscription and signature, because she had died young of cancer in 1967. But I wanted to be closer to the kind of criminals who read things like T.S. Eliot, and heard myself offering to give away my treasured volume.

Neither the attractive, low-key Rices nor anyone else in the group had much idea of how to solve what was going on in Korea. I saw in them the same frustrated concern I felt, and to me that was like a shot in the arm. I wasn't crazy! Contrary to being a "communist-style cell group," as I had stereotyped them, here were good ordinary people reacting to a crazy situation very much like I was, talking about it, wondering what to do. And they could laugh and joke and give courage to one another.

I made up my mind to attend more of these Monday Night Group meetings, and the next week I brought the T.S. Eliot book to the meeting. It somehow tied me in to this "subversive cell" – that, and the feeling the group gave me of being, like me, frustrated, upset, and very near to helpless... yet wanting to try to do something. It was like an alcoholic finally going to an AA meeting and finding fellow sufferers like himself.

I attended again the next week. This time it was held in the home of Louise and Butch Durst, a Methodist couple in their late twenties. Butch held the honor of being the first missionary arrested during these months of protests. The arrest was meant to frighten him away from involvement. It did not. Small-boned, blonde Louise from Tennessee worked first for her church in Japan and upon return to the U.S. had met the man from Colorado called Butch, a gentle, concerned man who fit neither the nickname "Butch" nor the westerner stereotype.

My presence doubled the Catholic attendance at the meeting. We listened to more reports of students disappearing, being detained by the secret police and intimidated physically. Schools were being forced to expel activist students and to discipline teachers who spoke too liberally.

More than Witnesses

The following Monday night, the meeting was held in one of the big, stone, western-style houses on the campus of Yonsei, a Protestant mission school that had grown into a prestigious university. Sue and Randy, Louise and Butch, and a dozen others joined Marty and me at the big drafty house in a special session where we played host to a delegate from a group who promised to out-do the Billy Graham performance of 1973. The high-powered salesman-type young churchman in our presence was a frontrunner for Explo '74, a gathering that advertised itself as the most multinational religious event since Pentecost. Explo '74 was to take place in Seoul in August, offering proof positive that the Korean regime fostered freedom of religion. More proof was needed this year, because so many religious leaders, seminarians, and Christian students were in jail!

Bill Bright, famed organizer for the Campus Crusade for Christ, had sent a preparatory committee to get Explo '74 off the ground, and on this May Monday evening, the well-tailored, shiny faced young man sat and told us what a grand affair was planned. Our plan was to push a bit against his confidence and make him aware of the government manipulation of his affair. For our efforts, all we got from the young optimist was an airy reply, "as far as governments go, we follow Romans Chapter 13, Verse One."

❧ ⬥ ❧

Marty and I looked at each other. Catholics were not very adept at pulling out scripture quotes by chapter and verse. That is a Protestant Sunday School and summer Bible camp specialty. Someone noticed we priests were at a loss and quoted for us St. Paul's letter to the Romans, Chapter 13, verse one: "All governments come from God. Obey your government."

"That's all you need to say," the Bill Bright delegate piped up, and went on with delight to describe all the generous government help

– space in schools, buses to be lent to them for transport of people to the meetings, Army tents and kitchens to be made available. (If the Roman soldiers had given such help, Pentecost would have been a much bigger happening.)

The bright young man and his scripture quote stayed on my mind, and a few days later, sure enough, Prime Minister Kim Jong-Pil (Kim Chongp'il) quoted the same chapter and verse to a Christian gathering, and added all on his own, "That means if you don't obey us, it's a sin."

In those warm spring months, I was doing a lot less ferry-boat traveling to my parish islands than I ought, and spending a lot more time in Seoul. It was there in early May that I was bombarded by another visual image, a poster announcing the annual Rat Catching Day. On the designated day all the people of the realm were to rise up as one body and "do in" the rodent population. This year's poster showed a hairy, fat-bodied, long-toothed, gimlet-eyed rat gnawing its way through a sack of rice. I had no argument against the campaign, but wished I had the wherewithal to mount one like it about my new concerns and frustrations, which seemed to be multiplying like rats.

I mentioned to Ben Zweber, fellow priest at another cluster of islands, a silly idea I had about the rat posters. I had taken to imagining the head of the hairy rat covered over with the portrait of one or another of the more intractable government leaders. "Let's do it," Ben said, to my surprise. Ben was a short, stocky, feisty man, full of energy and unstoppable. I used to get tired just watching him. My mere mention of rat posters set Ben into motion, leafing through newspapers, scissoring out appropriate photos, and, after full dark, leading me out onto the streets of Inchon, armed with a bottle of glue.

More than Witnesses

Our first stop was the nearest police station. At its gloomy side door entrance that led to the policemen's latrine, there was a rat poster. "Pretend we're drunk if anybody comes near," I suggested. But to spread the glue on the face of the buck-toothed rat and cover it with a photo of the Chief of the National Police took only a moment, and we walked quickly from there to a central community bulletin board at a busy crossroads. There we enshrined the photo of the former attorney general and now head of the KCIA, Mr. Shin Jik-su (Sin Chiksu), the man behind the phony plot blaming all dissent on communists. While Ben was pasting, a car's headlights caught him. "Pretend you're taking a leak!" I whispered hastily from my hiding place behind a light pole. Ben did more than pretend, so instead of quickly making a getaway, we had to wait until he finished his business.

The midnight curfew hour was approaching, and we still had our main piece of work to do. There was a newly painted brick wall along the main road into town that cried out for a poster. The last piece of the road was being asphalted at that late hour. There were white paper Chinese lanterns hung all along the street. All the signs and facades of shops around Inchon had been repaired and repainted in recent weeks, under police duress. The reason was not the approach of Rat Catching Day, but the coincidental impending visit of President Park Chung Hee, who was due in Inchon the next morning to grace with his presence the opening of a new harbor basin tidal lock – a great technological, navigational, and commercial advance. Ben and I earlier had spotted a loosely attached rat poster. As midnight approached, we peeled it off the wall and brought it out onto the lantern-decked main street. Scarcely a hundred yards away was the steamroller and the asphalting crew. We edged along the brick wall, newly painted red. In our hands were the glue and our last picture, not of the President, but of the brains behind him,

Now You Are Free to Speak Out

Prime Minister Kim Jong-Pil, also a former army major. Swiftly and liberally, we spread our remaining glue and with rapidly moving warm hands pressed it securely on the freshly painted glistening red brick wall. No time to stop and admire our work, we hurriedly ran away to get back inside the Bishop's house before the midnight curfew.

Next morning, Ben had taken a dawn boat back to his island, so I walked about town and checked the three sites. The police chief's head was still in place, a surprise because that poster was directly on the well-traveled path to the latrine. The KCIA chief's head was also still visible from its busy street corner location. The prime minister, however, poster and all, had been scraped from the bright red wall. Only traces of the paper marred the red paint. I stepped up close and saw the torn poster on the ground just in front of where we'd pasted it. The head of the prime minister, un-torn, had been carefully placed atop the wreckage. It was as if the evidence of the crime laid waiting for inspection.

I stepped back and looked about. Two stocky, full-bodied men in the casual slacks and windbreaker outfits of plainclothesmen were looking at me. I tried to assume nonchalance and strolled away. One of them followed. I turned into a short alley that led to another street, and despite my clerical garb, high-tailed it through the alley and hailed a passing taxi the good Lord sent by at that moment, returning to the safety of the Bishop's house. Nobody raided the premises, and I relaxed after an hour or so before catching the ferry back to my island parish.

〜 ❦❦ 〜

The decline of democracy and the abuse of human rights, ever the theme of student protest prompted the Park government to come up with a move to discredit the student protest as communist-inspired. Hence the invention of the so-called People's Revolutionary Party, a group of thirty-two supposedly communist sympathizers who allegedly were directly behind the students, orchestrating them to overthrow the Park government. These 32 men had all been picked up quite by surprise and hauled off by the authorities.

Imagine what it must have been like for the families of the PRP men. Picture for yourself a woman on a May morning in 1974, getting the family off for the day. Before your husband leaves the house, a stranger comes to the door and asks your husband to show him where an acquaintance of the husband lives. He leaves the house with the stranger and does not return to finish his breakfast. Nor does he return that night. Next morning, the secret police search your small house thoroughly.

This is what is happening in thirty-two houses in the cities of Seoul and Taegu, to the wives of a lumberyard foreman, a bathhouse manager, a clerk-bookkeeper, a high school English teacher. The wives are homemakers, not well-educated, members of no church or organization. They are told, "Say nothing. Just be quiet and nothing will happen to your husbands." The house searches yield little – in one house, some opposition party election campaign literature; in another, a book entitled, "The Russian Revolution," published with the approval of the Minister of Education; in a third house, a transistor radio, an item sold openly in stores. (These items will become the "evidence" against the men, proving that they are communists.)

Three weeks after the searches, you hear on the radio that your husband is on trial for having attempted to overthrow the government. "Overthrow a government?! My husband wouldn't know what to do with a government if they gave it to him!" you cry in astonishment. Your children come home from school, disheveled from fights, sulky or crying. The talk in school, even from teachers, is about criminals and traitors unmasked, referring to the children's father. Neighbors begin to shy away from you, but there is a man who stays close to you and follows you wherever you go.

Now You Are Free to Speak Out

In early August you are given a pass to the army court to attend the trial of the thirty-two men. Before you enter the courtroom you are told: "If you say one word, cry, or show any emotion, you will be taken from the courtroom." Around you are thirty-one other women who look as frightened and lost as you feel. Finally, surrounded by military policemen, you are ushered into the courtroom. When the "trial" is over, all are pronounced guilty. It is over. You are told to leave.

Women, unknown to each other half an hour before, cling together. Out in the air the sunlight seems cruel. You don't want to separate. Many of you go together to a tearoom. Some of you arrange to meet again. Next morning you learn from the radio why you were allowed to attend yesterday's sham. You hear the government report that your husband was tried not at a secret trial, but a "public" one. Men come to your house again and tell you to stay away from the other wives, to keep silent and everything will be all right.

One member of our Monday Night Group, George Ogle, a western Pennsylvania Methodist minister, was an evangelist to laborers and a founder of the Protestant Urban Industrial Mission. On a night in late September, George received a phone call from a woman who did not identify herself, but asked to see him the next day. Imagine his surprise when he opened the door of his home the next morning and found not one woman but eight. They introduced themselves as the wives of seven and the mother of one – representing eight of the thirty-two convicted PRP men. George listened as one after the other they told their stories.

"The police keep telling us to be quiet and everything will be all right, but what is all right about a death sentence?" one said. "My third-grader refuses to go to school anymore. The other children tease her about her criminal father," another said. George asked why they had come to see him. "None of us are Christians, but the women we meet at the prison when we bring money and clean clothes to our husbands, many of them are Christians. Some of them, the wives of ministers, told us to come see you. We were afraid, but what do we have to lose now?" "All we ask is that you look at the facts for yourself," Mrs. Woo, a spare, straight, alert-looking woman of 40 said in a controlled, cultured voice. "My husband is a quiet, scholarly man like you are, not a revolutionary."

⁂

Our brother Christian churches call themselves Protestant, and elements in each of their denominations "protested" – not against Catholics, but *with* Catholics – in open confrontation of the state. They preceded us, and they escalated their call for justice: "You are the monolith, always a rock to withstand persecution," a leader of the Protestant National Council of Churches in Korea told Cardinal Kim. "We smaller groups engage in the guerilla activities."

Guerilla means small war. The Protestants started small, with Thursday Morning Prayer meetings in the Christian Building, a six-story ecumenical structure on Chongno, the "Street of the Bell," in downtown Seoul. From praying together around a desk or two, the growing group moved into a conference room. By the autumn of the 1974, they had to reserve the five-hundred-seat auditorium above the lobby, on the second floor, where they met every Thursday at 10 a.m. The riot police met outside the lobby doors, plainclothesmen drifted through the lobby, and informers infiltrated the meetings where wives of jailed churchmen and mothers of jailed students gave the latest news of their loved ones, sang hymns, and prayed with their growing number of supporters.

On the first Thursday in November, Reverend George Ogle, our Monday nighter, took his turn at prayer and broke new ground. He prayed that God would move the powers to grant an open, civil, fair trial for the so-called People's Revolutionary Party, especially for the eight under sentence of death. He had researched the case and was convinced that the eight were innocent.

If there had been any lingering doubts about the sensitivity of the PRP case, they ended that day. George Ogle was taken away to Namsan, headquarters of the dreaded Korean Central Intelligence Agency.

George had the attention of us all at the following Monday Night Group meeting: "Five men came for me at home Thursday evening after the Prayer Meeting, and took me on a very wild and careless jeep ride. They meant to frighten me, and they did!" Ogle said. "After long and repetitive questioning, they led me down stairs and made me stand in front of a gorilla of a man who shouted at me for an hour. He was full of fanatical hatred of communism. All night long I was shouted at, questioned, and then shouted at again. Finally they ordered me never to talk in public of the PRP again. They said it was a gross interference of mine in the judicial system of the country in which I was a guest. They let me go, after forbidding me ever to pray again about the PRP. I asked them if that ban also covered private prayer. That caused a flurry and some discussion. None of them seemed to know what I meant by private prayer, so the subject was dropped," Ogle told the group.

The KCIA action against George Ogle served to bring others to a decision point. To quote the parable of Jesus about true works of mercy, the PRP were "the least of my brethren – what you do to them, you do to me."

The Korean Pastors' Organization and the Protestants came to the same decision – to include the PRP in their prayers and support, even if it complicated gaining the release from prison of those with less serious charges. We Monday Nighters felt proud that we'd already made that decision.

More than Witnesses

In the first Monday Night Group meeting in November 1974, after listening to George's account, Linda Jones of Rockford, Illinois, our constant chairperson, called us to pull in the reins and take account, because events seemed to be rushing by us too fast. Linda and her husband Dave were just finishing a two-year Frontier Internship with the Presbyterian Church. As usual, Linda had a list for the group. "Where we stand" was the title of her latest attempt to bring form and direction to our erratic if good-hearted efforts. Linda sat on the floor midst her papers and told us, "I've divided our efforts into sections. First, let's look at our relation with the United States government."

Linda had a trick of getting our attention, making us feel good about ourselves. Now she made us feel like a nation demanding diplomatic recognition. "President Ford is due here in less than a month. We've written to him, asking for an audience with someone in his large party," Linda said. (There were ninety signatures on our letter, representing a cumulative one thousand years of American missionary experience.) "No reply yet," she said, "though three weeks have passed. A copy of our request will be lodged with our American ambassador. We have selected a committee of five to meet with him to explain our request, which is simply to state what we've seen happening in the last six months. That meeting is next week."

Linda, allowing no elaborations, quickly moved into her second section entitled "Labor." "Our year-long effort for medical investigation of eyestrain and eye damage to the young women doing assembly-line microscope work has all been contradicted by company-hired doctors. We expected as much," Linda said. "We trust the facts gathered by our teams and will continue to send such information back home to the cities where these electronic and computer firms are headquartered."

Now You Are Free to Speak Out

"My third and final section has to do with the students." Here Linda's voice softened. She knew well many of the young people in jail. "By now we have overwhelming evidence that many were tortured after their arrests last April; they had to promise never to criticize the regime again under pain of expulsion from school. The amount of force needed to extract that promise ranged from words, to threats of physical punishment, to actual torture, depending on each student's resistance. We know that two hundred remain in jail, and we have to assume they have been treated most cruelly of all, yet they refuse to submit to pressure."

Linda had done her homework. She'd put our rambling reports and thoughts into order, and finished by saying, "I'm only sorry I have to end my stay with you and go home in a week, but we'll be doing things back there as well."

It was becoming clearer to us that "there" – back in "God's country" – was where "things" had to be done. A week later, when our delegation went to the U.S. Embassy regarding our letter to President Ford, a good hunk of our naïveté slipped away. Our group was graciously welcomed by Ambassador Richard Sneider, the recently installed successor to Philip Habib. He led us five into a reception room already populated by five others, standard Christian types who stay with the guys in power and tend heavily to identify God's will with that of the American electorate.

Our graduate of the KICA's Namsan, Rev. George Ogle, was chosen spokesman, but before he was given the floor, the ambassador took drink orders. When George's turn came to speak, and he began to tell of the number and quality of the regime's political prisoners, our Chief Envoy Ambassador Sneider got up from his seat and passed the peanuts around.

George was not a man who ever got livid, but he had trouble maintaining his composure when he reported all this at the following Monday night meeting.

More than Witnesses

There seemed to be frustratingly little we could do about the upcoming international event. Gerald Ford, newly appointed president of the United States, was coming to Korea in late November 1974 to put the seal of approval on a regime that persecuted just about everyone America was supposed to support. Giant twin posters were erected: portraits of the friendly U.S. and south Korean presidents, arranged so they seemed to be smiling at each other. It was painful to see. Wood and paper arches were constructed that read, "Welcome, His Excellency, President Gerald Ford." Korean and U.S. flags were in all the store windows.

The Monday Night Group met four days before the Ford-Kissinger visit. We discussed with some alarm how Kissinger, more than Ford, seemed to be setting the agenda and tone for their talks with the Park government. We were beginning to realize that the only word Henry Kissinger knew was "stability," even if that included putting Christians in jail and torturing them. Henry was using up a lot of good feeling that Koreans had about Americans – good feeling that missionaries, mostly Protestant, had cultivated by coming to and living in Korea, building and running schools and hospitals; 90 years of good works were being squandered for the declared "Vital National Interests" of U.S. foreign policy. The embassy, in my newly formed opinion, was half CIA and half U.S. Chamber of Commerce and cared not a damn for the Korean people. It looked like Ford and Kissinger would sail through their state visit, shake the hands of the jailers and torturers, reaffirm our friendly support in the war against communism, admire the good climate for U.S. corporate profits, then fly out again. It began to dawn on me that there was a bit of a contradiction between a good safe place to make money, as Seoul was advertised, and the imminent threat of Seoul being gobbled up by Red Hordes, as the U.S. also claimed. The fear of invasion had to be watered and tended like a fragile plant; it was the excuse for so many things.

Now You Are Free to Speak Out

On November 26, 1974, the *New York Times* carried a story that immediately affected all of us. The three-deck headline read: "Dissidents Doomed by Seoul, Said to be Spies." "Convictions Lack Credibility." "Present KCIA Chief had Role in Failed Case 10 Years Ago." Four days after the story appeared, Korean Immigration began proceedings against George Ogle, who had first listened to the eight PRP wives then prayed publicly for an open trial in the civil court for their condemned husbands. On the telephone, George was told by a U.S. Embassy person that the Koreans would allow him to remain in Korea only if he declared that he would not again criticize the constitution of the country. The American embassy man was go-between for the Korean regime, enticing George to forget his conscience and merely obey. George had a four-year visa, a privilege Methodist missionaries enjoyed. Legally he could stay in Korea three more years. But he would not agree to their demands. On Wednesday the officials of George's church called a meeting. I walked over with him. At the door I said goodbye, and headed for the islands, a four-day pre-Christmas excursion to several of my long-neglected churches.

On Saturday, December 14, the radio brought the news that "Ogle Moksanim [Rev. Ogle] is being deported today." There was nothing I could do but wait for the boat, so while waiting, I walked the country paths with the setting sun behind me. On a soft winter evening I watched the stars come out one by one. It was full dark when word came that "Ogle Moksanim is gone. They put him on a plane just a few minutes ago."

George, I felt, had not been deported in vain. The case now had wide international publicity. The men might not be freed very readily, but at least their lives were safer, exposed to the light.

More than Witnesses

To control all dissent meant that the Park government had to control the domestic media. Such control did not come easily. A "Declaration of Conscience" appeared in several Korean newspapers on October 26, 1974: "We reporters are ashamed that we have bowed to pressure. Henceforth we shall report news as it happens, not as we are ordered to." Among Korean newspapers, the *Dong-A Ilbo* had a long history of independence to protect. During the Japanese occupation of Korea, the rulers shut down the paper for six months for its brazen reporting. Since that 1935 incident, the *Dong-A* always stocked up a six-month supply of necessities, and after their recent publishing of the "Declaration of Conscience," and subsequent grumblings from the government, they prepared for a siege.

Besides stocking the storerooms, the *Dong-A* launched a subscription drive and hired extra newsboys to boost sales in order to cover expected loss of revenue. Sure enough, in the last week of December, advertisers both large and small – from shoe stores and restaurants to General Motors and Ford – all withdrew their ads.

The *Dong-A* reacted by publishing large blank white spaces where the ads had been. Within a week there was only one lone ad left, a postcard size blurb for Dr. Lee's Cough Remedy, surrounded by white space. Evidently, the authorities had not been able to reach Dr. Lee to cancel his prepaid ad.

Then the countermeasures began. The Korean Catholic Priests' Association for the Restoration of Democracy was among the first to march to the rescue. They took out a full-page ad, printing the best of the declarations and statements made by the church since July. All of the formerly underground literature was now available for all to see! More ads began to flow in: "Long Live the *Dong-A*!" Preserve Freedom of Expression" And soon, "I drink only Dr.

Lee's." As days went by, the ads got bolder, more humorous, ironic, and devious. Some were anonymous, most were signed. "If the *Dong-A Ilbo* dies, the country dies with it!" Another ad, mild in content but boldly signed "an officer of the ROK Army," precipitated a four-day-four-night session at KCIA headquarters for the manager of the advertising department.

The courageous struggle for press freedom waged by and for the *Dong-A Ilbo* is covered in other chapters of this book (see especially Marion Current's chapter). What I want to share here are several personal stories.

I enjoyed reading the ads but felt no call to participate until one day when I was at the U.S. Army Library, stocking up on books to take back to my island. While I browsed, music tapes were being played, but the melodies barely registered on my consciousness until I heard the strains of the Korean protest song "Seung Ni (Sŭngni)." This version had English words, however, and the words were "We Shall Overcome." Moments later I heard a strong, emotional, familiar voice start the speech that contained the words, "I have a dream." It was January 15, Martin Luther King's birthday. He would have been forty-six. I was forty-five, six months younger; George Ogle would be forty-six two days after King's birthday.

On more than one occasion since that year I'd been asked what prompted me to take certain actions. Borrowing shamelessly from Joan of Arc I replied to inquirers: "I listen to my voices. They tell me what to do." And it was true. I did listen to voices, and one of those was the voice of Martin Luther King. On that afternoon of his birthday anniversary in 1975, Dr. King's voice called me out of the library and sent me to the *Dong-A Ilbo*.

I had no idea where the newspaper's offices were located, but a taxi took me to downtown Seoul to the four-story structure of solid yellow brick. The building filled all the space between the two cross streets, appearing strong and proud to be where it was. I went up to the building and found myself at the tail of a long line of people waiting to do just what I planned: place an ad. I was the only foreigner, and soon someone took me inside where I was offered tea. The pleasant dark-faced man who ordered the tea told me how the lines of ad-placers grew longer every day. "There are students with penny collections gathered from classmates, well-dressed women, laboring people, all smiling and happy. You know, this is the first crack in the wall of public silence since the declaration of martial law in 1972," he said proudly. "We are the envy of all the other newspapers in Korea."

I told people what had motivated me to place an ad – that today was Martin Luther King's birthday, and that he and George Ogle and I had all been born in the same year. They didn't know until then that I was Father Sinnott. When they learned that, it caused quite a flurry of excitement. "May we take your picture and include it with the ad?" Not at all displeased, I said grandly, "I suppose you may." Next day the ad was twice the size I had paid for, my face in the picture had a leering drunken cast, and the names of Ogle and Sinnott were done in oversize black letters. I have since regretted that bit of braggadocio, because it gave ammunition to some of my more straight-laced missioner colleagues, who found me a bit too colorful and a mite flamboyant. But that first session at the *Dong-A* remains a good memory, the beginning of my education in police state journalism.

❧ ❧ ❧ ❧

I had written an article about the PRP wives for the *Dong-A* magazine. It hadn't been published, and I had assumed that Mr. Hwang, who had asked me to write the article, must not have liked what I wrote. This seemed like a good excuse to go back to the *Dong-A* and find out what was going on. When I made my way back to the yellow brick building, I soon learned that the magazine wasn't being printed at all, let alone PRP articles by dissident priests. The small office, filled with back issues of the magazine, was deserted except for one young woman. When I stated my business and asked for the publisher, she said, "Oh yes. We have your article right here, Father. Mr. Hwang was quite anxious to publish it. He'll be very glad to see you." It turned out that Mr. Hwang was one of the 20 protesting men who were occupying the pressroom, and I was told how to get past the guards to the room. "You're an American, so they are sure to let you by. For four days now he and nineteen others have held the printing presses captive," she said proudly.

I followed the route to the newsroom, got through the guards without even having to prevaricate, ascended the stairs to the third-floor newsroom and stated my business with Mr. Hwang. For four days now, I was told by a proud reporter, the twenty had sealed off the second floor and decided to fast; they had existed on barley water sent down a tube through the message chute, to which I was now directed. The reporter got down on the floor, put his mouth over the hole in the floor and called for Mr. Hwang, saying that a visitor was there for him. When the reporter got up off his belly, he motioned me over and, as if offering me a chair of honor, waited for me to assume that undignified position. I tossed decorum to the wind and flattened myself so that my eye was right over the hole. Sure enough, there was the beaming, polite, very pleased face of Mr. Hwang in the tiny circle of affordable view. "Hello, Mr. Hwang. Good to see you!"

"Sorry about the delay with your article, Father, but you know they shut down our magazine," he said.

I think I was beginning to understand. What my friends at the ad section passed over as a temporary difficulty was a matter of life and death up here in the newsroom. For these people, putting out a paper was more than a way to make money. I wished Mr. Hwang the best, and he asked me to visit again soon, repeating the theme I'd heard often before, that the more interest westerners showed, the less chance of a swift crackdown. I hurried down the dark narrow stairs from the newsroom and headed for the last ferry of the day that would take me back to my island parish.

March 15th, two months after Martin Luther King's birthday and my first visit to the *Dong-A*, seemed like an opportune time to visit again. No place in Seoul was under more police surveillance. When I reached the *Dong-A* building, one of the reporters came up to me and with a certain urgency invited me up to the third-floor newsroom. We quickly went up, past the second-floor presses still firmly held by the twenty strikers, including my friend Mr. Hwang.

On the third floor, no one was doing any work. Fifty reporters had taken this newsroom captive "until the four fired reporters are reinstated." I was very impressed. Even if I wasn't yet fully convinced of the practicality of shutting down the one voice of free speech, it struck me as a good, defiant act, and I was in the mood for defiance. I learned that the non-striking reporters, however, were still printing the paper at another location, as if nothing had happened; pretending the same Freedom of the Press crusade, with the Ad Section still functioning. I promised the striking 50 that I wouldn't place any more ads until they said it was all right, and many of them expressed their approval.

Next they took me up to the fourth floor, the offices of the *Dong-A* radio station. Again nobody was doing any work, just defiantly occupying the premises. The strikers applauded me when they learned that I was half of the "Sinnott and Zweber" ad team. (I had extracted funds from Benny Zweber to pay for my *Dong-A* ads, and he agreed to help me out – but only if his name also appeared on the ads!). There were thirty-five persons in the room – a dozen of them women – all holed up in common cause with the twenty on the second floor and the fifty on the third. Half the writing staff was aligned against management, the ad section, and the hundreds of non-news reporting employees from printers to truck drivers to newsboys. The broadcasting equipment lay silent and unused. Management had shut off the electricity and the heat, but the mid-March weather was mild and the strikers were still free to go and come to bring in food, candles, and kerosene for a few small portable stoves. My admiration for them knew no bounds.

The next day was Sunday and in the afternoon I stopped by Bishop Chi's residence. I described to the Bishop the *Dong-A* strike, and he was in full sympathy with their motives. The Bishop knew that, if not for the *Dong-A* these last few months, the Korean public would have no news of church stands on the justice issues. Once again I felt his support for the less than conventional life I'd been leading, and was grateful for it. His charming secretary, my friend Brother Justin Joyce, told me that some were placing bets that I would not get a new visa in April. But it didn't make sense to me that the Park regime would confront the Holy Roman Catholic Church over one priest; I had a lot of people on my side.

The evening sky was fully dark when I again approached the *Dong-A* building that night. The building itself took on a soft golden glow from the streetlights. I was glad to see some faint illumination inside – the strikers must still be there. A feeling came over me: "this is the place where I should be right now."

"We are going to be raided tonight and thrown out," Mr. Lee told me when I was finally allowed into the building. Mr. Lee motioned us over to the window. Below us, grouped like carolers at Christmas, were twenty or so well-wishers. Under a streetlight I could see the long white hair of Hahm Suk Hon (Ham Sŏkhŏn). A Quaker and longtime leader of justice-oriented Koreans, Hahm was sometimes referred to as the Gandhi of Korea. In his lifetime, he had resisted three different regimes of oppression – colonial Japanese, collectivist north Korean, and now 'democratic' south Korean. Almost 80 now, dressed always in traditional Korean garb, he struck deep chords in Catholics and Protestants alike with his great messages on nonviolence and justice. Seeing Hahm there fortified my convictions that tonight the *Dong-A* was the place to be.

As the midnight curfew neared, our well-wishers dispersed, some promising to be back first thing in the morning. Back in the long, cavernous newsroom, candles had been lit around a blackboard on which was chalked the words to a fiery old Methodist hymn: "Once to every man and nation, comes the moment to decide," a reminder of the sacred duty to oppose the Powers and Dominations. The Korean Student Christian Federation (KSCF) had made "Once to Every Man and Nation" their official hymn. Many students, picked up and arrested, would go over its words in their lonely travail in the basement dungeons of the KCIA headquarters or in their prison cells. As I stood now with the *Dong-A* men and women in this room, I learned the Korean words to the hymn and sang with them in the candlelight. The dim light made the singers seem as young and innocent as school children.

I soon learned from the group, which included seven brave women, what our "being thrown out" of the building would probably entail. Thugs hired at government expense, masquerading as newsboys or sales personnel interested in preserving their jobs, would come and challenge the strikers; they would charge the strikers with "destroying the newspaper" and take possession of the building. The eviction would appear to be an internal settling of differences, with no government interference.

Lookouts were posted at each window. I had fallen asleep when at 2:55 a.m. I was startled awake with shouts, "They are here!" Next I heard the reporters calling out, "Stay away from the windows. Get ready with the fire extinguishers. Turn out all the lamps!" Then all was quiet again until a sudden, harsh burst of sound came from the floor below us. The tiny hole of the message chute gave no clue to the action going on, but we heard shouting, things falling, people being dragged out, yelling in resistance. Then again soon, complete silence.

Someone said, "We will be next. Stay back from the windows." The long silence was painful. Suddenly the plywood barriers fell away, windows were smashed, wire was ripped away. Three of our men let loose at the trespassers with fire extinguishers, but it was a quick, forceless gesture. Soon a strong voice shouted to the three reporters standing in front: Mr. Lee, Miss Hwon, and Mr. Song. The man shook hands with them and bowed a greeting. He then apologized that as a street sales manager he was driven to this action, compelled to keep the paper alive.

"It won't *be* a newspaper unless our demands are met" Mr. Song replied. "*We* are not killing the paper but trying to keep it alive."

The intruders herded us toward the stairway door, now unlocked. As the first of the 45, some carrying cameras, others with unbound manuscripts under their arms, started down the stairs, they began – with deliberate slowness of stride and voice – singing the National Anthem. All lively spirit was gone from the beautiful words and music; it sounded like a dirge, a lament for things lost. There were free-flowing tears from men and women alike. How honored I felt, slowly treading down those stairs with such splendid people.

I learned there had been violence both below and above the third floor peaceable eviction. The twenty men on the second floor were carted away to a hospital on a truck. Because dawn was approaching, the fourth-floor men and women were herded out summarily, blows were struck, and one man was hospitalized.

Back in possession of the building, management and the non-strikers went to press pretending nothing had changed. The paper was even allowed to print a few innocuous articles more liberal than those found in the five or six other dailies, so that the abject surrender would be less apparent to the reading public.

The evicted *Dong-A* reporters picketed outside the building, and I joined them. One morning a short beaming man on the picket line tugged at my sleeve, "Don't you recognize me? I'm Hwang from the magazine! I'm sorry about your article. It's there in the office, but I'm not allowed in to claim it." "I'm sorry I didn't recognize you," I said. "It's different seeing you out in the open instead of through a hole in the floor."

⌒ 🐝 🐝 ⌒

In very early April, 1975: "There are no human rights denials in south Korea," stated Prime Minister Kim Jong Pil, the brains and strong arm behind the throne ever since the 1961 coup by Park Chung Hee. He had allowed three investigating groups into Korea: (1) Congressman Donald Fraser, U.S. House of Representatives Human Rights Subcommittee Chair, and his aides. (Yes, the same man to whom the Monday Night Group had sent that grammatically tortured, boring letter eleven months before.) Prime Minister Kim tried to keep Rep. Fraser totally occupied, but the Monday Night Group arranged basement meetings and a late-night rendezvous that provided Fraser a lot of firsthand information about political prisoners and about torture. Prime Minister Kim told the press that Rep. Fraser was an 'impolite visitor.' Sorry, Mr. Kim, it was our fault! The Monday Night Group even made Rep. Fraser late for one of his big-shot meetings.

2) The second group was from the BBC, the world-renowned

state-operated British Broadcasting Corporation. Their team consisted of a film crew headed up by Vanya Kewley, small-boned with hair a rich chestnut hue. Her job took her all over the world, meeting people and examining trends in religious expression, for a staple of Sunday evening broadcasts in Britain, called "Anno Domini." The Korean government was allowing the BBC crew to research and "tell the Korea story." But before the crew arrived, Prime Minister Kim had ordered all students who had done prison time to take a chaperoned bus tour to the south, far from Seoul, to see the "economic growth."

The BBC crew attended our Monday Night Group meeting on April 7, 1975, the night before the Supreme Court was to meet and decide the fates of the PRP men. Monday Nighters Willa Kernen, Butch Durst, and Gene Matthews all spoke eloquently and were immortalized in a BBC episode of "Anno Domini" that was seen worldwide – except, of course, in Korea.

3) The third group allowed in to investigate the situation was Amnesty International, the eminently credible watchdog on any government that mistreats its prisoners of conscience. Represented by a Danish doctor, Dr. Petersen, and a British lawyer, Brian Wroble, they got to see a few brave victims, including an ROK army general tortured for daring to criticize the regime. Gen. Lee Sei Jyu (Yi Seju), a battle veteran, showed Dr. Petersen his torture wounds. Wroble was the man who rushed from the Supreme Court on April 8 to make sure the appeal for the PRP – a legal right in all death sentence cases – was lodged at dawn. Despite this right, the eight men were hanged. That was after Kim Jong Pil made his "no right denied" statement. The prime minister didn't know the Monday Night Group had urged Wroble to extend his stay and investigation.

The next Monday Night Group meeting reflected the ghastliness of the preceding days. We were emotionally stunned, but not inactivated. Women were assigned to sew eight black hoods and eight thick plaits of heavy Korean rope for eight MNG men to wear over their heads and around their necks. They went to the U.S. Embassy grounds holding a big white banner with these words, "Is this the result of quiet diplomacy?" That was the U.S. Embassy's excuse, often offered to us, for doing nothing to influence a corrupt regime very much under American influence.

The *New Yorker Magazine* had summed up the situation following Emergency Decree #5 in 1974: "The United States offers democracy for its own citizens but prefers to support dictatorships overseas as safe havens for its own interests."

On one of my last evenings in Seoul in April 1975, my fellow Monday Nighter Ben Zweber and I were on a crowded bus. If there are memorial awards to be given, Ben should get the MNG award for the longest commute. His assignment, a little archipelago well out in the Yellow Sea, made his Monday night attendance sporadic, but he was there to grieve with the widows outside the West Gate Prison after the hangings and at the U.S. Embassy as well, with black hood donned and rope around his neck.

Riding along on the bus that night, Ben and I talked of the newly-widowed wives and children – twenty-three of them – of the eight hanged men. From our seat we could see the faces of those standing in the aisle of the packed bus, all properly aloof and quiet. Without any signal to each other, Ben and I switched into Korean and started reeling off facts of the PRP case in voices loud enough for our silent traveling companions to hear.

As we talked, faces froze, backs turned away from us. But from the seat just behind us, a man started to speak: "You two are right. It's terrible here now," he repeated in so many words. As foreigners, Ben and I had certain advantages that Koreans didn't have, and we had no right to get him in trouble by agreeing with us. There were informers everywhere, full-time paid ones and others rewarded for any information. Korea had then (and still does now) a National Security Law comparable to something out of the medieval Spain or the U.S. "Patriot Act." Ben turned to the man and said in a low voice: "You mustn't talk like that!"

"Why not? It's the truth!" the man replied.

"You don't mean it," I said loudly. "You've been drinking! You're drunk!"

"Yes, I'm drunk" he said. "I stay drunk. That's how I can stand what's happening to my country."

ꙭ ꙮ ꙭ

On April 28, 1975, I was told by Mr. Kou, Chief of Immigration in Inchon, that not only was my application for a year-long residence permit refused, but also that I had to be out of Korea in 48 hours. "Any country reserves the right not to renew a visa and to expel the applicant. You are not being deported," Mr. Kou explained. "We have expelled other people before you." "Thieves, murderers, drug sellers, yes!" I exclaimed in reply, "but not a priest!" He reminded me that I was not being deported, but expelled. (They had broken diplomatic rules when they had forced George Ogle on to a plane, deporting him while he was in possession of a valid visa, and the U.S. Embassy had lodged a complaint. Immigration knew not to do that again.) Mr. Kou was on solid legal ground and offered no further explanation.

My superiors agreed with me that I shouldn't go without getting a stated reason. They told this to the immigration chief when he called to remind my superiors that they would be breaking the law if they harbored me after April 30th. As with George Ogle, the U.S. Embassy played go-between, making their usual face-saving attempt to rescue me – negotiating an impossible deal that amounted to public, abject surrender on my part, followed by "possible reconsideration " of my case. The embassy delivered a message to me from the Korean authorities: "Sign that you'll obey all our laws and we might reconsider...." George had refused that bait; now, four months later, so did I.

Cardinal Kim called for a protest at the Cathedral on April 28th. He presided at the evening Mass, claiming I was guilty of no crime. Two hundred concelebrating priests stood around the altar, with Bishop Danny Chi at my side. The Cathedral on the hill was as full as at the height of summer, but it seemed darker to me. In conclusion, the two hundred priests proceeded down the main aisle. I bowed to the altar, turned to follow them, and was met by a wave of thunderous applause. Walking down that aisle provided a review of my life over the previous twelve months. Strangers and friends reached out their hands to me; fresh faces in student uniforms handed me pen and paper for autographs. I'll never have a funeral to match an event like that.

I never got back to my island parish where a gala anniversary picnic, celebrating my tenth year as their priest, was to be held May 3rd. Just as well I wasn't there – all I would have done was cry. My parishioners had a suit made – an anniversary gift that became a going-away gift. "A sentimental thought," I mentioned to the chubby, successful proprietor of the Seoul Emporium, which occasioned a lecture from him on the beauties of silence in the face of oppression.

I left on the last plane on the last day possible, April 30th. After midnight I would be an illegal alien, and anyone who fed or protected me would be breaking the law. Mr. Kou from immigration was there with the following written reasons for my expulsion: (1) having applied late for the yearly renewal of my residence permit in 1968; (2) interfering with police on the street; (3) defiling the dignity of the Supreme Court.

The first reason was bureaucratic nonsense, of course. The last two were not nonsense, but were not the real reason, I feel sure, that I was being shipped out. My sin was doing what George did, talking publicly about the "Peoples' Revolutionary Party," calling it a sham.

It's true that I had "interfered with police on the street," but so had many others. I presume the reference was to what has become known as "helmet-flipping," a technique acquired quite by accident in a desperate moment at one large street engagement. We in the front line had foolishly linked arms, then when pushed from behind by large numbers, lost our footing as the police pushed back. Finally, settling into a tight crushing line with no space between, I was trapped between the riot police and another priest who was trying to remove the wooden club from the hands of the police. As the police reacted, his club shot up and pressed against my throat. I was immobilized except for one hand that was wedged just under the edge of his helmet. I flicked my wrist and off rolled his protective head gear. It was immediate disarmament! He let go of me and bent down seeking his lost head covering.

I must admit I used this unplanned peacemaking method more than once, and after a subsequent arrest, the chief in a police station asked me where I learned it. Anxious to cooperate, I began, "Well, at the seminary." He reacted with delighted surprise: "They taught you that at Maryknoll Seminary?" "No, no," I quickly corrected, "I mean at the demonstration at Seoul Seminary." He wasn't listening. He was making notes. Since then, riot police wear better anchored plastic headgear with the neck protection attached. I sometimes like to think I had a part in that innovation.

The third and last reason for my expulsion still causes me revulsion: defiling the dignity of the Supreme Court. No! They defiled their own dignity – all thirteen Supreme Court justices in their straight, high, red-backed chairs – by confirming the death sentences of the eight men, unfairly convicted by an army court. I was carried out of that court after the wives were dragged out for objecting, with outcries and tears, shouting *"Cho jag i da (Chojak ida)!"* ("It's a lie; it's a fabrication!") I would have left after that, but I turned around and saw Monday Night Group stalwart Louise (Morris) Durst lying on the floor. Her husband, Butch, knelt by her side. She wasn't hurt, as I'd thought. She was just protesting. "I had to do something," she said.

Roy Whang, an American newspaperman, joined us. The room was suddenly quiet. We were alone. After an interval, 16 building guards, four for each of us, carried us out and down a back stairway and dropped us in the alley. *"Cho jag i da!"* we shouted all the way, picking up where the wives had left off – "It's a lie!" The Supreme Court's PRP judgment and the absolutely shocking executions at dawn the next day had crushed us all.

Leaving Korea was anti-climactic in an awful way – almost a relief. I took only an overnight bag, and no souvenirs, unless you count a black hood from the U.S. Embassy demonstration, which I had in the pocket of my new suit. For symbolic reasons and for the sake of the media, I put the hood over my head at the airport just before saying goodbye to my friends. Gene, Willa, Louise, Butch, and the whole Monday Night Group were there. They and all my clergy friends, Protestant and Catholic, as well as the families of men still in jail and the bereaved of the eight men – they all had the same orders for me: "Now you are free to speak out. Go and tell our story far and wide."

Chapter 14

From Service to Solidarity

Linda Jones

Once to every one and nation, comes the moment to decide,
In the strife of truth with falsehood, for the good or evil side;
Some great cause, some great decision, offering each the bloom
or blight,
And the choice goes by forever, 'twixt that darkness and that
light.[1]

I grew up in a lower-middle-class, suburban, Midwestern
family. I attended Millikin University 1962-66 and spent my junior

---

[1] *Once to Every Man* [now *One*] *and Nation,* an 1849 James Russell Lowell hymn, was sung
in Korean at most prayer meetings and gatherings during south Korea's struggle for democracy in the early 1970's. The full text is at the end of this chapter.

year abroad at the University of Ibadan in Nigeria. There I discovered that lower middle-class in the United States meant extraordinarily rich in Nigeria. I visited South Africa, where I came to appreciate the struggles and the solidarity of the anti-apartheid movement. Before returning to the U.S., I spent ten weeks traveling up the east coast of Africa.

Back in the U.S, I pursued a Masters in Teaching degree from Antioch College in Ohio. The degree program placed us graduate students in inner-city Washington, D.C. high school classrooms. We taught two-thirds time and did our course work at night with Antioch professors. The combination of teaching, reflecting, and learning was education at its best.

Dr. Martin Luther King, Jr. was killed while I was teaching in D.C. I lived through the trauma of being white in a black city whose neighborhoods were burning with rage. Yet I also knew the solidarity and safety of entering the particular African-American neighborhood where my school was located. All the teenagers on the street there knew me – I had nothing to fear among them. They would protect me.

After marrying David Jones, we moved into a rapidly changing (white to black) neighborhood on Chicago's south side where David was a Presbyterian pastor. I studied Urban Studies at Roosevelt University—a school funded by Jews for minority students (Jewish and Black). I also worked with international students as an intern in International Student Relations at the Crossroads (Roman Catholic) student center at the University of Chicago. There I learned the importance of extending genuine and careful hospitality. It was also there that I learned more deeply the ins and outs of the U.S. war policy in Vietnam.

From Service to Solidarity

One summer of my D.C. teaching years I traveled to Asia on a ten-week trip with other graduate students from Asia and the U.S. We visited seven Asian countries: Japan, Hong Kong, Thailand, Cambodia, Indonesia, the Philippines, and Taiwan. Our hosts in each country were members of the University Christian Movement (UCM). They taught us about the realities of U.S. foreign policy, local politics and economics, and the response and work of each Christian community. I made a pact with myself to go back to Asia someday.

In 1972 my husband David and I were two of 1sixteen persons accepted into the two-year Frontier Internship Program sponsored by three U.S. denominations: the United Methodist Church, Presbyterian Church (U.S.A.) and the United Church of Christ. Following a month of orientation in Geneva, Switzerland, we flew to Korea via Lahore, Pakistan, then at thirty thousand feet over Vietnam. I sobbed as we flew over burned-out villages and pock-marked jungles that had been fire-bombed by U.S. planes financed by my family's taxes.

I was a politically and theologically progressive, Democratic, Presbyterian, anti-apartheid, anti-Vietnam war, pro-civil rights, feminist teacher. For seven of the previous ten years I had lived and worked as a minority white person, in Africa, Washington, D.C., and Chicago. Now I was going to Korea, knowing nothing about Korean politics, not one word of Korean, and having talked extensively with only two Koreans in my life.

Was I ready for what was to come? Could anybody have been?

David and I were stopped in our tracks on our usual morning trek over the foothill to the language school at Yonsei University just five days into studies there. We had passed the shacks where displaced Koreans from the countryside lived, lured to the city by hopes for economic gain. Then we looked down on the sprawling Yonsei campus and saw an armed camp—army trucks and tents, men in uniform, tanks, but no students. The front gate was closed, heavily guarded by troops armed with rifles and shields. What was going on?

It was October 1972. We had been in Korea only a few weeks, hardly time to get used to "Korea as usual", and now we had been thrust into circumstances that not even the south Koreans understood. All campuses had been closed, and the military was visible everywhere. Park Chung Hee, who had ruled since 1961, had now grabbed complete power. Soon he would promulgate a new constitution and draconian "national security" laws permitting the government to label as "communist" any citizen who spoke out for democracy and a return to citizen's rights. Such persons were now to be considered sympathizers with north Korea. But before we knew all of *that*, our heads were swimming with what we were seeing, and with all that we did not understand about Korea.

❧ ❧ ❧ ❧

...the choice goes by forever, 'twixt that darkness and that light.

The U.S. Presbyterian church's Korea mission office tried to be helpful. The old office, still headed by non-Koreans, was our "business center" in terms of financial and logistical support, including help with documents for our stay in Korea. Being officially tied to the Presbyterian mission meant that we were expected to participate in the monthly meetings of the Seoul mission (made up then of perhaps 25-30 long-term missionaries).

Ties with the missionaries proved to be both negative and positive. One gentleman took us under his wing during our first week in Korea by treating us to dinner at the Officer's Club at the 8th Army Headquarters in Seoul. He must have thought we already needed good, cheap American food. The experience was a real eye-opener, seeing how well the army officers lived in their compound. But we were also struck by the realization that U.S. missionaries could use the officer's club, shop at the PX, watch movies at the army's theater, and use the army's library.

The missionary then took us to his brick house on a hill near Yonsei that was a "missionary compound"— an area with several Western homes, complete with Korean housemaids, security guards, and lawn-care personnel. As Frontier Interns, David and I had been oriented to live with "economic discipline," like the people with whom we would be working. We knew we could not and would not live at the level of most American missionaries in Korea.

The mission office helped us find and negotiate our housing in the upper floor of a westernized Korean house in a neighborhood near Yonsei. We shared the bathroom and kitchen with a Korean family of three, and we had a bedroom and a living room to ourselves upstairs. This was a good compromise between how Westerners usually lived in Seoul and how we could live as a full-time working couple who didn't want full-time housework.

We quickly learned that as a pastor David would be looked up to by Koreans with a level of respect much higher than that accorded pastors in the U.S. And we suspected that Linda's work would not be considered important—certainly by Koreans, and possibly also by the missionaries, most of whose spouses were doing volunteer work considered secondary to their husbands' jobs.

Our primary Korean contacts were Dr. No Chung Hyun (No Chŏnghyŏn) and others at the Institute for Urban Studies and Development at Yonsei University; and Park Se Il (Pak Seil), a Korean Frontier Intern who was waiting for his Japanese visa so he could begin work among Koreans in Japan.

Our other regular contacts were the Presbyterian missionaries in Seoul, persons so diverse they could not possibly be put under one umbrella.

When the university was closed by the military, we sought advice from all of these major contacts. Dr. No's institute was also shut down, and he had no idea when things would return to normal. Much of the institute's work in the urban slums was also stopped. The missionaries were making lots of guesses about the military takeover, but they had no inside track on what might lay ahead. They urged fellow missionaries to exercise a great deal of caution, saying, "don't rock the boat; things are tense enough already."

Park Se Il helped us understand what was happening. Park was a recent graduate of the prestigious Seoul National University (SNU). He was a bright, articulate young man with many talented, activist friends, among them student leaders in the various schools of study at SNU.

All the student leaders had been caught off guard by President Park Chung Hee's actions, including his changing the constitution to allow him to continue as president. But students were already sure that President Park was corrupt and conniving, so they saw no good in what must be ahead.

While waiting for his visa, Park Se Il introduced David and me to some of his student-activist friends. This would ensure that, even after he was in Japan, we would have excellent contacts in the Korean community to help us find our way.

One of these friends, Suh Kyung Suk (Sŏ Kyŏngsŏk), and his girlfriend, Shin Heisoo (Sin Hŭisu), became our close friends and led us into our three work connections – with the Korean Student Christian Federation (KSCF), with urban poor slum dwellers, and with laborers through the Urban Industrial Mission (UIM). Suh was in the military full-time, but his nine-to-five job five days a week as an army engineer allowed time for him to meet with us and others on weekends. Shin was a graduate student at Ewha Women's University; she had an undergraduate degree in English, which greatly facilitated our ability to communicate.

Within a few weeks of meeting Suh, he took us to meet Rev. Park Hyung Kyu, then pastor of Seoul's First Presbyterian Church in Seoul. Rev. Park had served as executive secretary of the KSCF in the late 1960's. Suh told us that if we ever got into trouble, we should call upon Rev. Park.

Today we still chuckle when we recall that introduction to Rev. Park, because, though we *did* get into trouble, Rev. Park got into much more trouble than we did. In fact, he was in prison most of the time we were in Korea.

Park Se Il and his friends were very busy people. Because they had been student leaders at their universities, current students looked up to them for help in understanding what was going on in Korea and how they might respond to the growing dictatorship. So Park and his friends had little time to spend teaching us about Korean culture, economics, history, or about the Korean church. As the political situation got worse, we came to understand that we could not be seen with these new friends, because either they were being watched by the ever-present Korean Central Intelligence Agency (KCIA), or we were.

The students, realizing we wanted to help, tried to figure out how we might do so. Initially, they asked us to do things like host "study groups" at our apartment. This was easy for us, simply offering the space. It was necessary for us to be uninvolved: David and I knew neither the names of most of the students who came, nor what they talked about. Only many months later did we realize that we were hosting Christian student leaders from many universities. They used our place to share information and decide how to respond to President Park Chung Hee's draconian measures.

417

More than Witnesses

...to side with truth is noble

David and I were very lonely during our first months in Korea. The language study was extremely difficult, and we were in a class by ourselves because we had not arrived in time to join a regular class. Our new Korean student friends were often too busy to meet with us. Yonsei University, including the Urban Institute, had reopened after several weeks of closure. But the institute was not able to do much outside of its walls except research in the slums. David was willing to work in the institute office, freeing me to assist groups working among the poor and oppressed.

I told Suh Kyung Suk of my desire for this kind of work. He told me there were some things I could do, but he was unsure whether to ask me for that kind of involvement. He told me that an anti-government student demonstration was going to take place at a certain day and time at one university. He told me to tell no one – the demonstration needed to be kept secret; it had to be a surprise to the government.

Within two days, another of Suh's friends whom I knew met me in another setting and asked if I knew anything about plans for a demo. I told him I did not.

From that day forward the flood gates opened. I began to receive more and more information, and I was given one job after another to help the movement. The meeting with Suh's friend had been a test. And I had passed. The student leaders knew there was work I could do, but they needed to know that I was trustworthy, politically aware, and level-headed. They had decided that I was not a member of the U.S. Central Intelligence Agency. And they realized that I had certain value to them both as a woman and as an American. As a woman I was less likely to be taken seriously by the police. As an American I could take some risks that they could not.

From Service to Solidarity

Though the cause of evil prosper,
yet the truth alone is strong;
though her portion be the scaffold,
and upon the throne be wrong

Ahn Jae Woong (An Chaeung) was the executive staff person for the Korean Student Christian Federation (KSCF). Hwang In Sung (Hwang Insŏng) was student leader of KSCF's Social Development Service Corps. The two of them asked me to write a series of essays on the church's involvement in human rights movements in other parts of the world. I would do the research and writing, which they would translate and present at monthly forums of student Christian leaders from several universities.

The assignment was a perfect fit for me. I could get information from international newspapers and organizations, human rights solidarity groups, the international church, even the U.S. 8th Army library. All of these sources were unavailable to the average Korean, because martial law meant strict monitoring of the Korean press and heavy censorship of all media from abroad. One of my sources of information was *The Guardian*, a leftist independent newspaper that, surprisingly, was arriving from New York unopened. How did it get past the Korean censors? Because it came tightly rolled up, looking like a calendar or set of posters.

The KSCF study forums became lively discussions of human rights in black America, South Africa under apartheid, China, Brazil, Chile, and the Philippines. Students discussed similarities and differences between the Korean student movement and those in other countries. They noted and discussed patterns in U.S. and Japanese foreign policy. One monthly forum dealt with Chile, including my prediction that the government would be overthrown. When the U.S. assisted in the fall of the Allende government two weeks later, it led to another focus on Chile at the next month's forum.

A book of these studies was published by KSCF. Because it's in Korean, I have never read the only book I have ever written!

≈ ≋≋ ≈

One of the many things I did not know at the time was that, in addition to discussing human rights struggles in other national contexts, the student leaders devoted part of each forum to discussing and planning for a massive all-campuses-in-Seoul student response to the Yushin Constitution of President Park Chung Hee. The forums gave them the cover they needed to get together — because the KCIA had not yet figured out the significance of the monthly meetings nor, apparently, could they keep up with the students as they surreptitiously made their way to the forums via so many back alleys.

The huge and well-planned student demonstration against the Park Chung Hee dictatorship took place simultaneously on campuses across Seoul in the fall of 1973. The KCIA and other security groups were taken by surprise. The foreign press covered the story heavily, making the government even more determined to find and arrest all who had planned the embarrassing display of citizen displeasure.

Our next forum did not happen. All the students were in hiding.

≈ ≋≋ ≈

By the light of burning martyrs,
Christ, thy bleeding feet we track

Thus began a second major piece of my work in Korea. Students needed to be hidden from the KCIA. Though some could find safety and protection in the slums, many others could not find safe places. Certainly their homes and the homes of their friends, relatives, or church members were not safe. Meanwhile, most middle- and upper-class Koreans, not yet convinced that the Park regime was moving toward dictatorship, would not consider harboring anti-government citizens – especially if they believed the government when it said the students were pro-communist dissidents.

For many months, then, it fell on the families of foreigners in Seoul to harbor some of the students on the run. Naturally, the topic became part of the Monday Night Group meetings. We began finding safe places for those needing to hide. The point was not to hide students indefinitely, but to hide them long enough so the police and KCIA would have plenty of time to get information from other sources. Then *these* leaders in hiding, when caught, would not be tortured out of their minds for information that the government had already obtained. Because our student contacts were so crucial to the democratic movement at that time, it was very important to keep them safe and able to continue in their leadership roles.

Sharing our homes with student activists provided us foreigners with rich opportunities for growth – including in our commitment to justice and our understanding of social, as opposed to individual, salvation. We were privileged to host people in our homes. Students taught us about the history of student protest in Korea, about other patriots who had taken grave risks in the past, about massacres done by foreign powers in Korea, and other stories that we had never heard before.

The students we protected told us they felt they were insignificant persons in the long line of Koreans who had stood tall in times of national crisis. Christians believed that all persons were made in the image of God, that all persons had value. Thus, the reaching out to and walking with those in the slums, the impoverished, the disenfranchised, the enslaved factory workers, widows, prostitutes, the imprisoned—all of this solidarity with the people of "han" (suffering) was a logical part of what students expected of themselves at this grave juncture in Korean history. (See broader definition of "han" in glossary.) It was a matter of praxis—living the Gospel and reflecting on that instead of merely preaching and talking about it.

David and I had moved to a private apartment not shared with Koreans, so we were able to participate in hosting people on the run. The longest-standing guest we were privileged to host was Hwang In Sung, whose faithfulness in trying to help us learn about Korea went beyond the call of duty. Just as he had once spent several hours bringing me a package that I had left by mistake at the KSCF office, he would painstakingly take the time to explain matters of U.S. and Japanese policy toward Korea. This young man's demeanor resembled more a kind and soft-spoken Korean choir boy than a leading strategist and organizer of hundreds of students struggling for democracy.

It was difficult saying good-bye to him when it was decided the police were getting too close and that he should be moved. For everyone's sake, only one other person ever knew the locations of persons in hiding. This meant that, as soon as Hwang left our apartment, we lost track of him. But it also meant that we could not possibly make a mistake and reveal his whereabouts.

Monday Night Group members were continually hiding persons or finding places for them to hide, but we never shared the names of the people we were harboring or working with. We were learning how to be faithful and smart – "wise as serpents and gentle as doves" – as we began moving from service to solidarity with our Korean friends and co-workers.

From Service to Solidarity

❧ ❧❧ ❧

They must upward still and onward,
who would keep abreast of truth.

Another job that came my way was to transport materials that were being brought secretly into Korea. Key Korean Christians in the struggle for democracy needed to keep abreast of what the world was learning about and saying about the Korean struggle. Reactions in the Japanese and U.S. media were especially important, since the governments of those two nations were closely tied to the Park Chung Hee regime.

My delivery route included Rev. Kim Kwan Suk (Kim Kwansŏk), president of the Christian Broadcasting System (CBS); Rev. Park Hyung Kyu (Pak Hyonggyu), pastor of Cheil (First) Presbyterian Church, former executive secretary of Korean Student Christian Federation (KSCF), and board member of the Korean Christian Action Organization's slum-organizing program; a professors' group at Ewha Women's University; the National Council of Churches of Korea; KSCF; the Urban Industrial Mission; Church Women United; and the YMCA. Each packet of materials I delivered was then passed among those who could be trusted in each of those organizations. Only one person in each group knew who was delivering the materials, and none of the recipients knew how the materials were getting into Korea.

The packets consisted of articles written about the Korean crisis in Japanese, American, and European magazines and newspapers, statements made before the U.S. Congress or the Japanese Diet, statements by world churches, and other documents. All of these would have been censored if carried openly into Korea, or Koreans caught carrying them would have been imprisoned. As an American, the worst thing that could happen to me was to be deported. So I was the right person for the job.

Most of the materials came to Korea via Japan, where Koreans (including Frontier Intern Colleague, Park Se Il) and others in the National Council of Churches of Japan, the East Asia Christian Conference (now the Christian Conference of Asia), and Documentation for Action Groups in Asia (DAGA) selected and copied the materials. They arrived in Korea via various routes, including missionaries and other western couriers who were working with human right groups in Japan.

The heaviest traffic route was through Faye Moon (see her chapter). Faye, married to seminary professor and Korean activist Dr. Stephen (Tong Whan) Moon, was an American social worker working for the U.S. Army as a drug and alcohol rehabilitation counselor among U.S. soldiers in Korea. Faye had access to the Army Post Office (APO) which, unlike the Korean postal system, was uncensored. She would receive package after package of material and lug them all off the base. Then I would go to her house, sort them, and head out on my delivery route.

We also aided in the movement of sensitive information out of Korea. Sometimes we carried important documents to Tokyo. Sometimes we wrote in code and mailed things out. Sometimes we used the APO. Sometimes we found other foreigners who would carry them out – but this was not the safest route. More than once these persons were stopped and questioned at the airport, and sometimes our documents were found and taken by the authorities.

The Monday Night Group became a great information source for foreign reporters when they came to Seoul. Reporters were seldom invited to our clandestine meetings, but they would find one of us and pepper us with questions. We would give them leads on breaking stories, including which Koreans they needed to interview and how to contact them. Of course the media's hotel phones and the phones of all Korean activist leaders were tapped, so all the arrangements for clandestine meetings between reporters and Korean leaders had to be made by word of mouth.

Often it was necessary for us to provide translators for interviews of Koreans by foreign correspondents. I spent many hours and days in Korea setting up meetings among Korean democratic leaders, translators, and reporters from major international English-language newspapers and magazines. Because all phone conversations needed to be carried on in code, sometimes things did not work out. We would say "meet in front of East Gate at 1 p.m.," which meant meet at West Gate at 2 p.m. If a reporter forgot the code, a busy, risk-taking Korean leader or translator would get rudely stood up – and an important story might not get reported overseas.

The name "Jones" kept coming up in KCIA files as someone involved in the movement. Under pressure from their interrogators, arrested students sometimes had to come up with names of people in whose homes they had been hiding. To name a Korean would land that person in prison. To name a foreigner would not. So our name was used. We may have been partners in the movement, but we were dispensable partners.

The KCIA was also "on" to us because we appeared often at prayer meetings for the imprisoned, at trials, at the KSCF office, and at UIM activities where workers were organizing for changes in the workplace.

The hymn *Once to Every One and Nation* was sung in Korean at many Christian gatherings. It became our "marching song," and we all stood tall as we sang it together. The words expressed both what we believed and why we were assembled – without revealing exactly what we meant to the KCIA agents listening in the back of the room.

To this day, I get tearful when I sing that hymn, as I remember the pathos and the diligence with which we sang it. We sang it with Korean women and men, young and old, who had endured imprisonment and torture; with people who could be arrested any moment; with people who were hiding others in their homes or working hard to find hiding places; with mothers and wives whose sons and daughters or spouses were in prison for their truth-telling and their actions in solidarity with the suffering *minjung* (oppressed common people); with elderly patriots and professors; with women who did not get named, but who were, in many ways, the backbone of the movement; with people willing to risk arrest by telling the truth to the international press.

Government agents would write down the names of persons attending these events. And they would write down the words of our hymns, but, unless they were Christian, they never understood what we were singing. How could they know what we meant by "though the cause of evil prosper, yet the truth alone is strong"? How could they understand us when we confidently sang that, some day in the future, the sway of the scaffold would undo those presently in control of the scaffolds?

It would take more than twenty years, but those who suffered the scaffolds *did* undo those in control.

⁂

With David's and my names surfacing every now and then in KCIA files, the agency twice sent serious-minded, low-level operatives to our apartment to question us. Both times, I headed for the bedroom, and they interviewed David in the living room. By all common Korean standards, David must have been the one who made the decisions in this family. The questioning would get comical as everybody, in broken English or broken Korean, tried to establish David's main Korean contacts and who he was seeing on a regular basis. It turned out that his quiet and unobtrusive work at the Urban Institute really paid off. It proved effective "cover" for my ongoing work.

David truthfully named everyone at the institute and people at the English-language Seoul Union Church as his main contacts. None of these persons was active in the movement. The operatives never asked about me or my activities or contacts—or found the piles of materials that were waiting to be delivered to leaders in the movement. On both visits, the KCIA agents left our apartment mystified as to why they had been sent to interview the Joneses.

More disturbing to us was an urgent call we received from R. Stanton Wilson, head of the Presbyterian Church (USA)'s mission in Korea. Stan Wilson had friends in the Korean government as well as in the U.S. Embassy and American business community. He knew well all of the Presbyterian missionaries and many of the Koreans in the institutions where the missionaries worked. Like many of those missionaries, however, he was not knowledgeable about the student movement or some other aspects of the movement for democracy. At the monthly Presbyterian mission meetings, long-term missionaries often asked *us*, who had been in Korea only a few months, what was going on among the students or with the outside press.

Mr. Wilson called to invite us to his home (supposedly not wire-tapped) to tell us that he had received a warning from the Korean government: If the Joneses kept supporting Koreans in the movement for democracy, and kept opposing the government, the Joneses would jeopardize the continuation of the work of all the

Presbyterian missionaries in Korea. In other words, not only might we get deported from Korea, but so might all the long-term missionaries – the doctors, health workers, professors, evangelists, social workers, and mission leaders. Surely we young short-term mission workers would not want to cause the deportation of persons with decades of ties with Korea, he said.

Mr. Wilson urged us to keep a lower profile and to make very discreet choices about what we were doing—for the sake of the whole PCUSA mission. We listened to his warning, politely thanked him, and went back to our usual activities – things requested of us by our Korean co-workers and friends

At such times, the support and solidarity of the Monday Night Group was most important to us both. We could bring information, let off steam, laugh, cry, and plan for our next actions, always following the lead of Koreans working for democracy and human rights. The Monday Night Group helped to erase the isolation we sometimes felt – isolation caused by the great limitations on how much face-to-face contact we could have with our closest Korean friends, all of whom were deeply involved in the movement and needed not to be seen in public with us.

⁓ ⁓⁓⁓ ⁓

One of the best stories of the KCIA getting all tangled up in itself was the remarkable story of the 1979 wedding-that-wasn't. A male leader in the movement was getting married at Rev. Park Hyung Kyu's church. All the Christian leaders in the movement showed up. The church was buzzing like a beehive. People who may not have seen each other face-to-face for many months had so much news to share.

The police and KCIA were fully aware of the event and were very present in their black-leather jackets. But for strategic reasons (bad press overseas?) they had decided not to disrupt such a large Christian gathering.

The informal discussions and friendly greetings went on and on because, for some reason, the bride was delayed. The KCIA got more and more nervous; all the key people in the movement were having this unexpected opportunity to talk and analyze and plan together. The people were having a wonderful time moving around the sanctuary and starting new conversations. The police were now sweating. Some two hours after the appointed hour for the wedding, it was announced that, regrettably, the bride would not be coming. At that moment, the police and KCIA realized they had been snookered—that a wedding never had been a part of the plan. Within days, several people were jailed for allegedly planning the wedding-that-wasn't. (See Marion Kim's chapter.)

‿ ⁓⁓ ‿

At one point, I was leaving Korea for a short period and taking an "orphan flight." This meant that three other adults and I were accompanying eighteen babies to their adoptive families in the U.S. – and receiving two-thirds off our airfare. The arrangement made me uncomfortable: I needed the cheap airfare, but I regretted carrying babies out of their homeland into a culture in which they would be a minority and in which it would be difficult to stay in touch with Korean culture.

Knowing we had a stopover in Tokyo, Korean Christian human rights leaders gave me a packet of time-sensitive documents, statements, information, and letters about three inches thick. Its immediate destination was the Documentation for Action Groups in Asia (DAGA) office in Tokyo, which served then as a key communication hub linking the Korean Christians and the world press and world church.

More than Witnesses

I was to meet Dr. Kim Yong Bock, director of DAGA at the Tokyo airport. I was instructed to hand over the papers through stylized holes in the cement wall between the in-transit passenger lounge and the airport visitors area. The transfer method had worked well in the past.

During the stopover, the babies were cared for by Japanese volunteers. I got off the airplane without my passport, which was being carried by the airline in the briefcase with the babies' papers. But, to my horror, I discovered that the open wall had been changed— people could no longer pass anything to others in the airport without leaving the in-transit lounge. It had been made clear to me in Korea that these papers were both very important and very time-sensitive. I had to get them delivered!

In a momentary and momentous decision, I decided to leave the in-transit lounge without my passport or my air ticket; I would find Kim Yong Bock, give him the papers, then figure out how to get back on the plane. I think my reasoning was that the airline would very much want me back on the plane, as I was the only one of the four adults who knew how to (and was willing to) change diapers.

The airport was packed. Everyone was Asian and had dark hair. It was noisy. How would I ever find Dr. Kim? I fought my way up to an information desk to try to make a public announcement calling his name – when I looked at the person shoving next to me. It was Dr. Kim, preparing to call me over the public address system!

We were both greatly relieved. I thrust the papers into his hands and gave him several verbal messages with which I had been entrusted. Then I asked him to help me get back on the plane. We discovered it was impossible at this in-transit terminal. We would have to walk to the next terminal where ticketed passengers enter planes. We were running out of time, so we ran. While airport security then was not as tough as it is today, it was impossible even then to get on a plane with no ticket and no passport.

My Japanese was nonexistent and his was nontechnical, so we tried to explain my problem in English first to a ticket agent and then to an immigration clerk. Everyone we dealt with was astounded that I had left the plane without my papers, and they insisted on knowing why. I was panicking. All I could say was, "How do I get back on the plane to help with the babies?" Finally, and just in the nick of time, we convinced a ticket agent to call into the plane by phone and ask if someone who looked like me had been on board caring for babies. Once the truth of it was established, flight attendants on board realized it was in their best interest to facilitate my reentry (remember, I was the diaper person). So the passport and ticket were found, carried off the plane, and delivered to me in the ticketing area.

A miracle. Documents delivered. Verbal messages given. Plane re-entry achieved. Dry bottoms guaranteed for 18 babies. But I could not fully process the miracle until almost 24 hours and scores of changed diapers later, when all the babies had been placed safely into the hands of their new parents in Seattle, Minneapolis, and Chicago.

When I finally arrived at my Chicago home, I slept for three days in a foggy zone between the dream world and the real world. Had what transpired in Tokyo been a crazy dream? But I knew it had been real when I began reading stories written by Tokyo-based correspondents of U.S. newspapers. The stories contained quotes from the official documents and statements I had delivered in Tokyo.

Part of what was going back and forth between Korea and Japan was information for, and articles by, an anonymous writer in Japan identified only by the byline TK. Each month he wrote a "letters from

Korea" column for the respected Japanese monthly magazine *Sekai* (The World) analyzing the Korean democratic struggle. I consider it an honor to have been involved in a small way in the transfer of information for his critically important writing, which was later published in an English-language book, *Letters from South Korea* by TK.

TK's identity was made public in 2004. He is Chi Myung Kwan (Chi Myŏngkwan), a professor at a Japanese university. When I heard who TK was, I realized that I had met him twice in Tokyo. He was one of the softest-spoken and wisest persons I ever met. Finally, he has been identified and can be acknowledged as one of the heroes in south Korea's march to democracy.

Toiling up new Calv'ries ever
with the cross that turns not back

In the spring of 1974, when we had been in Korea for eighteen months, the Park Chung Hee dictatorship initiated a huge crackdown against students. Although Park had closed the universities again months ago, he still feared organized demonstrations like those the students had pulled off in the fall of 1973. By spring, Emergency Decrees 1 through 3 had been issued (see Glossary). The latter would imprison people for fifteen years to life for planning public anti-government rallies. Many student leaders had already been in hiding for much of the winter.

We had gotten to know Hwang In Sung well when I was writing the human rights book for KSCF. The soft-spoken student hid in our apartment for almost six weeks in 1973. Mr. Hwang was a critical leader in the movement, because his Social Service Development Corps of the KSCF had placed many students in slum and factory settings to learn of the plight of the poor. The government claimed that such work was intended only to organize the poor for open, violent, communist-style rebellion. The government also suspected Hwang because he was a student leader – and according to the Park regime, students were planning open rebellion and revolution against the government.

Mr. Hwang could not hide at our house when the dragnet started in the spring of 1974. By then we were too well-known as his friends and as supporters of others in the democratic movement. But I was involved from time to time in finding new places for him to hide. For example, I did not know where he was currently staying that spring, but I had been asked to find a new, safe place for him. I was to meet him at a certain *tabang* (tea room) at a certain day and time to tell him where to go. Homes safe for hiding had become very tough to find, as the whole Monday Night Group either already had "house guests" or were too well-known by the government to invite anyone. Most foreigners would not help, and it was not our place to try to get Koreans to help.

One day before I was to meet Mr. Hwang there was considerable tension. Everybody was uptight about what the government was planning to do next. It was a critical time in the struggle.

A young, male typist whom I had often seen working at the KSCF office came knocking on my door all sweaty and in a panic. My limited Korean picked up that this was a matter of life and death and that he *had* to see Mr. Hwang and give him an urgent message as soon as possible. Did I know where he was? No, I did not, but I knew where he was going to be tomorrow. I named the place of the tabang and the time and told the office worker he could see Mr. Hwang then.

As soon as the young man left, I realized what had just happened. I had led the police straight to Mr. Hwang through this young office worker, who likely was sweaty and anxious not because he had a life-and-death message for Mr. Hwang, but because he had been threatened by the police to get the information out of me *or else*. My heart sank. I went to visit a family in the Monday Night Group, and they agreed that I had likely been fooled. There was nothing we could do. I did not know how to contact Hwang and tell him not to come. I did contact some of his best friends, who hurriedly cleaned all materials about the democratic movement out of their homes and who were able to warn others, fully expecting that they would be arrested next. For Hwang would likely be beaten and tortured enough to extract from him information the government sought about other key leaders in the movement.

That night was one of the longest and worst nights of my life. How could I live with myself after making a mistake that would lead to the arrests not only of Hwang but probably also of other brilliant, kind, and resourceful young leaders?

As morning came, the hour was upon us. With the heaviest rock in my stomach that I had ever felt, I arrived at the tea room. The office worker was already there—as were possibly a dozen other Korean men sitting at separate tables, reading their newspapers and having tea. The scene was completely usual for that place.

As Mr. Hwang entered the tearoom, his hair cut short and wearing sunglasses to help hide his identity on the streets, the office boy greeted him. Immediately a look of terror came over Hwang's angelic face. In a flash every man in the tearoom jumped up with a scowl and ran toward Hwang flashing pistols, screaming at him to hold still, roughing him up, and placing handcuffs on him as if he were a dangerous murderer. The office boy stood by, head hanging low. I screamed, "I'm sorry; I'm sorry," as they dragged Mr. Hwang away.

Then all was quiet. The office boy had left. I never saw him again. Nor did I see Mr. Hwang again while we were in Korea.

It was the week before Passion Week in the Easter season. Never had I felt so deeply the Passion of Christ's being double-crossed and turned in to the authorities as I did that next week. I could imagine all that was being done to Mr. Hwang. One by one, his friends were arrested too. These included Suh Kyung Suk, his brother, Suh Chang Suk (Sŏ Ch'angsŏk), and several others whom I knew from the study group in our apartment or from the human rights seminars at KSCF. I prayed for Mr. Hwang and the others. I prayed for forgiveness. I prayed that they would come out alive and with all their senses. In the past some of the tortured students had come out of prison psychologically very fragile.

On Maundy Thursday night, I attended church and took communion offered by Dr. Stephen (Tong Whan) Moon, the preacher that night. As we dipped the rice ball into the wine, he said to each of us, "Your sins are forgiven." I did not feel forgiven. I felt sick—and still could not eat or sleep. On Easter morning, it did not feel like a resurrection. It was more like the world had turned dark on Good Friday and would stay that way forever.

Ten days after Easter, someone knocked on our apartment door. A total stranger said a doctor had told him to deliver this small package to me. Inside the package? Two little pieces of paper. On one side of the first note it said, "Suh Kyung Suk (Sŏ Kyŏnsŏk) — urine sample" and a date in Korean. On the other side, "If you will, please deliver this note to Ms. Linda Jones," followed by my address. The second note said, "Dear Ms. Linda Jones, We hope you are well. We are sorry for all the difficulties our movement has caused you. From your friends." The paper for the first note originally had been wrapped around a urine sample bottle that Suh Kyung Suk had handed to a doctor in the prison.

I learned later that the students were told in prison that I had been deported for working with them.

Yet that scaffold sways the future

Can you realize what that note meant to me? First of all, it meant that Mr. Suh had not been tortured out of his mind. It meant that he was in touch with other incarcerated friends. It meant that they forgave me for my mistake that landed them all in prison. And it meant that the movement ran much deeper than anyone knew—as at least one guard and one doctor and one messenger had all done their part in seeing to it that Mr. Suh's message clandestinely got out of the prison and found its way to me.

What elation I felt! How thankful I was! I wanted to sing and dance! "Is this how it feels when one is resurrected?" I wondered. I was so moved, to realize that so many persons would take so many chances just to get a message to me. When my dear friends went through all of that, the least I and our friends in the Monday Night Group could do was to support them in every possible way. I became even more deeply involved in the movement.

The students were given long prison terms, but most were let out by President Park Chung Hee for political reasons related to the Korea visit of U.S. President Gerald Ford in 1974. That's when I knew my worst fears had been true: Mr. Hwang had been tortured. He never told me about it, but his friends did.

Although I was no longer living in Korea when the students were released, I have seen Mr. Hwang several times in the years since then. He has worked consistently over the years on issues related to reunification of south and north Korea. Until the mid-1990's, that kind of work was risky, and he was imprisoned more than once for it.

At the time of this writing, Mr. Hwang worked in the Blue House (equivalent to U.S. White House) with the democratically-elected President Roh Moo Hyun whose term ended in 2008. It was my deep pleasure to have a wonderful Korean lunch with him in the fall of 2003, when I and other members of the Monday Night Group were in Korea as honored guests of the Korea Democracy Foundation.

I was honored to know Mr. Hwang in the 1970's, and I am honored to know him today.

≈ ≋≋ ≈

Till the multitude make virtue
of the faith they had denied.

With so many students in prison from the dragnet that extended throughout south Korea, it was their mothers who stepped forward at the public prayer meetings, rallies, and interviews with the press. Suh Kyung Suk's mother, Kim Myung Jin (Kim Myŏngjin), became an international figure when the prayer she offered at a Seoul prayer meeting was published around the world.

In 1982, Kim Myung Jin, Suh Kyung Suk's wife Shin Heisoo (Sin Hŭisu) (see book endorsements), Faye Moon and I (plus other members of the Monday Night Group) were among five thousand women who attended an assembly for Christian women held at Purdue University campus in Indiana (see Faye Moon's chapter). We learned a great deal about how to get American church women interested in and involved in struggles for human rights and democracy. And we succeeded: women in various U.S. denominations led the way in demanding that the U.S. government and Congress stop supporting the dictatorship in south Korea.

Korean mothers were not the only Koreans transformed when their sons and daughters went off to jail. Wives and girlfriends joined solidarity groups to get decent food and warm blankets to prisoners during the harsh winter months. They wrote letters, led prayer meetings, talked with the press, and demonstrated at City Hall and in front of courthouses where judges were rubber-stamping the government's sentences.

Wives of twelve political prisoners, the March First Group (1976), refused to enter the kangaroo courtrooms simply for opportunities to see their husbands. Instead, they stood outside along one of Seoul's busiest streets and raised parasols that said, "Restoration of Democracy."

One result of the activism by Korean women was their own enhanced self-esteem. Before their husbands were imprisoned, those husbands had been the public figures – the spokespersons, the writers, the pray-ers, the actors on church and other stages. When their husbands were imprisoned, these women stepped up and began filling the void, becoming public figures themselves, speaking up and speaking out. More than one released male political prisoner was very surprised to come home and find a wife or mother who had become as strong a public figure as he had been. The women could not just go back to hosting and cooking. I've been told that, for some, it was quite an adjustment in family life.

New occasions teach new duties

Because their men were in prison when our two-year assignment ended and we left Korea in 1974, it was the women who said "good-bye" to me at the airport. They told me very clearly, "We have taught you all that we could in two years. You speak English. You are a trained teacher. Now go back to the U.S.A. and go into mission. Tell what you have seen and heard. Make your democracy work. If yours is working, ours has a much better chance of coming into being here."

I thought I had been in mission in Korea. Now I realized it had all been a preparation time, a training period for what was to come. Just as in my early days in Korea – when I had to pass a test to join people in the movement – I would need to go back to the U.S. and see if I could find a footing in Korea solidarity work there.

I had arrived in Korea thinking I could be of service in some way. What had happened in the process of being of *service* was that the work grew into *solidarity*. I grew to love the people I worked with, to feel such deep respect for them. I had learned to cry with them, be anxious with them, laugh with them, and plan and analyze and listen and talk with them. We had worked as a team, as one. I had learned the importance of community – and of friendships that defy outside forces. I had joined one of God's visible communities of good in the world, and it had become a part of me.

I went back to the U.S. and similar blessings happened again, in new ways. I found a small community of like-minded Korean-Americans and other Christians with whom I worked for the next 18 years. Our Korea solidarity work held no promise that democracy would come to Korea in our lifetimes. But it did in the 1990's. For that, for the deep friendships, for all that was learned and for all of the growth, I praise God, who has consistently stood "within the shadow, keeping watch above God's own."

More than Witnesses

Hymn: **Once to Every One and Nation**

Once to every one and nation, comes the moment to decide,
In the strife of truth with falsehood, for the good or evil side;
Some great cause, some great decision, offering each the bloom or blight,
And the choice goes by forever, 'twixt that darkness and that light.

Then to side with truth is noble, when we share her wretched crust,
Ere her cause bring fame and profit, and 'tis prosperous to be just;
Then it is the brave man (sic) chooses while the coward stands aside,
Till the multitude make virtue of the faith they had denied.

By the light of burning martyrs, Christ, Thy bleeding feet we track,
Toiling up new Calv'ries ever with the cross that turns not back;
New occasions teach new duties, time makes ancient good uncouth,
They must upward still and onward, who would keep abreast of truth.

Though the cause of evil prosper, yet the truth alone is strong;
Though her portion be the scaffold, and upon the throne be wrong;
Yet that scaffold sways the future, and behind the dim unknown,
Standeth God within the shadow, keeping watch above God's own.

Words: James Russell Lowell, 1849
Music: Ton-y-Botel (Ebenezer), Yn y glyn
Meter: 87 87 D

Chapter 15

1979-80: When Violence Peaked And Dictatorship Began to Crumble

The Editors

By 1975 President Park Chung Hee's dictatorship was firmly in place. He had complete control of the military, the KCIA, the police, the National Assembly, and the courts. By using the nine Emergency Decrees and other repressive laws to harass, intimidate, and arrest opponents, Park also effectively controlled the media, the universities, the labor movement, and even the vast majority of churches. Still, pockets of opposition remained, especially in places where Monday Night Group members were well-connected: in ecumenical church circles, on college campuses, and in the factories.

By the summer of 1979 tension levels were rising in south Korea. An increasingly paranoid Park Chung Hee seemed obsessed with eliminating all opposition, real and imaginary. The KCIA, well experienced as Park's enforcement agency, was eager to oblige. Attempts by exploited workers to obtain better working conditions and a living wage were met with extreme police brutality. The government launched a concerted campaign to convince the populace that Urban Industrial Mission (UIM) and others concerned with the rights of workers were motivated by communist ideology.

The Park government was shocked when workers, students, and others joined in massive uprisings in southeastern Korea's industrialized centers of Pusan and Masan. Those cities had received favorable treatment under the regime's economic development plan. Differences of opinion arose within the Park government concerning how to deal with the uprisings. A group headed by President Park wanted to impose even more stringent controls, while others favored some relaxation of the Yushin restrictions.

On October 29, 1979, Park visited one of several existing KCIA "safe houses" near the Blue House to discuss the matter with KCIA Director Kim Chaegyu. As the discussion became heated, Kim Chaegyu drew his side arm and shot to death both President Park and Park's bodyguard.

The country was plunged into a period of uncertainty. News about the assassination was carefully controlled and trickled out only bits at a time. At first it was reported only that Park had been wounded and incapacitated after a mysterious gun battle near the Blue House. Eventually we learned that he was dead, shot to death by his long-time friend and KCIA chief. There was considerable anxiety and fear that the dreaded KCIA might now be running the country.

After the initial shock and period of uncertainty, Monday Night Group members, along with our Korean friends and colleagues, were greatly relieved. We realized that the assassination had finally ended the reign of an increasingly oppressive tyrant. We welcomed the possibility that south Korea's long period of oppression and gross human rights violations would end with Park's death.

In the weeks that followed, our relief seemed warranted. As provided for in south Korea's constitution, Prime Minister Choi Kyu Ha (Ch'oe Kyuha) became acting president. He was a former professor at the Teachers College of Seoul National University who had entered government service in 1946 and served in a variety of bureaucratic positions until being named prime minister in 1976. Choi appeared to be a good-hearted, well-intentioned man – qualities that did not prepare him well for the tough infighting that followed Park's assassination.

Choi gave the country every impression of moving in the right direction. He canceled Emergency Decree Number Nine, which had criminalized criticism of the government or of the Yusin Constitution. Many of our friends were released from prison. Laborers began to enjoy more freedom of expression. The rigidly controlled press began to open up a bit. President Choi even appointed south Korea's first woman cabinet minister, Dr. Kim Okgil, former president of Ewha Woman's University. Shortly after being named minister of education, she began a series of steps to ease campus restrictions.

One interesting aspect of that brief period was the ease with which some governmental and media personalities – persons who had spent the stifling years of the Park regime fawning over him – suddenly began publicly faulting him and his regime.

These developments had some of us in the Monday Night Group beginning to wonder if our reason for existence was coming to an end. For the first time, we reveled in reporting *good* news. But lurking in the background was Chun Doo Hwan.

❧ ❧❧ ❧

Chun, a major general in the ROK Army, was serving as chief of the Defense Security Command when he was named to head the investigation into the murder of Park Chung Hee. From this position of power, Chun and his close friend, General Roh Tae Woo, began plotting a government takeover. The first step was taken December 12, 1979, when the two joined forces with other officers to stage a military uprising. Army units massed in front of the ROK Army headquarters, and soon ROK Army Chief of Staff General Chong Sung Wha (Chŏng Sŭnghwa) was wounded and arrested.

At the time, the ROK Army units were ostensibly under command of U.S. General John Wickham, head of the United Nations Combined Forces Command. The ROK units were not to be pulled from their front-line positions without notifying Wickham and getting his permission. Because such a move exposed the flanks of American troops guarding one part of the border with north Korea, Wickham needed to know. In a different environment, Chun's illegal deployment of troops would have been punishable as the most dangerous kind of treason. In Chun's case, however, the result was his complete takeover of the Korean military.

During the uprising, General Wickham and U.S. Ambassador William Gleysteen were forced to take refuge in a bunker in the U.S. Army Headquarters compound. Quite likely they feared civil war. Later public reports indicate that Wickham and Gleysteen were furious at Chun and Roh, but they chose to take no action against them.

Chun and Roh essentially began running the government from behind the scenes, retaining Acting President Choi Kyu Ha as a figurehead.

We were greatly sobered by this turn of events. Our days of enjoying good news appeared to be coming to an end. But once again we were pleasantly surprised: the political atmosphere seemed to move in a positive direction through the early part of 1980. Acting President Choi canceled President Park's Emergency Decrees and restored opposition leader Kim Dae Jung's political rights. Work began on a new constitution. College professors and students were released from prison and reinstated in their colleges and universities.

The long-oppressed labor movement also began to breathe more freely. Workers finally felt free to express dissatisfaction with the decades of government-enforced exploitation. Strikes became fairly common and were, for the most part, allowed to occur without the brutal police crackdowns that characterized the Park years.

But Chun Doo Hwan was simply biding his time. When a group of miners on the east coast protested dangerous conditions and low pay, Chun used the occasion to have himself named head of the KCIA, while retaining his military post as head of the Defense Security Command. Most of us in the Monday Night group were still naively hoping for the best, but some Koreans, especially the students, quickly caught on to Chun's intentions. They were angered in part because of highly publicized statements by General Wickham that appeared to express support for a military takeover. Through a most unfortunate choice of metaphors, Wickham likened the Korean people to lemmings who blindly follow their leader, and he called for a strong leader who would take Koreans in the proper direction. Such a leader could be found only in the military, he declared.

Because lemmings are not native to Korea, reporters had difficulty explaining just what Wickham meant. They came up with the expression "field rats." The unfortunate choice of words, plus Wickham's calling for a strong military leader to take control, came as an unexpected bonus for the unpopular Chun, who at the time was facing fierce resistance in his efforts to assume leadership. One can only hope that Wickham has repented for his "lemming" interview, but the damage was done. Combined with the lack of U.S. sanctions against Chun and Roh for pulling troops out of front-line positions during the December 12 coup, the United States emerged with a major black eye in the opinion of many south Koreans.

When Chun declared himself director of the KCIA, it ignited large-scale demonstrations throughout the country. Gene Matthews, who lived in downtown Seoul, recalls opening the gates of his residence compound to allow rioting students to pump water from the well in his front yard so they could wash the tear gas from their faces and eyes.

In reaction to this massive show of resistance, Chun suddenly declared martial law, closed the universities, shut down the National Assembly, and ordered the arrests of large numbers of students and politicians during the night of May 17-18, 1980. In doing so, Chun added another totally new equation to the formula of oppression: he brought the military directly into the process of civilian control. Although Park Chung Hee had taken over the country in a military coup, and had relied heavily on the army during imposition of martial law, he was, for the most part, content to utilize the KCIA and the National Police to control the populace. Following Chun's imposition of martial law, thousands of political and academic leaders, including many of our friends, were rounded up by the military, taken into dark cells on military compounds, stripped naked, and beaten violently. Victims of these terrible beatings included Kim Yong-Bock (Kim Yŏngbok), husband of Monday Night Group member Marion Kim. In many cases, no charges were brought against those arrested. The victims were simply horribly beaten then released to crawl home. The obvious intent was to frighten people, and in most parts of the country it succeeded. There was one remarkable exception: Kwangju.

≈ ≋≋≋ ≈

For complex historical reasons, residents of the southwestern section of the country, consisting of North and South Chulla (Chŏlla) Provinces, have been discriminated against for centuries, especially by the so-called elite of North and South Kyoung Sang (Kyŏngsang) Provinces, the home provinces of both Chun Doo Hwan and Park Chung Hee. President Park discriminated against the Chŏlla provinces by promoting industrial development in other parts of the country. Chun, like Park, also had a special dislike of opposition leader Kim Dae Jung, who came from South Chŏlla.

The people of Kwangju, south Korea's fourth-largest city and the capital of South Chulla, never passively accepted such discrimination. In fact, they have long been noted for their rebellious nature. When the rest of the nation more or less acquiesced to Chun's final military takeover, the citizens of Kwangju, behaving in a most "un-lemming-like" manner, rose up in rebellion and staged massive demonstrations in the heart of the city. On May 18, General Chun ordered the arrest of Kim Dae Jung, blaming him for the demonstrations. When news spread that their native son had been arrested, the Kwangju demonstrators swelled to more than 100,000 – students, workers, and ordinary citizens – demanding an end to martial law and a timetable for democratic elections.

Chun responded to the uprising by dispatching to Kwangju crack troops from the ROK Airborne Brigades. The troops were not only highly trained; they also had reputations for ferocity in battle. Chun apparently chose them to instill fear in the hearts of demonstrators.

The fully armed troops advanced on the crowds with fixed bayonets and began firing their rifles into the mass of people. What ensued was so brutal that people had great difficulty believing reports of the carnage. Demonstrators were beaten to death with rifles and bayonets; women, including the elderly, were raped; and people were stripped and forced to lie on the pavements. One eyewitness saw soldiers chasing a pregnant woman down a side alley, ripping her belly open with bayonets, and thrusting the bloodied fetus in the air. American missionaries in Kwangju described how arrested persons were brutalized. One report (*New York Times*, May 22, 1980) said a student was dragged through the streets with a rope around his neck, and that dead protestors were hung upside-down by the police in a city park. Civilians reported that paratroopers stomped on the faces of victims to prevent them from being identified. Stories began to circulate that the soldiers had been drugged or gotten drunk before the crackdown, because people could not otherwise believe that Korean soldiers could be so cruel to fellow citizens. One father, whose son was among those killed, said, watching the brutalities, "It was like a dog that becomes so crazed, it can't recognize even its owner." Hospitals in Kwangju quickly overflowed with severely wounded citizens, and dead bodies littered the streets.

Incredibly, in the midst of the violence and chaos, the citizens of Kwangju, led by the students, were able to gain control of the city on May 21. When the troops again fired on the demonstrators, killing 11, some 200,000 protestors, armed with kitchen knives, sections of lead pipes, rocks, and broken bottles, confronted the troops. A group of protestors broke into armories and police stations, seizing weapons with which they drove out the paratroops and took over the city. At the same time, in solidarity, demonstrators in 16 other Chulla province cities rose up, and many Chulla police officers laid down their arms. The citizens of Kwangju had effectively freed the city from military rule.

Military units retreated to positions surrounding the city and set up barricades restricting traffic in and out. Within the city itself, citizens organized themselves into efficient neighborhood units to keep order, direct traffic, transport the wounded to the hospitals, canvass for blood donations for the injured, bury the dead, and ensure distribution of food and water. A 30-member Citizen's Committee, composed of clergy, university professors, and student and civic leaders, was formed to negotiate with martial law officials.

1979-80: When Violence Peaked
And Dictatorship Began to Crumble

The committee declared a truce and offered to negotiate a peaceful settlement with government forces. It also appealed indirectly to the U.S. Embassy for mediation.

Chun Doo Hwan was outraged by this successful challenge to his authority. He immediately began making plans to retake Kwangju and punish those who had dared defy him. The way he went about it created yet another black eye for the United States.

On Monday, May 26, following several days of isolation and siege, Kwangju was invaded by 17,000 army troops. Citizens were forced to surrender in the early morning hours of May 27.

We learned later that General Wickham, U.S. commander of the United Nations Joint Forces in Korea, had released large numbers of Korean troops under his command for the express purpose of putting down the Kwangju protests. In addition to releasing the ROK Army's 20th Division, U.S.-supplied weapons and tanks accompanied the ROK paratroopers into Kwangju.

≈ ≋ ≈

Marion Pope, a Monday Night Group member and Canadian missionary nurse/educator, witnessed the Kwangju massacre. A musician, diaconal minister, and woman of deep faith, Marion served in Korea from 1957 to 1993. At the time of the May 1980 uprising, she was working at the Community College of Nursing in Kwangju. The following account was transcribed and edited from a 2005 telephone interview. Marion said that, 25 years later, her memories of the massacre remain fresh and still evoke pain and grief. Her account:

"The paratroopers came into Kwangju on Sunday, May 18. At church that morning (Yangrimdong Church of the Presbyterian Church ROK denomination), we heard about students demonstrating against the closing of the universities in Kwangju and how their actions had been suppressed. One church member, Professor Myung

More than Witnesses

Noh Gon (Myŏng Nogŏn), had just finished a year's imprisonment for signing a statement revealing that professors had been forced by the government authorities to spy on their students. He had just been reappointed to his professorship at South Chulla (Chonnam) National University after being released from prison. The elders of the church urged Professor Myŏng to leave town quickly, because the universities were again under close scrutiny and he, no doubt, would become a target because of his past activities.

"After church I went downtown with one of the church elders to see what was happening. There were some gravel-size rocks on the street in front of the police station, indicating that perhaps a scuffle had taken place, but members of the special police force were just sitting there eating their box lunches. We saw no other activity there, so we made our way to the YWCA where several Christian leaders were gathered. The leaders were deeply worried about what had happened in the last few days – the imprisonment of student leaders throughout the country, the declaration of martial law, the heightened military alert, the demonstrations in Seoul, the peaceful demonstrations in Kwangju the last few nights, the closing of the universities in Kwangju and other cities, and just that morning, the Kwangju student demonstration against the closing of their universities.

"When we left there, we stood for a while at the end of the street near the Provincial Parliament buildings. Since nothing new seemed to be happening, we both left downtown to walk back home. The invasion by the paratroopers took place just 15 minutes after I started home. We did not know then, but were later told by people in the rural areas, that soldiers had been sent into many towns and villages throughout the province two weeks prior to the 18th and that skirmishes had taken place in some of the other towns.

"The paratroopers stormed down the central street. First they just beat people, but then they started using their bayonets, and finally they began shooting. (According to a Buddhist priest, one of the paratroopers confessed to him that the soldiers had been told there were communists in the city and that each soldier was to kill five communists. The troops were then starved and given alcohol to impair their senses, the priest said.)

"Even though the U.S. government denied knowing anything about plans for the invasion of Kwangju and refused to admit any connection with it, it is now known that the Korean military units that went into Kwangju were at the U.S. airbase two weeks before the action, and again two weeks afterward.

"On May 22, four days after the military first entered the city, the students were able to obtain arms from a police station in a town south of Kwangju, enabling them to commandeer jeeps and military equipment and take control of the city again. The whole city rose up in support of the students and against the military brutality. The students felt a tremendous responsibility to protect the citizens. They organized themselves to provide for the needs of the wounded and the rest of the citizens as best they could. There was no looting or vandalism. The only property destroyed was the radio station, which had refused to report what was happening and instead kept playing sentimental music that everyone felt was totally inappropriate. (It is not known whether the radio station was burned by the students or perhaps by the paratroopers for fear that if the citizens got control of it, they could broadcast to the rest of Korea what was happening in Kwangju.)

"The vice mayor asked several church elders and ministers, as well as elders from the YMCA and our hospital, to intervene between the military and the students, and on May 25th a truce was arranged. But at dawn on the 26th soldiers re-entered the city through the Presbyterian missionary compound. Next they entered the old YWCA building, dragged people out of the building and shot them. Two middle-school girls standing guard in front of the building were shot and killed. Then the soldiers made their way to the center of the city. They went to the Provincial Government building where the students had stocked arms and ammunition and were trying to protect the people.

"One of the young men in Kwangju that week was a student at Seoul's Hanshin Seminary who just happened to be home at the time. His father was the minister of the Kwangju Holiness Church. The boy had joined the struggle against the invading paratroopers and had been arrested, then released and allowed to return home. His mother begged him not to go back. But he knew he couldn't just stay quietly at home. He felt he had to be with the other students and help them protect the city. He tried to calm his mother, telling her that everything would be okay because there was a truce and things were quiet now. However, that was the day (May 26) that the soldiers re-entered the city. As they made their way to the Provincial Government building, they sprayed it with machine gun fire, killing many, including this boy. People who saw him said he was tortured before he was shot.

"When the military was in control of the city, the wounded were taken to the South Chulla (Chonnam) University Hospital or to the private hospitals within the city. The hospital where I was working was outside the city limits. We had set up a blood transfusion unit to help the wounded, but at first no one came. We later learned it was because the soldiers were preventing anyone from leaving the city. However, around noon on Wednesday, May 21, the wounded started showing up at our hospital. The paratroopers had been replaced by regular soldiers the day before, and the students began to bring the wounded to us in commandeered jeeps. One wounded young woman begged us to treat her first because she had to get back to town to help the others. We treated her and she hurried off. But we soon learned that, as she entered Kwangju, she was shot and killed.

"After the students had finally been defeated by the military, all the ministers and church elders who had tried to help them were accused of treason by the government. Professor Myung Noh Gon was one of those sentenced to prison. Four others were given the death sentence, including my own minister, Reverend Un Myung Gi (Un sMyŏnggi). Fortunately, Reverend Un was able to go into hiding to avoid apprehension. He hid in Kwangju for about two months, until it became too dangerous and he had to leave. The police were desperate to find him, and the children in the home where he was hiding were beginning to ask questions.

"I was able to arrange for him to stay with Walter and Lenore Beecham, Canadian missionaries in Seoul. At an opportune time, Reverend Un was spirited out of Kwangju in an ambulance and taken to Seoul. He stayed with the Beechams for six months, hiding in their attic. All that time, Reverend Ŭn's wife did not know where he was and was terribly worried about him. We felt we could not reveal his whereabouts to her, however, because it might put her in danger. All I could tell her was that we were sure he was being taken care of by someone and not to worry. Months later, I was able to give her a note from her husband, but I did so in a way that she would not know where it had come from or how it had gotten to her. (Eventually the sentences of all the ministers and church leaders were reduced, and finally they were released.)

"During the days of the siege, the elders of my church asked me not to go downtown because rumors were being spread (including broadcasts from helicopters and low-flying planes) that this "uprising" was being instigated by foreigners and communists. The church elders were afraid that if I was seen in public or my picture was taken, it would fuel the rumors. All communication was cut off during those days, but there was one telephone line in one of the missionary houses that could still receive (but not make) long-distance calls. There were many people taking refuge in that home, and word was that among them was a relative of one of General Chun Doo Hwan's bodyguards. The woman, from Seoul, was in Kwangju visiting a friend when in the middle of the night she heard several bursts of machinegun fire in the house next door. She thought the gunfire was meant for her, so she came to this missionary family, terrified and seeking safety. While she was staying there a phone call came for her from the Blue House (the Korean White House), telling her to stay there. Obviously, the authorities in Seoul knew she was there. At some point another missionary family received a call, telling them to leave town and suggesting they tell 'that Canadian woman' (referring to me) to leave town too. They told the caller that they would not leave, and the Canadian would not leave either.

"The University Hospital staff laid out bodies in a makeshift outdoor morgue, but soldiers came and took the bodies. The soldiers also took some badly beaten patients who were still alive. They put them in trucks and drove away. Later we heard that a nearby farmer had been ordered to use his tractor to clear out a space in a field, and then was told to go away. We know now that the military held artillery practice in that and other farmers' fields, and it's possible that soldiers also buried persons there.

"When the paratroopers withdrew, they were replaced by regular soldiers who set up camp in the school yards in our neighborhood and throughout the city. The soldiers guarded the school gates and the perimeter of the school grounds where their camps had been set up. But, surprisingly, these soldiers had no idea what was going on in Kwangju. No one had informed them of anything. For example, they did not know that citizens throughout the city had been attacked without cause by the paratroopers. So some church people went around to the camps to let the soldiers know what had happened. They also took food to the camps, because the soldiers had nothing to eat.

"Among the remarkable and moving things that happened during those days were the many acts of kindness by the citizens of Kwangju. In fact, the whole town rose up in support of the students and against the military brutality. When the military had taken the city over the second time, the troops blocked the entrances to the city so no one could go in or out. But farmers would use back roads to enter the city and deliver milk for the people. They warned us that the milk was un-pasteurized, and to boil it before drinking.

"The soldiers ordered all stores to close, in an effort to starve people into submission. But shopkeepers quietly opened the back doors of their stores and provided people with basic needs. Many women from churches and community groups outside the city made lunches and brought them in for the students. The poorest person in my church, a woman who worked in a shoe store, made some delicious soybean milk and gave it to the students. Even the prostitutes in town used their money to buy soft drinks and snacks for the students.

"Our hospital staff went on half-rations so that we would have enough food for everyone. The hospital population had doubled, in part because so many came seeking refuge when they couldn't get back home safely. I remember the overwhelming feeling that this must be what the Kingdom of God was like: everyone helping and caring for everyone else.

"Many photos were taken during this time by Koreans and others. Presbyterian missionaries Martha and Betts Huntley tried to send photos with someone who was leaving Korea, with strict instructions about how to get them out safely. Unfortunately, the person wasn't able to comply with their instructions, and the photos were confiscated at the airport. Little by little, however, others were able to get photos out of the city. Monday Night Group member Marion Current was able to take some in her luggage when she returned to Canada for a short trip. The photos were of people shot by bullets that fragmented into many pieces once they entered the body. The photographer's identity was purposely not revealed to Marion, so that if she were questioned at the airport she could honestly say she didn't know who had taken the pictures.

"We believe that three to four thousand persons were killed during the Kwangju massacre. Several years later, someone studying census figures noted that a very high number of deaths – many more than the normal number – were recorded in Kwangju during May 1980. The person who reported these figures, however, was said to have lost his job, and the figures were consequently "corrected."

"The Kwangju Massacre is now considered a pivotal point in Korea's 5,000-year history. It is still hard to believe that such a horrific tragedy could have occurred in today's supposedly advanced and civilized world. If I had not seen it with my own eyes, I still might not believe it," Marion Pope said.

∽ ⊚⊜ ⌒

While many Monday Night Group members, like Marion Pope, lived and worked in Korea for decades, others, like Linda Jones, were in Korea for only a few years. With remarkable consistency, MNG members who returned to their home countries did not stop assisting the democracy and human rights movements. Linda is a prime example. In 1975 she returned to Chicago where she promptly established the Church Committee for Human Rights in Asia (CCHRA). Her continuing close communication with other Monday Night Group members and Korean leaders put her in a unique position to inform U.S. citizens, particularly American Christians, about what was happening in Korea and to urge Americans to take action in support of Korea's struggle for democracy. The CCHRA monthly newsletter, *Asian Rights Advocate,* provided an ongoing chronicle of the human rights struggle and often was the world's most up-to-date source of news direct from the Korean movement.

The headline of the January-February 1980 issue of the *Advocate* read, "Korea: Anything Could Happen." It described the new martial law government of hardliner General Chun Doo Hwan, the complete muzzling of the Korean press once again, and the rise to power of Kim Jong Pil (Kim Chongp'il), architect of the Korean CIA and new head of the powerful ruling party. In the April 1980 *Advocate,* a news "flash" warned readers about Chun Doo Hwan, who had overseen the worst tortures in recent Korean history. The news alert reported how Chun had become head of the KCIA as well as martial law commander, and it concluded, "It looks as though Korea's political 'time in between' is drawing to a close and the suffering begins in earnest." "Little did we know how true those words were to become," Linda Jones recalls today. Just as the 1980 Memorial Day holiday was approaching in the U.S., she began receiving urgent phone calls from Korea. The situation in Kwangju was desperate; thousands of Korean troops were amassed outside of Kwangju, ready to retake the city. Those Koreans who realized what was happening (most were unaware) were frantic to get word out to someone in the U.S. government. They wanted U.S. assistance in negotiations between Chun Doo Hwan and the Kwangju citizenry – and they wanted the U.S. Army to intervene before disaster hit Kwangju.

The state of Illinois, where Linda and the Church Committee for Human Rights in Asia were based, had a capable and well-placed member of the U.S. Senate, Charles Percy, a member of the powerful Senate Foreign Relations Committee. However, because it was Memorial Day, congressional offices were closed for the three-day holiday weekend. Repeated calls by Linda and her committee failed to reach Senator Percy.

More than Witnesses

Two hours before the May 26 re-invasion of Kwangju by south Korean troops, a U.S. State Department spokesperson in Washington said that, although the U.S. had urged maximum efforts toward a peaceful solution, "total disorder and disruption cannot go on indefinitely." Apparently the State Department had not heard of the calm in Kwangju after the troops had left the city and the police had laid down their weapons. Asked about the U.S. viewpoint three days prior to the invasion, the State Department had expressed concern that democratization would have to be postponed until calm had been restored in Kwangju. General Chun Doo Hwan needed no brighter green light than that for a violent retaking of the city.

As Americans were sleeping off their Memorial Day partying, Chun's troops re-entered Kwangju. Linda Jones recalls, "Just as Passion Week carried new meaning for me after the imprisonment and torture of my Korean student friends at Easter in 1975, five years later Memorial Day would hold a deeper feeling of mourning and sorrow. My feelings of helplessness within our own U.S. democracy were overwhelming. It was as though a part of me also died in Kwangju."

The *Asian Rights Advocate* newsletter reported in June 1980 that Koreans in the U.S. – usually conservative, reserved, and quiet about political reforms needed in their homeland – put aside their normal activities and held rallies in cities across the U.S. in solidarity with the Kwangju citizens. Hundreds attended rallies in Los Angeles, Washington, D.C., Chicago, and Cambridge, Massachusetts. A memorial service for the massacred of Kwangju, held at Riverside Church in New York City on May 29, was attended by hundreds of Koreans and Americans.

Details of the massacre were slow to come. For days Kwangju was isolated – foreign reporters found it difficult to enter, and citizens found it hard to exit. Eventually word began to spread inside

1979-80: When Violence Peaked
And Dictatorship Began to Crumble

Korea. People began telling what they had seen and heard, and the international press carried more details of the massacre. Because all Kwangju news was suppressed in the Korean media, part of Linda's role at the CCHRA was to gather international news and opinion pieces about events in Korea and feed them back into Korea. Koreans deeply involved in the struggle needed to know what was being reported outside Korea.

The tragedy in Kwangju led international human rights groups to launch huge efforts in the following years to get Korean prisoners released, to re-evaluate U.S. foreign policy toward Korea, to analyze the activities of Western corporations that were taking advantage of cheap Korean labor, and to take a new look at the realities of north and south Korea, divided by the U.S. and the Soviet Union after World War II. Military rule would not end in south Korea for many more years. But the blood of the martyrs of Kwangju gave new life, energy, and determination to democracy and human rights movements inside and outside Korea.

❧ ❧ ❧ ❧

Gene Matthews offers this personal reflection:

"The Kwangju uprising and the way it was handled represented a time of great personal sorrow for me and for many friends and colleagues. My grief and bitter disappointment extended beyond Kwangju to the general crackdown, the massive arrests, the stories of torture and mistreatment that continued all over south Korea. Through it all, I was distressed by the perceived involvement of the United States government through its envoys in Seoul at the time, Ambassador William F. Gleysteen and General John A. Wickham.

"I met Ambassador Gleysteen frequently and General Wickham less often. I feel that both were good, well-intentioned people. Gleysteen, who died in 2002, and Wickham have each written books describing their actions and inactions during 1979 and 1980. Both men believe strongly that what they did or didn't do was driven by a necessity to preserve peace on the Korean peninsula. Unfortunately, their actions and their public statements at that time created a strong impression that the United States officially supported Chun Doo Hwan in his military takeover of the nation and his brutal suppression of a democratic uprising in Kwangju.

"Debates continue to this day over how many people were killed by the Korean army in its putdown of Kwangju. Concerned historians estimate that approximately 2,000 citizens were killed in Kwangju; countless others were severely wounded, including some crippled for life. Apologists for the Chun government claim the death toll was "only" two hundred. Apparently Chun and his generals could sleep better at night using that figure. But I believe that one death was one too many when its only purpose was to please the ego of a power-hungry general.

"In 2003 many of us who were part of the Monday Night Group, along with other supporters of Korean democracy, were invited back to Korea by the Korea Democracy Foundation. During that remarkable trip we were taken to Kwangju and shown scenes of the military's massacre of citizens. We saw the little prison room into which far too many students and young people were stuffed with no food, water, or toilet facilities. We were taken to the cemeteries where the dead are buried. At one point I wandered off alone among the many graves and stood for a moment shedding tears. They were tears of great sorrow, because I genuinely mourned the deaths. But they were also tears of pride in the Korean people, because for a few brief days a city had caught a vision of freedom. They stood up to the guns and bayonets of a powerful force. They paid the ultimate price for an ultimate prize. The soldiers are gone, and beautiful Kwangju stands as a beacon for freedom," Gene Matthews said.

1979-80: When Violence Peaked
And Dictatorship Began to Crumble

With Kwangju as a beacon, south Koreans still had much work to do to establish democracy and human rights in south Korea. First they suffered the rule of Chun Doo Hwan, who took over as president in August 1980. Following Chun's tumultuous reign, he handpicked his coconspirator in the 1979 military coup, Roh Tae Woo, to succeed him as president. By this time, however, the public had become intolerant of top-down rule and was craving a democratic voice. The public soon joined the student-led demonstrations against the authoritarian selection of Roh, forcing him to back out of his presidential appointment. Thus in 1987, Korea engaged in its first-ever open and relatively free presidential election, with Roh running against two long-time champions of democracy, Kim Young Sam and Kim Dae Jung. The two Kims initially spoke of joining forces, but factional strife and division prevented this. The pro-democracy vote was divided by the two Kims, and Roh emerged as president with only 36 percent of the vote.

Without a strong mandate, Roh's term was marked by a degree of relaxation, even though many of the harsh policies established by his predecessors were continued. Any credibility that Chun and Roh may have had when their terms ended was wiped out when investigations later revealed that both men had amassed vast personal fortunes while in office. Both were sentenced to prison (and eventually were pardoned).

By 1992 the popular yearning for democracy was unstoppable, and Kim Young Sam finally was elected to a five-year presidential terms that began in 1993. He was followed by Kim Dae Jung, who was inaugurated in 1998.

❧ ❦❦ ❧

During the last two decades of the 20th century, democracy slowly, sometimes painstakingly, deepened its roots in south Korea's political culture. The power of the military over the state gradually declined. The roles of the KCIA and police changed with the political culture. The courts were gradually freed from government control. The media finally could begin to report freely.

Through it all, the Monday Night Group kept meeting. Membership slowly dwindled, however, and the sense of urgency that motivated the group in the 1970s gave way to less political, more social needs. Today the Monday Night Group sometimes meets just once a month. Issues are still discussed, but now there is time to relax and enjoy one another's company, and to celebrate a new day in Korea's long and storied history.

During the 20th century the Republic of Korea survived occupation by a brutal foreign power, tragic division of their country, rule by the U.S. military, a devastating war, a succession of rigid military dictators, and a long, continuing occupation by American military forces – and, remarkably, managed to achieve democracy. The people of south Korea reached this goal because their desire for freedom came from within. The seeds of democracy were planted by a handful of courageous people, many of whom you have met in these stories. The seeds grew and thrived over several decades until the march to democracy became unstoppable.

We members of the Monday Night Group are eternally grateful for having known and worked with these heroes; they blessed our lives beyond measure.

Long live Korea, the Mighty Nation of Han.

Where Are They Now
Fact Sheets

Introduction to Facts Sheets
Repression Brings Response
The "Yushin" Constitution of South Korea
and Its Consequences
Letter to President Ford
The Struggle Continues

Emergency Decree Number Nine
A Tract for Our Times

Where They Are Now

And What They're Doing
Summer 2008

Jean Basinger and her husband, Bill, reside in Des Moines, Iowa, where she served twelve years as a registered nurse at the Iowa Methodist Hospital Chemical Dependency Center. She is involved in issues ranging from ministries to prisoners and immigrants to protests against U.S. military and nuclear policies.

Marion Current resides in Toronto, Ontario, where she is an active member of both an English-speaking and a Korean church. She travels to Korea every two years. Between those visits she surfs the web for Korea news (south and north) to forward to interested friends.

Walter "Butch" Durst resides in Nashville, Tennessee, where for nineteen years he has worked for United Methodist Communications. He enjoys Eastern Europe folk dancing, translating Korean stories into English and playing with his grandchildren.

Linda Jones and her husband, David, reside in Rockford, Illinois. She continues to inspire friends and family with her courageous eight-year battle with leukemia. She graduated from McCormick Theological Seminary in 2001 and preaches and teaches in area churches. Linda remains involved in Korean and women's issues.

Willa Kernen resides in the Oliver Lodge Nursing Home in Saskatoon, Saskatchewan, where she celebrated her 80th shortly after moving there. She knows the nursing home well because she served as a volunteer at the United Church of Canada facility for nearly 15 years.

Marion Kim resides in Seoul, Korea with her husband and his mother. She teaches English to elementary-school children. She supplements the regular school curriculum with lessons promoting a culture of peace – for example, sharing stories of persons who have overcome situations of injustice.

Gene Matthews and his wife, Insook, reside in Iowa City, Iowa. He is active in Kiwanis International, a service organization focusing on the needs of children. He serves on five committees at his local United Methodist Church and is active in the Methodist Federation for Social Action and the United Methodist Missionary Association.

Faye Moon and her husband, Stephen, reside in Bloomfield, New Jersey, where she is involved in the social action team of her local church. She works two days per week at an after-school childcare program, where she is in charge of a program bringing together kindergarten children and senior citizens. Her daughter wrote a biography of Faye that will soon go into publication.

Louise Morris resides in Nashville, Tennessee, where for eight years she directed a state-wide grant-funded program advocating access to health care for uninsured Tennessee children and teens. She is currently Lay Leader at Edgehill United Methodist Church and she continues to raise concerns about U.S. government actions.

Fran Nelson resides in Lincolnton, North Carolina, where she is a member of the First Presbyterian Church. She enjoys family and friends, attending many reunions, and organizing photos and memorabilia. She also takes advantage of every opportunity to appreciate the North Carolina mountains.

George Ogle and his wife, Dorothy, reside in Lafayette, Colorado, near two of their daughters and four grandchildren. He is a member of the Boulder United Methodist Church and vice president of the Lafayette Historical Society. His newest book, *The Price of Colorado Coal,* is available from Xlibris.com.

Marion Pope (quoted extensively in Chapter 15) resides in Toronto, Ontario, where she participates in her local church's women's study group, choir, worship planning, and Public Witness Circle. She edits sermons, liturgies, and papers for Korean ministers and theology students who have immigrated to Canada.

Randy Rice resides in Lincoln, Vermont. He is pastor-emeritus of the United Church of Lincoln, which he served from 1991-2002. In retirement he enjoys occasional preaching, counseling, teaching, and volunteering at the Lincoln Library where he headed the Board of Trustees from 1992-2005.

Sue Rice resides in Lincoln, Vermont, and is a Clinical Social Worker at the Counseling Service of Addison County. She works primarily with clients with major mental illness under the Community Rehabilitation Treatment program with a specialization in intercultural counseling. In her spare time Sue and her husband raise angora goats to produce fine knitting yarn.

Jim Sinnott resides at the Maryknoll Center in Seoul, Korea where he writes and continues to monitor the political and spiritual condition of his beloved Korea. He enjoys being able to say "I told you so" as truths about the Park Chung Hee regime are revealed. He finds great joy in recent court decisions which fully exonerated the names of the so-called members of the PRP who were executed in 1975 and granted a large financial compensation to the surviving family members.

Jim Stentzel is a retired United Church of Christ pastor residing with his wife, Cathy, in Key West, Florida. In addition to hosting many visitors who flock to his home during winter months, he serves as a board member, program chair, and treasurer of the Florida Keys Chapter of the American Civil Liberties Union. He preaches occasionally at the Metropolitan Community Church of Key West, where he also assists in delivering hot meals to home-bound seniors.

Introduction to Fact Sheets

Editor's Note: Between 1973 and 1981, the Monday Night Group wrote periodic "Fact Sheets" for worldwide distribution through church and other international networks. They were also distributed to other missionaries within Korea to help inform them of things they otherwise may not have been aware of. This being before the days of word processing, email, fax machines, and with limited access to copy machines, each issue was typed using several layers of carbon paper for additional copies.

Though written, compiled and distributed by members of the Monday Night Group, authors' names were never mentioned, so as not to reveal their identities in case the articles somehow became known to the Korean authorities. Subjects covered everything from arrests of prominent Koreans, student demonstrations, the plight of factory workers, government's efforts to silence the church, the Yushin Constitution and Emergency Decrees, to numerous monthly chronologies of human rights abuses.

Many in our overseas networks relied on these Fact Sheets for "inside" up-to-date information, and were able to distribute them far and wide to their own constituencies, including to members of the U.S. Congress. As for other missionaries in Korea who received them, the impact was hard to assess, but we were fully aware that there was a wide range of opinion regarding our involvement in these issues – from various degrees of support to opposition and outright anger.

Four examples of the total of 63 Fact Sheets are reproduced here in their original forms. Korean names in these documents sometimes use the Western style, putting the family name last (e.g. Hyung Kyu Park) and sometimes uses the Korean style, putting the family names first (e.g. Kim Dae Jung).

REPRESSION BRINGS RESPONSE

The Case of Rev. Hyung Kyu Park
Seoul, Korea

After almost four months of sitting in a damp prison room, Rev. Hyung Kyu Park's sentence was pronounced on Sept. 25, 1973. The outcome of five very tedious trial sessions was a two-year prison sentence, pronounced at a closed session with a large crowd prohibited entry.

Rev. Hyung Kyu Park was arrested on July 6, 1973, for "attempting to overthrow the government by force." According to the Park Administration, fifteen agitators led by a Presbyterian pastor had distributed leaflets at April's Easter Sunrise Service in Seoul's South Mountain public park. The leaflets called for the "revival of democracy," according to the government report.

What frightened and annoyed the government was not the scattering of leaflets among the 100,000 worshippers at the Easter service, but the fact that Rev. Park and his followers were organizing the one million people who live in Seoul's slum neighborhoods. Rev. Park is head of a community action committee whose purpose is to organize the slum dwellers to demand basic necessities, such as a place for their families to live and school privileges for their children. The government report did not mention its concern about this type of activity; it stated only that those arrested had been "organizing action groups of malcontent Christians to topple the present government by force."

The most recent case in Seoul took place in March, when the Seoul City government ordered the 1,500 dwellers in the Song Dong

Slum to vacate their shacks by the end of June. The reason given was that the land was needed to build a roundhouse for a subway presently under construction in that area. Rev. Hyung Kyu Park's committee sent in a number of organizers to help the slum dwellers resist such governmental action. By May, the community had solidified enough to draw up a petition to President Chung Hee Park, asking for compensation. The result was that the community leader, Mr. Kang, was arrested, beaten and told not to organize any more petition drives. Since Rev. Park's arrest, one district of the slum community has already been moved (<u>without</u> monetary compensation).

The slum dwellers' next step was a letter of appeal sent to the foreign diplomatic missions in Seoul, as well as to church groups abroad, asking for support. This action angered the government because it revealed this embarrassing situation to foreigners whose support is needed in the UN "battle" against North Korea. Also, the government knew that if Rev. Park's committee succeeded in making this oppressed class of slum dwellers aware of their situation, it could be a threat to the present government. Immediately after the letter was sent, Rev. Park's committee members were repeatedly picked up, questioned and released, though no charges were brought.

Since there is no specific law against community organizing, the government remained silent until it was able to force one of Rev. Park's workers, under duress, to say that he was involved in an attempt to overthrow the government, led by Rev. Park. While it seems certain that the Easter morning leaflet distribution was, indeed, carried out by some of Park's young followers, it does not explain the charge of plotting to overthrow the government, or the arrest of the community organizers.

Rev. Hyung Kyu Park, a very respected minister in Seoul, is the pastor of Seoul's First Presbyterian Church. He is well known for <u>acting</u> upon his Christian beliefs. During the Japanese rule over Korea, as a young man he started a night school in Pusan for children who could not afford an education. One of the courses taught was Korean language – forbidden by the Japanese.

In addition to his pastorate he currently holds several other important positions: chair of the Church and Society Committee of the National Council of Churches in Korea, member of the editorial staff of the *Christian Thought* magazine, head of the Korean Urban Industrial Mission committee of the World Council of Churches, and lecturer at Hankuk Theological Seminary. In addition, he has been guiding a young ministers association in Seoul into researching the future mission of the church in Korea.

Since Rev. Park's arrest in July, there have been five trial sessions held. Each of these sessions has been well attended by an estimated 350 people, including well-known church leaders such as Mr. Hahm Suk Hun, a Quaker writer and poet; students; members of Rev. Park's congregation; concerned foreigners; and family members of the arrested. Inter-denominational worship services have been held before almost every trial session.

In addition to accusing Park and his followers of trying to overthrow the government, the prosecution has also tried to establish links between Rev. Park and the aborted coup de e'tat by General Pil Young Yun. (However, General Yun was under arrest for the alleged coup attempt – though without public charge – for several weeks before Easter.)

The defense states that an Easter crowd of 70% women carrying only Bibles and hymnals is hardly the crowd to demonstrate, or to march to the Blue House (Korea's equivalent of the White House) to overtake it. Rev. Park states that he never met General Yun but only heard about him and his arrest. He said his plan was only intended to inform the worshippers of the need to restore democracy and regain human rights and freedom. He felt, however, that the public should know about Yun's arrest, since keeping such knowledge from the people is a misuse of democracy.

It is evident that Rev. Park and his followers have been given severe physical punishment and that Rev. Park's physical condition has deteriorated. At the third trial session he looked pale and it was difficult for him to answer the defense lawyer as quickly as he had in previous trial sessions. He also was coughing, seeming to have caught cold, so his family sent warm underwear to the prison for him, which was refused at the prison gate.

The irony of the entire case is that, in the government's attempt to limit freedom of speech and publication, it has triggered the very opposite reaction. There are church leaders, students, housewives, lay people, churchwomen's organizations, ministers associations, and groups of Westerners, who have become even more aware of the <u>repression</u> of freedom in this country. Out of this awareness has come <u>response</u>. Cooperating across denominational and other factional lines, these people have begun to speak out courageously, whereas before they had been relatively quiet.

Because of the number and quality of people supporting Rev. Park, we can hope that amidst a very difficult and tight situation, President Park Chung Hee will realize that his so-called "Korean-style democracy" <u>must</u> allow the people to have more individual freedom and justice.

What Can We Do?

If you are interested in <u>doing</u> something about this situation, here are some suggestions for starters.

1. Join us in prayer.

2. Write to congressmen (especially the U.S. Foreign Relations Committee).

3. Send money or other support to the Korean National Council of Churches: Rev. Kwan Suk Kim, c/o Korean National Council of Churches, ChongNo-Ku, YunChi-Dong 136-46, Seoul, Korea.

4. Affiliate with and/or write to groups concerned about human rights (e.g. Amnesty International, Korean groups in your local area, Fellowship of Reconciliation, etc.) to inform them of the situation in Korea and to ask for their support for Rev. Park and his colleagues.

Fact Sheet # 5
February 20, 1974

THE "YUSHIN" CONSTITUTION OF SOUTH KOREA AND ITS CONSEQUENCES

❦ ❦❦ ❦

In October, 1972, south Korean President Park Chung Hee enacted Martial Law, and shortly afterwards instituted a new constitution called the "Yushin Constitution," translated as "Revitalizing Reforms." This constitution essentially gives Park virtually unchecked presidential powers and prolongs his tenure indefinitely (having already been in office 13 years). As reported in a brochure produced by the Ministry of Culture and Information, "The President has the right to select 1/3 of the National Assembly," and "...will have the right to dissolve the National Assembly." President Park's explanation of the need for the new constitution was its necessity to facilitate dialogue with the North, in hopes for the earliest possible unification of the country. Although it was reported that Yushin received 90% approval of those who voted, there has been much evidence of irregularities in the balloting.

Along with Martial Law came the closing of the universities, an effort to prevent students from assembling and organizing to protest the new measures. In Korea, according to the Confucian tradition, "scholars" have always been a highly respected class in society, and students have long been considered a strong political force, especially when basic democratic rights are threatened. It was a student revolution which overthrew the dictatorial administration of former president Syngman Rhee and sent him into exile in April of 1960.

After Martial Law was declared, outwardly the atmosphere was relatively quiet for nearly a year, until the students of Seoul National University staged demonstrations beginning on Oct.

2, 1973. These were followed by similar demonstrations on other campuses demanding that the government explain the kidnapping of opposition politician Kim Dae Jung, that the Korea CIA be done away with, that democracy be restored, and that the "selling out" of the nation to Japanese investors be halted. At the same time religious and literary leaders began making similar protests, and reporters protested the tight government control of the news media. Also, the North-South Talks seemed to be stalled, with the North demanding the removal of south Korean representative Lee Hu Rak (head of the KCIA).

In December there was a general shake-up in Park's Cabinet, which saw Lee removed both from his KCIA post and from the North-South Talks, and eventually his mysterious disappearance from the country. At this time Park also allowed some relaxation on the controls of the press, and made some efforts toward dialogue with groups such as university presidents, press reporters, etc. During this time increasing numbers spoke out for civil rights and specifically called on President Park to change the Yushin Constitution (without which there can be no change in power through election). Chief among these efforts was the drive to collect a million signatures on a petition demanding constitutional changes. Also, the newspapers began printing articles about unjust labor practices, problems of slum dwellers, and the "prostitution industry" which was being provided for Japanese male tourist groups.

This brief respite lasted less than a month, and on Jan. 8, 1974, President Park clamped down with renewed vigor by issuing his presidential Emergency Measures, making it illegal to "oppose, deny, misrepresent, or defame" the Yushin Constitution, or even to criticize the new Emergency Measures themselves. These Measures also provide for punishment of offenders through a military court-martial of up to 15 years imprisonment and loss of all civil rights. Law enforcement agencies were given authority to "arrest, search or seizure without warrant." A new angle to these latest Emergency

Measures is their application to foreign residents (foreign reporters being the primary target) as well as Koreans.

The measures have brought a definite lull to previous activities, with heavy surveillance on many leaders and other "potential" critics, but within only 3 weeks after the decree was issued, 19 were arrested, 15 of whom have received prison sentences of 5-15 years. Among the 15 are 2 former politicians, 7 university students, and 6 Protestant ministers who were involved in work helping poor laborers and slum dwellers. Many feel, at this point, that the situation in Korea is tighter now than at any previous time during Park's presidency, and that underneath the lid things are far from being calm. One Korean who was quoted in Newsweek (Feb. 18, 1974) analyzed the situation as, "beyond the point of no return. I don't know when it will all happen, but I'm quite sure that it's going to happen."

Suggestions for What You Can Do

1. Send contributions toward legal defense and support of families for the 6 ministers and others who may need similar assistance.

Send contributions to:
Korea National Council of Churches
c/o Christian Building, Room 765
136-46 Yonji-dong
Tongdaemun-ku
Seoul, Korea

Note: Please designate what the money is to be used for.

2. Send letters to President Park Chung Hee requesting the immediate release of those imprisoned under the Jan. 8 Emergency Measures.

3. Contact Amnesty International for information on the continuing plight of these political prisoners, and other actions that might help bring about their release.

4. Write to U.S. officials concerning the present situation in south Korea (refer to attached "Sample Letter").

5. Write to U.S. State Department asking about the relationship between the 42,000 American troops in Korea and the continuation of the present trend of oppressive events in that country.

SAMPLE LETTER FORM

Below is a sample letter form, which we would urge you to copy, sign, and send to any or all of the following persons:

1) Your senators and/or representatives

2) Chairman of the Senate Foreign Relations Committee: the Hon. J. William Fulbright (D. Arkansas), 2527 Belmont Rd. Washington, D.C. 20008.

3) Chairman of the Senate Armed Services Committee: the Hon. John Stennis (D. Mississippi), Room 205 Senate Office Building, Washington D.C.

In writing this letter we would make two suggestions:

1) Adapt or change the content as you wish, but keep your letter factual and brief.

2) Do not allude to the origin of this letter—in other words, offer it as <u>your</u> letter written out of your own personal motivation.

Dear_____:

As a member of (your constituency)* I am writing you out of concern for the present condition of democracy in south Korea.

For the past 28 years our nation has made heavy investments of troops and money in order to create favorable conditions for the development of a strong democratic system and a stable economy in Korea. Yet according to <u>Newsweek</u> (2/18/74, Asia Edition) any growth in this hoped-for direction is now threatened by the dictatorial policies of President Park Chung Hee.

Not only does the present government of Korea forbid political reform through democratic processes, in addition it is now sentencing responsible critics, including respected religious, civic, political and literary leaders to long prison terms of up to fifteen years.

I am disturbed by this trend, and I would respectfully request that you use all means available to you as (insert appropriate title here) to bring pressure to bear on President Park and the governing authorities of south Korea for the immediate re-establishment of democracy in that nation.

Sincerely yours,

Your Name(s) and Signatures

*Insert if writing to congressmen; delete if writing to chair of Foreign Relations or Armed Services Committees.

LETTER TO PRESIDENT FORD
From Mothers of Korean Political Prisoners

The following is a translation of a letter to President Gerald Ford, protesting his visit to Korea in November, 1974. It is written by a group of mothers of students who are now serving long prison terms as political prisoners in South Korea. Their "crime" was criticizing or demonstrating against the oppressive policies of the present South Korean dictatorship. Though the Emergency Measures under which they were sentenced were abolished in late August, these students and others (over 200 total) have been held in prison since March and are now facing the cold winter ahead in unheated concrete cells. As of yet they have not been allowed to communicate in any way with even the closest members of their families.

Dear Mr. President:

God bless you and your family in this abundant season. We especially pray for your wife's complete recovery. We also pray for our friends, the American people, and for their limitless prosperity.

We, who are addressing ourselves to you in this letter, are mothers of young people who have been sentenced to death, life imprisonment or prison terms of 7, 10, 15 or 20 years for political reasons.

According to news reports, you will soon be visiting Korea. The people of Korea are pleased with your interest in our nation. However, the circumstances in which we now find ourselves mean that there are some in Korea to whom your visit will bring sadness instead of happiness. In 1960 when former President Eisenhower visited our nation, we welcomed him with great excitement. Even today, the affection we feel for you is no different from that time. However, circumstances today make it difficult to express the feelings, which lie deep in our hearts. To speak frankly, we are frightened about the possible results of your visit. We are, in fact, so overcome with fear and concern that we are sending this letter to you.

Our children, attempting to pattern their lives after Jesus Christ, have worked through student organizations to renew Korea. Because of this they are in prison, convicted of being communists and anti-government activists. They have all chosen to live and serve with the oppressed and rejected, the poor who labor in farms and rural areas. They have done this out of the deep conviction of their Christian faith. They have sought to assist poor people in achieving a sense of pride and individual worth and to help them become independent members of society. Impressed by the lessons they have learned in school, they have worked to make democracy a reality.

Believing that God created man in His own image, that all are blessed in His sight and that He wishes all to be free, our children have given of their sweat and tears to help free people from the injustices of our society.

However, the Park regime, during its 13 years in power, has demonstrated no real concern for the needs of the people, but has only been concerned for its own political survival. To this end, it has enforced its so-called Yushin Constitution with the use of tanks and fabricated elections, which have violated the rights of the people. Even one word spoken in opposition to these actions endangers the spokesman as being branded a communist.

Our children felt they could not tolerate this situation and called upon the government to withdraw its Yushin Constitution. They were arrested and subjected to endless mental and physical tortures. Half dead from the torture, they were forced to sign confessions, which have been used as "evidence" against them. Even now, behind prison bars and facing continued beatings and electric torture, they are determined to continue their efforts to create a democratic Korea, believing that true freedom and peace for all are the will of God for society.

Therefore, we are concerned and deeply distressed by the possibility that President Park will use your visit to prolong his regime and will lie to the Korean people about the extent of your support for him. The prolongation of the Park regime can only mean continued unhappiness and despair for the people of Korea with no real security. We beg you to understand these feelings.

Because we mothers publicly revealed what our sons actually said at their trials, we too have been arrested by the police and the Korean Central Intelligence Agency and have experienced severe interrogation. During interrogation some of us were beaten to unconsciousness and had to be hospitalized. Even while undergoing treatment in the hospital, agents of the C.I.A. came to interrogate us. They tormented us in our hospital beds and kept us from sleeping. One of the nurses broke down and wept at the treatment we were receiving.

Perhaps you will ask why students are involved in such activity while most citizens remain quiet. For 13 years, the government has effectively prevented the citizens of Korea from seeing what they ought to see, hearing what they ought to hear, and saying what they ought to say. They have been powerless under this merciless oppression. However, in their hearts they thirst for the day when they will be free and at peace.

Faced with the dread reality of the present, we mothers await your wise judgment and decision on our behalf. With a prayer for your peace and good health, we close our sad letter.

Signed by Representatives of Mothers of Prisoners:

KYUNG JO JUNG: mother of <u>Chul Lee</u>, 3rd year student in Sociology, College of Liberal Arts, Seoul National University (sentenced to life imprisonment).

MYUNG JIN KIM: mother of <u>Kyung Suk Suh</u>, graduate of Engineering College, Seoul National University (20 year sentence) and Chang Suk Suh, 3rd year student, College of Engineering, Yonsei University (20 year sentence)

EUN SOON PAIK: mother of <u>Kwang Il Lee</u>, 2nd year student of Hankuk Theological Seminary (20 year sentence)

TUK NAM LEE: mother of <u>Hyung Ki Kim</u>, graduate of Teachers College, Seoul National University (12 year sentence).

HAN LIM KIM: mother <u>Yun Kim</u>, (only girl sentenced), 4th year student in English Literature at Sogang University (5 year sentence)

Similar letters of protest have been sent by other individuals and groups, including one letter signed by 62 foreigners living and serving in Korea. It is evident to those who are struggling for human rights and justice in this country that President Ford's visit will bring much more harm than good, and will only work toward strengthening and prolonging the oppressive dictatorship in Seoul.

Recently the ROK Government has again cracked down against the students with heavy surveillance, harassment, illegal arrests and harsh interrogations. In addition, the Ministry of Education called a meeting of all university presidents in Seoul, placing full blame and responsibility on them for any student protest actions, and threatening to close all schools for up to a year. Local newspaper reporters have been called in for special "education" sessions and warned to "co-operate." Political prisoners who had previously been allowed short (5 minute) visits with their wives twice a week, are now allowed visits only once every two weeks, or in some cases, only once a month.

It has usually been the case that during this particular period of the year (especially before and during the U.N. Hearings), the government has relaxed its tight grip somewhat, only to draw in the reins even tighter around the end of the year. However, this year the period of "leniency" has been slight if any at all. Many observers of the situation here believe this to be a direct result of the U.S. House of Representatives' failure to pass the bill proposed to cut military aid to South Korea. The approval of the original $167 million in aid to Korea seems to have bolstered the Park regime's self-confidence to carry on in the same fashion as before. It seems certain that Ford's visit will be interpreted and used in the same way, if not to an even greater extent. Therefore we urge you to join with the Koreans in their struggle to prevent this further tragedy from occurring.

What Can We Do?

1. Write to <u>President Ford</u>; Senate Foreign Relations Committee Chairman, <u>J.W. Fulbright</u>; House of Representatives Committee on Foreign Affairs Chairman, <u>Thomas E. Morgan</u>; and other concerned Congressmen (especially Sen. <u>Frank Church</u>, Sen. <u>James Abourezk</u>, Sen. <u>Harold Hughes</u>, Rep. <u>Robert Nix</u>, Rep. <u>Donald Fraser</u>, Rep. <u>John Anderson</u>, Rep. <u>Michael Harrington</u>, and Rep. <u>Thomas P. O'Neill</u>) URGING PRESIDENT FORD TO CANCEL HIS SCHEDULED NOVEMVBER 22, 23 VISIT TO KOREA, pointing out that this only shows support for the Park Government and will be used by Park to reinforce his oppressive policies.

2. If President Ford must come to Korea, urge him to take an open stand against repressive acts being practiced here, by requesting that: (1) the remaining Emergency Measures be lifted, (2) all political prisoners since October 1972 be released, (3) surveillance and harassment of citizens by the KCIA and police be stopped, (4) control of the press be lifted, and (5) the Yushin Constitution be rescinded, reinstating in its place the democratic constitution which existed up to October, 1972.

3. For an excellent analysis of the U.S. involvement in South Korea and its future direction, read "The Korean Connection" by Edwin O. Reischauer, in the New York Times Magazine, September 22, 1974.

4. Write to Thomas E. Morgan, Chairman of the House Committee on Foreign Affairs, expressing displeasure over the passing of the $167 million in military aid to South Korea.

THE STRUGGLE CONTINUES

President Ford's visit was awaited with anticipation and hope, but also with a nagging feeling of gloom. Those who are under the thumb of the Park regime – those with relatives in prison, those whose husbands still carry the death sentence, those who continue to be harassed by the CIA, and those common citizens who feel the wrongness of this oppressive government more strongly each day, rallied together in some extremely courageous actions before Ford's visit, with the dim hope that he might influence President Park in some way to ease up on the internal pressure which has become so unbearable this year.

President Ford has come and gone, and those who hoped that things in Korea might see a change for the better have been sorely disappointed. Ford's visit seems to have done exactly what many predicted – show unconditional support for Park and his policies. The newspapers since then present a bold and confident Park making daily public threats to his opponents. The Koreans are disappointed and tired, but they do not give up. The struggle goes on.

The following article is an excellent description of some of the events that took place prior to Ford's visit. These events are representative of the many prayer meetings, masses, fasts and demonstrations that continue to be held, even more frequently than before. And the pressure of the authorities continues to be applied, in many cases more strongly than before.

THREE DAYS IN KOREA — by Jim Stentzel

JCAN (*Japan Christian Activity News*) co-editor Stentzel returned this week from a journalistic visit to South Korea, where he met with church, government, press, labor and academic people. Below, in diary form, are his notes on several religious experiences he had on 3 consecutive days. The Bishop Chi he refers to is Chi Hak Soun, Catholic Bishop of the Wonju Diocese, who was given a 15-year prison term in August. George Ogle, 45, is an American missionary (and Methodist minister) who has served in Korea since 1954. The "People's Revolutionary Party" (PRP) according to the ROK government, is a communist group whose members were planning a violent overthrow of the government last April. The Korean Student Christian Federation (KSCF) is a long-standing Christian student group whose office has been shut down since the mass arrests of students in early April. Twenty KSCF students, 3 national staff members and 3 KSCF supporters are now serving prison terms ranging from 7-20 years.

Wednesday, October 9: A beautiful, clear fall day – a national holiday – in Seoul. The Pope himself couldn't have hoped for a better day to celebrate the beginning of a special Catholic Holy Year. Some 20,000 Korean Catholics from all over South Korea gathered for an outdoor mass to kick off the once-every-25-years emphasis. The 2 and 1/2 hour mass included a sermon that was surprisingly blunt – for a Korean in public – about the plight of hundreds of political prisoners in this country.

I was preparing to leave about 4:30 when a South Korean flag, several banners and a dozen signs suddenly sprouted like fall flowers from the priestly recessional. A friend explained that the signs all said "Release Bishop Chi." Before I knew it, I was caught in the middle of one of the largest anti-government demonstrations in Korea in 10 years. Five bishops, some 100 priests, 300 nuns, 50 seminary students and 3,000 lay Catholics willingly followed the signs. Thousands of others looked on. Some looked shocked, and many other faces showed fear. The group was marching out of the Catholic seminary toward the street, singing hymns as they went.

Near the street, however, about two dozen plainclothes policemen hurriedly closed the heavy iron gate. The procession halted for a moment, then an equal number of priests in their colorful robes, took hold of their side of the gate and overpowered the policemen after several coordinated heave-hoes. A loud cheer erupted from the heretofore-solemn people. But one step outside and the first of some 800 helmeted riot policemen rushed in from the street. The marchers were halted only 5 meters past the gate. Brief scuffles ensued in which the police smashed some of the signs. Some foreign priests broke through the first police cordon only to find themselves isolated from their Korean brethren. It was a stand-off for 2 hours, during which ringing hymns were interspersed with slogans: Restore democracy, Stop repression, Free the prisoners, Restore basic human rights, Help laborers and poor people, Restore freedom of speech.

Their numbers, their vigor, their unity and their dignity, under the circumstances, struck me. And I was struck by the gravity of the occasion when, as the demonstrators were dispersing at dusk, many stopped to sing more hymns at a nearby intersection. Police trucks rolled up and tear gas guns began spewing forth the government's brand of communion wine, sending the last several hundred worshippers scurrying back to homes throughout the South.

Thursday, October 10: I raced to get to the Christian Building by 10 a.m. only to discover that the prayer meeting was beginning "on Korean time" – 15 minutes later than scheduled! The small room was packed. Hahm Suk Hon, the white-haired "Mahatma Gandhi of Korea," looking as majestic as he is wise, sat among a dozen or so rather well-dressed mothers and wives of imprisoned Christians. I stood alongside several plainly dressed women with ruddy complexions. A missionary explained that they were wives of the alleged "PRP" communists, several of whom have been sentenced to death. None of the women are Christian, yet they come because the community shares their pain and struggle.

Rev. Yun, a Presbyterian minister, stood up to announce that the meeting was about to begin, but that first he wanted to advise the participants: "For my prayer last week I was harshly interrogated by the KCIA. If anyone here is not willing to risk similar treatment, perhaps he or she should leave now." No one among the 40 present moved, and the service began.

I missed at least 80% of what was being said, but was gripped by the profound depths of emotion in the prayers, most of which concerned the some 200 men imprisoned this year for their political, religious and social concerns. Coming from Japan, I tried hard to fight back my tears - and not blow my nose in public! - until I noticed that nearly everyone else in the room was in tears. A wave of inspiration – of judgment and redemption – swept through my body. I was no longer an American from Japan passing through Korea. I prayed like I haven't prayed in years. The prisoners' bondage and their families' suffering, became mine – became ours – in a prayer of confession that rose from our collective souls. But I should not imply that my encrusted soul took flight in some ecstasy-fantasy. What happened to all of us this morning was very earthbound: a physical and spiritual rising, standing up to say: "Yes, Lord, we rise to your occasions with our feet firmly planted. Despite our fear, we know your purposes."

George Ogle gave the sermon (in Korean) using Matthew 25:34-40. He mentioned well-known Koreans who have suffered and some who have died in the struggle for justice, saying that such men symbolize Christ's incarnation. But, he argued, Christians have not shown much awareness or concern for lesser-known men who also symbolize the incarnation: particularly the alleged members of the PRP who had committed no crimes worthy of the death sentence. He said that these men are experiencing more suffering and greater injustice than many of the well-prayed-for Christians in prison, and he pleaded for Christian love and compassion for all of God's children.

After several more resounding hymns and prayers, the minister who had been picked up the week before talked about his experience with the KCIA. Since there were no aisles, nobody could roll in them, but his account was utterly hilarious. He is a short, squat man and he illustrated how he had stood firm, tried to stand tall and put up his fists every time a 6-foot tall, 200 lb. KCIA man threatened to beat him into confessing the "error" of his prayers. His faith and courage then were matched only by his daring to come and tell his story today.

Afterwards I met Ms. Lee Oo Jung, head of Korean Church Women United. She, too, in the midst of filling me in on the utter seriousness of her own CIA interrogations and prison experiences, was able to laugh at some of the ridiculousness of the government's rule. One story concerned how early this year she had worked hard to organize CWU groups to boycott Hitachi products (because of the discrimination case against a Korean in Japan). A CIA man threatened her, forcing her to promise to stop her "anti-Japanese protest." Then, in August, when the ROK government helped organize and fund anti-Japanese riots in Seoul (because a Korean from Japan had killed the President's wife), another CIA man visited Ms. Lee. He demanded to know why CWU wasn't supporting these demonstrations. She calmly explained that she was a woman of her word and mentioned the promise to the other CIA man. Devastated, the agent went away without saying another word.

Friday, October 11: For several weeks the Board of Directors of KSCF has been planning a prayer service for prisoners. It was to be the first major KSCF meeting in more than 6 months since police cracked down on the committed young Christians. The CIA heard of the plans and threatened to stop it. When 2000 postcards were ordered announcing the meeting, the CIA stopped the printer from doing the job. Word of mouth was used to announce the evening prayer service, and no one knew if more than 20 people would show up.

But tonight more than 200 people – some 175 students,

13 relatives of imprisoned students and an estimated dozen CIA agents met and prayed up a storm in the Christian Building. For the second time in two days I was moved to tears, first by a prayer by the mother of two student prisoners, then by a prayer from one of the few released prisoners. The sermon brought Mark 10:32-34 to powerful life. It made all the feelings in the room – amazement, fear, oppression, death and new life – unbelievably real. As on yesterday, I was amazed, strengthened and encouraged by the depths of courage and faith that motivate these people. With new eyes I could see the beauty amidst pain, the affirmations of life in the face of death, that these Christians carry in their struggle to be free men and women. There is something about this Korean Christianity, the likes of which I have never experienced in the U.S. or Japan. Life is brought to worship and worship to life, all with extraordinary integrity to the Gospel.

As I left the building I felt drained and yet filled. I passed two of the CIA men who are on permanent assignment at the Christian Center. Outside I passed three buses of riot police who were wondering, "If the Catholics can do it, why not the Protestants?" Then first word came that George Ogle had been picked up and taken to CIA headquarters for interrogation. Later I heard that Rev. Park, a Presbyterian minister who also prayed yesterday, had also been taken in.

(Note: Both men were released the next morning. Ogle was held for 19 hours, including 2 hours of sleep. An unknown CIA agent at the Thursday prayer meeting had transcribed Ogle's sermon. Ogle was told that Christians shouldn't show concern for "proven communists," and he was forced to sign a pledge that he would never again refer to the PRP in a sermon. He was lectured on where the government draws the line between religion and politics. And once more a humorous note in the midst of a terrifying experience: after an agent read the CIA sermon transcript to Ogle, Ogle told him had done a very good job and invited him to preach at his church some time. The agent didn't laugh.)

Taken from: *Japan Christian Activity News*
No. 462, October 25, 1974

Since the writing of the above article, Rev. Ogle has continued to show his concern and mutual commitment to the struggle being waged for civil liberties and social justice. He has been frequently requested to preach or speak at prayer services, student meetings, etc. The PRP wives continue to seek his support, advice and help in their own, somewhat isolated struggle. And he continues to feel pressure. . . . Recently he has received word through the U.S. Embassy that the Korean Ministry of Foreign Affairs has voted to have him deported form Korea. The reason given is related to his preaching and his contact with the PRP women. *

The prisoners have seen certain changes in their own situations – all for the worse. The severe cold of winter has struck many prisoners hard, causing physical discomforts ranging from frostbite to more serious illnesses. Recently there was a general transfer of many of the prisoners, separating them from each other and sending them to prisons all over the country. This has made it much more difficult, if not impossible, for their relatives to go the prisons to leave money, warm clothes, books, etc. for their loved ones. (Except in a few cases, most have still not been allowed visitation privileges, even with their closest relatives).

President Park continually holds out the "release of the prisoners" like a carrot on a stick – first it was hinted that they would be released in connection with Ford's visit, next by Christmas and now the papers are saying maybe early next year. Perhaps the next deadline will be spring, so that they can use the prisoners' release as bargaining power against any student action, which is traditionally strongest at that time of year.

* Rev. Ogle was deported on Dec. 14, 1974. He can be reached via Mr. Edwin Fisher, Board of Global Ministries, United Methodist Church, Room 1540, 475 Riverside Drive, New York, N.Y. 10027. Various written or TV and radio recorded interviews of Rev. Ogle are available from Mr. Fisher or from the Institute for the Church in Urban-Industrial Society, 800 W. Belden, Chicago, Illinois 60614.

WHAT CAN WE DO?

1) Send letters of support and concern (and/or money contributions) to heads of groups working for the restoration of democracy in Korea. Such leaders include:

(a) Kim Yong Sam, Chairman,

(b) Kim Dae Jung

New Democratic Party Headquarters

Ankuk Dong, Seoul, Korea

(c) Chairman, Korean Student Christian Federation,

(d) Chairman, Korean National Council of Churches,

(e) Relatives of Political Prisoners, c/o Korean National Council of Churches,

(f) Chairman, Church Woman United

The Christian Building

Chongo 5-Ga, Seoul, Korea

(g) Cardinal Stephen Kim

1 2-Ga, Myeong Dong,

Jungku, Seoul, Korea

2) Read the January 20, 1975 *Washington Post* editorial page account of the plight of the *Tong-A-Ilbo* independent Korean newspaper and join thousands of others in sending any amount for an advertisement of encouragement. Sign it with the name of the group you represent – or any individuals, or anonymously. It is only encouragement gifts like this that are keeping the *Tong-A Ilbo* alive after massive cancellation of advertisements by major Korean and Korean-American-owned companies. The address for your gift (by check):

The Tong-A Ilbo
139 Seichong-No
Chong-no Ku
Seoul 110, Korea

Emergency Decree Number Nine

Editor's Note: Between January 1974 and May 1975, President Park Chung-hee issued a total of nine emergency decrees in increasingly paranoid attempts to stifle opposition to his authoritarian rule. The decrees were all similar in that they made it illegal to oppose the government. But they also differed, in both their targeted groups of citizens and the scope of their inclusion. Perhaps most onerous of all was the final decree, Number Nine, issued May 13, 1975.

This sweeping decree essentially criminalized any criticism of the government. It was so vaguely worded that virtually any individual or organization could be accused of violating some aspect of it. Authority was granted to "the ministry in charge" to determine whether or not there had been a violation.

Particularly noteworthy in the decree was Article 7 spelling out the penalty for violation of the decree. Previous decrees had specifically listed years in prison and ultimately execution. Number nine simply noted that violation would result in "imprisonment for a period of not less than one year." People realized that "not less than one year" could mean a very long time.

The decree achieved its intended results. The struggling opposition lost its public voice as the Korean media caved in and essentially became a voice for the government. In this context the meager efforts of the Monday Night Group to inform the world took on greater significance.

The Decree

Article 1. It shall be prohibited for any person to engage in any of the following acts:

1. Fabricating, disseminating falsehoods or making false presentation of fact.

2. Denying, opposing, distorting or defaming the Constitution, or asserting, petitioning, instigating or propagating revision or repeal thereof, by means of assembly, demonstration, or by using mass-communication media such as newspapers, broadcasts or news correspondence, or by making documents, pictures, records or other publications.

3. Assemblies, demonstrations or other activities by students which interfere with politics, with the exceptions of (a) classroom or research activities conducted under guidance and supervision of school authorities, (b) activities conducted with prior approval by president or principal of school, or, (c) other ordinary, non-political activities.

4. Publicly defaming the present Emergency Measure.

Article 2. It shall be prohibited for any person to broadcast report or otherwise disseminate publicly the content of any act or acts which violate Article 1 of the present Emergency Measure; or producing, distributing, selling, possessing or displaying publications the content of which violates Article 1 of the present Emergency Measure.

Article 3. It shall be prohibited for any person, with intent to perpetrate a property flight, to move property or properties of the Republic of Korea or of its national to a foreign country; or to conceal or dispose of, in a foreign country, property or properties which are due to be introduced into the Republic of Korea.

Article 4. It shall be prohibited for any person to obtain an emigration permit or to escape to a foreign country, by means of entering false information in application documents or by other improper means.

Article 5. The Minister in charge may issue orders or take measures, against violators of the present Emergency Measure, against the school, organization or company to which the violator is attached at the time of violation, or against its representative or head, as follows:

1. Issuing order directed to representative or head of school, organization or company, requiring dismissal or expulsion of its officers, teachers or students.

2. Dismissal or expulsion of representatives, heads, officers, teachers or students.

3. Banning of broadcasting, reporting, producing, selling or distributing.

4. Suspension of activity, closing of school, suspension of publication, discontinuance of publication, disbandment or shutdown.

5. Revocation of approval, registration, permission, authorization or license.

Article 6. The prohibition under the present Emergency Measure should not be construed to provide punishment to members of the National Assembly for their opinions officially expressed in the National Assembly: provided, however, that this exemption does not cover a person who broadcasts, reports or otherwise disseminates publicly the said opinion.

Article 7. Any person who violates any of the provisions of the present Emergency Measure and any person who does not observe measures taken by the Minister in charge by the authority of the present Emergency Measure, shall be punished by imprisonment for a period of not less than 1 year. Suspension of qualification for a period of not more than 10 years shall be concurrently imposed. Any attempt, preparation or conspiracy to commit violation of the present Emergency Measures shall be punished in the same manner.

Article 8. Any person who violates any of the provisions of the present Emergency Measure, and any person who does not observe measures taken by the Minister in charge by the authority of the present Emergency Measure, shall be subjected to arrest, detention, search or seizure, without warrant thereto.

Article 9. Any government official or officer of government-managed enterprises, who violates, after the present Emergency Measure becomes effective, the provision of Article 2 of the *Law Providing Aggravated Punishment Against Specific Types a/Crimes* (Law No. 1744 of February 2, 1966, as revised on February 24, 1973) which provides aggravated punishment for the crimes of bribery, or any government accountant who violates Article 5 of the said law which provides aggravated punishment for acts incurring loss to the national treasury, shall be punished, in addition to punishments set forth in each article of the said law, by fine, equivalent to 10 times of the amount taken in bribery or amount of loss incurred to the national treasury.

Article 10. Violators of the present Emergency Measure shall be tried and sentenced in civilian courts.

Article 11. Matters which are deemed necessary to enforce the present Emergency Measures shall be promulgated by the Minister in charge.

Article 12. The Minister of National Defense may assist the Mayor of Seoul, the Mayor of Pusan and Provincial Governors, if request for mobilization of the Armed Forces is made for the purpose of maintaining public order.

Article 13. Orders issued or measures taken by the Minister in charge by the authority of the present Emergency Measure shall not be subjected to judicial review.

Article 14. The present Emergency Measure shall be effectivefrom 15: 00 hours, May 13, 1975.

A Tract for Our Times

Editor's Note: Perhaps inevitably, the involvement of the Monday Night Group in Korea's struggle for justice and democracy caused consternation in the missionary community at large. Members of the group began hearing comments ranging from mild curiosity to outright anger. In extreme cases we were accused of jeopardizing the entire missionary effort in Korea.

In response to these criticisms the Monday Night Group drafted a letter to be mailed to all missionaries in Korea. The letter, signed by 23 Catholic and Protestant missionaries, was an attempt to explain, in as gentle and loving manner as possible, why we felt our understanding of the Christian faith demanded our involvement in the struggle.

We were not so naïve as to expect that critics would be converted to our position. But we did hope that at least some missionary colleagues would become more understanding. We were right on both counts. Many responded with appreciation, and a few with scathing criticism. One missionary said we should all leave the country and let the work of the Lord continue.

A copy of the letter was shared with Dr. Edwin O. Fisher, Jr., then Executive Secretary for East Asia of the World Division, General Board of Global Ministries, United Methodist Church. Dr. Fisher was so impressed with the letter that he persuaded various denominational leaders to publish it in a pamphlet titled *A Tract for Our Times*. In October 1975 10,000 copies were printed for distribution to churches throughout the United States.

Foreword

Historically, Korean Christians have stood firmly against political oppression, whether from Japanese imperialists, totalitarian Communists, or from their own government. Today, the Korean population is subjected to harsh and repressive measures decreed by the government of President Park, Chung Hee. Within this tragic situation many Koreans have spoken and acted heroically in spite of government surveillance, intimidation, brutality and sometimes criticism from fellow Koreans.

The following testimony was given by a group of Protestant and Roman Catholic missionaries in Korea.

Statement of Position

The following letter is an effort to clarify to ourselves and to others the reasons, both personal and theological, on which we base our actions. It is a statement on our position and the interpretation of our role as Christian missionaries in the Republic of Korea at this particular time and in these particular circumstances in the history of this country.

As Christians and missionaries we are all a part of a common community, though representing differing opinions and ways of practicing our common mission. In light of these diversities we offer this letter as an effort to share our particular understanding of the Scriptures that has led us to our present position. We hope that these expressions will be accepted in the spirit of trust and love in which they are offered and, although we do not anticipate complete agreement with our point of view, we hope that at least a door will remain open between us.

We realize that many understand this position and may be in sympathy with our point of view, but there are others who do not and who feel that our stand on certain issues has caused inconveniences to some members of the foreign missionary community. We address this letter to all who are interested.

With all Christians we share the conviction that the practice of the Christian life must be consistent with the teachings of Scripture. It is our belief that the forms of witness we have been engaged in are in harmony with and are required by these teachings. Though it is not possible in this limited space to provide a full thesis, our understanding of Scripture which provides the rationale for a so-called "political" witness, may be summarized generally as follows:

We believe that the ultimate source of power and authority is God Himself. Eternal God, the Father, has created the world and people in it so that they might respond to Him in free, obedient love, thus becoming His sons and daughters. In so responding to His goodness and grace, they are also required to create and maintain among themselves personal and social relationships of the same quality as those which characterize the relationship each has with the Father. In other words, God's will is to be done not only in personal-individual terms, but also in the larger groupings and communities that characterize societies.

By their free choice, people have chosen to be disobedient and unbelieving. They have sinned against God, and endeavored to erect an independent society and life centered around themselves. From this primal disobedience comes all the other divisions and separations which are the fabric of every individual life and all societies—individuals against themselves, people against people, people against nature. The effects of this rebellion against God pervade all areas of human society, including institutions. Nothing has escaped the domination of sin. The forces of evil, personified in the being of Satan, have found access into the world through human disobedience, and working through human beings have established a kingdom counter to that which the Father intends.

God sent Jesus Christ into the world to restore the relationship between Himself and humanity. Christ lived a life of perfect obedience to the Father. He was the one true human being who exhibited in His daily life, in His words and works, what it means to do God's will. By His death on the cross, and resurrection from death, He broke the power of Satan and sin over humanity, and made it possible to return to a life of fellowship with, and obedience to the Father. By faith in Christ's act, persons are reconciled to God, freed from the dominion of darkness, and transferred to God's kingdom. Faith comes by the preaching and teaching, the hearing and the acting out of God's message of salvation in Jesus Christ.

Freed from this trap of his own and Satan's making, mankind is summoned to a life of obedience. The pattern for this life is Jesus Christ, and the power to live it is generated by Christ, who lives in the believer as the Holy Spirit. The Christian life, which begins in the individual, must extend outward into all areas of human society—into marriage and family relationships, and ultimately into all spheres of life: cultural, social, economic and political. There is no pocket or zone of human experience which is of unconcern to the Christian. He lives as the herald of God's Good News in a still-unbelieving world, witnessing to the message of salvation in both word and deed. In so living out this obedient life, the Christian confronts the entrenched power of sin and Satan which, though broken by Jesus Christ, still operates where people submit to its dominion. This results in conflict and struggle, usually experienced first in personal terms, and then in wider social and relational terms. The struggle is not only one of overcoming sin personally and socially, it is also one of building and restoring those personal and social conditions which will, in accordance with God's original and continuing intention, make it possible for all people to live the abundant life which Jesus promised.

One of the structures which God has provided for the benefit and well-being of His children is government, the so-called "political" realm. This is certainly the teaching of Romans 13. However, because government has also become the sphere of Satan's activity, the political realm is also one in which the Christian, in living an obedient life, becomes engaged in struggle and conflict. It is precisely at those points where government:

1. requires an obedience and loyalty that only God Himself can demand

2. requires of the Christian a behavior that is prohibited by Scripture or by the Spirit-informed Christian conscience

3. ceases to function as the agent of God (Romans 13:6) and engages instead in brutal or unjust acts against its citizens (be they Christian or non-Christian)

—that the Christian is called upon to bear witness. The witness which he bears is that Jesus Christ is the Lord of Lords, that only He can command total obedience. It is a warning that God Himself will judge governments and the human agents who wield political power by the way in which they exercise that power in the laws, policies and practices which they establish. The Christian is compelled to act, in accordance with the example and Spirit of Jesus Christ, not only to point out such evils, but also to correct them. The Christian will speak truth to power; will obey God rather than people; and will submit to whatever penalty or punishment may come as a result of this witness.

This is the political segment of life in which we have, by our actions, attempted to emulate faithfully our Lord's example.

There has been specific criticism leveled against us because of the kind of activity in which we have found ourselves involved. Although detailed and involved response to this criticism is obviously impossible in a statement of this nature, we nevertheless are obligated to express to our fellow missionary colleagues our own feelings about the issues raised by them.

1 The first criticism is that as foreign missionaries we are guests in Korea and ought, therefore, to behave like guests. The inference is that engaging in "political

activity" does not become the role of a guest, and that what we are doing is political activity.

Aside from the fact that the presence of any foreigner in Korea today is in itself of deep political significance, we feel that this issue could be approached from a number of directions. Perhaps the simplest way to respond, however, would be to ask some relevant questions:

How long, for example, must missionaries live in a foreign land before they cease to be guests?

If missionaries choose to identify themselves as guests, does this mean that the demands which the Lord places upon them become secondary to those which the Korean government places upon them? (Consider Amos, who journeyed to a foreign land and spoke prophetically.)

If we are really guests, who is the host—the rulers of this nation or its people?

What is the responsibility of the guest to the host?

Do the guests sit quietly even if they discover that their host has become ill or is dying?

Why do guests have the right to "meddle" in the most crucial aspect of life—the religious—but not the human?

Look at the story of the Good Samaritan as an example of a foreigner who intervened in the affairs of others. Suppose the Good Samaritan had responded to the situation in which he found himself by saying, "I am a guest in your land and cannot get involved. You can be certain, however, that I will pray for you and also for those thieves who treated you so poorly."

2 A second criticism leveled against us is based on the biblical injunction expressed in the 13th chapter of Paul's letter to the Romans, urging us to be subject to the governing authorities, for their authority is from God.

Obviously, in a letter of this sort we cannot hope to exhaust debate on this complex subject, but a few comments are in order.

We wonder why this particular passage is singled out of all relevant biblical texts on the subject. The Revelation of John, for example, written much later than Paul's Epistle and under a much more severe government, presents an effective diatribe against the ruling authorities and uses such expressions as "throne of the beast" in taking evil and corrupt rulers to task. The Old Testament abounds with instances of resistance to evil rulers: Moses in Egypt, Daniel and his friends, Samuel's rebukes of Saul when he got out of hand, to mention only a few. Why, then, among all the passages of the Bible concerning this issue must we single out this particular one in the New Testament as our ultimate guide?

We wonder also how far those who uphold this particular passage of Scripture would go in adhering to it. Would they consistently apply it to every ruler who has ever existed or would they admit that there might be room for exceptions? Is it never wrong to serve an evil king? Does submission mean blind obedience? Is it not true that our ultimate obedience is always to God and that, although we ought to uphold our earthly rulers to the end of preserving order, we will ultimately find our allegiance to the Lord taking precedence? And is it not true also that those whose authority is from God are in turn subject to God?

What do we do when the rulers in power have arrived there by forcibly overthrowing the previously existing powers, as is the case with our present government? Why were they not subservient to the previous rulers?

This statement must be applied to any nation which insists that it is still a democracy, where the governing authorities are the people themselves and it is improper for any one person or group of persons to assume absolute power.

3 Issue number three deals with the theological understanding of the role of the missionary and finds the foreign missionary required to "limit himself or herself to religious activity" or to "stick to preaching the gospel."

Those who raise this issue, be they missionary colleagues or government officials, have their own understandings of what that means. Basically it is an attempt to radically dichotomize what are usually called "evangelism" and "social action." We regret the separation of these two because we find them to be common and inseparable concerns of Christ in the New Testament. While calling people of all walks of life to a new birth, a new life and a new community, Christ healed the sick, fed the hungry and ministered to the poor, and at the same time also directly challenged the authorities on such matters as working and healing on the Sabbath. We frankly see no way to live in Korea as missionaries attempting to be true to Christ's example without sharing these concerns for the total life of every human being.

We are also bemused by an understanding of our role which seems to imply that the "religious" aspect of life is relatively unimportant and that, therefore, we can meddle in it as much as we please. One would think that those who insist on separating the "religious" from the "physical" or "earthly" would also insist that the religious is of most crucial importance. Nevertheless, we are offered free rein in this area even to the extent of government support of activities which it decides are genuinely religious.

This raises a challenging question: are we willing to let this or any other government determine what is or is not proper religious activity?

4 Another area of concern which has recently gained tremendous publicity and emphasis is the "national security" question. Many say that while freedom, justice and civil liberties are important, these must take second place to defense against the expansion of Communism in Asia, and that therefore, those who are working actively for those issues must postpone their efforts in light of the more important priority of defense and security. We can only take this statement as a contradiction in terms.

Without denying either the existence of the Communist threat or its severity, we would make certain observations:

We have observed recently the collapse of Vietnam, not because of lack of foreign aid in finances or man-power, but because the people of Vietnam were not sufficiently inspired by a succession of totalitarian leaders to resist aggression.

We believe that Korea's greatest asset in countering Communist aggression has long been the fierce anti-Communist stance of the Korean people (and especially the Christians) based on a great desire for freedom and justice. By destroying freedom and justice, by trampling on human rights, by outlawing all voices of opposition or differing opinions, the Park regime is destroying the only hope of unity and common commitment to its goals, even to one as important as national security. The goals of national security are actually dependent upon an atmosphere and genuine support of democratic freedoms and justice, but these are the very things which present government practices tend to smother out. This in itself is, in our opinion, the real threat to national security.

5 The fifth criticism with which we attempt to deal is what has been phrased "don't stick our necks out." Actions by some missionaries which upset the government result in inconveniences for all missionaries who suddenly find that they are under surveillance and that it is more difficult than previously to obtain visas, residence permits and tax exemptions. This is perhaps the most difficult of all the criticisms to answer because we are sensitive to what is happening and we are sorry that our involvement has caused inconvenience to others.

But let us place the issue in the most glaring light possible. Through exhaustive research, prayer and personal involvement based on our own understanding of Jesus' words in Matthew 25:31 ff, we came to feel that eight essentially innocent men were executed by the Korean government. Could we honorably remain quiet in such a situation? In other words, which is ultimately more important, innocent death or inconvenience?

We ask for your understanding as we turn this issue around and point out that others' actions and involvement affect us also. Those who support this government either directly or through indifference and silence, make it extremely difficult not only for us, but even more important, for the millions of Korean citizens who long for a just and humane life.

We hope that this statement will foster a greater understanding and cooperation in the Lord's work. We hope that you will accept it in a spirit of love, knowing that it is not meant to be a closed or final comment, but that we offer it as an open-ended statement, realizing our need for continuing growth, new insights and open dialogue with all our brothers and sisters in Christ. The Spirit gives each of us a special and different function in His service, and yet we believe that out of this diversity we are, each one, working to build up the Body of Christ which is the Church.

If you are interested in getting together for a more personal dialogue, either for further exploration or clarification, please contact us:

W. Ransom Rice, Jr.	Christine Ortis
Suzanne Rice	Jo-anne Fisher
Basil M. Price	Madeleine Guisto
Robert J. Kelly	Richard Peterson
Gene Matthews	Dorothea Schweizer
William A. Basinger	Fran Dunne
Charles A. Krauth	Martin J. Lowery
Fran Krauth	Delores C. Geier
Walter F. Durst	John Daly
Louise M. Durst	Sean Dwan
Willa Kernen	Dolores Congdon
Marion Current	

Korea Joint Action Group

East Asia Working Group

Division of Overseas Ministries

National Council of Churches of Christ in the U.S.A.

475 Riverside Drive, New York, N.Y. 10027

Update

Several of the stories in this book relate to the plight of eight men who were executed in April 1975. They were accused of being ringleaders of a "People's Revolutionary Party" (PRP) plotting to overthrow the government. Members of the Monday Night Group were convinced of their innocence and felt the case against them had been fabricated by the dictatorial government of Park Chung Hee. Several of the stories recounted in More Than Witnesses deal with attempts to minister to these men and their families.

In January 2007, almost 32 years later the case was retried. All of the men were found innocent of any wrongdoing, and the case was declared a government fabrication. On August 21, 2007, the Seoul Central District Court awarded a large sum of money to compensate the families for their losses.

Thus was justice finally achieved, but it was in many respects a hollow justice. Family members of the eight men suffered immense hardship and humiliation during the 30 years since the executions. They had great difficulty supporting themselves financially. Their children were taunted and bullied in school because their fathers were "evil, communist spies." They faced constant harassment by the government and were prevented from getting jobs or opening small businesses. Ministering to the families during this period became a major focus of the Monday Night Group.

Members of the Monday Night Group who supported the families and believed in the innocence of the accused, are happy that the government has finally admitted the truth, has officially cleared the names of these men, and has sought to "right the wrong" by awarding a monetary compensation to the families. We also understand, however, that the families would have much preferred to have their husbands and fathers alive and well and that loss bears a price too steep to be covered by any compensation.

9 781933 449623

Printed in the
136442LV00C